GOT ENERGY

?

Increase Your Potential
with Renewable Life Energy

3 Musts to Igniting
Your Passion

Tim Hooper

This publication is designed to provide authoritative information with regard to the subject matter covered. It is sold as a self-help and personal improvement resource with the understanding that the author and publisher are not engaged in rendering professional advice. If advice or expert assistance is needed including but not limited to financial, physical, mental or emotional, the services of a competent and licensed professional should be sought.

The author and publication team have given every effort to credit quotes and thoughts that aren't original with the author.

Cover Design: Black Card Books Design
Interior Design: Energy4PR

ISBN: 978-1-64255-427-4
"Got Energy? ... 3 Musts to Igniting Your Passion!"
www.timehooper.com

Write to:
Time4Energy, LLC
PO Box 332798
Murfreesboro, Tennessee 37133

TABLE OF CONTENTS

Energizers
Foreward
Dedication
Introduction

ENERGY　　　　　　　　　　　　　　Chapter

Energy Defined – Reclaiming a powerful meaning　　　　　1
Energy's Harmony – Deeper understanding to live fully　　2
Energy's Motivation – Igniting your internal flame　　　　3
Energy's Attraction – Abundance mentality to love deeply　4
Energizer – Becoming a power source　　　　　　　　　　5

MUST # 1 - PERSPECTIVE

Bonus – Living fully present today　　　　　　　　　　　6
Legend You – You're worth more than you think　　　　　7
Visionart – Simply, start painting your life picture　　　　8
Sunrise – How to wake up giddy every day　　　　　　　9

MUST # 2 - OWNERSHIP

Energy Mapping – Fullness: sources, switches and swindlers　10
Energy Equation – A 4,000-year-old secret　　　　　　　11
Time Machine – Creation and redemption formula　　　　12
Energy Budget – A focused investment　　　　　　　　　13
Energy Zone – Cubicles, surfing and intervals　　　　　14
Balancing Act – The amplitude of wholeness　　　　　　15
Tortoise Tuff – Huge power in "little" consistency　　　16
WW[ ]D – Becoming CEO　　　　　　　　　　　　　　17
200 Percent Heart – Living like it's your big moment　　18

MUST # 3 - ACCOUNTABILITY

Synergize – Energetic learner - all are my teachers　　　19
Scrum Time – Unleashing vulnerability – 10X accountability　20
160,000 Eyes – Lighting the way for others　　　　　　21
Paying Dividends – Creating raving shareholders　　　　22
Second Bonus – The beginning of a journey　　　　　　23

Index
Sponsors

ENERGIZERS

to the leaders and mentors who've poured themselves into me and have given their time to write an endorsement for my book, thank you ...

"Surround yourself with the dreamers and the doers, the believers and thinkers, but most of all, surround yourself with those who see the greatness within you, even when you don't see it yourself." — *Edmund Lee*

"50 percent or more of success has nothing to do with price, product, systems and processes. 50+ percent of success has to do with your attitude and energy. Tim Hooper's book, 'Got Energy?' will fast track you to achieving that oftentimes elusive 50+ percent. Get your dose of calorie-free energy – buy this book!"
Jack Daly, Amazon and Forbes Best Selling Author, www.jackdaily.net

"Tim's the most energetic person I've ever met. His constant smile and positive attitude are a nonstop inspiration. This book will fill you up and push you forward. Cars need to refuel. Phones need to recharge. People need to renew. I promise, Tim will help you get to 100 %."
David Rendall, Speaker and Author of The Freak Factor, www.drendall.com

"Energy is an economic driver of success. Tim is the definition of energy and how to funnel it for positive. Want to make a difference in your life and the life of others – read this book, take lots of notes and take action. Tim will lead you through a journey of personal discovery – get ready to add energy to your life!"
Andy Bailey, PETRA COACH, Four Decisions™ Certified, www.petracoach.com

"Tim's book offers a fresh look at how to build and sustain high energy levels that can change your life and impact all people that come into your sphere of influence."
Shane Reeves, CEO TwelveStone Health, Pharm.D., www.12stonehealth.com

"At the end of the day most people are selling commodities that can be gotten anywhere and sold by anybody. What's hard to measure and what is clearly the differential for some is an INTANGIBLE. For Tim Hooper that intangible has always been his energy and mindset of attack toward life. His contagious spirit leaves a residue you'll never forget. Buy this book and have that residue rub off on you. You'll be glad you did."
Micheal Burt, SUPER COACH, Amazon Best Selling Author of Everybody Needs A Coach in Life

"During the years I've known Tim, I've never met a more driven, positive, goal-oriented person in my life. His "can-do" attitude and unrelenting will power to achieve his goals is an inspiration to all those around him. If you want to change your attitude and change your life you need to BUY THIS BOOK!"
Jim Tracy, Tennessee State Senator

"Tim Hooper's one of those rare people in life that just make you want to be the best version of yourself. Not by telling you how, but by showing you every day what that truly looks like. His clarity on the topic of energy comes from walking the talk. Thank you, Tim. You, my friend, inspire me to be a better man!"
Monte Mohr, Broker, Owner EXIT Realty The Mohr Group & Associates

"As a reader of 'Got Energy?' you can trust in the consistency of the person behind the words. Tim is authentic, genuine, and thrives in seeing people reach their highest potential. It's my honor to endorse Tim's new book 'Got Energy?'. I hope you find Tim's passion as infectious as I have."
Kevin E. O'Dea, Headmaster Lancaster Christian Academy

"Have you ever heard of an Energy Coach? Meet my friend Tim Hooper. Tim's an incredible promoter of the words 'Coachable' and 'Accountable' as a teacher and a student. He truly practices what he preaches and shows us how to do the same."
Rod Key, Gunnery Sergeant, USMC, Wellness Coach

I know Tim personally and I know this is going to be a great book. I am ordering mine and you should order yours. I hear people say about children, "I wish I had their energy or I wish I wasn't so tired all the time!" Well your wish is Tim's command. Buy this book and get energized! Congratulations Tim! I'm proud of you my friend!
Don Day, Speaker at Don Day Speaks & President at Intero Real Estate Services

"Inspiration and energy have never been more powerful than when Tim Hooper is present. He is a tireless coach, mentor, and friend. Tim's life of ridiculous efficiency is what I initially hired him to teach me. What I discovered was the depth of his heart in everything else in life."
Ray Singer, Corporate Vice President at New York Life

"Tim's world-class at what he does. His ability to provide not just energy (which he has in abundance) but clear and deeply intelligent insight, is remarkable. He's able to combine story-telling with data-driven insight. Everything Tim does is about serving people, which directly translated to how much value he added to the work our team is doing. I would highly recommend inviting Tim to your workplace as a speaker, author, and mentor. He's the real deal and you, and your team, will be better having worked with him."
Jake Nicolle, International Speaker, Novel Podcast Host

"From the very first time I was in the same room as Tim for a quarterly planning session, you could feel the positive energy. He literally lit up the room. For the next four-plus years through today, I got to witness personally, the energy he transferred to our clients, team, company, his family and everyone around him. From the Sunday school children on the buses with their enormous smiles, to the 5K runners that felt his glow as he cheered them on. Like the sun, his energy source is limitless! Tim is truly the "Energy Guy" and I'm fortunate enough to have him in my life, providing that spark on a continual basis. Just like most any object in the world today, "plug-in" to this enormous power source through this book and Tim's many platforms. You won't be sorry."
David Oliphant, Energy4Sales, Sales Performance Head Coach

ENERGIZERS

to those blessing me with your audience, thank you! I love seeing the sparkle of dreams in your eyes, feeling the energy radiating from your soul, hearing you laugh, seeing your tears and feeling the love flood right back! Blessed to speak globally offering healing and hope through this message of energy ...

"There is only one excuse for a speaker's asking the attention of his audience: he must have either truth or entertainment for them." – Dale Carnegie

"Awesome job and great stories. Thank you for joining us and speaking to the team. Each one of them benefited. Let's connect and stay in touch!" - Shannon Y.

"Thanks again for the enthusiasm and passion! You have great voice projection, and stage presence, and I look forward to watching your future success!" - Stacy B.

"I've heard Tim speak several times and his energy and motivational spirit is consuming! If you need to be motivated, Tim Hooper is the man to call to speak to your group or organization. He is one of a kind for sure!" - Myra S.

"Tim spoke at our event to a group of 500. He was passionate about our cause. His heart was evident, and our people were moved. His energy was contagious to say the least! Thanks!" - Jennifer H.

"You inspired me! Your optimism and enthusiasm are contagious!" - Mike N.

"Tim is a motivating and high performing coach. He knows when and how to challenge you, and when its time to show compassion. He can see the bigger picture. His enthusiasm is captivating and inspiring. Tim's coaching has changed my life for the better forever" - Jay L.

"Energy – Exciting, Never-Ending, Rejuvenating, God-given, Youth. Thanks for your coaching." - Chris C.

"So glad that Travis and I found you, Tim! I'm thankful for the time you invested in Travis, and that he in turn invested back into our family." - Brittany T.

"Your motivation has kept me going! I love following you now and staying inspired!" - Molly M.

"You have an upbeat attitude and great outlook! I appreciate all your energy you put in! Without you & your persevering personality, I would not be working here!" - Shannon C.

"I have worked with Tim in business and as volunteers, and he gives 110% at whatever he is doing. He is extremely passionate about anything that he gets involved with and has more energy than anyone else I've been around. The main thing that I've enjoyed about Tim is his positivity. He is second to none and inspires me greatly in this realm. He is always fun and high energy and will inspire you and your team."- Joel P.

"I worked with Tim for almost two years; during that time, he was always able to make my day brighter. I feel confident and humbled when saying that I've never met anyone as positive, motivated and inspiring as him in my life. It was a pleasure, Tim." - Rachel C.

"So blessed to call you friend!! Thank you for always encouraging and speaking life to me (and to everyone)! You make a difference, and I love watching you inspire and energize everyone around you!" - Jenny H.

"Timspiration is what has been a part of keeping me going every morning! Love your motivational posts! So much fun, too." - Rita Y.

ENERGIZERS

to our sponsors who support our vision of "igniting energy to live fully and love deeply," thank you! It's my privilege to list your name as an author recommended resource ...

"Alone we can do so little; together we can do so much!"
— Helen Keller

GoHooper Web Design
Gale Stoner Images
TwelveStone Health Partners
Magnolia Medical Center
UFit Murfreesboro
Ashley Benson Fitness
Peachtree Financial Planning
Growability
Isagenix - Gary Brever
Tom James
St. Jude Children's Research Hospital

ENERGIZERS

to the Energizer Tribe who pre-ordered this book committing to share the energy with their teams, families and friends, thank you ...

"Commit to live fully and love deeply –
igniting energy every day!"

Shane Reeves
Rod Key
Travis Tipton
Brittany Tipton
Ray Singer
John Turner
Tracy Turner
Glenda Victory
Kylejay Lee
Monte Mohr
Brian Chalmers
Chris Clayton
City Auto Sales, LLC
Chattanooga Head Start Program
Middle Tennessee State University
Lynsey Nail
Lissette Lister
Hannah Hooper
Rachel Garvin

Rita York
Patti Jenkins
Nicole Remkus
Adam Skelton
Todd Griffin
Tammy Anderson
Gina Lennon
Annette Lane
Michelle North
Kathy Stout
Kristi Ankrom
Jeff Molnar
Andrew Hooper
Sarah Ingram
Sandi Solomon
Jen Hooper
David Oliphant
Talie Weir
John Hooper

... to those who have since bought this book and all who will, welcome to the **Energizer Tribe**. Thank you for investing in your energy – your very lifeforce ...

- Invite your friends to grab their copy @ www.timehooper.com
- Follow us on social media @ timehooper.com

FOREWORD

by Jen Hooper

" ... realizing what true energy is all about changed him – and me!" – Jen Hooper

Tim's always had an amazing outlook on life. For the fourteen years I've known him, I've always seen him smile and whistle even while doing jobs such as cleaning a bathroom or fueling a furnace – one of the farm's chores he did when we first met. Much of his upbringing and even coming into our marriage, he had very little confidence. He would apologize quite often for just about everything – even things outside of his control. I've always known God had something big in store for him, and sure enough, when he turned 25, his whole mindset changed. Our lives changed – drastically. He became more intentional about his outlook. He started valuing himself as God values him. He made peace with his past and somewhat daunting plans for our future. He's always been a terrific husband, father, son, brother, and employee, but realizing what true energy is all about changed him – and me. He's become more fully present in our lives. I can say Tim lives every word in this book, and I believe "Got Energy" will impact and change your life! ~ Jen

DEDICATION
to some of the special people in my life

"There's a destiny that makes us brothers: none goes his way alone: all that we send into the lives of others, comes back into our own." – Edwin Markham

Jennifer Dawn, my love! Thank you for faithfully supporting me and encouraging me through the brainstorming, writing, editing and application of this book. I love you and the energy we share! You've taught me so much about patience, meaningful relationships and deep trust. Thanks for going on this journey with me! To many more amazing years together!

Nikki, Jeremy, Ethan and Kaylee, thank you for the many snuggles, precious notes, paintings of *Time4Energy* logos, your two, four, six and seven-year-old encouragement, love, and perfect examples of unfettered energy. You remind me constantly that, too often, we grow up and let life beat us down, when instead, we could be living like you: resilient and full of life! I trust you read this book and use it as your guide to think and dream big about an abundant life full of opportunity to create value – living fully and loving deeply! I will always love you for you!

Mom, thank you for your love and support, and for flunking me in English in the fourth grade so I'd understand the basics of writing. Thanks, too, for teaching this hyper kid to be diligent. The power of one handwritten, meaningful note is your story! I love you!

Dad, the work ethic and positive attitude you taught made life much easier and set me up to succeed. I love you, believe in you and always will.

To my brother Paul, I miss you, and hope telling your story sparks the same bonus mentality that visiting your grave sparked in me. I love you and will see you soon.

To all my siblings, John, Stephen, Hannah, Ruth, Rachel, Sarah, Rebekah, Andrew, Naomi, Esther, Joanna and Abigail, thank you for your support, love and for being your authentic selves, chasing your dreams and loving life! I love each of you dearly!

To my pastor, Dr. Norris, who counselled me as a young guy to find myself and get rooted and grounded. Thank you for your edification and love. Your power in the pulpit stirs my soul; the most significant moments, perhaps, being those when the service left script – unrehearsed – tears were shed, hearts were squeezed, and spirits revived. Thanks for your purity and energy!

To my accountability partners, coaches and mentors, Kevin, Joe, Joel, Shane, John, Rod, and Gale, for your consistent lives and belief in me. For accepting me as imperfectly perfect and continually inspiring me to grow! "Scrum Times" are epic!

To my former employers, Mark, Jeff, and Stephen, for being go-getters and investing confidence and skill in me. Thanks for giving me a shot. I hope your lives and businesses are richly blessed by this book.

To Matt and Christa, Dave and Debbie, Dave and Michelle, Jeremy and Colleen, and others who invested huge love deposits in some of the most crucial moments of my teenage years. Thank you for being fully present when it counted the most!

To all my extended family and friends, thanks for journeying with me. Your support means more than words will ever have the capacity to express!

INTRODUCTION
why write this book

"The message is rich, it's powerful, and most importantly, it's needed now more than ever."

Dear Energizer, thank you for investing in your energy by scooping up this copy of *"Got Energy? … 3 Musts to Igniting Your Passion"* Connect with us at **www.timehooper.com** and leave us your feedback of how this book helped you. I want to thank you in advance. I also want to thank the countless people who invested in me and inspired me to write this book.

We started *Time4Energy* in 2013 with the goal of reviving excitement and enthusiasm for passionately engaging life and the contribution we get to make through it. But why start *Time4Energy*, research and write this book? Statistics tell us people are worn-out, stressed, anxious, overwhelmed and burned-out. People say all the time, "I wish I had more energy." In our technologically advancing age, we are plugged in – constantly being drained.

This book is not an exhaustive work on energy, nor does it even profess to come close. As vast as the sun and universe are, so is the subject and idea of energy. Here's what we know. We all wish for a tad more energy. Deep down, we all want to maximize our potential and have an impact in the years of our life. We want to live, but not just live. We want to enjoy the experience of feeling fully awakened to life. People want to thrive as human-beings. Our clients, corporations we speak for, communities we live in and people across our world have this one thing in common – we want to thrive! We want to have our needs met and meet the needs of others, love, be at peace and do good in this world. *Simply stated, thriving could be defined as living fully and loving deeply.*

Realizing the universal longing for more energy and passionately living each day to the fullest, I share some of my life experiences, ideas and research on personal energy. I've put these simple, powerful truths into practice and have found healing in my own life. I've been privileged to coach executives and watch the tremendous effects in their lives and those of the people they lead. I've been moved as I watch tears flow from stages as I speak. The message is rich, it's powerful, and most importantly, it's needed now more than ever.

Do you want to feel more passionate about life and what you do?

Know this. The things you do to increase, focus and fortify your energy can drive a lasting passion. So, if there's a small spark ignited deep in your soul, if I can get you to envision life with more meaning, if your energy is improved by a fraction, and if the seeds of greater awakening to life are sown, then I will count the hours of writing to have been successful. Let's dive in and take a closer look.

Breakdown of the book
philosophy, then practical

The first five chapters give us the philosophy of energy. We reason what fullness looks like. Jot notes in these chapters and dream with me. Envision what passionate, abundant and vibrant life looks like for you. I speak vulnerably throughout the book and ask you to unfetter your emotions by breaking down any walls or defensive barriers. Life leaves many of us with scars and wounds. I want to understand and feel your pain. I want to reach through these pages, gently squeeze your arm, look you in the eyes and tell you, "I believe in you." Please open your heart in these first five chapters and consider the power of an energized life. **When our hearts are stirred, our energy begins to flow again.** When energy is tapped into, we begin enthusiastically engaging life. So, in these first five chapters, realize your life can be awakened, abundant and attractive. You can feel and be energized and best of all, you CAN be a source of energy to love and illuminate our world!

The remaining chapters of this book give very practical steps to become so passionate about your energy - building and bolstering it. It's like runners who begin demanding more of their bodies. They naturally begin craving more water and more pure nutrition; they detest empty calories. My goal is sparking a passion for showing up fully, engaging with everything you've got and getting results – truly energized! Craving wholeness, fullness and abundance. Finding internal calm for powerful action – focused, channeled, and vibrant! When you truly start living, being fully present, connecting, energy ignited, you'll detest emptiness – energy swindlers – literally. The "empty calories" of life won't appeal to you, because you're demanding more out of life. You'll begin to ask of everything, "Is it worth my energy?"

Goals of the book

there are eight of them, and all their acronyms form T.I.M.E. (as in *Time4Energy*) for ease of memory – so that you can get more out of life

1. To Ignite More Energy – Why? So that you can live every moment fully present – powerfully effective.
2. To Inspire More Enthusiasm – Why? So that you can choose to live and work passionately.
3. To Increase More Engagement – Why? So that your life's work creates maximum value.
4. To Infuse More Excitement – Why? So that you can realize anticipation and experience joy in life.
5. To Invigorate More Empowerment – Why? So that your mind can be stimulated to think powerfully, imagine, dream and believe.
6. To Invest More Encouragement – Why? So that you can offer hope and belief to others.
7. To Interface More Emotion – Why? So that you're intelligently understanding feelings and able to nurture relationships.
8. To Influence More Effectiveness – Why? So that you can better lead those following your example.

Interacting with the book

share it, use it, write in it, and coffee stain it

We want to share the joy of your journey igniting energy in your life! Would you get the biggest smile you can (hint: laugh a little and imagine being a kid again). Hold your book up. Snap a selfie and post on social media (tag: timehooper on any social platform and hashtag #GotEnergy

When you see something you love, highlight it, and go a step further by sharing it. Treat it like seed and plant it – it will come back to you. If it speaks to you, share it. Chances are someone else needs it, too. Snap a picture of the page. Post it. Hashtag #GotEnergy

Go to **www.timehooper.com** and subscribe. We don't clutter your inbox. Subscribe so you can stay inspired with weekly episodes of "The Juice" as well as our speaking schedule so you can attend when we're in your area of the world.

Write in this book, tear it up, spill your coffee on it. It can remap life for you; it did for me. Use it as a tool.

Here's to your energy and passion to live fully and love deeply! I love you and can't wait to meet you … Tim

ENERGY

*Understanding
the depth of energy
& resolving to feel
fully awakened to life,
living abundantly
with purpose & passion,
& loving others deeply!*

What could this mean for you?

CHAPTER 1
ENERGY DEFINED
reclaiming a powerful meaning

"Energy is the internal force that transforms anxiety into abundance, burnout into boundless zeal, exhaustion into enthusiasm, fatigue into fullness, judgement into joy, overwhelm into overflowing, and stress into serenity!"

Mascot

Can you guess what this is? It's big, pink, furry, wears sunglasses, plays a drum – more like pounds a drum – and has this little hole in the back. In this hole is a black, plastic box and in the box, you insert two AA-batteries to make it run. Chuckling, you've figured out that I'm talking about the infamous Energizer Bunny! You know – the friendly rabbit we see on top of the Energizer battery section in the Walmart aisle, or in the comical, TV commercials. Now, would a book on energy be complete without eluding to this universal mascot of energy? No. So, I want to start right here with this *simple and perfect example*. Many of us have either been called an Energizer Bunny, or we've called someone the Energizer Bunny. Perhaps this big, furry, fun-loving bunny has come to mind when we've met some charismatic, active and perhaps slightly hyper individual, or little kid! "I want his energy," we've thought to ourselves.

The names "Energizer Bunny" and "Energy Guy" labelled me when I first entered the workforce as a janitor and official errand boy. I could've been called worse; fortunately, these names stuck causing me to join millions in their quest for more energy. The statistics blew me away. One in every five Americans claims an energy deficiency severe enough to detract from daily normal living according to *Medical News Today*. I wasn't particularly fond of the names at first. Being a low-confidence eighteen-year-old, I'd determined, after a couple rough patches as a kid, to keep a positive attitude in all life's situations. Growing up on a horse farm and in a military family, hard work and discipline formed the underlying mantra of our home. There are a ton of wonderful memories and good things I learned growing up, and I practice being grateful for these things. Too often, a negative, self-depreciating and harsh, heavily-disciplined environment existed. I left home at eighteen and joined the workforce out of high school. At nine dollars per hour and motivated to provide for my new bride, Jennifer, I picked up a bucket of Pine-Sol, a wool rag, and began cleaning bathrooms in a Smyrna, Tennessee machine shop. I love to sing and not wanting to be distracting at work, I'd step it down a notch by whistling. Across the hallway sat Ms. Deb, our purchasing manager whose role I'd assume a few months later. "Hey, energy guy," she'd say, "will you clean my house, too?" I'd sometimes whistle softer or worry about whistling at all. Was I acting too happy? Was it showing too much? What did people think? Do they think I'm trying to outdo them? Am I? "Maybe you should tone it down …" my mind would say. The mental battle ensued. I was thankful for my job, and whether I felt it or not, I was going to act happy. *I became a positive and passionate façade.*

Other times, I worked through lunch to get a project done and coworkers labelled me the "Energizer Bunny." They saw a great smile, positive attitude, and being number seven of fourteen siblings, I tended to be a friendly relater. I was very happy for a great job, an employer who believed in me and the feeling of contribution and meaningful work. Right here and right now mark this down. Meaningful contribution is wired into our DNA. When we shirk from working or finding meaningful contribution, then we too will shirk the work that a truly energized life will require. A passionate heart and positive attitude will take you to great places. It will! Even a passionate heart with a negative attitude has taken people to great places. Corporate America and Corporate Global is filled with passionate people. Many of us "passionates" pull on a mask every day we get up. The party is great, but alone in the shadows, we must face reality. Here's where true energy is going be so meaningful to so many. Now, without wanting to make a meaningful contribution through our life's work, the desire to ignite our energy is pretty much nonexistent. Work is part of the energy equation. When you get energy right – work becomes fun! However, if you feel passionate about something and have a good work ethic, but you feel stuck, drained, overwhelmed, burned-out, unenthused, stagnant, or empty, read on. For me, unfortunately, the affirmations of "energetic" and "passionate" came from all other places and arenas of life, too. I sucked it up. I enhanced my performance every chance I had. Owned it and crushed it at work and went home to crash on the couch. I didn't have a lot of energy left for family, community, or even exercising. My existence was consumed with playing the part, beating the drum, and looking like energy. Fortunately, I was young and could coast in my health a good long while yet, right? That extra community or social involvement I wanted could and would have to wait. Maybe by the time I'm retired. Positive and passionate performance was great and put me ahead for sure, but without a firm foundation and being real and genuine inside, passion doesn't and won't last.

Completely Wrong

When I turned twenty-five, a life changing event occurred in my life and I decided to change some things – a lot of things. One thing I decided was to start bottling up some of my "energy" to give to others. I'd write a book on energy! That's when I ran smack into the face of reality. What I thought I knew about energy and what I'd been labelled for was completely – completely – wrong! Passion and energy are not the same, though we often confuse the two. We've interchanged the words so regularly as a society that *we rarely think of energy as anything more than external power, excitement and passion.* Energy's meaning is so much deeper than our casual use of the word, and grasping its meaning can literally change your life. It changed mine.

Here I was, amplifying the drum beating, the marching, the nodding my pink furry head up and down. I was the "Energizer Bunny" all right. The sunglasses fortunately saved me the embarrassment of anyone looking too deeply past my grin and deep into my soul. My soul was the little black box with those batteries. That was the place where Tim – the real Tim – sat quaking, shaking and scared of his own shadow. Could I have changed my past to be a confident young man? Like many out there who have past wounds and scars, no. We can't change the past. The point here is, too often, energy's mislabeled in our society. *Instead of focusing on the small, quiet, powerful, and seemingly insignificant, internal battery*, energy is misconstrued as the outward expressions: waving of the arms, charismatic demeanor, smiling and active persona. These outward attributes may very well be the result of a deep-rooted love of life, an inner peace and being a renewed source of energy.

However, in our fast-paced, technologically-advanced, information-overloaded and instantly-gratified society, the renewal, the healing, the fortitude and wholeness that we as human beings need, too often doesn't happen. We rush through life "putting it on." In his book, *Quiet Talks on Service*, S.D. Gordon writes, "We all admire the beauty of the trees that rear their heads, and send out their branches, and make the world so beautiful with their soft green foliage. But, have you thought about the twin tree, the unseen tree that belongs to these we see? For every tree that grows up and out with its beauty and fruit, there must be another – the twin tree that goes down and out." Energy's internal!

Inevitable Burnout

In the example of the tree, often, the twin tree – the tap root and roots go down further than the tree grows upward. The unseen tree's constantly tapped into the sources of energy in the soil, transferring these to the branches and yielding abundant fruit. Too often in life, we look like energy but have very little root. Our tree – our life – is shriveling away. We look like energy until we get one-on-one with someone or by ourselves. It's then we're not real sure what drives us or what our life's all about. We're beating the drum, marching and nodding our furry pink head up and down. We're thankful for the sunglasses to hide the past wounds and hurts, the stress, the overwhelmed feelings, and the internal anxiety about our future. Oh my, and the sunglasses, they come in all different shades: ego, position, title, money, power, prestige, need for validation and the list goes on. Internally, our battery – our energy – is drained and unrenewed. We're dying for the weekend just to get some reprieve. Instead of a renewing and even a surging opportunity, our vacations are an escape from life. We're gasping for breath. We're on "E" and almost tapped out. We're at the point of burnout. Perhaps we're on a prescription drug simply to cope with the anxiety of it all – many are. According to a *CNN Health* article, the average American fills twelve prescriptions per year. This is an annual expenditure of over $234 billion! Americans spend the most globally on healthcare and statistically are some of the unhealthiest and stressed. We can't find the energy to break free let alone transform and fortify our ever-dwindling energy – all rooted in our mental, physical, spiritual and emotional wellbeing. We know we should, but we're stuck. We need energy badly and we know it – deep down.

What is this life we're living? Whose is this life we're living? It's ours. We've lost focus of the battery, our internal personal power, our driver, the foundation – our energy. We've emphasized the façade and are going through the motions. It's not entirely our fault. Our environment and culture today emphasize the outward appearance, the bandwagon, and fitting-in. Think about this. In a generation's time, *we've shifted our inner sense of peace and being fully present enjoying time in the physical presence of family and friends to thinking in terms of Instagram posts, Facebook captures and tweets.* Again, there's nothing inherently wrong with social media, but are we building what counts or chasing a virtual mirage? Energy's foundational! How's our internal foundation? How's our taproot – our energy? Like Cicero wisely wrote in his work De Amicitia, "To be; rather than to seem." Each of us must analyze our own foundation and ask, "How are we really doing deep down inside?" Like Epictetus said, "First, say to yourself what you would be; and then, do what you have to do."

Reclaiming Energy's Definition

In defining ourselves or others, we use and coin words we believe synonymous with energy. I've heard them and used them: intense, powerful, dynamic, spirited, strong, a force, vibrant, driven, lively, the juice, zealous, charismatic, enthusiastic and passionate. Exactly opposite lurks a dreaded list: drained, apathetic, lazy, lethargic, burned-out, empty, and disengaged. While we often use the word "energy" interchangeably with other illustrious terms, the concept of energy is far deeper. Energy is the difference between enthusiasm and exhaustion, boundless zeal and burnout. If dwindling energy equals feeling drained, what would ignited personal energy do for us? Ignited energy is the best driver; the internal force enabling us to act - a force working for us! *Lasting passion (the feeling) and effectiveness (our work) are driven and sustained by an ignited energy (the foundation).* Energy's a fact; a state of being; the reality of inside. Let's look at the exact definition and origin of energy so we can better understand it. With a better understanding, we can change the way we look at energy and subsequently, everything.

Let's turn to *Merriam-Webster's* for the purest definition of energy. Here it is, plain and simple. "Capacity to do work." Another definition states: "Capacity or power for work or vigorous activity." Still, other sources give additional meaning: "Internal or inherent power; the power of operating … the effectual operation … strength or force producing the effect." Finally, we find, "Capacity to perform work (such as causing motion or the interaction of molecules)." When I first read and studied the definition of energy, I was shocked! Shocked! Heartbroken in fact. I wanted it to mean all the externals. To embody the busy, active and passionate person I was. Here's when I realized my preconceived ideas were totally wrong. I was thinking external exertion without any regard to internal capacity - fullness! Our society often uses the term "energetic person" for appearance and initial impression without considering the depth of its meaning. Inner capacity? How boring, right? Not quite. Fully understanding this word, this concept of energy, can bring one's life so much clarity, healing and purpose. How? Let's break the definition down.

Sponge, Camel, Battery & Sun Tzu's Bow

"Capacity to do work." What if we lived and operated at full capacity? How much more effective would we be? Imagine knowing who you are, what your purpose is and showing up in power - fully charged! Fact is, many of us are drained - not fully charged. What does capacity mean? Capacity holds a double meaning. First, "the maximum containable amount." Second, "the capacity or ability do something." In energy's case, both variations become meaningful, because being at capacity (full and not empty; charged and not drained) gives you the capacity (ability; stamina; endurance) to do work.

Think of scrubbing the kitchen floor as a kid. The capacity of water the sponge held dictated your ability to get the job done. You may have used a tiny sponge, or a great big sponge. This is ability. You may have barely dipped the corner of the sponge into the bucket of water and scrubbed mostly dry. This is capacity. I'd find the largest sponge, submerge the porous fibers beneath the suds and slosh it all over the floor to get the dirt soaking for easier removal! This way I could move on to the next chore, or grab my BMX and pedal down the street to play soccer with my friends.

Imagine a camel deciding to trek across the desert without first having drank its thirty – yes thirty – gallons of water. This typically water-guzzling creature's depleted capacity would greatly hamper its ability to do its work. So with energy, your inner capacity – fullness – dictates your capacity – ability – to do work.

Have you ever had to replace your car battery? You went out to start your car one morning. Turning the key, you received no response. The charge was gone. We say a dead battery "won't hold a charge." Its capacity is empty and therefore, it has no capacity or ability to provide the ignition to your car's starter.

In his epic work, *The Art of War*, Sun Tzu states, "Energy may be likened to the bending of a crossbow." Consider an archer's bow for a second. Elasticity in the limbs determine the success of sending an arrow down the range to penetrate the target. Should the tensile strength be insufficient and a bow limb shatters, the energy is immediately transferred out of the bow through the weak limb. Subsequently, the arrow receives very little energy if any at all. It may fly a short way or fall to the ground, but most definitely won't be successful in its mission. Our level of energy – our inner capacity and fullness – dictates our effectiveness, our impact in life, and our very ability to fully enjoy life. *Our level of energy determines how fully we will live and how deeply we will love!*

Personal Capacity

Let's think now in terms of personal capacity. Do you remember a time when you felt on top of your game? Everything was good at home, you spent some recharge time over a weekend, on a trip, or perhaps with family. You were consistently exercising, eating great, and guzzling the water. You were in good spirits and charged into work to conquer a new project you were excited about doing. Consistently feeling energized and enthusiastic comes when our inner capacity – our battery – is filled up, charged, fully awakened, full of power and very little is detracting or corroding our energy! This fullness drives our passion and we're excited. So, why not feel this way all the time? We want to, right? What happens? Life happens. Our world is full of distractions, interruptions and vices. Incapacitators – energy swindlers – lurk on every corner. Think back to the bow illustration. The bow is our life, the limbs represent our energy and the ability to fully bend depicts our capacity. The arrow is metaphorical of our life work – our meaningful endeavors. If energy is low, the bow can bend only slightly, and the arrow is slow, ineffective and falls short of its target. However, if the bow has the capacity to bend fully, the arrow – your life's work – will hit the target every time.

When we analyze capacity, we must look at our own capacity. We are all different and have different abilities. This world is like Grandma's cupboard. My goodness. She has every size glass, dozens of coffee cups, plastic Scooby-Doo cups for the grandkids, and just about something for every season, not to mention the fifteen you've bought her with family pictures the last fifteen holidays. All of us are different. My capacity is not your capacity, and neither is yours mine. We'll look at comparison later. Comparing ourselves to anyone else or anyone else's standard is only detrimental to our energy! Some have been through incredible tragedy in life. Perhaps their physical capacity has been decreased. Others have been affected by trauma and their mental capacity is limited. I feel for these dear friends – deeply. Life is not a bed of roses for sure. So, as we ask ourselves where we're at and where we want to be, let's be honest with ourselves. How energized do you feel today in relation to where you think you can be (your potential)? You may think your capacity is one pint. Until you accept and determine to maximize your capacity – this pint – you won't know for sure what your capacity is. *We must determine today to increase our potential by expanding our capacity, for then, we can and will be in the position (have the ability) to splash over on this world in a greater way!* Purpose today to strengthen your bow so you can maximize your effectiveness!

Work

"Capacity to do work." Work. Yes, there's the dreaded word. In fact, many people look at work as a necessary evil. We've seen the quote that states, "Create a life you don't need a vacation from," but for so many of us, over 900 million according to the *Huffington Post*, we don't know what this looks like. We can't fathom this. We look at our jobs as boring, difficult and unfulfilling. We save, hope, dream and work all our life so that we have enough for retirement. We can't wait to escape the job we hate. I remember an old "Andy Griffith" episode satirically depicting this unending quest. Howard Sprague decides he's going to go buy a condo on the beach. Poor guy. Doesn't last a week. He has no purpose. We've heard the stories of retirement boredom. The struggle to find purpose and fulfillment after leaving a career is real. If you're retired and reading this, know one thing. Working a job should be no different than living life. Man was created to find and fulfill his divine purpose. Whether you have a clearly defined purpose, or your purpose becomes finding your purpose, have a purpose.

Living in Germany, I was privileged to visit some historical and sobering landmarks like Auschwitz. One of my heroes is Viktor Frankl. Chronicling his experiences as this concentration camp's prisoner during World War II, he describes his psychotherapeutic method as defining a life purpose and immersing yourself in imagining its outcome. In his book, *Man's Search for Meaning*, he writes, "The prisoner who lost faith in the future – his future – was doomed. With his loss of belief in the future, he also lost his spiritual hold; he let himself decline and became subject to mental and physical decay." Our life and our job should never be a prison. What's your purpose – your work? *Your work, your meaningful endeavors, your personal mission statement should be clear in your mind.* In future chapters we'll write this down. Many today are looking to get out of work because we've conditioned ourselves to believe work is a necessary evil. Let's recondition our thinking. Finding and embracing your life work is crucial to your energy. It's in the definition – IN THE DEFINITION! If you hate work, you'll struggle increasing capacity (igniting energy). Embracing and expanding your effort in your work, today, is necessary to ignite your energy - whether you currently love your work, or not.

Origins of the Word

Why would "capacity to do work" be the purest definition of energy? Consider the origin of the word "energy." Coming from a "mid sixteenth century French word "énergie," it finds its roots in the Greek word "Energeia." Two parts make up this Greek word. First, the word "en" (in, within), and second, the word "ergon" (work). Therefore, we have the internal capacity enabling the external ability to do work. We find three very interesting and important concepts from the origins of energy: condition, transference and work. Remember these.

Condition

From its Greek origins, Aristotle took "energeia" and formulated the concept of energy around 300 BC. Energy was and is best described as a condition. The condition of "being at work." English speaking people first used the word "energy" in the 1600's, but solely in reference to power.

Thus, we still treat the words as close relatives today. However, the idea of energy being a condition was formulated shortly after and introduced to physics in the 1800's by Thomas Young. This idea brought clarity to a word that's mistaken as something we get or lose. Energy is present in all living things. Like health, we can't necessarily get health; we can, however, be in poor health or great health. We can improve our health. Our energy condition is either poor, great or somewhere in between. Like health, our energy is inherent to life. We can either ignore or improve our energy. ***Energy is no longer a cheap word, it's our very lifeforce; it's responsible for the condition of our lives!*** In the 1900's Albert Einstein established the general concept of "energy" into scientific form used today. "Energy is a condition that describes the capacity to do work." When we realize that energy is a condition (state of being) and the laws that govern energy improve or worsen this condition, we then realize that our quest for quick energy is futile. So, instead of saying, "I want more energy," what we should be saying is, "How do I improve my energy?" The condition of having full, maximized and abundant capacity to do purposeful work – ignited energy!

Transference

Transference simply means that energy is transferred from a body to another body, or from a body to an object or vice versa. Say a person uses a certain amount of force to move an object, complete a task, and so on. Energy is transferred from that person to the object or task. When you eat, drink, sleep or think, energy is transferred from an object or idea into your body. There's this fancy law in physics that states, "Energy cannot be created or destroyed; it can only be transformed from one form to another." This is known as *The Law of Conservation of Energy*. One is not required to study or master the vast science of physics to understand this transformational concept. I'd be hopeless for sure. Very simply, energy is transferred. It's not created or destroyed. Consider the situations in your life when energy is transferred to and from you. Becoming more keenly aware of this principle sets us up for success. We must begin seeing our energy as this flow – this transference – and it's in a flow state all the time.

Work (In Physics)

Of similar interest, the term "work" was defined in the 1800's as well. Since then, work has come to mean the "mental or physical effort done in order to achieve a result." This is how we view our career and occupation. While we've analyzed finding meaning and purpose in the gift called work, in physics, a very similar definition exists. In physics, however, it has a defined prerequisite. Simply stated, work is the "transference of energy to create movement." Movement – a result – must occur to qualify the transfer of energy as work. "Movement – a result – must occur to qualify the transfer of energy as work." Fortunately, we aren't compensated based on a physics definition. Hmmm, what if we were? Employers take risks on our ability to "get the job done," and if we show good enough attempt, or even just show up nowadays, we receive compensation. Wow! What if this changed? Would we be more careful to make sure our activity - our energy transference - effected movement and achieved a result? It begs the question that if our energy, our capacity to do work, is to be improved, increased and maximized, we should explore the areas worth transferring energy to – our work. We'll dig deep into mapping the constant flow – the transference of energy – in chapter 10.

Measuring Energy's Flow

Let's look at some numbers as we begin to understand we can chart and measure our energy flow. The "energy" industry's numbers aren't that energizing, though. Over thirteen billion in Monster Energy, Red Bull and Rockstar "energy" drinks sell annually, and sales are on the rise! Does this statistic scream, "Thriving"? Or is drained more like it? Coffee houses boom; the industry ranking only second to oil production on a global scale. Yes, Starbucks, Dunkin Donuts and our local coffee shops make great hangouts, but are we overindulging or dependent on caffeine? According to a recent *Forbes* article, **seventy percent of employees attest they feel disengaged in their careers.** Just ask ten people in passing if they could use more energy. For most, it would be a definite, "Yes!" I've asked hundreds what energy means to them. It's "I need more energy", or "If I had more energy, I'd be able to do _____". *Energy is a condition, and with the three powerful and basic principles of perspective, ownership, and accountability – POA (the following core sections of this book build upon each of these) – we can build and bolster ours!*

What you and I need to do – must do – is pause and think. Quiet our minds. Stop. Turn everything and everybody off and think. We don't do this much anymore. We don't even know who lives upstairs many days. We've not taken the time to introduce ourselves to our amazing minds that live in our heads right behind our eyes and between our ears. We must create space to think. Not just right here and now about who we are, what our purpose is and how fulfilled and energized we feel, but also every day. So, think ... think about your life. Who are you? THINK! Are you thriving? Do you feel energized? Do you feel enthusiastic - alive and fully awakened? Does your purpose in life uplift you? Are you passionately going after your dreams and goals? Are you engaging every arena of your life with all your gusto? Do you connect deeply with others? Or are you like I was? Hurting deep down in your soul; your energy feeling constantly depleted? Friend, at a time when loneliness is becoming epidemic, you're not alone. Just the fact that you've picked up this book means that you want more out of life, and you realize we all have tremendous potential – more than we ever thought possible. We have amazing dreams, ideas and hopes for a better life. Passionately engaging life is a daily challenge and choice – a daily one. We have tremendous potential; yet, mediocrity pulls on all of us to level off – to coast.

Secret Sauce

I ask that you read this section and then close your eyes. Seriously. You wouldn't believe how many of my audiences give a nervous smile and hardly close their eyes – it's more of a suspicious squint. I'm laughing because as part of many past audiences, I'm guilty of having my guard up as a speaker walks on stage. Since it's just you and me, please read this section and then close your eyes. I want you to imagine. Imagination is something we did all the time as kids. ***Imagination is literally the magic – the secret sauce of our minds.*** Our logical brains condition our imagining. Our logical brains conform our beliefs and behaviors to what we've experienced in our environments. Our imaginations can take us out of our brains' self-imposed conditions and barriers. Imagination questions everything.

Question your potential. Question whether you're maximizing it. Imagination can stretch our perception of what we're capable of. What we believe we're capable of will drastically impact how much energy we ignite in our lives. It's like a gas grill. You don't have to ignite all the burners. Depends on how much your grilling, right? Company comes over, you light them all. If you desire to make a lasting impact on the lives you touch and experience life to the fullest measure, you'll ignite your deepest energies. You'll light all the burners. Your energy level dictates how fully awakened you are to every dimension of your life, your family, your kids, your occupation and in every other arena.

Imagine Living Life:

- Understanding your value, your uniqueness, your purpose – Imagine living with a deep, inner peace.
- Operating with an ownership mentality, making no excuses, just consistent forward action. - Imagine a powerful drive knowing exactly where you're going and excited about it.
- Passionately living from a heart full of love and sharing a contagious enthusiasm – Imagine being an abundant source of encouragement.
- Learning to welcome and embrace the incredible resource of accountability – Imagine the ability of vulnerability and getting along with everyone.
- Attracting team members, referral partners, clients, friends and family members through daily renewal and ignited energy – Imagine inspiring the best in yourself and all those around you.

So, close your eyes and imagine. Take three solid minutes. They can be excruciatingly slow when you're this intentional. But, take three minutes. Close your eyes and imagine … Open your eyes. What does life look like? What's different than it is today? What must change? What's possible? Scribble something that came to mind:

_____

_____

_____

_____

Hyper-Drained vs. Deep-Overflowing

Establishing what's possible is essential in measuring energy in our life. Similarly, knowing what energy's not is necessary. Think of a past memory of someone you've labelled as "high-energy." Were they a quiet, peaceful and powerful force whose presence you craved in your life; or, were they loud, rambunctious and forceful? What kind of "energy" do you want to be? I remember this saying my mom would tell us as kids. She'd remind us to "stay cool, calm and collected." The evidence is over-whelming that many feel fatigued with burnout just around the corner. What's worse, many won't make the time to stop pounding the drum, stop marching to everyone else's beat and hiding behind the sunglasses – the masks. *Many want to look like energy instead of taking the time to learn how to be whole – truly energized.* Instead of committing to the long-term fortification of fullness – the real work of living energized – many try to fake it; and, their mindsets, focus and relationships all suffer. Those who aren't deeply energized won't fully live!

What we must do with this book – any book – is pick them up as mirrors. Be the "Man in the Mirror" like the old song's lyrics. It's written for me, Tim. I must look in this mirror to check in with myself – no one else. How's my energy? Is my energy flowing up from within and spilling over, or do I have to force myself to contribute in life? Am I squeezing for all I'm worth – knuckles turning white – to show up with any sort of passion? Is Monday dreaded, hump-day celebrated and "TGIF!" shouted on Friday? Is life a drag? We must make an honest assessment and ask ourselves, "Is this really the way I want to live?"

Energy Reading

The electric company used to come by and read our meter, now it's done remotely. Interestingly, I've never called to argue my electric bill. They measure it and bill it. Shouldn't we take a reading of our energy if we hope to improve it? Do you want to improve your energy? Why? What's your reason? Who's your reason? Reasons are powerful sources of inspiration that keep us commited when the going gets tough. We'll take the first small step if we have a powerful enough reason. With that in mind, jot your powerful reason here:

_____

_____

_____

But, how do we quantify our energy? If we want to increase energy, how do we first measure where we're at today? Let's set a benchmark against which we can measure. *Imagine bounding out of bed, enthusiastically engaging life and everyone in it. Imagine the energy to show up fully present and abundant for those you love and care for!* How would you feel consistently operating at full capacity? Here's the start of the benchmark.

Emotions and Feelings

Now, how do you feel today? Are you in touch with your emotions? Our "e-motions" are our energy in motion. Our energy is moving constantly. It's our lifeforce. Our ability to perform. Like high - performance business coach, Andy Bailey, says, "Energy is our economic driver of success." This flow state – this motion – produces our emotions, and our emotions create our feelings. This is so powerful to understand. Our emotions (energy in motion) literally signal the brain to create feelings. Our emotions show which way our energy is flowing – negatively or positively. Our feelings gage how much of our energy is flowing in a positive or negative direction. It's why feelings of disgust turn to jealousy, then to bitterness, and then to hate. Negative energy starts flowing and gains momentum – the wrong way! On a positive note, soaking in feelings of gratitude leads to happiness, which leads to abundance and then to a prosperous mindset. ***Positive energy starts flowing and gains momentum – the right way!***

Measure to Improve

What gets measured gets done, right? Improving your energy in the slightest way is going to change so much of how you feel about yourself and others. Even a sliver of more energy in your day would change things for most people. Are you ready for a fruitful journey of igniting your energy? It's not going to be an overnight deal. That's what "energy" manufacturers like Monster want us to think. To begin the journey, let's measure how energized we feel against our benchmark of operating consistently at full capacity. So, how alive and thriving do you feel about every arena in your life from your job to your personal relationships? How powerful do you feel to take on anything from eating healthy, sleeping more, completing a new project, making a needed change, breaking an addiction, letting go of anxiety and worry, exercising, being fully present with your spouse or children, investing into your team members, getting involved in a charity, starting a business, chasing a dream to finding your passion? A feeling can be misleading by itself as our brains are stimulated from multiple sources, but the conglomerate of our feelings will gage how energized we are.

Energy Defined

Grab your pen and circle on a scale of positive 10 to negative 10 how energized you feel on a consistent basis:

10. Operating consistently at "Abundant"

9. Vibrant

8. Powerful

7. Enthusiastic

6. Engaged

5. Full

4. Excited

3. Driven

2. Passionate

1. Hopeful

0. Stuck

-1. Stressed

-2. Anxious

-3. Tired

-4. Exhausted

-5. Drained

-6. Overwhelmed

-7. Powerless

-8. Burned out

-9. Depressed

-10. Operating consistently at "Empty"

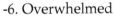

Download a copy or multiple copies from our website as well. www.timehooper.com If you've attended our *Signature Energy4Life Workshop*, you know how empowering a simple benchmarking activity can be. Someone said, "When you name it, it no longer has power over you." Diagnosing our energy condition is a powerful first step!

Ignite Your Energy!

Fifty percent of igniting our energy is identifying the need and deciding to do something about it. We're already half way there. Now, determine to study, learn and take action to improve your energy. No matter how small an improvement, determine to yourself and those you love to dig in and enhance your energy! Energy is life! Imagine your life fully awakened – your soul on fire! In the following chapters, you'll find some simple – not easy – but simple and practical truths to doing just this – igniting your energy which will increase your enthusiasm for passionately engaging life!

As we dig deeper into igniting our energy, we will use the purest definition and look at our energy as a condition. May the following pages improve each of our conditions. May we take a close, hard look at increasing our capacity and transfer our energy to the best use and highest calling – our life's meaningful contribution – our work. Our capacity for doing our life's work is maximized when we are consistently stretching and growing our potential. This quest to reach our greatest potential requires we ignite our deepest energy reserves; for, when energy's ignited, capacity is maximized and our full potential - to live fully and love deeply - is reached!

May we look at our condition, our inner capacity, our ability – our energy – as the priceless treasure it is. We look at our health as a condition in the terms of "poor," "good" and "best of." Or the condition of our homes as well kept and organized, or cluttered and completely disheveled. When we look at energy as a condition, we realize we can improve it to be more efficient, engaged and effective in life's purpose. Conversely, we can discover those areas in our condition we're incapacitated and thus, ineffectual. Why seek to understand the deep and transformational meaning of energy? Why measure each of our current conditions? Why even bother? Because your life is worth living fully awakened! Experiencing the joy of abundant life is incredible! ***When we maximize the amount of time we're fully present in life, we maximize our lives!*** We maximize our impact. We live to the fullest – truly energized! Developing enthusiasm for life will create a need for more of its lifeforce – your energy – and, when you create the need for more, you'll receive more!

CHAPTER 2
ENERGY'S HARMONY
deeper understanding to live fully

"Learn this from water: loud splashes the brook but the oceans depth are calm." - Buddha

A Gut-Wrenching Kick

Wham! I heard it. It wasn't the kick I intended. It was supposed to be a solid but much gentler kick in my brother's direction. Nope. This one contacted his shinbone, and to make matters worse, I was wearing my suede leather, steel-toed, very heavy and clumsy work boots. My brother, my own flesh and blood, let out a sharp cry of pain and collapsed to the blue couch in our recreation room. *The fight that I was determined to win seconds earlier became one of the deepest gut-wrenches I've ever had.* My gut still wrenches remembering the tears and the anger I caused in my brother's eyes. Andrew was four years younger than I was and we did everything together – including fighting. That day, it was a pool stick. Believe that? A pool stick that as a twelve-year-old, I decided was more important than an eternal relationship! I remember that incident so well, because while we'd wrestle all the time, that was the first time I had pained him so badly. I heard it and I felt it; but what I felt the most was the emotional wound rip through his heart as it ripped through mine.

Since then, Andrew's grown past me in height by nearly a foot and could squash me without breaking a sweat. In fact, he's working on his pilot's license to fly the Time4Energy team to speaking engagements and events. We did make up shortly after that fight, and I'm thankful – very thankful – for his grace and mercy! I'll be even more thankful when I'm on the jet with him in the cockpit – trust me!

As we both married and climbed corporate ladders, we'd share conversations over the gut-wrenches of discord and severed relationships at executive levels. Yes, grown-ups fight, and we've figured out how to be more professional about it. We don't always intend to connect the kick. We get so passionate about winning that we forget what's really important. We forget our own power; and the steel-toe makes gut-wrenching connection. What energizes this sort of detrimental behavior? Let's take a look at the discord and harmony of life as it pertains to our energy.

What Energy's Not

Sometimes, the best way to understand what something is starts with figuring out what it's not. We all have ideas and thoughts about energy, how to be energetic and how to feel more empowered. In the previous chapter, we defined energy and its origin. Just being able to grasp the powerful concept that our energy is a condition means that *we firmly hold the key to unlocking some ideas and practical steps we can take to improve and maximize our energy condition.*

First, let's look at a few important aspects of our energy. This chapter will take common ideas about energy and analyze them. Very possibly you've experienced some of these thoughts as you've witnessed passionate people plow through life. Properly understanding energy will help us gain a whole new insight into optimizing our life. Properly understanding what it is not will help guide our thinking.

The deeper – and more basic – our understanding of energy, the simpler it's going to be tapping into and igniting as we decide and commit to live fully – with our whole being! The more uncluttered our inner capacity, the greater potential we have for fresh, daily filling and tremendous effect! Understanding the following sections sets the remaining chapters and principles of perspective, ownership and accountably – POA – up for successful exploration.

Kind of Energy

When we look at energy as simply a charge, a rush of sugar, or ability to perform, then sure – all kinds of "energy" is good. In fact, the word energy has become extremely popular to use in marketing, and in turn, by us as consumers. When we understand energy as a deep, whole-life condition, then it demands a more thorough investigation.

There's negative and positive energy. We've all heard and seen the quote, "They told me I couldn't, so I did it anyway!" While this mindset is popular and can be very emotionally stimulating and motivating, ask yourself this question, "Am I best served by negative energy?" We can all relate to the negative and dramatic stories that tend to come up time and time again at family reunions, certain kinds of environments, or in some social gathering. We wonder inwardly if this person will ever be able to heal and move on. Often, they don't want to, because pain can be a great motivator and somehow, it keeps them going. They live in the toxicity instead of experiencing the thrill of rising above and realizing how much life their bitter, negative energy was actually syphoning away from them.

When we're out to prove someone wrong, prove ourselves right, or to get even, our ability to do life's work may spike for a time or a lifetime, but this negative energy can only detract from others' lives and limits deep relationships.

Dale Carnegie shares the story of entrepreneur and businessman extraordinaire, the oil baron, John D. Rockefeller Sr. Carnegie shares that Rockefeller was pursuing his goal with such "grim determination at the early age of 23," and, according to those who knew him, "nothing lifted his countenance like the good news of a good bargain." Carnegie said, "He could never put his head on his pillow without worrying about losing his fortune." Rockefeller confessed to a neighbor in Cleveland, Ohio, that he "wanted to be loved," yet he was "so cold and suspicious," according to Carnegie, "that few people even liked him." When reading of this sad and lonely existence, I wondered what drove Rockefeller. Not surprising, history tells the story of his father, William, abandoning the family when John was just a teenager. John's father once bragged, "I cheat my boys every chance I get. I want to make 'em sharp." Perhaps this deep hole in John's heart filled him with the passion that drove him!

Shakespearean plays, love triangles and I'm sure a host of relationships in our lives are reflective of negative energy. A limited, backward-flowing, energy headed for burnout. We see instances of negative energy daily. Just stand in a fast-food line, and before long, you'll witness someone who's made it their life mission to teach the up-and-coming, young worker how not-to "throw" a hamburger on a bun, or what "lite" ice means. Did you feel super comfortable and pleased witnessing this confrontation, or were you uneasy. Sure! The negative vibes went everywhere stressing everyone out. This is negative energy.

Negative energy is powerful. The swindlers of gossip, bitterness and hate belong to this family. It can spread like wildfire, too. As humans, we already have what's called a negativity-bias (more prone to zoom in on the negatives than we are to look for the positives), and thus, when someone is wronged, and they let us in on it, our energy gets going as well. Often times in the same negative direction as the gossipee's. Gossip literally feeds on negative energy. That's why we have the urge to not just tell one or a dozen people, but as many as we feel we can "confide" in. We never get filled when we gossip. It's always energy-swindling, draining and negative-flowing. We have to be super intentional to pause and ask, "Which direction is my energy running here?" We quickly find negative energy detracts internally! It's one of the harshest task-masters! We are looking for filling externally and swindle other's energy just to survive.

Positive energy, on the other hand, is harder to stimulate internally, because it requires super intentionality and rising to a higher frequency. Once stimulated, though, positive energy will look for the good, find common ground and compel others to join. It's giving, not detracting. I very much wonder if this is why Jesus instructed his followers to "turn the other cheek and bless them that wrong you." In the end, positively-energized people will be at peace with themselves (internally) and able to walk away. The negatively-energized person must stay trying to fill the void left inside, must win at all costs, or will find another human being to swindle and drain energy from.

Let's not condemn the person who exudes negative energy. Chances are someone or some unfortunate experience in their past has wounded them deeply. It's our call to overflow grace and love to them while we guard against absorbing their toxic energy. These hurts are very real and when we allow them in, they drain our real capacity while motivating our outward ability. We transfer energy from negative motivation into our actions. We wonder about some of our favorites; some of our heroes. What causes someone like a Robin Williams, as driven to make people laugh as he was, to be so alone and empty in the end? Others like Elvis and Prince come to mind. Why a drug overdose? My heart goes out to anyone who somehow feels driven to spend their life singing for and entertaining others while attesting to emptiness inside. Or tennis legend like Andre Agassi who spends a lifetime building his net worth to approx. 170 million, only to admit he hated the game. What I love about his story, is his about-face where he writes in his book, *Open,* "One day, your entire way of life ends." He's since opened a foundation for kids and works heavily in philanthropy.

When the motivations of running-from-something, or proving-some-body-wrong dominate us, we allow a negative force to run through us and our energy flow is negative. We check out into our one drive – winning! We find our thrill in competing in business and can't find any joy looking deep into the eyes of our own kids on a quiet evening walk. This is a stark sign that our energy is flowing in a negative direction leaving us empty and looking for filling externally. In his lifechanging book, *Linchpin,* critical-thinker and the world's leading blogger, Seth Godin states, "The problem with being outwardly focused is that we have no center, nothing to return to … there is no compass, no normal, no way to tell if we're in balance."

To overcome the backward current of negative-energy, one must first realize it exists and then root out and replace the emotions causing it. Og Mandino, inspirational sales maestro and author, suggests, "You will succeed best when you put the restless, anxious side of affairs out of mind and allow the restful side to live in your thoughts." Life's too short and there's too much joy and true happiness to miss out on. When we go through life building something to prove somebody wrong, or living a life seeking and needing validation, we miss deep inner peace and the renewing flow of positive energy rising from within. Rising above to forgive freely brings with it a wonderful validation – you won't need anyone to validate you. In full and free forgiveness is a wonderful peace and freedom.

Tennis star, Arthur Ashe, said it like this, "True heroism is remarkably sober, very undramatic. It's not the urge to surpass all others at whatever cost, but the urge to serve others at whatever the cost." Negative energy reveals itself in reactive people. They're passionate, but about things they can't control. They bemoan the past and stress over the future. This is drama-passion. This is negative energy. Positive energy manifests itself in proactive people. They're passionate about what they can control and thrive in the present. This is calm-passion. This is positive energy.

The backward flow of negative energy ends at emptiness creating insecurity and driving defensiveness. *Energizers, on the other hand, are secure in who they are and always growing.* They are full and energy flows in a positive direction – up and over! Just because it's energy, doesn't mean it's the right kind of energy.

Explosive Energy

Negative in their very nature, to be sure, anger and righteous indignation are emotional dynamite. You will unleash energy, this is guaranteed. A lot of it. Anger, even when absolutely necessary, will drain yours and a lot of people's energy – and quickly. Your engine will blow when operation is sustained in the red zone. Some well-directed anger over an oncoming negative result can shake some things up and disrupt already negative patterns - sure. But, run from living in the red zone. Use righteous indignation only as a temporary stomping on the gas to break free of your own mediocrity! Anger, when used permanently will cause permanent damage; even when used frequently, it will require frequent emotional and relational repairs.

Anger is a motivator. Enormous energies lie within us and when we get angry enough, these energies can surface – however, it's usually in a negative way: explosive, disruptive and often hurtful. When Lee Iacocca was interviewed by *The Wall Street Journal* about turning Chrysler around, he said this, "We got so mad, we banded together, we talked things over, and working together, we fixed what was wrong at Chrysler." Alan Loy McGinnis states that "A little righteous indignation seems to bring out the best in the national personality when you consider 56 patriots got angry enough to sign *The Declaration of Independence*."

Creating takes time, destroying takes little time. While rooting out some legitimate wrong, many people and even leaders have rooted out and destroyed many a relationship. A volcano and a stream are both forces; one disruptive, negative energy, the other calm, positive energy.

3 Toxic C's

Competitive, comparative and condemning are what I call the three "C's" of negative energy's modus operandi. They are all reactive and limited modes of thinking and responding. They do not raise us or others to our best selves or a better way. Let's examine each.

Competitive. Competition can be structured in a healthy framework, but too often, it's subtractive and places a governor on abundance. In business and life, we often need the motivation of competition to raise our own standards. A rare few will consistently and proactively raise their own bar to compete with their previous best. Alan Loy McGinnis writes, "This instinct to compete appears to be inborn in most of us; otherwise the world would not enjoy games … and therein lies a very strong – and equally dangerous – basis for motivating people." Competition is typically structured to beat another person or team. In sports, healthy competition can teach teamwork and good sportsmanship. Competition, when used to validate ourselves, can quickly go horribly wrong! "I'll beat them," "I'll show you," and "Watch what I can do" reflect a backward flow of energy – limited and draining.

Business leader, Charles Schwab, encouraged competition in healthy boundaries, stating, "The way to get things done is to stimulate competition … not in a sordid, money-getting way, but in the desire to excel." So, when anyone competes outside of the lane of striving for excellence, competition turns dangerous. The best energies aren't ignited when competing outside of excellence. Excellence is growth and growth is a positive flow of energy. It's attractive. Competing to prove something, derive satisfaction, or gain approval is unhealthy. It's self-centered and a negative flow of energy.

David Niven Ph.D., in his Hallmark book, *The 100 Simple Secrets of Happy People* says that, "Ultra-competitive people rate their successes with lower marks than some people rate their failures." Wow! When you're living as an energizer instead, you're fully present in everything you choose to do! The energizer doesn't compete. The energizer asks, "Did I do my best?" "Did I give my best?" "What did I learn to make next time better?" Have fun giving your best, not making everything a competition!

Were we born into this world to beat somebody? Were you born into this world to get a larger ____ whatever than your friend or neighbor? Why do we feel this way? Are we unsure of our value or worth maybe? Set meaningful goals and go after them. Let their realization be your winning, not outdoing someone. In the end, what does winning mean to you? Check in where you compete. Does the competition invoke motivation to be the storm and sink them; or motivation to be the tide and raise all ships to do better?

Comparison is a close relative to competition. It's the glance over your shoulder while you're competing. Comparison will not only drain energy as we're constantly wasting our energy on fear of what others think, judgment, searching for self-worth, etc., but comparison also allows us to drink the poison of mediocrity. *Instead of looking inward and deep for our greatest potentials, we look outward and wide for someone we positionally look better than.* School of Greatness founder, top-podcaster and all around amazing guy, Lewis Howes shares this in his epic book, *The Mask of Masculinity*, "The people who care about you the most have been waiting to see what's behind your mask. It's time to reveal the real you." Comparison stems from fear and lack or self-worth. Be cool with you. As we'll discuss in chapter 8, "You're pretty special!"

Comparison is kin to fear. Rick Warren says it like this in his book, *The Purpose Driven Life*, "Insecure people are always worrying about how they appear to others. They fear exposure of their weaknesses and hide beneath layers of protective pride and pretentions." The more insecure that people are with themselves, the more they will work for the approval of others. Comparison is the enemy of living an energized existence.

When we courageously face our fears of what others think and let go of comparison, we receive a rush of positive energy. The defensive walls are torn down and the emotional flow brings up from the buried reserves of our hearts blessings of inner peace, emotional intelligence, emotional control, patience, deep strength, and free forgiveness.

There's only two times in life when comparison should exhibit itself.

The first is when you see someone in need. Then, let us stop and compare, not to prove we're any better, but to realize how much better we have it, and how much more we can be, live, give and love! The second is in benchmarking ourselves in growth. Compared to where I'm supposed to be, I'm here today. McGinnins writes, "We do much less than we are capable of until someone else shows us greater possibilities!" Comparative benchmarks are positive as they inspire growth. Any comparison that's fear based is negative. Let comparing never motivate us to be better than someone else; rather, let the comparison to a higher standard motivate us to be our best.

Condemnation is the evilest of the three "C's". We kind of have this built-in hate for the "bad guys". We compete with them, we compare ourselves to them and because either we just can't play at they're level, or we set ourselves up to be judge of some character flaw, we condemn them! If we are in the right, and they are in the wrong, then should we not live in patience that good will always triumph over evil. Love always wins over hate. We really don't believe in the Cinderella story deep down. We take it into our own hands to condemn. We live our "better than you" existence kind of out of spite. We're ultra-quick to judge and condemn others. We think inwardly that if we can just succeed, our winning will be their condemnation. *Rooted in unhealed hurt, inwardly condemning themselves, and drowning in a sea of negative energy, the calloused soul grasps tightly to condemnation simply to stay afloat.*

When I was growing up, we grew several gardens. I always remember with the most endearing love, Mr. and Mrs. Dean. They were expert gardeners and patiently taught us how to grow fruits and vegetables. There was this one section where Mr. Dean grew flowers. One autumn day, I noticed one whose leaves were falling off and it was no longer flowering. That one has "gone to seed," said Mr. Dean. I didn't quite understand 'til some time later, that "gone to seed," meant the flower had died and it was time for rebirth. Many people become complacent in their own lives, stop growing and begin condemning others. They're not spending their energy blossoming, just condemning. They've literally "gone to seed." They need rebirth.

Energizers, on the other hand go through life overflowing love. That's it. They grow – grow. They respond consistently at the highest frequency of love. Every fact or principle they learn is not to analyze another's shortcomings through the glasses of judgment, but to continually grow themselves. They offer grace consistently. These empowering energizers, according to Stephen Covey, don't overreact to negative behaviors, criticism or human weakness. "They're quick to forgive. They don't carry grudges. They refuse to label, stereotype, categorize or prejudge. They're genuinely happy for and help facilitate the successes of others. They believe in the unseen potential of all people. They help create climates of growth and opportunity."

Passion a Close Relative

Passion is great, but it's not the same as energy. Passion is simply the outpouring of a strong emotion. *When enthusiasm, excitement and passion overflow from an inner fullness of positive emotion, then you can be sure they're genuine expressions.* They are energy's children if you will. Passion can be aroused by external force as well. Someone else can ignite passion within you, or to say it another way, you can tap into someone else's fullness of positive emotion and exhibit passion. The new sales professional will often tap into another sales professional's passion for the product until he has a chance to sense the value of the product, install that emotion and truly internalize the belief that he's selling the best product in the world. This "tapping-into" happens all the time when great leaders cast empowering visions and attract a strong following. It's called "buy-in." Followers believe in a leader's passion and tap into it. Unless one or some of the followers has internalized the same vision, you take the leader or the reason for passion away and – poof! Gone. Take a friend's wedding for example. You've probably experienced feeling the strong emotion of love during the ceremony. You possibly even shed some tears. This is passion. The outpouring of a strong emotion. However, the rice is thrown, the bubbles blown, and the car drives away and so did the passion. All that's left is the "Father of the Bride," Steve-Martin look of exhaustion.

Borrowed passion and excitement is abundant in our society, and it feels good. Just look at consistently packed sports' stadiums. There's nothing wrong with tapping into someone else's fullness or organizational fullness of positive emotion. Just know the difference between energy and passion so you can understand the depth and richness of being whole and full of life. Energy is inner capacity; being energized is fullness of positive emotion. Passion is simply the feeling of one or more strong emotions.

The secret for sustained and powerful life passion is building and bolstering positive, strong emotions in all four parts of self. Your passion then, will be the synergized and powerful overflow of positive emotional fullness.

Looks Can Be Deceiving

Going back to what we discovered in chapter one, energy isn't the outward appearance of force and show, but instead, an inward depth of power. Energy is the harnessed emotions and focused mind. I like how Buddha said, "Learn this from water: loud splashes the brook but the oceans depth are calm."Many of us are acting like energy, and we're good at it. Yet, we're really energy deficient. Again, evidence shows our drain. We are on the distraction-rich treadmill of life and it's only getting faster.

Energy is so much more. Energy isn't necessarily flashy, talking fast, a lot of movement, or the lightning bolt. It is always true fullness and genuine wholeness regardless of how it's displayed. There are some people that come onto the scene of life and make a big splash. We've seen the new salesman arrive with a grand introduction, bold statements and big promises - two weeks later he was gone. We've had that person come into our life (boyfriend or girlfriend maybe) promising grand things and "playing with our emotions." When we scratched below the surface we found it was a facade. It's the storyline of the ages. Mostly evidenced by salespeople, politicians, lawyers, religious teachers, and other extroverted types, humans have the ability, with just enough charisma and going through all the correct motions, to garner trust and sell other humans on something. Buyer's remorse sets in when we leave feeling like they got the better end of the deal. They pressured and pushed. In our psyche, we feel a violation of the small bit of trust we gave them. Perhaps someone promised to be your friend and instead, you felt used. They violated the trust you gave. We've all had our trust violated at some point and those feelings of hurt go deep.

Whether by a "friend" or a professional, we've all felt sold a time or two or dozen or more in the past, and it's why these professions suffer so low trust. I like how national sales coach and best-selling author Jack Daly admonishes sales people that there are no tactics – "people like to buy; they hate to be sold." So, in sales as in life, we must continually make decisions and choose responses that fortify emotional fullness and inner wholeness! It's becoming a true source of power. Learning our product and developing our skill set will set us on the path to becoming a trusted advisor. Be okay with not knowing something and ask questions to constantly learn. Be real and build fullness. Don't settle for going through the motions with charisma as your mask. See the difference?

I love how S.D. Gordon, in his book, *Quiet Talks on Service*, states, "Some men who have seemed quite unattractive in the light of some modern standards have been found on touch to be charged with a life current of tremendous power. And some others, outwardly more attractive, have been found to be as powerless as a dead wire. And some there have been, and are, very winsome and attractive in themselves, and charged with the life current, too." **The great secret of the energizer is that deep, inner connections are being carefully maintained with the source of power.**

In later chapters, we'll discuss enthusiasm - the overflowing nature of positive, deep, internal energy. However, like energy, enthusiasm can also be faked. Feigned enthusiasm doesn't laugh. It's seen as a tool to get people to do something for another. It's as deep as Tom Sawyer's love for painting fences. Feigned enthusiasm creates a lot of noise. Watch out for noise! Our society is full of noise makers, screaming loudly, selling their wares, cluttering our inboxes, mailboxes to build their empires and garner a following instead of creating true value. I love how Flora Plummer, in her book, *The Spirit of the Teacher*, states, "Noise is not a necessary accompaniment of enthusiasm. The loud talker, the turbulent agitator, the aggressive pusher, may stir up enthusiasm, but unless he has instilled into the hearts of the people a real love for the thing he champions, the structure he erects will tumble to the ground as surely as a pyramid set upon its apex."

So, let this guide you in all your life's relationships - business or personal - go for character over charisma. Go for the steady stream that beautifully carves rock as opposed to the flashy lightning bolt that shatters trees. *Our greatest barrier isn't our lack of energy; our greatest barrier is misunderstanding what energy is, how it's ignited and which direction it's flowing.* Simply put, it's living fully and loving deeply!

Bigger Is Not Always Better

In chapter one we defined energy as our internal capacity for fullness and power to be effectual in our life's work. We see this dominant mind-set in society and business today, "Go big or go home!" Take money for example. Money can be the energy within a business. Without a thriving culture of happy people, money becomes a negative energy propping up the externals. Without great customer service and truly adding value to your clients lives, business will dwindle. We've seen recent examples of scandal, fraud and corporate mischief. All the money in the world can't buy back the loss of momentum, reputation and trust when the external workings of business come screeching to a halt.

Negative energy can drive externals for a time, but the internals must be thriving and healthy. This may just be why Solomon made the wise statement on integrity and trust that, "A good name is rather to be chosen than great riches, and loving favor rather than silver and gold." There's nothing wrong with big and there's nothing wrong with money. Both are wonderful when overflowing from a vibrant internal source.

The careless pursuit to be the super-star or the narcissistic ego are things that get us into trouble. Mark this down. If we pride ourselves with the, "I did it my way" or "relentlessly pursuing that which sets my soul on fire" mindset without first making peace within our spirits and souls, then be assured we're incapacitating our energy. While these motivational clichés make us feel fearless and powerful, when we're not whole as a person then we aren't wholly experiencing life. That which sets our soul on fire should serve our inner fullness and capacity to be effectual in our life's work as an abundant source of love and light to those around us. This defines positive energy.

On the flip side, we mustn't criticize valiant leaders pressing forward and building great empires. I know some leaders like this and the ones I know deeply and personally are men of integrity and fullness. Men like Mike Pence, Randy Boyd, Shane Reeves, Andy Bailey, Lewis Howes, Brendon Burchard, Kevin O'Dea and the list could go on, who have carefully built and bolstered a solid foundation of wholeness and courageously charge out into the night of this world to abound with light!

If you're created for more and you decide to play it small, then call it for what it is - fear. *If you have the capacity and internal depth to step up to the plate and make a difference for yourself and this world and fear is holding you back, then continue reading so that you can break free of fear and reach your God-given potential.* We each have a divine purpose and it may be that running a mega-billion-dollar industry is that purpose, or it may be a dishwasher at the homeless shelter. Bigger is not always better, but go big if you have the capacity of overflowing love to do this work! Live energized in your capacity. When we're each at peace with our purpose because that's exactly what we truly want to be doing, then we won't have to worry about having midlife crises.

Ask yourself this question. Do you have to do your role, or could you walk away if destiny changed your life's course? Ego is a huge trap and driver – a ruthless driver. Ego makes fools of people. If you trample on people, bad-mouth people or have to be right, chances are ego is ruling you. Your inner capacity may be empty, and your energy may be swindled, by ego.

Be egoless and shine brightly. Seek to be an overflowing abundant well of value creation. If this legitimately takes you to the top, then go big! Show up powerfully with purpose – YOUR purpose. If this is the course you're on, then be assured you will be attractive as we'll discuss in chapter four. I like how "The Rock" Dwayne Johnson says, "Stay humble and hungry." Be courageous and relentless to pursue your life goals. Be prepared to freely forgive every day, because you will have enemies if what your doing is worthwhile and going big is part of your calling.

Not All Strength

I remember professor Phillips from my public relations class who greeted us warmly on day one and then made this statement, "I'm a super creative person and love the ins-and-outs of mass communication; but, I'm terrible at keeping up with time." She said instead of fighting it, she'd bring a timer to class to buzz when she had ten minutes left. Throughout the semester, she gave no excuses and took no excuses. She was easy to get along with and I believe every student was a little easier going and open with feedback and quicker to share struggles and ask questions. She was perfectly honest with who she was – strengths, weaknesses and all. Wow! Don't waste energy trying to be perfect. Accept your weaknesses so you can maximize your strengths! And, in being ok with not being perfect, you actually open up more channels of genuine emotions and connect so much deeper with people.

Be cognizant of the temptation to paint flawlessness. When you see "perfection", or someone makes you feel like you come up short, don't "buy-in" to the feelings generated. Be ok with having weaknesses and play to your strengths. David Rendall says it beautifully in his book, *The Freak Factor*, "Your greatest weakness is also your greatest strength." Know and thrive in your purpose. Not to impress, but to abound. Someone said it this way, "We impress with our strengths, but we connect through our weaknesses." Be an extraordinary life that exemplifies and has no embarrassment overcoming obstacles – we all do. **When we're comfortable with ourselves – full acceptance of our strengths and weaknesses – we can connect fully, love deeply and stop hiding behind walls of painted perfection.** I love how social media writer & brand strategist, Amy Blaschka, once said, "Be ok with imperfectly perfect!"

Not More or Less Energy

Instead of "needing more energy," let's realize that while capacity can be expanded slowly over time, it must first come by maximizing our current capacity. This happens when we ignite the energies we already possess. We'll ignite them when we decide something is worth our energy. All the energy we need is already available to us. Energy is neither created or destroyed, remember. Focus instead on the transference of energy. Yes, where am I transferring my energy from and to whom and what? *We often transfer too much energy to the wrong people and activities and too little energy to the people and activities aligned with our life goals.*

Consider the fire escaping the fireplace. Too much energy is being transferred. No longer the warmth of heat; it becomes a destructive force. The scorching sun is debilitating. The uncontrolled child is exhausting, and so on. Unfocused, ineffective and wild energy are all examples of too much transference. We can transfer energy to all the wrong places and exhaust ourselves by getting very little return on our investment. We can transfer positive energy too quickly towards a hurting person expecting immediate change and disallow their feeling of deep pain. This can be damaging to relationships. Wisdom, therefore, must be used to determine the worthwhile nature of our investments and the pace of energy transference.

The sources from which we transfer our energy must be examined and improved as well. In order for us to improve our energy condition, the statement, "I need more energy" needs to evolve into a thought process, "Am I transferring my energies into worthwhile investments; and, am I transferring my energy from rich sources?"

Channeling Energy

Some say that they can't control their energy. This is false. You can. It may be more difficult for some of us, but you can. The largest amount of energy is transferred to us by way of our thoughts. The largest swindler of our energy, as we'll look at in Chapter 10, is our minds. Our decisions and responses are all mentally based. To claim we can't control our energy would be to claim we've lost control of our minds.

Attending a Nashville Mental Health Conference recently, I learned so much about the struggles and stigmas of mental health. First, let's lift the stigma, and my goodness, especially nowadays with all the technology, mental stimuli, modern warfare, and drug use in society. Mental handicaps are nothing to be treated lightly and they can be shear horror for those struggling with them. With the advance of medicine, the recognition and identification of mental disorders has also drastically advanced. Unimaginable trauma causes PTSD, and another common mental challenge is ADHD. In many cases, medical advice and medication may become necessary to assist in harnessing or regaining control of one's mental faculties. If you've experienced trauma in your past, professional help may be necessary. I love the show "Monk". We may chuckle during episodes of extreme-OCD like turning the umbrella handle around to match the others, but these things are very real swindling energy and leaving feelings of fear and anxiety.

Let's take an inside-out approach to this feeling of no control, though. Too often, we choose to consume violence through mediums of news channels, movies and TV. I'm not saying be an ostrich and never catch a news story. The point is, we're inundated with negative mental stimuli. This exposure doesn't speak peace and calm. Constantly plugged into our virtual worlds and technologies overloads our mental RAM. It's no wonder our minds aren't calm. Negativity planted in our minds swindles energy trying to show up in our physical reality.

We transfer a lot of energy into our thoughts, and ideas and thoughts transfer energy to us. Thoughts are literally energy-producing stimuli, and there is unlimited supply of this stimuli. When we choose to let our minds run on auto-pilot and aren't intentional with what we plant in our minds, and when we plant it, then we really aren't in control; we're simply being propped up by our environments. *Therefore, our feelings rise and fall with external forces and our energy feels uncontrollable.*

Sources Aren't Created Equal

All sources of energy aren't created equal. There are rich sources and poor sources. Do you want to be truly energized? Seek out natural sources of energy first. Nikki just walked up while I'm typing and reading over my shoulder asked, "Daddy, why aren't sources created equal?" I picked up a chocolate laying nearby and asked, "If I have this chocolate in this hand, and an apple in my other, which do you think is the best energy source?" Without a pause, she answered, "Apple!" Yes, Nikki's correct. Synthesized sources of energy will never compare to natural sources. Humans are natural beings and therefore should seek the richest, natural sources. In our lives, we should seek out the cleanest forms. The cleaner the energy, the cleaner the aftermath, the by-products and the result. Long-term, our capacity is increased and fortified.

Grandma's instruction to shop around the outsides of the store is great advice. The living produce and fresh breads are there. Science and evidence prove these to be the richest sources of vitamins, minerals and nutrients your body needs to be healthy. The packages of Twinkies, cookies, donuts, candy and sweet drinks line our aisles and have been manufactured using scientific research to appeal to tastes and to satisfy natural cravings, but they don't satisfy them in naturally, energy-transferring ways.

Poor sources give us a good feeling temporarily and trick our minds by releasing feel-good stimuli. In reality, they're empty calories and leave us empty. Why do we incapacitate ourselves like this if we truly want to be energized? I'm not recommending going extreme and not enjoying a donut from time to time. After a marathon, there's nothing more rewarding (temporarily rewarding), and I may choose to splurge. The wisdom we need is to seek out a good balance of the richest sources.

Imagine a heavy thunderstorm rolls through and knocks out the power to your house. You'd grab a few candles or flashlights. Your capacity to do work would be greatly inhibited, but you'd have some light – some capacity – to slowly perform a few tasks. Reporting the outage and tapping back into the main power source would greatly increase your capacity. Just like power isn't inbred in our cellphone batteries and thus, we plug them into the charger. Remember the old car charger from your college days? You know the one. That annoying cord that you had to wiggle back and forth. Once the lightning bolt appeared on your phone, you'd have to wrap the cord around the phone and tuck it under to hold the perfect charging position. Sound familiar? Back at home is the wall charger you just purchased. Perfect fit. Energy must be transferred. Which is the richest source?

So, when we think of sources let's think rich sources versus poor sources. There are plenty of sources of energy, but if we have access to rich sources, let's tap into those to truly maximize our capacity – ignite our energy condition! Synthetic energy is all around us. We could write a volume of books on all the processed, fried and sugar-filled foods presented to us, today. Basically, if it's packaged and can endure a very long time, chances are it has disproportionate levels of salt and preservatives inside. Think fresh as much as possible and get your fuel from great sources of dietary fats (fatty acids), proteins and carbohydrates.

Steroids are a form of energy. They enable us for a time to perform at greater levels, but are they worth it? Many have fallen from the sports scene having inflated their capacity but ruining energy. Why not enhance your inner drive – your true energy? Being at peace and having true strength is always worth it. Do you burn the candle on both ends? There's a certain amount of pride in that – sure there is. Sometimes we find it necessary. Kids up all night, term-paper due, etc. Is this habitual? When we skip sleep, we not only miss the rich source of energy that sleep is, we usually add stimulants to carry us through and only add to our unenergized state.

If you're having to rely on an energy drink, sugary pick-me-up or even coffee, chances are you're too plugged in and too drained. I'm not saying stop cold turkey, but you can start researching the effects artificial foods and stimulants have on your health. *This research will help shape the way you feel about adding pure sources of energy to your life and you'll be much more empowered to replace a certain belief and habit when you found the answer and reasoning than if someone gave you a blanket list.* Most don't stop to think, research or plan. They continue the rat-race, giving no priority to rich sources of energy (food or exercise), and their metabolisms are slowed as a result. So, break the rhythmic lull, awaken the deadened senses, get excited about what life can feel like and start researching and make a plan, today. Begin making small changes for pure energy sources and every time you do, breathe in the belief that someday you will – WILL – realize the tremendous effects of your diligence.

I've spent many a run with someone who decided to take ownership of their situation and stimulate a healthy metabolism by planning their fuel and exercise. I like how John Jubilee told me once that when your metabolism is a roaring fire – by fueling and exercising properly and routinely – then you can throw a wet log on that roaring fire and it'll burn right through it. I've heard runners say they run so they can eat whatever they want. While that's a little but of a stretch, the point I'm making is that tapping into the right sources of exercise and food (or fuel may be a better way to state this), you will begin to feel the change. You have to be committed to the change by first grounding your belief on the facts and then before long, the feeling will follow as the positive emotion of healthy diet and exercise is installed and grows stronger.

This book isn't an exhaustive resource on all the best fuel sources. It's not "Cut this out" and "Add this in." It's simply understanding how our wholeness ties to our energy – our full and awakened sense to life. ***When we realize that every little thought, every little bite, every little lifestyle action adds to or subtracts from our energy condition, we operate at a higher level of consciousness and choice.*** It's simply asking ourselves, "What do rich sources of energy look like for me?" It's simply igniting our energy! By pursuing a deep, real fullness and powerful existence – an increased capacity to do our life's work!

Not Mystical or Magical

Because of the industrialization of the West, we've lost touch with many healthy, natural practices – many of which are still practiced in Eastern tradition. Very recently, we've watched a resurgence of meditative and physical exercises such as Yoga and others with deep breathing routines, etc. I engage in daily meditation and breathing exercises, and perform several Yoga-style stretches for greater flexibility and to increase balance – something this flatfooted, crooked-spine guy isn't the best at.

Religions promoting peace and serenity put a much higher priority on bodily exercise. They understand you cannot separate body and spirit. However, with these forms of religion come foreign-sounding names of exercise. Mix that with candles and meditative thought, and some get skeptical. Sure, some go to greater lengths than others exploring "energy" and it's transference from the air, sunlight and ground. There's nothing mystical or magical about energy. Everything in the universe consists of matter and energy. Energy is constantly flowing. The better we can understand the sources of energy and our energy flow with our environments and the people in them, the better understanding and greater awareness of life we have.

With the introduction of energy healing in the West, many have found deeper sense of calm and greater awareness of life. It's very acceptance speaks to some stagnation in Western religious traditions. ***Whenever you single out one dimension of the whole person (spirit, mind, soul or body), practical application will be difficult to understand and experience.*** When we lose touch with the whole being of who we are as humans, we easily become robotic in one dimension. Think about it and you can see it happening all around us. Stagnation is real; it happens. We see this in not only our religious circles, workplaces, societies and families, but also our personal lives. We've been conditioned to think one part of us can operate independently without affecting the other parts of our whole being. We show up to "worship" and our minds are stimulated – maybe our spirits. We show up to work and our bodies and minds are stimulated, but our hearts (souls) are far away dreaming about vacation, hobbies, etc. We fail to bring engagement and emotional labor to our work. We check into our addictions with our body and numb our emotions, minds and spirit. We don't stop to realize that without bringing our spirit, our mind, our body and our soul into everything we do, we are literally deadening our existence in some way. When our choices are poor in one dimension, our whole being suffers. We simply are failing to live fully.

You hear people refer to the Great Depression of the 30's, the long lines at the gas stations in the 70's, the recession of the 80's and the Great Recession of the early 2000's. I remember the Y2K preparation. Of course, with a huge family "preparation" is an understatement. Dozens of 200-liter barrels were filled with water. Flour, oats, noodles and other dry goods, easily over hundreds of pounds, were stored away. Canned goods like split-pea soup and sardines – literally hundreds of tins of sardines. I can't remember if they were cheaper in Europe, or if the assumption was made that everyone shared the same delight for the oily, salty taste. They easily formed a majority in the rooms we transformed to pantries in our old brick, 4-story house built in the 1400's. In fact, the last tin was finally polished off five years later.

The tendency of human nature is rushing to the bread and milk aisles at the first sign of apocalyptic trouble. Do we realize how much of what we do is fear-based? Fear of poverty has driven us to a mad state of materialism. It's captured our souls that we've failed to care for our bodies. We then spend thousands and millions on insurance and doctors when we might have lived wholly and more fully awakened earlier on sparing us both extremes. We live in an industrialized and now, even more technologically advanced, fast-paced environment than ever before. The biomedical revolution along with artificial intelligence and internet of things will only further infuse our technology and industries. We will be offered – no, probably handed or drone-delivered – instant gratification before or as we're thinking about it. What horrors lay in store for our wholeness of living life if we don't understand it before the tread-mill gets any faster, or that pink bunny's drum beats any louder. We will be virtual emptiness merely coexisting on a cold planet if we don't finally realize why we can't get excited about life! Wholeness is real and it's fun! It was designed by our Creator this way! *We've lost touch with wholeness and the call to redeem life has never been louder than right now.* We must declare that the days of sacrificing our health and well-being for more career prominence and "success" are over. We must denounce partial existence in our own lives and embrace wholly living and fully thriving! We can and must demand abundant life. We must stop being okay settling for mediocre results! We must take responsibility for our energy and ignite it!

Eastern religions have taught their students the benefits of invigorating lifeforce energy and moving it throughout the spine and brain. All things in our universe consist of matter and energy - our bodies are no different. Lifeforce energy is directly connected to the condition and quality of our health as it is to our minds, souls and spirits. We're guilty of separating the four parts of self which were intelligently designed to form a synergistic being. Every day we live in separate parts of self, we block the flow of energy. Abundant and available to us, it lies dormant! The wisdom of lifeforce energy – life fully awakened and whole – has been around for thousands of years. The greatest teachers have taught it, some proclaiming to be in complete harmony with mother nature while teachers such as Jesus claimed God desired this harmony with man. In Japan - lifeforce energy is called *Ki* where we get the work *Reiki*. Taoists call lifeforce energy *Chi*. Indian yoga trainers call it *Prana*. Called *Mana* in Polynesia, *Ruach* in Hebrew and *Baraka* in Islamic countries, lifeforce is the spiritual essence of man. In this book, we use the word energy as defined – our inner capacity. In doing so, we understand living fully (at capacity and abounding) must – it must – include a harmony of spirit, mind, body and soul.

- The spirit – our eternal essence that thrives through hope and faith.
- The mind – our intellectual faculties that thrive through thoughts, creative imagination and ideas.
- The body – our physical being that thrives through health, movement and value creation.
- The soul – our heart of emotional flow that thrives through desire, belief, will, giving love and feeling loved.

Whether you believe in God, mother nature, another religion, or profess atheism, the fact the we consist of spirit, mind, body and soul is difficult to deny. *The fact that we feel joy, express hope, imagine, dream, create, and can live at a higher consciousness, choosing love over baser motivations, proves there is a greater lifeforce within us when our four parts of self are functioning in harmony.* Have you experienced that spark at one time or another? The spark of vibrancy, perfect harmony and total congruence of all four dimensions? Sadly, for many, being fully awakened to life started and ended in early childhood. It's this harmony that inspires an unstoppable drive within us to love and to do good to all. It's this depth of energy that inspires us to leave a legacy of good behind us, creating peace, abundance and vibrancy.

Energy heals. Yes. The freer your emotions flow and in a positive direction, the freer and more apt you are to love. You possess a respect for yourself and others. You'll love your body and you become a whole person understanding all four parts of you form gestalt, where the "whole is greater than the sum of the parts." If our spirit is blocked from accessing hope and faith, our soul won't feel love and our body will feel badly. We'll be tense, stressed and fatigued. We need not think there's anything mystical about energy. Energy is our inner capacity. How fully awakened (capable and able to live fully) are you? Simple? Let's keep it that way. When we overcomplicate energy, we'll in turn overcomplicate a simple decision like choosing water over Pepsi.

Feel the Vibes

Did you know that vibes exist? Most times we're too busy to pay attention to them. Then, someone enters our life and either leaves a really good feeling or a very bad feeling behind. We may say, "Man! I love her vibes!" Some people use names such as essence and aura to label the vibrations of our emotions. Call it what you will, vibes exist. We will call them vibes in this book as science proves our energy has vibration to it. On the other hand, an aura or essence define more of a spiritual dimension, neither of which is necessary in understanding the very real presence of thought and energy vibration.

You can't fake fullness. Your energy condition will manifest itself through your vibrations. You may look like energy, but those in touch with your vibrations will sense your true level of fullness. That's why we say, "I have a hunch," or "my gut's telling me ... " You're either energized, or you're not. There's no shame in being drained. We all get there. Accept it and realize there are practical steps to daily ignite your energy – perspective, ownership and accountability - POA! BOOM! *Vibes are simply the manifestation on the outside of what's happening on the inside.* You ever wonder what it would be like if cartoon bubbles really existed? You think something and buuuloooop – there it is in bubble form floating above your head for all to see. Vibes work this way. They're just felt as opposed to seen. Johann Wolfgang Von Goethe made a powerful statement when he said, "To think is easy. To act is difficult. To act as one thinks is the most difficult." Basically put, many act, but not in accordance to what's really going on inside their minds. Getting a gut feeling about something or someone is not totally absurd. Through body language and tone, they are saying more than just words. While their words are going one direction, your intuition is picking up thought waves going the complete opposite direction. Elbert Hubbard said, "We awaken in others the same attitude of mind we hold toward them." So, if you feel uneasy around someone, perhaps you're uneasy about yourself or they're uneasy about you. Consider.

This is a powerful concept and worthy of attention. The first thought, second thought, third thought and fourth won't necessarily create a vibe strong enough to cause emotional response from your intuition. Unless, of course, the thought is a strong emotion like "love at first sight." Two people see each other, the emotions send a strong – very strong – feeling out and there's instant magnetism. Emotions of desire create the strongest vibrations. That's why greed can create pushy salespeople. Ever experience this vibe? Immediately, right? I have nine sisters. Several of them were so in touch with their intuition, they'd literally know just by looking at the man's eyes, sensing his body language and how he acted whether his motives were pure and appreciating or self-centered and depreciating. See, when we think thoughts five, six, seven and on, we're beginning to form patterns. These become thought concentrations and go from our conscious minds into our subconscious minds. *Our subconscious mind never sleeps, and these brainwaves create a steady, consistent vibration.*

Our guts pick up on these vibrations and we can sense deep down when someone is off, hurting, or out to get us. Listen to your gut. Did you know your stomach is called your "little brain" because it contains millions of neurons and they're constantly in touch with what's going on in the rest of your body – especially in your subconscious mind. That's why your stomach can do somersaults when you meet "the one" you're supposed to marry. That's why you get a gut wrench when you realize you completely forgot your anniversary. Your subconscious knew all along and you didn't tap into it – then, it sent a strong surge out and your gut turned inside out. You may feel uneasy around someone and get a gut feeling that you decide to override. Here's the deal, their subconscious mind is making them act in certain ways which may be polar-opposite to what's coming out of their mouths. Your super-powerful subconscious mind is picking up on these vibes and your stomach's neuron radar detection is going bonkers. Former Navy Seal and author of, *The Way of The Seal*, Mark Divine states, "If danger lurks around the corner, or if something just isn't right, part of you knows it and feels it. Your stomach gets the signal and diverts blood to the extremities to prepare them for movement. Your brain may not register the threat, but you feel the tug in your stomach." So, trusting your gut simply means you've learned to listen this information.

Vibes do exist by the vibrations of our thoughts that are often masked by twitching, nervous smiling faces. When you leave someone, check in with your gut. What were you sensing? What did you experience? How'd the encounter make you feel? Did you feel inspired and encouraged, or did you feel on edge and in competition? Here's an easy-to-remember checkup when you walk in to meet with anyone. Any sort of profession with interpersonal communication involved will benefit from listening past what is being said to see if what's heard audibly and vibrationally are in agreement. It should be as easy as **ABC**, but could be as cold as **ICE**. Let our thoughts toward others be:

> **A** – Abundant
> **B** – Believing
> **C** – Caring

Let them never be:

> **I** – Insecure
> **C** – Competing
> **E** – Edgy (tense, nervous or irritable)

Psycologist Joyce Brothers said, "Trust your hunches." The beautiful thing is this. The more you work on your conscience, the inner person and whole you – becoming truly energized – the more your intuition will be sharpened. Intuition, hunches, and gut feelings will show up and be more reliable when you're in touch with your energy condition and it's positive, full and overflowing!

Staying energized and working to live fully – wholly in harmony – gives greater purpose, too. You're literally fun to be around! *Energy is in all matter and when energy's high, there's a certain electricity in the air.* Walk into any stadium when the fans are going crazy. Feel it? Remember that feeling? Their deepest energies have been called upon, and whether temporary or not, the enthusiasm bubbles over. There's nothing magical about vibes, it's simply electricity and excitement in the air resulting from the heightened frequency of positive energy flowing and enthusiasm overflowing! It can happen individually or in a crowd.

Eat Honey or Bounce

When it comes to energy, there's not one ignition or "fix" for the one feeling unenergized. We are all uniquely created; one size doesn't fit all.

Perhaps you've been blamed for being Tigger, bouncing everywhere, happy-go-lucky, positive and super-eccentric. On the other hand, maybe a Pooh Bear personality that's super-honey-driven-focused, methodical and steady mannered depicts your personality. Is there only one template for igniting energy? Can some people possess more energy than others?

Perhaps different levels of energy can be exhibited; however, each of us have the same opportunities for igniting energy that we'll teach through perspective, ownership and accountability – POA! Take a power plant for example. Some run efficiently while others run less efficiently. What we must understand is that each power plant has different levels of capacity and potential. Size of plant, availability to resources, level of skill, and the list goes on. As people, our capacities are all different. It's amazing what the human body can do! Science proves that aerobic exercise ignites a lot of energy; however, we cannot relegate energy to mere physical ability. While a physical illness or disability may prevent someone from showing the outward signs of an energetic powerhouse, I've seen time and time again these dear souls outwit the rest of us with a superb mental energy! That's right – mental energy!

Take a person with special needs who willingly shares the biggest smile and warmest heart! The energy of this expression exudes from their very presence! Everyone has some sort of capacity. Recently, I was supporting my good friends at the Zaxby's establishment when an employee rolled up to the counter in his wheelchair. The man, who appeared to be a veteran, was so joyful he literally made my day! Or, take a child with Down Syndrome like my friend Sarah. Her heart is so warm; she has no defenses up. When she hugs me, I'm challenged to up my hug-giving.

Tom James, my clothier, knows this concept well. One size doesn't fit all. They take elaborate measurements to be sure the coat is cut just the right angle and height. They want the clothes to truly fit you. You are unique. *Look inside and avoid modelling everything and everybody you see.* Yes, learn and grow, but always make application to your unique wholeness. Ask, "what's my capacity?" "Am I maximizing my potential?" "Am I living fully?" "Am I expressing my love?" If you're a singer, sing. If you're a dancer, dance. If you're a hugger, hug. If you're an encourager, encourage. If you're a somersaulter like my 4-year-old son, then do gymnastics. Don't let the swindler of fear suppress natural emotions. It's your energy in motion and it's you. Work to encourage, not limit, the outflowing of others' emotions as well. Be okay with Tigger and Pooh, and live fully YOU!

Simple; Not Easy

Some think enhancing your energy will make everything easy - no conflict. Let's learn a simple lesson from nature. Roots must dig deep into soil, the fish swim against current, forest fires happen, gold is refined in fire. It's the ebb and flow of life. Trials and difficulties come our way. People hurt you, toxicity exists, sickness happens. It's called the groan of nature. Our job is to press forward, embrace the good pain of growth and endure the pain of suffering when asked of us. Give grace and be willing to receive grace. Love everybody because you don't know what they're going through. Fight the internal battles to live in fullness.

Energy will make everything about life much simpler. You'll be deciding and responding at a much higher frequency. Life becomes uncluttered and energy keeps you flowing with the rhythm of it. Relationships work much better and good things are attracted to your life. Energy makes life so simple, it doesn't mean life's going to be easy. In fact, energizers never pray for an easy life, they pray that they'll live fully the one they have. Simple not easy. Are you the tree's roots hitting rock? Press on. Are you the branches experiencing storms? Forgive and hold fast.

No "Quick Fixes"

Energy is capacity and we must maximize our capacity. To do this, we must be charging and recharging daily. This takes time. Too often though, we look for a shortcut or stop improving altogether. We're used to quick fixes after all. However, if anything is quick in life, we should stop and question it. Truly energizing activities are not microwaveable. Be in your quest for abundant life for the long term! Fully awakened living takes time. Running for three years, I've just recently become comfortable running three miles each day. I realized that my first two years of running taught me a lot and prepared me for a greater challenge. You'll never know the joys of level two, until you fight the foes of level one. What gives you a rush? If a video game can give you a rush, imagine what real life feels like if you'll just purpose to start igniting your energy today! You'll grow if you'll stick with it. My lungs are just now opening to new levels. Singing's improved, speaking's improved, and breathing's improved. It's taken three years. So, stick with the consistent habits that tap you into rich energy sources.

Nothing truly great happens overnight. Some of the greatest companies took years of diligence, and take the same diligence today, to continue running at peak performance. Did you know kettle-heated tea is better for you? The microwave, as much as we love it, is a quick-fix. There have been times in Jen's and my personal journeys – and guaranteed to be more with new levels and phases of life – when we've experienced thoughts like "is this new endeavor or growth worth it?" Don't give up. Open up and support each other in your growth. Climb together and grow together consistently and patiently. ***The joys of the next level will far outweigh the pain to grow. Embrace growth-pain and grow. Avoid seeking out the quick charge to your energy.*** Avoid Band-Aiding a deeper problem, because, when it shows back up, it'll be greater and stronger. Get to the root of the problem – that thing that is draining your energy – right now. You may say, "Tim, I have a lot of drains on my energy." I hear you, but let's list the top three that keep coming up for you. The three that keep draining you. Together, we're claiming breakthrough on these as we continue reading. Are you with me? Okay. Good. Write your top three energy drains below:

Energy Drain # 1 _____
Energy Drain # 2 _____
Energy Drain # 3 _____

Declare today that you won't seek out the quick fix, but you're purposing to daily ignite your energy in some small way fully believing that this long obedience over time will gloriously compound into a full and abundant, deeply energized and harmoniously whole life!

CHAPTER 3
ENERGY'S MOTIVATION
igniting your internal flame

"The most powerful force on earth is the human soul on fire!" – Ferdinand Foch

First Car

"Daht, daht, daht, daht, daht, daht … " my '94 Cutlass Sierra, Oldsmobile was singing to me. I was rushing home to pick up my date for the Valentine banquet. Jen and I at ages 20 and 18 had just moved to Tennessee. I'd wash and wax that sleek, silver exterior and keep the plush burgundy interior spotless. Under the hood, though, another story was unfolding.

I'd heard a small "tap, tap, tapping" going on in the V6 engine a week earlier – just a small noise. I decided to get it checked out soon. I didn't make soon happen fast enough. Valentine's Day snuck up on me and now, I had my date waiting on me. This louder "daht, daht, dahting" really had me worried. *Alas! I didn't have time to stop and check what was going on.*

By the time I pulled into Jen's sister's driveway, where she was staying, the "daht, daht, dahting" had turned into an all-out banging! It was ear-shattering. As she emerged in her royal blue, gorgeous ballgown, my heart sank. What a "fine" carriage ride I was offering my princess. Opening her door and apologizing for the racket, we drove off hand-in-hand on that front bench seat to the Association of Realtors' building where the banquet was hosted.

I remember the night well – very well. Pulling in and leaving were the post painful memories as my rattletrap's commotion interrupted the perfect purrs of Tahoe, Cadillac and Suburban engines around us. The next morning, I thought if I could just make it to work, I could get shop foreman, Doug, to give me a diagnosis. En route, acceleration onto the interstate also accelerated the demise of my car's engine. The culprit to all that banging – a rod – decided to launch itself through the oil pan. Engine sputtered to off and my car rolled to a stop on the shoulder. Since Jen kept our only cellphone with her, I walked 5 miles to call my brother. He brought a tow strap and we pulled the car to his house. Within two weeks, we had that beauty up and rolling again.

Why tell this story? Let me tell you why. The incapacitated car is metaphorical of how many people spend life. Our engine has sputtered and died. We live our days always on the lookout for someone with a tow strap to give our life mobility. We need motivation constantly. We've put off preventive maintenance if you will. It's been said, "Familiarity breeds contempt; it's human nature." **We become contented at a certain operational level and fail to build and bolster our energy.** We must stop rushing off to the next event long enough to realize what's valuable – our life, our energy, our relationships. I love how author of the book, *No Try Only Do*, Andy Bailey calls energy, "Your economic driver of success." Is your economic driver of success driving today, or are you pulling out that tow strap pretty frequently? I love how Brendon Burchard puts it in his book, *The Charge*, when he writes, "In the best moments of your life, there was a spark. You felt it and you never completely forgot it. The question is, what drove that spark? What was it that made you feel so alive? And how do you bring that feeling into your everyday life? Better yet, how do you turn that spark into a lasting flame and fire in your soul – a charge within yourself that never goes out?"

Huge Value in Motivation

There are amazing motivational people in this world and many more from the past we read about, follow and draw inspiration from. YouTube and our social media streams contain thousands of inspirational stories if we just look for them. Motivation is key! We all need motivation. In fact, a daily dosage in some form or fashion may help us gain greater perspective or take action in some key area of life. Motivation can and should provoke us to thought. There are times we fall down or run out of gas. We need the tow-strap of a Good Samaritan to get us where we need to be. Solomon wisely states, "Two are better than one; if one falls, the other can help the fallen rise again."

Motivational conferences are wonderful. I always love being around the faith and hope of the speakers. Motivational conferences and content, however, have limited effects on us. Why? We must leave and go back to life. What happens when we leave a motivational event or seminar? Our old programming is still there. We were impressed by the external, and we even believed success could be ours. That is until we return to our own environments, routines, and we hear them. Hear who? *The internal voices that lives upstairs and make a racket every time we think about making a change or taking a step.* The voice on stage drowned them out – for a short while. I like how Zig Ziglar put it, "Motivation doesn't last, and neither does bathing; that's why we recommend them daily."

Here's what happens. We want to believe in the best, and we love inspirational stories and the hope they generate in our spirit. Hope keeps our spirit alive. Sometimes, though, we attend a conference or session to get motivated and leave feeling like listening and taking notes was the work. Perhaps our perspective changed a bit and we felt like we achieved something. If we do carry determination and commitment with us, how do we internalize to last more than just a few days? During the conference we chose positive thinking while we were around a positive charge. Then, when we faced real life and the work that stared us in the face, we froze. It doesn't always feel good to face reality and our sense of positivity was in the belief and vibes of the conference instead of in the fact that small hard daily steps would win the prize.

Many become too reliant on motivation. We become professional followers and conformists instead of leaders and thinkers – yes, thinkers. We are professional book grazers instead of book heeders and doers. In fact, motivation isn't even a scarcity. We are tapped into so many sources. Motivation is necessary, and reading is powerful. Many of us have become dependent on someone else's motivation. We simply fail to believe in ourselves or place enough stock in the good we desire. We don't give any credibility to our own words. Perhaps we have a track record of unfulfilled intentions and we can't trust ourselves. We haven't done in the past what we said we were going to do and the vicious cycle continues.

Hospital Blueprints

My friend is an electrical engineer and lays out massive schematics and detailed plans for hospital construction. He's in charge of all the wiring. Thick stacks of pages form the booklets that must be created just to encompass the undertaking. There are separate outlets for this, and special outlets for that. Different assortments of fuses are used. Isolated outlets for oxygen and critical care utilities are installed in case of circuit overage or power outages. In case the power to the hospital was ever lost, there must be generators and back-up generators in place according to regulations. He tells me that a hospital can run pretty well on backup power, but I'll assure you, if the power went out, the electricians would be working overtime to get back on the main line. They cannot live contentedly dependent on those generators.

Friend, motivation is like the generators and back-up generators of our lives. Many of us are content living on generators today. **We're not taking the time to prioritize great sources of energy, nor are we working to free our lives of the energy swindlers.** Many of us are unwilling to let go of bitterness. We stew daily over somebody or something and allow it to eat at us. It's killing our power. Instead of the internal power of energized living, we rely completely on the generators of external motivation to get us through.

Energy vs. Motivation

Energy's not motivation although they're related. Motivation can get you going, but energy (your internal driver) will keep you going. Motivation's external; energy's internal. Motivation's someone else's fire; energy's your fire – it's internal. Energy is inner fullness and personal power to move you in a focused direction. It's one's capacity to accomplish great things. Energy allows us to operate at peak performance every day from a place of abundance. As we've seen, we cannot "put on" fullness. You either enter someone else's life (spouse, child, client, and so on) from a place of abundance or a place of emptiness. And when your energy's lacking or empty, you and others suffer. You cannot give what you do not have!

Motivation must be viewed then as seeds planted in our minds that internalize to ignite our energy. We all want to do better and give our best. However, the obstacles, the unbelief, no internal fire, and ceaseless inner voices are holding us back. The seeds of motivation should enter our minds and help us to overcome the obstacles, add faith, ignite our flame and quiet the inner voices. Motivation must get us going to be useful, but we must not rely on it. *Why live catching motivational fires that blow by externally without igniting our own, down deep in our souls?* Let's ignite our energy to be firing on all cylinders and become a daily powerhouse.

Life happens though, and when some trial or tough situation has knocked the wind right out of us, we should tap into encouraging sources of motivation and inspiration. There's strength in numbers. Surround yourself with people who can help you back up. Being knocked down, however, is often the time people reevaluate their life's purpose and determine what's really important to them! So then, every time we're feeling down-and-out, unmotivated, or stagnant, wouldn't that also be an ideal time to reevaluate? What could YOU do every day that would literally add wood to YOUR internal fire? What beliefs could you overhaul that would pour oil into the V8, twin-turbo engine? Motivation can help us discover our gifts, eliminate our fears, and map out a powerful vision, but let's build the engine of energy!

Ignite Energy

Let's bring this all together. Don't become dependent on motivation. Use motivation any chance you get to protect, fortify and maximize your energy! Let your inner capacity be the highest priority to you. Stay motivated to build and bolster fully living and deeply loving. KEY: An abundant life is a self-motivating life. A full and overflowing soul leads a self-motivated life. Use motivation to help you get unstuck. Maybe the engine's good; you just froze not knowing which direction to go. Motivation can get us unstuck. If our energy isn't ignited, not fully unleashed, then we'll keep getting stuck. Ignite your energy! Use motivation to arouse dormant energies. We can tap into and unleash pent up energy by becoming emotionally whole. Like the Oldsmobile, let's allow external motivation to rebuild our energy condition quickly so that we're tapping into our internal motivation again.

We can train our minds and our actions to be replenishing sources of energy. When this is happening, we won't be dependent on external motivation. Motivational speaker extraordinaire, Brendon Burchard, clearly summarizes this concept when he wrote, "A hallmark of those who achieve greatness is the discovery that they can control the level of motivation they feel by better directing their own minds." The greatest source of energy is energy of thought. The evidence is overwhelming that one thought can drive us to immediate and massive action. I've seen people defy all forces of gravity as they launched themselves from a porch swing running faster than Roger Banister to snatch up a child who'd wandered into a busy street. I've seen someone lift themselves from a supermarket riding cart and dash after a twenty-dollar bill that escaped their purse. History is full of stories where people did all sorts of great feats simply by a channeled and focused thought process – no other options were available to them. Subsequently, every bit of energy was unleashed! Like Mr. Miyagi said to the karate kid when he got knocked down over and over, "You're best karate still inside - focus!"

Value Self-Motivation

How powerful do you feel right now? If a desire or goal is physically possible how much inner drive could you count on to go do what you decided needs done? I believe many of us don't have a base of solidity, a foundation for keeping commitments to ourselves. Interestingly enough, we'll jump through hoops and even break speed limits to do something for an employer, yet, we'll set on the couch instead of getting up and going for a walk which is a simple proven enhancement of your own vitality and power – your energy.

Where does this distorted valuation stem from? We assign value to the job, but little to ourselves – the one who performs the job. This isn't anything new. Humans tend to devaluate what's free and place value on that which cost us something. Earl Nightingale states, "Our life came free to us; it cost us nothing. The things that are truly worth the most, came to us free." With our life came our mind – standard equipment. Our mind is the most valuable of all our possessions according to Earl Nightingale's *Strangest Secret*, for it alone can determine the fulfillment of our life.

If we'd value our own ability for self-motivation, then we'd experience tremendous capacity to take on any task, commitment or goal with force and velocity, for we'd daily prepare and ignite our driver – our energy! Too often, we simply take life for granted, show up to our work and perform instead of thriving. We show up, tow strap in hand, banking on a manager or leader's motivation to pull us. We're looking for someone's fire to inspire us.

When we're banking on external motivation, we're more susceptible to someone's negative energy becoming a source of motivation to us. This can get our energy flowing in a negative direction – rushed, stressed, overwhelmed, etc. There's a high in enthusiastic living. After all, many people are attracted to the enthusiast. The only issue is that many enthusiasts forget what bolstered them and after becoming addicted to the high, they didn't go back to charging – they burnt out internally. Enthusiasm's necessary when you decide to live energized, to be an energizer and leave your all on the field. But, know this, you must recharge. You must stay plugged into sources of power constantly transferring positive energy into your life.

This is the great differentiating point between motivation and energy. People who are plugged in and people needing charged. One is like a car with working alternator. They literally stay charging as they run, knowing when to stop to refuel/recharge. The other is like a car with a faulty alternator that has to trickle charge overnight and hope to start the next cold morning. In his powerful book, *What To Say When You Talk To Yourself*, Shad Helmstetter Ph.D. wrote, "Imagine being able to rely on yourself to automatically and unconsciously energize your spirit, focus your attention, and keep you in tune, on top, in touch and going for it! You can, just by learning that all true motivation, the only kind that lasts, the only kind you can count on, is internal motivation."

Self-motivation would be wonderful, right? Ignited energy would completely change our lives. It sounds too simple, doesn't it? Lest we discredit the facts that you can become a deeply energized person, self-motivating, and valuing the commitments you make to yourself, let's look at why we don't. Let's consider some areas where we get stuck and fail in our commitments to ourselves. This is huge. When we identify what's holding us back we can climb to a higher perspective and find breakthrough. Let's look at what's holding us back and why we may be failing to start. Then, let's briefly *analyze how our beliefs, emotions, feelings and habits all work together to either stymie us, or propel us forward.* It's simple, but remember, it's not easy.

Potential or Kinetic

There are two states of energy in all matter: potential and kinetic. Let's grasp a basic overview. Potential energy is stopped – at rest. It's dormant. Potential energy is like water behind the dam. When energy's in motion, it's kinetic. It's happening! It's thriving! Kinetic energy is like water flowing over the dam.

I remember wanting to run, desiring to run, even planning and believing I'd run! All my attempts, and plans and wishes didn't achieve the goal! I was potential energy. When we get stuck, we usually have great potential, but we need that little extra, a raised perspective, or little nudge to get us over. When we get stuck, life's happening to us instead of us happening to life. Too often, great plans and big talk stifle the simple action needed to achieve the goal! Do we need more motivation? A challenge or dare? Definitely not another new year's resolution! The magical energy already resides within us, yet we fail to tap into its abundant supply. What is this energy, and what ignites it? What sparks the first flame that continues to grow into a roaring fire? What will turn your potential energy into kinetic energy?

Kinetic energy – energy in motion – does amazing and wonderful things in your life. One scientist stated, "All moving things have kinetic energy. It is energy possessed by an object due to its motion or movement. These include very large things, like planets, and very small ones, like atoms. The heavier a thing is, and the faster it moves, the more kinetic energy it has." The energy inside of us is our WHY, our picture of how rewarding the future can be! It may be getting healthy to better your ability to play with your kids, learning to swim so you can finally conquer that triathlon, or calling a distant relative to redeem a relationship. The activity itself is often not the obstacle. Finding a strong enough reason to do something – that's the obstacle we face. *All reasons have different weights. The stronger the WHY, the heavier it is and the more kinetic energy you'll have.*

When your work doesn't align with your vision or passion, your WHY may be hard to find, and without a strong WHY you'll need motivation. When your work means something to you – you simply decide you're showing up in force (no ifs, ands or buts)! You'll dig deep to unleash your energy. It becomes personal to you. Finding several WHYs comes easy to you. Overcome this obstacle; get a strong WHY or "ball of WHYs"! Put a picture of your kids on your mirror, and then a picture of your walking shoes just below it, and say to apathy and lethargy, "You're both toast"!

Art of Start

The magic is the start! Just go. Make that list, take one step at a time, and celebrate each time you check a completed action or checkpoint off! Spark that flame that begins a roaring fire within. Trigger that energy with your WHY, and move from a potential dreamer to a daily kinetic doer and achiever!

Someone asked this question, "If three birds are sitting on a wire and one decides to leave, how many are left?" Well, the answer is three. Until you go do – DO – the action, you're not internally driven. Motivation can help you decide, but when your internal fire kicks in, action, commitment and consistency result. A firm belief must set deep into your heart that this change is worth the effort.

Beliefs – the Engine

Mark Twain said something like this, "It's not what you don't know that gets you into trouble; it's what you know for sure that just isn't so." We all have beliefs in our minds that either empower us or hold us back. Carefully examine your beliefs. Test which beliefs empower you and which ones hold you back. Ask yourself, "Why do I do _____?" or "Why do I want to do _____?" If you'll be completely honest with yourself, you'll begin to unravel limiting beliefs.

Use motivation to raise your perspective to replace limiting beliefs and build your WHY. Develop a strong, impenetrable WHY! Beliefs are constituted through the internal faculties that will long endure after the motivation has left. Beliefs are formed when our emotional (limbic) brain is called upon over and over again until a belief has firmly formed and taken hold. The limbic brain generates all of our feelings and it drives all behavior. ***Remember, virtuous beliefs drive valuable behavior delivering volumous benefits to our world!*** Motivation doesn't engage the emotions. It only gives the WHAT that needs to get done and ends there. Motivation speaks to the neocortex of our brains – the portion of our brains that "generates rational and analytical thought and language". That's why we can know WHAT to do and never do it.

Simon Sinek, in his book, *Start With Why*, states, "Only when the WHY is clear, and when people believe what you believe, can a true loyal relationship develop." Anything less than a strong WHY causes us to resort to the many methods of motivation. Kraig Kramers put it like this, "An empowered associate does not need to be motivated, managed, or leveraged with top-down power." Empower yourself and others with a strong, emotionally-based WHY.

Ask yourself and others, "How do you feel about this?" Ask this often. When you don't feel good about something, chances are your mind's not wholly convinced. Understanding this incongruence allows us to understand the internal argument going on here. Sometimes you want to believe, but you really don't and so, a good practice never sticks. An example would be leaving the motivational seminar saying, "Sure, it worked for him, but _____." We can quickly talk ourselves out of some-thing because what we felt in the moment was never transferred into our own beliefs. We really didn't form our own, strong WHY! We weren't really feeling it. Ask, "Am I feeling it?" If not, why not? "Can I bring myself to feeling it?" If so, you can move into forming a strong WHY – a strong belief for lasting behavior. Again, if you start with WHY, you will ignite energy. It may be just a spark at first, but with some fanning, you will be a an energizer – a life on fire!

Emotions – the Ignition

Rick Warren, in his book, *The Purpose Driven Life*, said, "There are hundreds of circumstances, values, and emotions that can drive your life: problems, pressures, deadlines, guilt, resentment, anger, fear, materialism, need for approval." Understanding your emotions and the feelings they generate is key. ***People who understand their emotions will be able to replace negatively charged emotional generators with positive, more constructive ones.*** Emotions happen in your soul – your limbic brain. It's the generator of all emotion. Emotional patterns are learned and habitualized. An emotion is triggered and this thought in your limbic mind fires off an immediate signal called a feeling.

Consider this example. An argument occurs where two of your kids want the one red bowl for breakfast. You step in and resolve the issue with an awesome orange bowl. They don't think it was that awesome. The result is tears or a grumpy attitude. Maybe this same scenario has happened between adults over choice of restaurant or between students over a parking spot. Life is full of changing expectations. Negative emotions are stimulated by default when these changes aren't in our favor. These negative emotions trigger feelings which affect our mood. Our mood sets the tone of our life. Our mood is the predominant charge of our feelings. A positive mood means positive feelings are winning which means more positive emotions have been stimulated than their negative counterparts. A positive mood reflects energy flowing in the right direction, upward and overflowing. A prevailing negative mood would reflect energy flowing in the wrong direction, down and out, leaving emptiness.

Now, some negative emotions are healthy like standing back from the cliff's edge, slowing down in the rain, grieving loss or feeling guilt for a wrong we're responsible for. However, we can choose to shift quickly to the positive emotion. I'm staying a healthy distance from the edge so I can enjoy the gorgeous waterfall without getting hurt. I'm slowing down and going to be safe on the roadway. Life's a celebration and I will live fully knowing the greatest honor I can give those who have passed on before me is carrying a bright torch for all those who will come after me. This life isn't meant to be lived in guilt and shame; therefore, I'm righting my wrong, learning from my mistake and growing - constantly! Do you see? Negative emotions can be used to

catapult us quickly into a more powerful, positive emotion - if we so choose! With our kids, we make sure to acknowledge their pain but quickly point out the happiness they're creating in their sibling and that "give and it shall be given" is an irrefutable, divine law. They'll get a turn to use the red bowl. We then turn to discover the beauty of orange and talk about how all colors make life beautiful. They're not "bad" for wanting red, but we can leveage the grumpy emotion to find joy in orange - a more positive emotion!

Coffee delivered to you and it's too sweet? It's ok. Laugh! Someone cut you off in traffic? It's ok. Smile. Someone yells at you? Hold your tongue. Smile. It takes concentration and practice, but *the great news is, YOU can choose positive emotional responses when expectations change!* Positivity doesn't start externally, it starts inside of you. Our brains are phenomenal! Billions of neurons are triggered simply evaluating a complex situation. We can intentionally stimulate these neurons with positive signals! Use your greatest asset – the brain – to work for you to look for the positives in everything! Generate positive emotional signals no matter how difficult the situation! Watch your mindset change and become the generator of positive energy in your life! You will become a powerful internal motivator constantly igniting your energy!

James Allen once said, "As you think so you become." Control your thoughts and you control your life. Control your thoughts you control your energy. Energy is life. Consider someone honking at you for no apparent reason. A negative emotion is stimulated. If you stew on that emotion and honk back or react with a more escalated response (negative emotions are highly competitive little rascals), you transfer energy to that emotion and now it's being reinforced and habitualized. Your very energy doing the negative work. Complete swindle. You get to work upset and the person who honked and started this series of unchecked emotional responses is now miles away. It seems ridiculous to fall for this scheme, but society is full of emotionally-negative responders. Thoughts are designed to produce action. In fact, they will manifest themselves into reality eventually. So, *thinking on the "pure, powerful and positive", like Zig Ziglar would say, will enable energy enhancing emotions, sending positive feelings throughout our souls' electromagnetic, amplifying systems causing our mood to radiate, and eventually being sensed through our vibes.*

What thoughts are you investing energy into today? Are you getting a great return on your energy? When the thoughts are powerful, they will transfer positive energy to you. Have you considered any thought or emotional journaling? Here's a simple exercise:

What are some of my most prevalent, negative thoughts? The ones that occur over and over:

Now, write a replacing, positive thought for each one and resolve to think these instead. This simple exercise proves we can control our energy:

What are some of my most prevalent, negative emotions?

Now, write a replacing, positive emotion for each one and resolve to build and bolster these instead. This simple exercise proves we can control our energy:

Check back in here each day and reflect on your progress. You become what you think about, and where your focus goes, your energy flows and expands. People who choose their thoughts instead of reacting to emotional impulses will empower themselves. By choosing our thoughts, visualizations, and affirmations, we can replace old emotional generators with new and empowering ones!

Feelings – the Gas Pedal

Emotions are your energies in motion; feelings tell you which way it's flowing and how strong the flow. Your emotions produce your feelings. Listening to what our feelings are saying allows us to assess our energy. Feelings gage our energy from negative to positive, empty to full and drained to abundant.

We get the chance to process our feelings. There are a lot of feelings before, during and after every decision we make. Analyzing them is crucial – many don't! The emotional memory bank initiates our initial feelings. If we simply go with our initial feelings, they may lead us astray. Feelings can be deceiving. Or, we may already be feeling excited or happy which puts us in a good mood. It's possible to go with the flow right into something we may later regret. ***When we stop and analyze our feelings, the ones stimulated by our emotions through internal thought or external stimuli, we can imagine what the result will be for a certain choice or decision.*** We empower ourselves when we consider the end feelings that will most likely result by a certain emotional response. We should ask, "In the end, is this what I really want?" "Will this TRULY make me and others happy?" "Does it benefit all?" In their book, *Emotional Intelligence 2.0*, Travis Bradberry and Jean Greaves share great insight, "One person thinks apologies are for 'sissies' so he never learns to recognize when one is needed."

In this scenario, let's imagine a workplace manager makes an angry outburst in a team meeting. Pulling him aside, a colleague shares she was startled and hurt by the outburst. In his mind, apologies are for 'sissies'. So, a negative emotion of weakness signals the initial feeling of defensiveness. It's a learned algorithm of defense in his brain. His jaw clenches and folding his arms across his chest, he bristles, makes an excuse and brushes off the complaint. He returns to his office with a huff and shaking his head. The initial feeling told him, "You don't dare apologize," and he went with that initial feeling. Had he stopped and disrupted the thought pattern with a counter thought, "Why not apologize?", then he would've activated the frontal facts-based brain called the neocortex. This reasoning side of the brain would've acted like Siri and Alexa combined to quickly deliver a summation of all the possible outcomes. Siri would have highlighted one possible outcome, "If you apologize you may experience a better result in the manager-employee relationship." Of course, a little friendly competition from Alexa would've thrown in a side note stating, "There are no guarantees, but it's the best chance of resolving this relationship." This second feeling is analyzed by our friend who thinks, "I don't know about this; um … ok, let's try it." The neocortex-brain and the limbic-brain have a conversation and the emotion switches. *The rush of energy changing from negative to positive leaves his palms a little sweaty and he feels the nervousness gripping his larynx just a bit.* "Hehemmm!" Clearing his throat, he offers a very timid, out-of-practice apology. Surprisingly, the employee stops dead in her tracks, turns around, and a tear trickles down her cheek as she says, "Thank you." He's shocked! What in the world? One simple apology can touch someone so deeply? The positive feelings rush all throughout the limbic brain and embed themselves into that newly formed emotional generator. These feelings stay in his memory bank forever. The next apology comes a little easier as this positive emotion moves energy through him. Every time after, the energy flows a little freer and a little stronger, upward and outward, and the feeling lasts longer. The initial plunge was difficult, but the action became easier with practice.

Between the neurons signaling, and thought clusters circulating throughout the brain in complex, multi-layered loops and pathways, there is a lot of brain activity in any given nano-second of the day. When decisions need made, the neural-spiking just before the "eureka" moment is intense. So obviously, the previous mental conversation is a very drawn-out, yet over-simplified version of the billions of neurons firing during this one response. Understanding how new, positive emotional generators can be created is crucial. Creating a new, positive feeling is tough. It's tough because it's unproven and puts extra load on your brain – initially. When the ending feeling is positive and productive, the new emotional generator is strengthened, and responding in a positive manner gets easier and easier.

Choices and responses made with the end feeling in mind, tend to spare a ton of hurt feelings and negative emotions from happening. They generate more understanding and harmony, and they strengthen themselves with use, so let's **GLUE** them into our memory. Emotional responses that reside in the highest levels of consciousness are:

G – Gratitude
L – Love
U – Understanding
E – Empathy

Let's consider an example of choosing that initial, deceptively "good" feeling that gets us into trouble. How about a situation, I'm sure many of us have experienced, when the emotional generator called "need for security" triggered the feeling called "comfort" and sent the sensation throughout our body. ***The unanalyzed emotion makes a quick, easy and painless decision – stay in bed.*** An hour later, we fly out of bed when our subconscious mind sounds the alarm and it dawns on us, "I'm late!" The emotion of security and feelings of comfort are now quickly overridden by the much stronger emotion of loss and the feelings of emergency. Flying out of bed ignites our energy, but with the negative feelings of emergency, we're already transferring much higher rates of energy into every action compared with a calm, peaceful morning. We're now flying about here and there – in a negatively energized state. We dash out the door – wait – back in the door for the car keys – back out the door. Start the car, put it in reverse – wait – put it in park, back in the door for our iPad on the charger with the much needed presentation we're pitching – back out the door! Driving, talk-radio adds amperage to our already negative state. Traffic doesn't help. Arriving, the motorist taking the nearer parking space we really need is the straw that breaks the camel's back! We lay on the horn and sputter some names under our breath – or worse, shout them! We park, and flipping the sun visor down to glance at our face and make sure the whiskers aren't too unbecoming for this presentation, we scowl at ourselves. With furrowed brow, lowered eyebrows and squinted eyes, we mutter something to ourselves like, "What were you thinking?" Fortunately, the minute-long walk and brief elevator ride provide a slight transition period. The executive assistant greets us with a smile and that helps to lift our spirits. We begin recalling all the sales training tips to our minds, and taking a deep breath to calm ourselves, we regain enough composure to stride confidently in to pitch this deal. We work extra hard to exude confidence because we're feeling the lack of control inside. Our client senses it, too. Not quite sure what he's feeling, his gut isn't picking up on any positive vibes. In fact, they're picking up traces of negativity. Somehow, in just a small, unrecognizable way, we weren't fully present with the sort of calm confidence that listens and responds. We lose the deal.

Listen, it happens. Hopefully the specificity of this illustration let's you know that I've experienced this, too. And if not this illustration, each one of us can think of one. The question, "what was I thinking?" or perhaps someone asking you, "what were you thinking?" can be answered like this: "I went with the initial feeling instead of stopping to analyze and make a positively emotional choice with the end feeling in mind." Bradberry and Greaves continue, "Another person hates feeling down, so she constantly distracts herself with meaningless activity and never really feels content." The unapologetic manager, the illustration of sleeping in, and this unrealistic optimist would each be well served to analyze their initial feelings. *When we interrupt our initial feelings, we can analyze and imagine positive end feelings, and in so doing, motivate our emotional generators to change.* Consider why you're feeling a certain way and ask, "What are my alternatives?" Turn the chagrin of "What was I thinking?" into a satisfied "I thought this one through!"

If you feel hurt, let bitterness go and forgive freely. We can interrupt negative feelings by replacing emotional generators. Negative responses will only hurt us further. Let's make decisions and choose responses with the end feelings in mind. Shad Helmstetter Ph.D., had this to say about feelings, "Your feelings about anything you do will affect how you do it." All of your feelings combined affect your actions. How you feel in every arena of life will determine how well you perform in each of those arenas. If your feelings are positive and productive your actions will follow. Make emotionally intelligent decisions and initiate positive responses with the end and lasting, positive feeling in mind.

Habits – the Fuel

To form great habits, feelings and their generating emotions must be understood. To form great habits and especially to replace poor habits, end feelings must be analyzed. When we stop and analyze, we engage the neocortex allowing it to serve as check-and-balance to our limbic brain. Useful habits are switches that unleash your energy. The more infused your habits are with good feelings, the more successful you will be implementing them, and we all know, old habits can be hard to replace. Why? Well, they have powerful initial feelings being produced by deeply engrained emotional generators.

The initial plunge to replace a habit is always difficult. It's uncharted waters and your neural pathways have to be formed, feelings banked in memory and new, positive emotional generators installed, built and bolstered. We have to be extra intentional when desiring a new habit to build an emotional pathway and stimulate good feeling with the imagination and thought of what the future holds. It's so key to support any positive habit making process with invigorated and heightened positive emotions. Lean into the initial tough feelings (getting up early, running, eating healthy, holding your tongue, etc) knowing that the end feeling is powerful, fully awakened life – ignited energy!

To conclude our discussion of external motivation versus our internal energy working for us, let's keep this in mind. Motivation gets us going, and our habits keep us going! Habits are powerful switches that tap us into positive energy transferring activities and routines in our lives. *Instead of a viscous cycle of unproductive default feelings, we've created a victorious cycle - energy's ignited!*

CHAPTER 4
ENERGY'S ATTRACTION
abundance mentality to love deeply

"Positive energy attracts at the highest frequency of giving – abundance!"

New Tires

Who loves a cool tire store? I do. The chrome, aluminum, and black powder-coated rims and the fresh smell of rubber. Ah! Rubber has to be some of the most forgiving material, but still, 40,000 miles or sooner depending on road conditions, they're going to need replacing. We're supposed to measure the depth of remaining tread and make a new tire decision sooner than most do. However, does anyone remember being a young adult, working three jobs to make ends meet, and praying the metal mesh showing through the rubber wouldn't leak any air before you could buy new tires? Yep. Been there, done that. I thought I couldn't afford to; looking back, I shouldn't have afforded not to!

I left the machine shop one day to head home. It was late. I was ready to get home to spend a few hours with Jen before heading off to deliver pharmaceuticals to care centers across Tennessee. From a distance, I could see a drastic slant to the top of my Oldsmobile – yes, another Cutlass Sierra story. I went around to the passenger's rear side and to my dismay – flat tire! Opening the trunk, I retrieved the spare, thankful my father-in-law engrained in my brain to keep it checked for proper inflation. After installing, I drove home a bit slowly, also thankful the flat hadn't happened en route that morning.

The next day, the receptionist called me up to the front desk just about closing time. "Would you take the hole-punch kit to Jeff?" Hollie asked. "He's at Sam's Club and needs it." "Sure thing." I said. A bit confused why the CEO would need this hefty, hydraulic hole-punch kit anywhere in the world outside of our electric panel-build area, I asked, "When does he need it?"

"He asked that you leave immediately, and don't take a company truck. He said it's quicker for you to just go home from Sam's Club – wouldn't want you to have to waste the time coming all the way back." Inwardly, I was bummed. There was a good three hours' worth of over-time for me – and we needed it. I needed to buy a new tire. Outwardly, I jumped on it and soon was rolling toward Sam's Club.

Driving around looking for the white,Chevrolet truck our CEO drove, I spotted it on the side. I drove over and hopped out. No one was in it "Hmmm, he must be inside, I thought." Just then, I heard a whistle from one of the tire-change bays. There he stood motioning me to drive my car in. Wha-aaaaat? Sure enough, he had the manager all cued up and within an hour, I was heading home with not one, but four, top-of-the-line tires! Jen was blown away. I'd only been working there a few months.

Nine years later, Jeff and I were heading to Georgia to sign-on a large client, and we landed on the subject of giving. He told me he loved living within his means, saving and investing and doing well in business so that he could give. I reminded him about the new tires story. Thanking him again all those years later, and you know what? He seriously had to think about it. He was in such a habit of creating the ability to abound in giving, and he'd just about forgotten that one instance. I remembered every detail!

Abundant

Let's consider this principle of an abundant mentality, how it gives, and how it attracts. *An abundant mentality overflows: adds, multiplies, invests and gives. A limited mentality withholds: subtracts, divides, spends, holds back and takes.* When you're empty, it's hard to imagine abounding; when you're full, you have the ability to give. When energy's ignited and you become whole as a person, you're filled, and you expand your capacity in life. At this point you experience richer life and other people will experience a richer life because of you. You literally become a well of water springing up from within. This is where giving – in its purest form – comes from. Solomon wrote the proverb that says it like this, "There is that scatters, yet increases; there is that holds back more than is needed, yet is lacking." Another promise, "Give and it shall be given" is an irrefutable law, and there are many types of giving. This law promises a return – a universal attraction. This attractive force is powerful. *Many choose to think only of immediate needs in order to survive and get by, instead of thinking abundantly.* Let's dig into this powerful, life-changing principle.

Attractive

Have you ever met a truly attractive person? Our magazine covers and TV shows depict what we often hold as the standard for beauty or attraction. If we're not careful, we can mistake appearance or personality for attraction. Hair, clothes, makeup and styles all change – beauty as defined by our appearance fades. What's truly attractive and an enduring attraction are those people that make everyone feel loved. An attraction of the soul. Attractive people have the capacity to make everybody feel like a somebody. They aren't pre-absorbed with themselves. They spill over on people. You simply can't contain these people from blessing others. There is a certain magic in giving and the principle of attraction will always work under one condition – a truly abundant mentality. Let's look at abundance and attraction as seen in the beauty of nature.

Radiant, Thermal & Chemical Energies

Nature can be a great teacher. What comforts the heart and reinvigorates the spirit can prove exhilarating to study! Think of the awe of the sunrise and the comfort of a warm fire on a cold, winter night. The sunshine is radiant energy; the fire is thermal energy. When we eat food, our metabolism kicks in transforming it into chemical energy - fuel for our bodies. Consider a beautiful sunrise providing light to the world, rising every day on a consistent basis. Beaming its heat down to earth, it summons millions to sandy beaches. Scientists devote their lives to capture its abundance of solar power. It displays a quiet, attractive power boasting nothing when it rose this morning, and it will boast nothing tonight when it sets. The sun simply does its thing. It gives and attracts. The fire on a cold winter night will give warmth and attract humanity to its side. The smell of food on the stove will send forth its aroma and gather families around the table. All give; all attract.

Becoming Attractive

Add wood and the fire continues to roar. Add truths from this book and others like it to allow your fire, your inner drive, your energy, to roar! Your life can be a thriving source! Calm power, deep fullness, abundant giving! You'll be light. Energy will radiate from your face. You'll be warm and open. Your touch, your embrace your very presence and your vibes will give a harmonious presence to all you encounter. Attraction will project itself from your life without you speaking a word. We've all heard the saying, "Your walk talks louder than your talk talks," and I believe attractive living speaks louder than both. *Who you are on the inside – the truest form of you – is your energy. It's your capacity for life. And when you're living with a mindset and actions of abundance in everything, you're attractive.* You'll be the right things (virtuous), you'll do the right things (valuable), and you'll attract the right things into your life. You're a blessing and the blessing finds its way back in reciprocation. S.D. Gordon writes, "There is the life of sweet purity and gentle patience always so winsome, that speaks all the time in musical tones to one's circle."

When you add value to your life by building your mind through new skills, enhancing your health, developing your emotions, digging deeper into your spiritual well-being, and improving your thoughts and beliefs, you build attraction. When you find ways of adding value to people's lives around you, you build attraction. Add value to the universe, be the sunlight's radiant energy, be the fire's comforting warmth, have an aroma of value about you and you will be attractive.

Mentality of Abundance

Sometimes, the easiest way for some to think of giving is monetarily. Some people view the size of the gift as valid measurement. Giving can never be measured but by the fullness of heart from which the gift was given. I remember getting a used cap gun from my five-year-old brother. I was eight years old and I remember getting a lump in my throat. It was his only cap gun, and his favorite. We didn't have much, so he went and wrapped a toy he knew I'd love. There are those who'll write a large check to charity, those who'll fly to Africa to work in a mission, and yet those who'll pay it forward in the McDonald's drive-through. Can anyone be ranked higher than the other? No. The law of giving and receiving is irrefutable.

When giving is not in pure motivation, we can assume the attractive power is deteriorated. Consider, those giving to get something in return. They calculate. I like what Robert Jones Burdette said in the nineteenth century, "Don't believe the world owes you … the world owes you nothing – it was here first." Limited mindsets make bottom line decisions only. We know the story of Ebenezer Scrooge, the "tight-wad", right? These people hold back and aren't benevolent unless it benefits them. Have you ever met someone like this? Were they an attractive source? I love the quote that states, "Gold contracts; giving expands." Seth Godin discusses becoming indispensable in his book, *Linchpin*, and he states, "What capitalism has taught us is that every transaction has to be fair, an even trade for goods or services delivered. Linchpin thinking is about delivering gifts that can never be adequately paid for. Tribes can be built by giving gifts, not by taking. That's how it used to be done." *Abundance has no calculation. It's a well of water springing up from within and blessing all that come for a drink.* S.D. Gordon writes, "The stingy man thinks chiefly of the years making up his own present life; but, the man who takes into his reckoning not only the present generation, but all coming generations, in the disposing of his money is a shrewd financier."

While money practices can indicate a limited or abundant mindset, all other life practices tend to march to the same drum. Closed off versus open, loving versus calculating, warm and trusting versus cold and judgmental.

Yet, some of the biggest calculators and "Scrooges" are the ones who give large amounts. One of the largest reasons for failure in this area of giving is feeling guilted into giving or needing the validation of giving. One should avoid giving for these reasons. Some are addictive-givers and impoverish their own families. When giving is fear-based, it's calculating; it's not stemming from an abundant heart. Abundant-minded givers understand their gifts, utilize these gifts, and add the most value they can to the recipient. So then, giving may be money; but, it could also be time, a helping hand, a listening ear, wise counsel, a tool, and the list goes on.

Whether money or another medium, practice giving more value than required. The original form of money is value. What we trade for that money is our time. Use that traded time (like working a job) wisely, create more value than is expected and don't squander what you earn. Invest wisely, and create a lifestyle of giving. Give yourself to that which lasts. Make investments of your time, talents and treasure into valuable assets. Assets appreciate. Assets yield fruit. Think abundantly and build wealth so you can maximize giving. Give to yourself – to steward your finances investing in assets. Give to others – to sow your finances and invest in abundance. You build true wealth that keeps on giving from its abundance.

Entrepreneurs capitalize on opportunities to fulfil needs and create value for people. When they give more value than expected, they usually make more, or can ask more – look at modern examples of Starbucks, Apple, and other loved brands. Wise and diligent laborers should never doubt the next raise. They give more than is required and with this abundant mentality, they are confident the reciprocity will happen. This mindset is an abundant one. When you're living in a giving mentality all the time – giving your all in everything you do, then the attraction of abundance is your reward. Giving then is not a poor judgment call, but a blessed opportunity! If we'd look at our responsibility to give seriously, we'd invest our talents and abilities more wisely. Instead of wasting our resources, we'd busy ourselves creating value, building wells, and building good and true wholesome wealth – much more than just giving money to sooth an inward need.

When our motives are driven by love and abundance, then giving becomes a multiplying activity for us and to us. We won't settle to only cut a check for a certain amount if we're supposed to do more. It's like the business owner who told me he used to send a check to Africa each year to feel like he was doing his part for world hunger. Then, he discovered he could pay for his team to go for the same amount and install a clean water well together. Not only did he research and think bigger, he instilled something into the hearts of many more. His giving from abundance multiplied much further than simply cutting a check out of duty.

And lest we think we must have perfect motivations before we begin, begin now. You can give something right now. Stewardship seeks to grow this giving. Every small action either amplifies or diminishes your abundance. Give more of yourself, give your smile, give your time, give your talents, and give your treasure. Giving should become a habit; allow practice to perfect its motive. Fall in love with giving. Find ways to give. Giving opens your heart and expands it. Giving is a desire to overflow. Don't wait until your totally full because as we'll look at in the five levels of giving, you become full by giving. Living from a place of abundance motivates you to abound. You realize the truth of the proverb "he that waters will himself be watered."

Always splash out to others. *By splashing, you think fullness and abundance. You literally create the need to be full so you have more to splash.* This is the greatest blessing. Giving takes you along this beautiful journey of discovering so much more about yourself! Through this habitual splashing, you create the habit of expansion and it causes you to think bigger. Creating value comes easiest to the giver. Givers care. They realize the joys of caring. Caring people give. Before long, what you gave compounds and comes right back – in big and, oftentimes, unexpected ways! Let's rise higher than simply "cutting a check" or mindlessly easing our emotional need to give. Let's engage all of our energies into what is our best gift. What do we know about abundant givers? Abundant givers are happy people.

Chapter 4

Creating Value

One of my business mentors, Shane Reeves, has poured himself into my vision for business. He's enhanced my perspective. He's helped me and many young men find their gifts and calling. Is this a monetary gift? No. It's far greater. He's teaching us how to be profitable. I know Shane's a monetary giver as well, but abundant-giving encompasses our entire being. Giving our gifts and calling everything we've got, so that we can give this world everything we've got! In his famous and powerful book, *The Fred Factor*, Mark Sanborn declares, this abundance mentality, "takes ordinary products or job responsibilities and makes them extraordinary. These are the real-world alchemists who practice the art and science of value creation."

So, let's not only work hard, but work hard creating value. This is true wealth maximization – creating value. Let's curb extravagant tastes, and invest assets that prosper ourselves and others. If a charity is established to collect money, but isn't working to add maximum value to the local or global community, then they're not any more worthy of a gift than a thief. *The giver and the receiver together should create value – thus prospering together. This is synergy in giving!* Analyze the receiver's track record of trustworthiness in creating value, give to maximize them, and give with pure motivation – needing nothing in return. If we're lacking, and by giving we hope to get something in return, we're not giving with purity and abundant mentalities. Instead, step back, analyze the sources of income in your life and the swindlers of income. Increase the sources, cut the swindlers, and only invest in creating value. Everything should be an investment.

What about creating value in the sales process? Marketers will tell you that you must keep your products and services in front of people, and with technology and sponsored Ads, the tactics are at our finger tips. While it's true, we should stay in front of people, as people buy from those they see, know and trust, it's very possible to inundate people with needless information instead of finding out what their needs are and meeting those needs. Do daily emails inundate your inbox from the site you purchased a product from or attended a webinar with? This is tactic instead of needs. It simply creates more noise than value. With gimmicks, consumers jump in only to find there's a catch. They feel conned. Instead of gimmicks like a catchy pitch, a cool new app, or luring webinar, why not focus first on creating value that meets a need. How are you finding out the needs of those around you? Are we doing our research? Are we asking? Are we listening? Once needs are known, are we building a product that delivers a benefit and gives a specific result? Results speak for themselves. If you can truly touch lives, improve a condition or meet a need, then you can let your clients speak for you. This is the highest form of marketing. With genuine testimony, high trust is built and you never "hard-sell" anyone. You can move through the market explaining your services and offering those services. Like my friend, New York Life agent and achiever of the President's Circle, Ryan Denney, told me once, "Drip value to your clients." When you study hard and know your stuff, you're confident you can add value to people's lives. It's no longer a matter of if, it's just a matter of when. Drip value to your clients, your family, your kids, your community. When you create good content that's high value, they'll come. You won't have to oversell!

Get so secure in who you are that you don't have to ramble on and on trying to find yourself in every conversation. I did this as a young guy. I'd saturate conversations about me – ramble about my life. When you know where you're going, you'll find you're much more aware to the conversation and helping others find their path, and you can engage in their desires and needs. *I love how Benjamin Disraeli said, "The greatest good you can do for another is to not just share your riches, but to reveal to him his own."* One of the greatest forms of giving is the gift of identity. Be sincerely interested in people's lives, their dreams, their identities and their stories. We all want to feel like we're valued. In fact, it's the cry of humanity. It's why people love being listened to and we all need to be listened to in our lives. When you truly listen – not casual listening, but actually hearing – you give identity to people and show you care for their needs.

The salesperson who's so secure in their products rarely talk about their products, they discover needs and will match the best product when it's needed. They don't push catalogs, clutter inboxes and show features. They talk needs and then the benefits of your product or service to meet those needs. Like my friend, Jack Daly, says, "Help people to buy. People like to buy and hate being sold." Meet needs – create or add value!

Simple! And, it's super attractive! I remember meeting the Apple evangelist himself, Guy Kawasaki. His smile in itself was enchanting and when he signed and handed me his book, I wasn't at all surprised to see the title was, *Enchantment, The Art of Changing Hearts, Minds and Actions.* Guy writes in his book, "There are many tried and true methods to make a buck, yuan, euro, yen, rupee, peso, or drachma. Enchantment is on a different curve however. When you enchant people, your goal is not to make money from them or to get them to do what you want, but to fill them with great delight."

Sales is not the only arena for creating value; it's a desire within us – part of a higher consciousness. Analyze your activities in your life? Do they create value in your life and the lives of others? Every action in life should create or add value. Are you using your abilities in the highest and best use of your calling? Think of one non-value adding activity right now:

_____

_____

What value-adding activity could you replace it with:

_____

_____

Adding Value

Some may not immediately see what they could possibly create, but they can sure add value to everything and every life they touch. I spent a summer serving breakfast to the homeless in Nashville. I learned a lot from these dear people coming in off the street. Most of them are super-talented, and every now and then, you'll find one strumming a guitar on the corner of downtown. In his own way, he's adding value and I bet he's more prone to receiving a tip in the case, cup or hat setting on the cobblestones. My heart is compelled most by the person, without much, doing what they can.

It's like the story of the blind beggar who's sign read, "I'm blind, please help." Very few people empty their pockets of spare change. A kind stranger walks up, takes his sign, pulls out her Sharpie marker and on the other side of the cardboard, scribbles these words, "It's a beautiful day out, and I can't see it." The power of words is the point of this story, but did she add value to his life by leaving him no money? Clearly, this new message drew all sorts of people who received emotional value of gratitude and willingly emptied their pockets. This is adding value and is the start of an abundant mentality.

Ben Franklin was known to give the Philadelphia homeless population work as street sweepers. He convinced shop keepers that they could get more clerical work done instead of wasting their time sweeping their shops of dirt from the cobblestone streets. The homeless would add value around the city sweeping the streets. Less tracked-in dirt created value for the merchants. So, they'd take up a collection to pay the street sweepers. *We inherently recognize value and are drawn to it. The subject of adding value and attraction are inextricable!*

A Well, Fountain & Mountain Stream

Here's the attraction of abundance. Your life becomes full and abundant. You're a well of water in this world! You become a fountain as opposed to a drain. Wells and fountains draw people. I remember a crystal-clear mountain stream channeled into this hollowed out log when I was a kid. It was the perfect place to stop after a long bicycle ride up the mountain. The water was always so fresh flowing out of the mossy log's channel. You could splash it on your face, rinse the dirt from your hands, and scoop freshness to your mouth. It wasn't just a full bucket, it was an overflowing source powered by the velocity of water from the mountain above. Ah! Refreshing memories! Consider a well of cool water. People in ancient times built wells – wells attract people. People get thirsty and wells quench thirst; unless, they're dry. Dry wells repel people and have nothing to give. People become even more thirsty as they came expecting a drink only to find nothing. So today, be a full and abundant well, fountain or mountain stream. Some are bigger and more powerful. Size doesn't matter; abundance does. Let your heart be the power behind your giving. All of your emotional energy will be this power adding velocity to your life! Dig deep; be full so you can propel emotional giving. Dig deep to know who you are and what your gifts are – how you create value! Then be a source of water, flowing upward and outward to all. Be pure, fresh, clean water and you will attract. Don't concentrate on attracting, though. Concentrate on the well – building, bolstering and bubbling over!

Giving is an amazing thing. The act of giving feels amazing. The law of giving is irrefutable. And giving has so much more meaning when it comes from the heart. ***The ability to give and give abundantly is incredible and when our giving's abundant, it produces the greatest attraction.*** A magnet that's abundant gives an attractive charge. When giving is connected to the emotion of love, it will attract as well. Let's consider the five levels of abundant giving. Knowing and following these will amplify your attraction – guaranteed.

Giving Before ... Forgiving Before Giving

In order for giving to be attractive, no strings attached, completely pure and overflowing from an abundant heart, there's a first level of giving. It must take place for any other levels to be truly attractive. It's the concept of giving before, or pre-giving. It's the freest form, deepest form and must also be the first. Forgiving! Some give without first forgiving, but they miss out on the highest level of abundance – the fifth level. We have to start at this first level of forgiving. An unforgiving heart is limited in some reserve and can't attain the highest level. Author of, *The Five Love Languages*, Gary Chapman states, "Forgiveness is the way of love."

Forgiveness is the freest, and most powerful form of giving, yet it's proven throughout human history to be the most difficult. As much as it's difficult, it's vital. It's the start of a giving journey. Jesus taught that if we bring a gift and remember any negative attitude toward another like anger, hate or jealousy, we should leave our gift, and go forgive that person first. With a forgiving heart, there's no strings attached to giving. Emotional hurt won't be incurred as a result of giving. Someone doesn't thank us, we don't mind it. We didn't give for thanks. Someone doesn't repay our gift, we're none the wiser. We didn't give to benefit us.

... Giving Before Forgiving

Some look to giving for healing; only forgiving brings true healing and perpetuates abundant living. Some look for emotional healing in giving without first forgiving past wounds and hurts. See, giving was designed to be an abundance exercise – the outpouring of an abundant heart. Giving when we have nothing but the heart to give is a sign of faith knowing we will reap. However, giving from a place of obligation, or to feel better emotionally, without first forgiving is fruitless. Yes, we may get the feel-good of giving, until it wears us down and becomes a chore. We start resenting the people or places we're giving to, begin calculating, or lose the joy that giving is designed to immediately give back. Giving can be an obligation or an opportunity. When we think abundantly, we want to invest our gift.

So, why must forgiving come first. When we hold resentment or bitterness in our hearts, our energy is deteriorated. Our emotions are scarred in some way. Giving may be able to flow, but it won't flow freely. Only when we first forgive do these emotional barriers come down, and our gifts aren't tainted by impure motives, calculation, or insincerity. *Forgiving is free, but it's the hardest form of giving. Giving isn't free, but it's often easier than forgiveness because we can touch and feel giving something – and we can calculate it.* Until we forgive freely, we will not know the deep joy of giving! We will not recognize all the opportunities to give of ourselves whether that's listening, spending devoted time, emotional giving, financial giving, our talents, our smile, our love, service rendered, adding value, and the list is endless.

Giving can't bring the healing forgiving was designed to bring. When you first forgive, you will find healing through this ultimate form of giving; then, giving will flow freely from a healed and emotionally abundant heart. Giving without forgiving violates the energy principle of being first, then doing. Forgiving is an exercise of being – internal. Giving is an exercise of doing – external.

Giving Up ... Free but Difficult

The second level of giving – giving up. Giving up the things that swindle the quality of our lives is another free form of giving. And again, it's difficult. Yet, more quality life means more quality life to give! You ask a lady if she wants any bracelet or bracelet from Tiffany's and she'll choose the latter every time. You spend all day with your friend but don't them any attention, or spend two hours of deep listening and investment into them. They'll choose the latter. So, giving things up to improve the quality of your life, your health, and your time is so key. It's free; yet, it's terribly difficult! It means giving up jealousy, bitterness, and hate. Giving up talking badly about others. Giving up unhealthy expectations of yourself. Giving up debilitating habits. Giving up energy-swindling activities. *Give up, so you can give more!*

... Pruning Trees

My friend, Joshua, leads a consulting firm called, Growability. His decades of business study, consulting mastery and global work with other countries and their economies sums his training up into a beautifully painted tree and every function of business represents something on this tree. The depth of wisdom in this philosophy so closely tied to nature is incredible. Just like the orchardist, a wise leader knows you must prune in business: old systems, old technologies and underperforming employees. The same is true in life: old habits, toxic friends, and the list can go on. For a tree, a business or our lives to be healthy and grow, giving up must happen constantly throughout life. The wholeness of the tree is in direct proportion to the size of the fruit. A pruned and efficient tree is why I could pluck a grapefruit from Grandma's tree when we visited her in Florida. It was an abounding plant. Abundant! What can you point at and say, "that's the huge fruit in my life." Give something up so you can. Give yourself life (the tree's sap) so you can yield fruit.

One of my clients is a phenomenal speaker with tremendous

knowledge of Lean Management, he makes me more efficient just visiting him. Chris is known as the "Champion of Change." He teaches what he calls the "5-P Lean Benefit." The five P's are: personal, philanthropy, purpose, power and pattern. "When you're lean," he says, "you're more profitable, and can become a major player in the world of philanthropy." Instead of the mindset of just getting by, what if businesses pruned, built capacity, created raving value among shareholders and abounded! We all must prune. It's that simple, yet many won't because they feel obligated. They weigh their life down and expend energy like it grew on trees! Trust me, I've done it. Energy does not grow on trees. *Energy is sap being robbed by many unproductive twigs and unfruitful branches. Prune so you can transfer energy to fruitful activity and abound!*

Giving In ... My Cup Runs Over

The third level of giving – giving in. There's an ancient Hebrew saying, "My cup runs over," and it stems from a ceremonial practice where a family would invite strangers to the table. A cup was placed on a saucer, and as they filled it, the oil would reach the brim. They didn't stop pouring, but kept right on until the oil ran down and filled the saucer. This was symbolically saying, "As we've received and are abundant, may we share with the strangers that come to our table." It's a beautiful piture.

Notice, they had to fill the cup; so also, we must be filled to overflow. How are you filling? When you're healthy, you can encourage and give health, not to mention do more, earn more and give more. How are you giving health to yourself? When you're emotionally intelligent and know yourself, you can understand emotions and connect with others better. Are you getting in touch with your emotions to be more resilient, understanding and connecting? What makes you happy? Anne Frank said, "Whoever is happy will make others happy, too!"

Instead of being full, our cups are too full of holes. We transfer energy to so many meaningless thoughts, words and actions. We've bought into debt and are being swindled of the ability to be a blessing. The majority of Americans are too strapped financially to experience the joy of giving from a place of abundance. Change your mindset as quickly as possible.

Build internal wealth – a rich mindset – that never fade away! Henry Ward Beecher said it like this, "A man's ledger does not tell what he is, or what he is worth. Count what is in him, not what is on him, if you would know what he is worth – whether rich or poor." Build a life vision of true wealth. Dream, envision, set goals, and plan actions around getting to the place where you can be more and give more.

The airlines have a standard procedure they walk you through every time you board and prepare for takeoff. In case of emergency the oxygen masks will fall from the ceiling. "Install yours first; then help your neighbor," says the instructional video while being illustrated by the flight attendant. *The longer we remain stuck and refuse to invest in our capacity, our wholeness our fullness – our energy – the longer we delay the joy of doing the most good!*

Give in to yourself, your development, your ability so that you have greater ability. Give inwardly to build you. Spend money on education and use that education to bless your life and every life you touch. Spend money on books that will truly expand your capacity. Stay in the habit of giving so you can experience the joy of giving in every arena of life. This joy and fulfillment will increase your vision to do more so you can give more! Why not cut swindlers of health? Why not replace addiction with value creating activities? Why not let go of emotional wounds so we can feel more alive? When we realize the joy of being an overflowing source, then learning, growing, loving, forgiving, foregoing temporary happiness for eternal joy becomes easy. You'll continue to fortify and increase the capacity of your well! I love this quote by Dalai Lama "Every day, think as you wake up, 'Today I'm blessed to have woken up, I'm alive, I'm a precious human life and I'm not going to waste it. I'm going to use all my energies to develop myself, to expand my heart out to others. I'm going to benefit others as much as I can!'"

... Never Level Off – Abound

Never level off - abound! Grow – constantly! When you're an abundant source, you won't compete. You won't have to. You'll be you; you'll be different. Thrive in this! There will be takers in this world that don't like to see overflowing sources. They'll say things to discourage or diminish the overflow of your heart. Guard against the detractors and dividers of the world. Be a multiplier; commit to always be a fountain of blessing. Free up more of your time from busy work to give quality. Eliminate debt and create more monetary income by creating true wealth so that you can give more financially. Cast off the swindlers of your energy so that you can have energy – living fully – to love deeply! Cut the swindler of constant tech plug-in and go play with the kids. Abound to life!

... Fullness is Daily Growth

When you're growing, it's so much easier to feel the sap flowing through your branches and fruit being produced in your life that you don't get offended when someone compares to, competes with or condemns you. You're not disheartened because you know – you're not faking – that everyday you're growing! You're getting better and better, every day, and in every way. You're competing in your own lane to continually expand your potential. You're demanding you become your absolute best. You know everyone benefits when you operate this way. *Growing then is not a matter of filling a large glass, it's overflowing your small glass today and expanding the glass every day.* Overflow every day! It's when you level off and grow stagnant that the sap stops flowing. The trunk is wounded – hurt. The branches are tangled and fruitless. Criticism and judgement penetrate and hurt. We compare and compete because our satisfaction comes, not in the fresh growth we're experiencing, but in our stagnation looking just a bit better than someone else's stagnation.

Key to overcome stagnation; always stay hungry to grow. Are you hungry? We get hungry for a reason, and, deciphering through featured images on the outside of the package, hopefully we choose great, nutritious fuel. What about mental fuel, spiritual fuel, relational fuel, occupational fuel? Are you hungry today for growth in every arena of life? Life is not about mere existence. Nature itself teaches us that growth happens in living things! We must grow through life, not simply go through it. Are you hungry? If you're hungry, you will grow. Like the beattitudinal promise, "they that hunger and thirst after righteousness shall be filled;" when you're hungry for something, you're going to feed the appetite. It's a guarantee of nature. How are your appetites? Are they healthy? I must daily challenge myself to ensure my appetites are healthy! Healthy appetites are good! Remain hungry and grow in all areas of life!

Giving Thanks ... Magic Switch

The fourth level of giving – giving thanks! When you give thanks, you change your heart from limited to abundant and it overflows. It's the very switch to this entire mentality of abundance. Gratitude! When you're focused on becoming your best so you can give your best, and you're grateful for growth, you raise your frequency. Intentionality combined with gratitude is a powerful frequency!

Gratitude! Wow! What a day we live in when we get upset over being cut off in traffic, yet our very vehicle (whether executive-looking or a rattle-trap) proves we possess more than most of human population at this time. *An abundant mentality is when we decide to look at all we have, and all that we're able to create, instead of what we don't have, and the limitations and excuses for not creating.* When we rise to this perspective of gratitude, we see everything differently. Our vision is re-learned and we see things at a higher level. We operate on the frequency of gratitude – the electromagnet is finally turning on. The attraction is building. Gratitude is the switch that can immediately fill us. That's right. We become abundant almost immediately with gratitude. Perhaps this is why the commandment for gratitude is so drastic, "In everything give thanks," – everything!

... Attitude of Gratitude

Think of the last time somebody's done something nice. Remember having a grateful thought quickly pass through our minds? We don't always express it, or perhaps we don't know how to express it. Maybe, thankfulness doesn't come so naturally.

Consider our expectations of "the ideal shopping experience." Maybe criticizing the weak points of service or finding fault comes easily and we've missed an opportunity to thank another human being like a waitress, a store clerk, and so on. If we'd instead nurture an attitude of gratitude, and find something to be thankful for, we'd literally change the world. That's the power of finding the good! Like my good friend, Joe, likes to say, "You don't have to, but what if you did?"

Wouldn't someone stopping you, looking kindly and deeply into your eyes and giving you a sincere and heartfelt "Thank You" mean the world to you? What about a handwritten note in the mail? Do it for someone else. Text someone right now. Be the source of love, encouragement and gratitude! With the abundance of technology, we have no excuse not to abound in gratitude. Gratitude pent up inside is useless. So, let's give our **BEST** thanks:

> **B** – Be specific in naming what someone did for you.
> **E** – Express it through a text, handwritten note, phone call, Facebook post, lipstick on the mirror, or another creative medium.
> **S** – Sincerely thank them; let your heart flow.
> **T** – Think about how their act made you feel and how your gratitude made them feel. Invoke emotion so the generator of feeling thrives and you repeat BEST thanks again and again!

Remember, gratitude is a choice. Nurture the attitude of gratitude, and form habits of thankful expression! Invoke emotions into your gratitude. "Thoughts which are mixed with any of the feeling of emotions, constitute a magnetic force which attracts other similar or related thoughts," said Napolean Hill. Watch the energy ignite when you choose to find good and express it! See what gratitude does? It causes us to realize we don't have to have everything we think we need before we give something. *We give something, now, realizing how much we already have, and it's by this faith – the eyesight of gratitude – that giving attracts abundance to us.*

The grateful-giver isn't limited. The grateful-giver is so accustomed to looking for the good, they begin seeing good and value where others don't or won't. Their dreams, thinking and plans become richer! The grateful-giver thinks abundantly. There was a story of a poor orphan girl in nine-teenth century, London who had nothing but a crutch which she'd use to get around. She loved helping in all the ways she could, and did her best to balance on her crutch while filling bowls with soup. One day, a girl was carried into the orphanage by one of the volunteers. This girl couldn't walk. Maggie thought about giving her crutch to this girl, "but then," thought Maggie, "I can no longer stand to serve soup." So, Maggie went to the volunteer and asked him if he could ask someone outside of the orphanage for a wheel chair for this poor girl. So grateful was Maggie for her plight in life – as hard as it was for her to get around – that she never even thought once to ask for herself. The volunteering friend, so moved by her care for others, pulled a group of London's businessmen together and purchased the wheel chair and a new pair of crutches for Maggie.

This is the power of grateful-giving. You think gratefully, and your heart grows. It literally expands, and life becomes abundant. You think in terms of *"What can I do to create the most value for you,"* as opposed to, *"What's in this for me?"*

Giving Out

With grateful-giving, you're literally finding the good in every body and every situation. This lifts you to the ultimate level of giving – giving out! Giving out of what? Or, giving out to whom? It's giving out of an abundant and overflowing heart. It's giving out to everyone. It's the highest frequency of giving. It's giving out of a deep heart of love! You don't only find the good in everything and everyone through gratitude, you start seeing and believing the good in everyone – even when they can't see it in themselves. This giving gives a smile for a frown, a blessing for a curse and gives freely!

You keep your heart whole and your energy high so you can expand into every arena and amplify creating value, giving yourself and over-flowing kindness and love. Kindness and love are the overflow of the full and whole life. Why? Because both are given without expectation of anything in return. This started with your mentality of abundance and became an unstoppable fountain as you moved up the first four levels. At level five, you are overflowing with velocity at a high frequency. An overflowing, giving, loving life is a super attractive life.

... Kind of Kind

Be kind! I vividly remember Mom's frequent reminder – commandment is more like it! With five brothers, things could get ugly quickly. My idea of "kind" was to be kind of kind. As long as they showed kindness, I would reciprocate. However, the urban dictionary hits the definition spot on: "Kindness is doing something and not expecting anything in return ... it implies kindness no matter what." Kindness stems from a belief in others. A deep love for our fellow man. It's no surprise the apostle Paul says, "Love is kind." Kindness is an act that's so freeing! Unlike my childhood understanding of the term, true kindness eliminates expectations!

Like rays of sunshine energize the universe, unfettered kindness energizes the giver and receiver! Not kind of kind but whole-hearted kindness! How different would our marriages be if we'd truly be kind? What would they say about us at our places of employment if we'd work with kindness in our hearts? Think of the difference and impact we'd make! Reach out a hand of true kindness. Be intentional with acts of kindness not expecting anything in return. Let kindness be your keynote! Watch what happens.

... A Piano Teacher

We've all met those people that have made us feel amazing! Think of someone who showed up into your life from a place of abundance. They came running at a time you needed someone to believe in you. They didn't give to receive anything in return. They poured themselves into you, added value to your life and loved you unconditionally! They literally made all the difference in the world. Who were they? How old were you? How'd they enter your life? What did they say? How did it impact you?

Write their names below:

_____

_____

_____

For me, her name was Christa. I was 13 years old and struggling. Addiction and deep-rooted bitterness were sucking the very life out of me, and I had nowhere to turn. There was a night I packed my backpack, grabbed the last jar of peanut butter and some old Y2K sardines from the pantry shelf and climbed down the large brick chimney. Most of the chimney's in our village had metal rungs up the side for the chimney sweepers to access. I had a change of clothes and at 3 a.m. I was purposed to head for Matt's house.

My friend, Matt, who served in the military and worked for the JAG division was an extremely kind guy. He'd come by the house all the time, go cherry picking with us, shared my love of history, and best of all, he was engaged. We kids shared his excitement. He'd talk about Christa all the time and showed us the wallet-sized pictures (before cellphones and social media ... laugh out loud inserted here).

Heading toward Matt's house, I snuck past our horse barn and Marina let out a whinny. Marina was the same horse that had accidentally knocked me to the ground and stepped on my left shoulder as she escaped the attempted kick of another horse. Marina was also good at stepping on your foot and then shifting all her weight to that hoof, again, completely unbeknownst to her. A firm slap on the rump would set your foot free. When we'd go riding, she'd always lumber along and probably endured the most slaps of the reigns. She was the slowest, fattest, yet prettiest of all the German-bred, Haflinger horses we raised. *She was a good horse - meek, and mild-mannered.*

Marina's whinny stopped me. It was almost a knowing whinny. Kind of like, "Hey kid, I know how you feel ... people call you clumsy, they beat you, you get the raw end of the deal. It's ok. Hang in there. Just keep lumbering along and appreciate the dry stall, oats and hay you've always got in the barn. It'll all turn out ok." I remember dropping my backpack behind the barn and clambering over the stall door. Jumping up on Marina's back, I laid down with my head on her shifting flanks and my feet crossed over her shoulders and sank into deep thought.

I thought about my Mom crying when my oldest brother left, and what my leaving might cause. I thought about how trapped I felt with no one to listen or care. I thought about what I'd like to do with my life. I thought about why I was even alive, and what's the use. I felt so stuck. Yet, I decided to stay around long enough to meet Christa.

The day finally came when Matt flew back to the states to marry the lady of his dreams. I remember getting so excited the Sunday they came over for dinner. Christa had this laugh that was simply charming, and her dimpled cheek won my heart. I was proud of Matt. We kids would peek through the drive-way gate watching them go by on their evening walk – holding hands.

One day, Christa came over to help Mom out with grading our English books. Phew! That's another story for another day. Christa asked Mom if she'd ever considered giving us piano lessons. Most all of us sang and some of my older siblings had taught themselves to play by ear. Before long. We were taking piano lessons – eight of us. The rate at which my sisters took off and danced their fingers across the keys bringing Mozart to life was incredible! On the other hand, I invested very little time into practice. I really didn't care to play the piano – seriously. But, I stayed on taking lessons because of Christa. She invested more than lessons into me. She believed in me. She'd brag to Mom about my mastery of music theory. I did enjoy studying the chords, keys, and history of music. I don't even know if Christa knew this at the time, but she simply made us kids feel okay about who we were.

She praised us. She gave compliments. She invested love – unconditional love – into us. The space of time in our week known as a piano lesson became an oasis – a haven. **She showed up abundant. She was okay with who she was, and in turn, she was ok with who we were.** She demanded quality from us – trust me. She marked my English book full of Red-X's (meaning mistakes), but her and Matt's lives were filled with acts of genuine kindness to me and my siblings. Christa loved. Christa, in a very good sense of the word, saved my life. Think about the truly abundant, giving-for-nothing-in-return kinds of people in your life. Just a handful? These people are attractive people. They overflow living fully and loving deeply. This is true kindness – love in action.

... Love's Choice

True love isn't what we've come to refer to as "falling in love". This implies an accidental love. Yes, chemistry and sparks can and should happen (emotions should flow in a positive way), but love is a choice. "I choose to love you for who you are; plus nothing, minus nothing." Let's take a closer look at love! It's vitally important to understand the abundant nature of true love, especially as it's been cheapened in our society. When we cheapen love, then it's no longer the highest level of abundance – giving out. Cheap love is selfish love. True love on the other hand is abundant and attractive:

- Love is a verb.
- Love looks past differences.
- Love casts out all fear.
- Love forgives freely through faith.
- Love asks nothing in return.
- Love can't be jealous or boastful.
- Love never changes.
- Love endures forever.
- Love is a philosophy for life.
- Love is a journey - a lifetime journey.
- Love is the most powerful force in this universe.

Author Doug Reed powerfully states, "There's no defense to unconditional love." Paul the great apostle stated, "Love keeps no record of being wronged." Covey said it like this, "Love is a verb. Love, the feeling, is a fruit of love, the verb." We know these things, yet we must consider. Do we truly love people? Do we deeply love people? Do we love ourselves? We fear others when we look through our own insecurities. This perspective yields pride or it's evil twin - false humility. *We will only love others to the point we learn to love ourselves.* Anything else is a feigned love. Do we show our love to others through sincere words and acts of genuine kindness? Do we share our love freely with everyone - enemies included?

The greatest teacher, the carpenter from Galilee, Jesus, said it like this,

"Love your enemies, bless them that curse you and pray for them that despite-fully use you." Love wins because it flows freely requiring nothing in return. It's giving out – constantly! It's often opposed to the dominant way of thinking; therefore, let us constantly exercise ourselves in it. When we're giving out love freely we find a greater meaning to life. I love how Mother Theresa said, "Love is a fruit in season at all times, and within the reach of every hand!"

True love is the purest sense of all that's good and what we know of God. True love ignites the deepest energies in your life, fills your spirit and overflows from your soul! True love jumps out of bed with joy to overflow love – giving out to someone! True love doesn't wait for the feeling of love, but like Og Mandino puts it, "chooses to greet this day and every day with love in your heart." By choosing to love, you stimulate the groggy emotional generators with the feeling of love. You don't wait for the feeling - you create the first one. I guarantee a flood of positive feelings will follow the first choice every time!

Will your energy be pure, powerful and positive? Let it be powered by love. There's no greater force. We all desire to love and be loved. So, let every action, every task, every job be given out of love – the abundance of the heart. Flora Plummer states, "Services that are merely professional, even when skillfully ministered are not as effective … no imaginary, sentimental, pretended emotion will avail." Love breaks down the barriers of any reserve and distrust inside of hearts. True love compels; deep love attracts. *Until we've loved deeply, we've not lived fully; therefore, to live fully, let's determine to love deeply, today!*

... Diamond Dipper

And what about the people we don't feel like loving? Homelessness, poverty, hunger, drug-abuse, disease and famines exist in our world. If we get out of our own bubbles of conditional loving and look past the outward person that perhaps we've been taught or pressured by society to look down on, then, we'll make a difference by giving out love. We'll find that just by our noticing, people feel loved and often want to improve their condition – not always; but, wouldn't love attract the best from them? We can touch and bless humanity. What could you do? What squeezes your heart? Do you realize when we perform the smallest act of un-repayable service, we experience more fulfillment and gratitude in every dimension of life. Everything abounds.

We literally get to give out life to another human being. Like Toby Mac sings, "So speak life, speak life, to the deadest, darkest night ... just speak life!" We get to look into hollow faces and see sparkling eyes – beautiful souls. We get to feel the compassion come over us that here's a fellow human being not much different than me. We get to slow down. We get to reflect. We get to be thankful. We get to give freely requiring nothing in return.

Do you remember the parable of the diamond dipper? The little pioneer girl's mother lay sick with a fever, so she snatches the wooden dipper and runs to the mountain. There's been a drought, but after searching all day, she finds a tiny trickle high up in the mountain. Slowly filling the dipper, she rushes home. On her return, a small dog lay panting on the side of the road. Her heart's squeezed and she gives it a drink from the dipper. Magically, the dipper turns to silver. She runs to her mother's side and gives her the much-needed drink. The dipper turns to gold. Just as she's lifting the dipper to her own lips to drink the last of the water, a stranger stumbles through the doors gasping for a drink. She runs to him and gives him the last of the water. He drinks and then lifting the dipper to the sky, he blesses her and says, "Because you gave of your very little and of your last to those who could never repay your kindness, you shall have water forever." The gold dipper, then, becomes a solid diamond and water flows from it like a fountain.

... Big Dippers

When you look at life as a channel to give, every decision will be to give more. This choice raises our frequency; the choice is ours. *Living and giving from a place of abundance takes personal healing, courage and faith. It's a higher level of thinking and living. It requires constant tuning, yet the tune of your life is attractive and attracts everything you'll need for this journey.* I like how Albert Schweitzer said, "I don't know what your destiny will be, but one thing I know: the only ones among you who will be really happy are those who will have sought and found how to serve." I know wealthy and happy people with huge homes who know how to give out love and service. Their pattern for giving didn't start when they "got rich." Rich is a mindset. What are you going to do with riches? Spend them? Steward them? Steward means to make more of. To multiply. To create and add value. To abound.

And with life, if we steward our talents and gifts, we won't level off. We'd be appalled to level off. We will abound. *We will constantly strive to be our best, so that we can give our best!* Give more influence, more impact, and more value. When we add value, we leave open an equation that's filled with reciprocity – it's guaranteed. We love on people. We go forth into this world and bless. Zig Ziglar said, "You help enough people get what they want out of life, and you'll get everything you want out of it, too." Live to bless. Let every decision increase value in this universe for you and those around you.

Attraction happens when we overflow material things from abundant emotions of the heart. Similarly, withholding material things starts in limited emotions of the heart. Thinking of the story of the diamond dipper, there've been many nights when Jen's and my eyes were drawn to the shape of those seven unfailing stars - the Big Dipper. Oh, that we'd long to have abundant hearts. We'd experience an attractive life! Let's be big dippers of blessing in our world!

The mentality of creating and adding value thrives in the abundance of the five levels of love: forgiving, giving up, giving in, giving thanks and giving out love! See how all of these add and multiply value? Attraction is understanding that value is magnetic. Be the sunrise; be the warmth of the fire. Attract through abundance! The mentality of abundance ignites our energy – maximizing our capacity to do more! Remember, you cannot give what you do not have. Be a smile, be a hug and be full so you can overflow and pour out love and service on our world! Give out!
Love - constantly!

CHAPTER 5
ENERGIZER
becoming a power source

"If you want to awaken all of humanity, then first awaken all of yourself!" - Lao Tzu

Charging

I remember leaving a tourist attraction on a vacation with my wife and four kids. After loading and buckling everyone, we were ready to make our journey home. Key in the ignition, no normal dinging sound, and what's worse, upon turning the key – nothing. In disbelief, I realized I'd left the lights on. Being broad daylight, this made no sense. A Kentucky tunnel had prompted me to manually switch them on and subsequently, I'd forgotten to turn them off. "Clickkkkk, clickkkk," – nothing. You know the feeling. Jumper cables – phew! We packed them! And, the parking lot had about two hundred cars so no problem asking for a jump! Relieved can't describe how I felt!

Today, people are drained, fatigued, exhausted and stressed. We're running here and there, worrying, fearful, anxious or sick. People are looking for identity and someone to believe in them more today than ever before. *Showing up into someone's life, your workplace and your family full of energy, while not always easy to do and maintain, would make you the game changer for so many people.* You'll not only change the lives of people stranded powerless and desperately needing somebody to simply show up and listen, care and heal them; you'll also change your own life! You'll gain so much clarity on life's meaning when you start looking past your own set of problems and circumstances and realize there are people with the same problems or worse. Energizers are compelled to make a difference no matter how small.

What's interesting, one of the smallest cars obliged us and jumped our van's battery in a matter of minutes. Its battery was small, but it was full – fully charged – and it made all the difference for me and my family. I think of corporate cultures that teach their people to reach out a hand of blessing. I think of Mark, who works for Hampton Inn and created consistent outstanding experiences for a tired sales representative checking in after hours. I think of the consistent happiness on the faces of Starbucks' baristas. I think of the heartfelt connection from the Publix associates and how it literally makes all the difference in the world. Question is, are we as individuals longing to connect – to be a constant source of power? To stay charged and be the charge!

The world is languishing for want of good energy: people so engaged and enthusiastic to be the charge, to be the light! *Not because they have to be, or it's only in their best interest, but because they get to be, and it's in the best interest of all they get to touch and serve!* Be charged, stay charged, so that you can charge those who've run out of juice!

David Wagner, best-selling author and salon owner who is a charge of power to our world and literally saving lives through small, kind deeds, wrote a must read called, *Life as a Daymaker*! He shares the poem "Beauty Tips" by Sam Levenson:

"For attractive lips,
Speak words of kindness.
For lovely eyes,
Seek out the good in people!
For a slim figure,
Share your food with the hungry.
For beautiful hair,
Let a child run his fingers through yours once a day.
For poise,
Walk with the knowledge that you'll never walk alone.
People, even more than things, have to be restored, renewed, revived, reclaimed and redeemed. Never throw out anybody.

Remember: if you ever need a helping hand, you'll find one at the end of your arm. As you grow older you'll discover that you have two hands. One for helping yourself, and one for helping others."

Experience - Wooden's

The famous football coach, John Wooden, ranked by ESPN as "the greatest coach of all time, across all sports," serves as prime example of the energizer. In describing Wooden, people talk about his championships, his intense focus on what worked, cutting everything that didn't, and his immense love for his team! After 40 years at UCLA though, one person described the beloved coach best when they, "you can't really describe Wooden, you had to have experienced him." In a TED Talk that Wooden gave, he shared this poem that had made an impression on him in the 1930's. It shaped more of his life, and started him in pursuit of inner fullness than all of the coaching manuals combined:

> "No written word, no spoken plea,
> Can teach our youth what they should be;
> Nor all the books on all the shelves,
> It's what the teachers are themselves."

His definition for success came directly from that inner fullness, personal peace and quiet effort to do your absolute best. Wooden said, "Success is peace of mind which is a direct result of self-satisfaction in knowing you made the effort to become the best that you are capable of becoming." Many leaders bring out the best in their people by their very presence. People perform better because their leader is there – they're fully present. The leader's presence breathes on an inward spark and sets it aflame.

An Energizer breathes hope and sparks dreams. An Energizer calls upon dormant energies. The energized leader's emotions flow freely and positively and allow their people to experience feeling. *Energized leaders perform the best kind of work – pouring their heart and emotion into it.* They realize they can motivate or inspire and they choose inspiration. Inspiration takes longer than tactics of traditional motivation. Inspiration is the Energizer's highest calling! We may feel like being an Energizer is reserved for a few gifted individuals. It isn't. Are you a mother, father, business leader, teacher, college student, teenager, child? Are you a factory worker, grocer, waitress, doctor, dentist or nurse? When we choose to live in the freedom of faith, vision and belief, we will inspire people! Whether we ever say a word or not. There is someone no one will be able to touch like you're able. Therefore, if you'd agree with me that we shouldn't discount any one person, then I'm here to tell you, we shouldn't discount the story that inspired that one person – yours! I guarantee you touch countless people, but touching just one other human being makes you an energizer! There's nothing more energizing than when one human genuinely and authentically believes in another human being!

Experience - Your's

When a client walks through your door, do you have to put on a show? Do you have to be anything that you aren't already? The best influencers today do their thing and move crowds and people. At the very heart of humanity, they want someone who is true to themselves and authentic with them. We no longer want dressed up, guarded, so-called "professionalism" that we really can't experience. The person with airs about them. The person who tries to impress. Some are comfortable in a suit and many events and occasions call for dressing up. It can be fun and energizing to dress up by putting yourself in a fresh state of mind, but you may want to be like Mark Zuckerberg and wear a T-shirt, or Steve Jobs and wear your sneakers. It's telling how many professionals are okay dressing up for the role without bringing the experience. Am I saying not to dress up here? No. Am I saying ask why we're dressing up? Absolutely. *Am I bringing a genuine fullness, peace, calm and my entire presence – my unique experience?*

Company's coming over so we clean every nook and cranny. Cool beans. We're showing respect to the company. That's nice and thoughtful. But are we flustered by the time they get there and so exhausted and drained we don't have an experience of deep connection left for them?

What experience do we bring to people's lives? Or do we work extra hard to impress? If dusting is something you do on a regular basis, then dust. But if it's dusting to forego the embarrassment of cobwebs that have been growing for a month then it's probably good to analyze our WHYs in life. We need to ask ourselves, "Where's our focus?" and "What's important?" "External or internal?"

Someone once said that the external is all men have to go by. For the sake of first impressions, or your professional role in your career, a nicely dry-cleaned shirt or blouse, crisp sportscoat or jacket, or pressed slacks or pencil skirt may be what your culture expects. Awesome. Just invest more on your internal being, and bring your experience!

When I first started speaking, I was so worried what I'd wear, how'd I look and so on. I learned that people long for real connection. I learned to work first on the speech and power of the message. Then, package it nicely. There's huge truth to this. Here's the takeaway. What experience are we bringing that no one else can offer? When we're authentic and true to ourselves, no one else can be like us. We have this experience that only we can give. When we copy someone else, we spend our energy fitting in. We're often too busy being like everyone else or putting on the status quo. *Instead, tap into the energy of living in our authenticity, gifts, calling, and bringing an experience that only our DNA can create – being okay with our own skin and shining as our incredibly unique personality!* This mindset carries confidence in any corridor of our professional and personal lives – it's super attractive.

Egoless

An Energizer isn't concerned with who receives the credit. An Energizer inspires people to thrive, to innovate, to grow into their best selves. An Energizer's mantra is, "Your thriving is thanks enough!" An Energizer helps people think, imagine, dream and achieve. An Energizer wants others to get the emotional deposit of praise or credit which may encourage them to reach for greater heights of growth. An Energizer becomes so consumed with being whole, emotionally stable and grateful for life at this higher frequency. They see the good in others and help others see this gold in themselves!

Empowering

In our age of industrialization, technology and automation, too often, we blur the lines of processes and people. Our assembly lines and work-spaces demand a certain set of actions and often a standard operating procedure on how to get the job done. Trust me, after ten years and writing many SOP's, I know the fear and angst my team possessed as they sought to follow all the rules. They didn't want to mess up, or do something the wrong way. Often, customers went untouched and creativity internally dwindled because of cookie-cutter syndrome. Systems and processes are extremely important, but many times they aren't built to empower but control.

In society, people are quick to buy into a system like a diet, new app, etc. While there's nothing inherently wrong with creating a working process, and getting hundreds to tap into it, what happens is we allow the cookie-cutter syndrome to set in. We want someone to lay out the exact steps and tasks for us. We get the process and can't keep up either because the pace is too fast, the process too complicated, too simple, or we don't truly believe the results they promise will pan out for us. So, we give up and search for the next cookie-cutter. *Cookie-cutter syndrome steals creativity, swindles energies, encourages conformity and adopts an "easy-way" mentality.* We show up to the assembly lines and, too often, don't engage fully.

Why discuss the cookie-cutter syndrome? Because, by identifying it, we can avoid it, even in the most automated and processed tasks and static environments, we can foster creativity, innovation and growth. If we're in leadership, then our chief job as Energizers isn't simply spelling out a list of tasks or steps to follow; we must also inspire people with the WHY of what they're doing and empower them to think for themselves. An Energizer doesn't get bogged down creating the perfect cookie-cutter. By the time it's perfected, another better cookie-cutter comes along. An Energizer shows the outcome, delivers his process, and empowers thought and innovation. The Energizer encourages and supports process improvement. Chances are, the customer is empowered with a better product in the long run because someone creates an experience like none other.

An Energizer, therefore, teaches people how to be their best so they can give their best. An Energizer realizes every person is unique and wondrously gifted. An Energizer is firm with goals and flexible with methods. Humans are each magical creations with intriguing DNA's. We all see things just a little bit differently than each other. Appreciating this, an Energizer will empower people to create a better way. Like Antoine De Saint-Exupery stated, "If you want to build a ship, don't drum up people together to collect wood and don't assign them tasks and work, but rather teach them to long for the endless immensity of the sea."

Freedom and fear are involved in the dominant motives of humans. Brendon Burchard calls these two forces the greatest motivational forces known to man. "One inspires full, whole-hearted engagement leading us to growth, happiness and transcends all fear that would hold us back. The other causes us to avoid challenges, resent conflict and adopt mediocre thinking." We'll run only as far as fear incites us to run and in turn, we grow complacent, accept a victim mentality, stagnate and experience our demise. Fear never instills independent thought and empowering vision; on the other hand, freedom does. Freedom inspires one to think for them-selves leading to continual growth. Motivators often choose to use fear. When you choose freedom and empowerment, you become an Energizer!

Do you inspire those around you to grow into their best selves and greatest potential? Or, do you live your life in fear and use fear to demand those around you to act their best selves? Both are passionate motivators, but only one has the energy, the wholeness, the genuine spirit that truly inspires. How do coaches like Bear Bryant, businessmen like Lee Iacocca and religious leaders like Mother Teresa consistently bring out the best in people? Best-selling author, Alan Loy McGinnis, wrote that most "use the same tools" for energizing their people. People can be inspired by the right leader – inspiration itself implies a mental stimulation to think, believe and achieve. Energizers realize that body and mind must not ever be separated and they inspire people to think and act.

Is your presence encouraging or intimidating to people? Ask yourself, "Is my life and the experience I leave compelling people to think, to hope, believe; or, do they feel belittled, or not good enough?" An Energizer helps others think for themselves and about themselves. An Energizer asks, "What do you want?" and "What would you love doing?" An Energizer helps people define their vision. An Energizer seeks to understand what people want and why they want it. An Energizer teaches and empowers people to acquire the skill, the tools and the principles necessary to achieve their vision. An Energizer is one that inspires people to dream! They inspire enthusiasm!

Conscious to Life

Are you living fully alive? Are you totally aware of your life – the whole person? Or are you ok to just get by? What parts of life are we numbing? There are levels of consciousness as described by thought and inspirational leaders. The strongest drives form the basic level of consciousness – acquiring and defending. Things like survival, finding food or a mate, protecting our family and defending our group, ideas or beliefs. The higher levels of consciousness form human drives that aren't necessary for life but allow a greater sense of meaning and purpose – bonding and comprehending. Things like forming trusting relationships, learning, creating and making sense of our purpose in this world.

Many numb themselves because of past pain, wounds or anxiety about the future and with this numbing, stop striving for a heightened awareness of life. *Choosing not to numb themselves with any vice, but to pursue their highest potential, Energizers pursue that which makes them and others come alive!* While consciousness describes an awareness to life, our conscience serves as an internal feeling – an inner guide – that directs us to a higher consciousness. Our conscience. What a gift. What is your heart saying? Do you listen and pursue more life – higher living? Seeking to connect and form trusting relationships, or learning, creating and understanding others? Have you stopped listening or tuned out that voice? Trying to please everyone else? Living in fear of others' opinions? Our consciences guide us to form virtuous beliefs and with them experience a higher awareness to life! Higher consciousness inspires deeper energies of thought and of heart. Becoming a genuine person of character. Becoming a person of your word. Becoming an Energizer who is so open to life and so full of life. Living at a higher frequency lowers defenses and allows for deep, authentic connection – the Energizer's experience.

George Washington was one of my heroes growing up and perhaps one of my most prized possessions is a book my dad gave me. It was published in 1860 by an author who met George Washington as a kid and was captivated by his virtuous, gracious and magnetic personality. He shares how English and French leadership were literally attracted to Washington's personality which were the combination of "a fiery nature that loved excitement, didn't fear danger, a union of the imaginative and reflective faculties, of energy and discretion, impulse and great accuracy." It was this man who displayed the decisiveness to cross the Delaware, yet possessed tenacious patience to endure Valley Forge. Washington's attraction flourished from his inward fullness of virtue.

The more virtuous your mind, soul and spirit, the more valuable your action, your influence and your entire essence becomes to all those around you. You become an overflowing and abundant person. Here, we see deep alliances and lifelong friendships form when there is an outpouring of heart to heart. Interestingly, on a recent trip to Washington D.C., Dr. Chuck Harding led several hundred ministers, pastors, and spiritual leaders through the capitol and into the chambers of Congress. I was privileged to sit in the seat of House Representative, Nancy Pelosi, and take in the splendor of architecture and engravings. Encased in the paneling to the left of the speaker of the house is a portrait of the first foreign dignitary to address a Joint Session of Congress – Lafayette himself. What Lafayette did for America was nothing short of spectacular. Yet, it all stemmed from his attraction to the power of George Washington – the essence and genuine nature of this man. Historic recordings say that, "The bond between the two men grew so strong that they were more like a father and son, rather than a commanding general and his top-ranking officer." In fact, the key to the Bastille, the symbol of France overthrowing tyranny, hangs not in the corridors of France's capitol, but in the home of the beloved George Washington. His dear friend, Lafayette, sent this priceless gift as a token of his love.

From where did this character, this depth of virtue blossom? Did Washington become an attractive force of true power – an Energizer – overnight? No. Writing of Washington's youth, the Honorable J.T.

Headley states, "At thirteen, he formed little manuscript books, into which he copied poems and snippets from his mother's teachings … evidently not such as a boy would naturally prefer." One such creed of Washington's was this, "Labor to keep alive in your heart that little spark of celestial fire called conscience." Conscience! Wow! When a person looks up and out past their own basic desires, and acts in the interest of humanity, an Energizer is born. Integrity and service matter to those who commit to live as Energizers. They don't have anything to prove; their presence makes you better. They are an abundant source. Their lives back up everything they say in perfect harmony. They are genuine, real and deep. They live fully and love deeply with no apology. I love how James Allen said, "Let there be nothing within thee that is not very beautiful and very gentle, and there will be nothing without thee that is not beautiful and softened by the spell of thy presence." *People are looking, searching, longing for wholeness.* In every interaction, interview or communication, humans ask for or give trust. An energizer realizes that authentic living is the only way to lead.

Energizers long for a pureness of heart for fullness of life, and also to benefit the poeple they are serving whether a child, client, employee or pupil. When you operate in purity of benefiting others, you will in turn receive the highest benefit. How many times as a father have I told my son to quiet himself without paying attention to why it was he was crying or whining. Taking the time to look deeply into his eyes, experience his needs, and help him overcome would, in the long run, pay the greater dividend to both of us. "Taking the time" being the operative phrase here. Oh, how we preabsorb ourselves with the affairs of this life and take little thought to life and lives. Charles Schwab was the first man to make a million dollars in someone's employ, and he did it by calling on the best energies in all of those he managed – he took time to inspire people. Napoleon Hill called it, "the magic of the Schwab personality." Whatever we exude from our being will be reflected back. We attract what we are. Negative internal dialogue projects and attracts negativity. Positive faith-filled thoughts projects and attracts positivity!

Creed

The desire of the Energizer's heart is to live with a greater awareness to life and to possess a stronger sense of purpose and connection. Consider rising higher than a mere existence in the basic drives of human nature. Rising higher than our basic drives, and reaching deeper for fuller life and meaning, let us love deeply and live fully so that we may experience ignited energy! This poem formulated in my mind one morning out running. Let's call this the "**The Energizer's Creed**,"

> "A higher consciousness I claim,
> Not of doubt, fear or shame,
> Nor of greed, pride or fame;
> But a life lived fully,
> Loving others deeply.
> Fully igniting energy!"

Yet, there's a universal weakness called lack of ambition. It results in mediocrity, complacency and apathy. People who lack ambition have a hard time breaking free for the obvious reason of lacking ambition. If you're reading this book, then it means you've scheduled your spare time to invest in yourself and open your way to an upward climb! I am so grateful for you! I believe in you, Energizer! Whatever level of ambition you feel you may have, keep growing and nurturing it! *Keep alive your celestial fire called "Conscience" to guide you to the highest consciousness of living!* You're a force! An Energizer! A leader! This ambition of yours to experience life to its fullest degree possible and love at the deepest level possible will remove every obstacle from your path and will attract the friendly interest of the people who have the power to put you center stage at the intersection of preparation and opportunity! Fan ambition's flame, Energizer! I believe in you! Never settle and never stop growing!

Believe

Do you want to change your family tree, do things, travel, live fully, love deeply, give and receive love, have meaningful connections, be less stressed and overcome fear in your life? You can. Do you believe you can? You must believe. Only believe. *Belief takes faith and faith is opposite of fear. Faith is a non-conformist. Faith doesn't stop for the barking hounds of fear. Faith soars; fear anchors.* Will you believe, by faith, that you can be an Energizer? Be prepared for the pull of those around you who don't want to be uncomfortable. Be prepared for the pull of your own fears. Know they'll come so you can be better prepared.

I remember watching this short video of this kid who went into the middle of a park where people were running playing, sharing picnics, and so on. It's a pretty crowded and popular place. He begins to dance – I mean really dance. People gather on the sidewalks, they point, call for their friends and start videoing and some begin laughing. Some look annoyed; others don't even mind him. That kid keeps right on dancing. Just about the time you think he might be wrapping up, he just keeps on going. He's hopping all about, making eye contact, smiling, and just keeps dancing. About five minutes later, someone begins to dance with him. The look of pure joy on his face signals that was his intent. Only half a minute later the third person joins, then seconds later the fourth until one after another are standing up and joining in. Apply this same principle to life. Be prepared for the pull, but never stop dancing - keep being the charge in our world!

Energizers believe deeply! And, they don't condemn others for not sharing their depth of belief – they remember the struggle. Therefore, they internalize grace and they abound in grace to this world! Energizers never use the corrosion of judgment, and they suit up before entering any toxic environment. An Energizer refreshes and renews to keep the emotion of gratitude flowing freely so that every aspect of life is lived fully awakened and every person is loved deeply! Now is the time to fully thrive and feel alive.

Energizers charge through the power of authenticity. Dr. Mike Norris, my spiritual guide and pastor once told me, "Inner purity brings external power!" Aristotle concluded, "Happiness belongs more to those who have cultivated their character and mind to the uttermost, than to those who have managed to acquire more external goods than they could possibly use, and are lacking in the goods of the soul." The internal purity of soul, spirit, and mind is important to Energizers. They work to be congruent in what they believe internally and how they behave externally.

Energizers work constantly on raising the standards of their beliefs – what they believe about themselves, others, the world and their place in it. Shad Helmstetter Ph.D. wrote, "Belief does not require something to be true it only requires us to believe that it's true." This is powerful! How are our beliefs? Are they tried and tested? What we believe – deeply believe – forms our inner world. Our inner world creates our outer world. Work on building and bolstering your energy – your inner world. Be an Energizer because what you are inside dictates what you do outside, and what comes to you is a combination of both. Zig Ziglar said "It's impossible to consistently behave in a manner inconsistent with how we see ourselves. We can do very few things in a positive way if we feel negative about ourselves." Shad Helmstetter Ph.D. encouraged affirming powerful beliefs. It's with a powerful belief about ourselves that we'll be the charge others long for and need. Helmstetter writes,

> "I am full of life. I like life and I'm glad to be alive. I'm a very special person living at a very special time. I have a lot of energy and enthusiasm and vitality. I am exciting, and I really enjoy being me. I smile a lot. I'm happy on the inside and I'm happy on the outside."

What do you think? Do you belive the best about yourself? Do you believe the best about others? It's when we don't believe we can be the charge to this world that we stop. We settle down. We stop dancing because no one joined us. Why settle? Why not at least fight to feel alive, and if you were to fail, at least you can boldly say, you tried! Why settle for less than that? Alan Loy McGinnis wrote, "In the end, the ability to give inspiring leadership is an inner quality of spirit; it requires people who live from a great depth of being ... such spirituality doesn't come upon us suddenly ... it accrues gradually from persistent study and regular cultivation." In his classic, *Speed of Trust*, Stephen M.R. Covey describes the Energizer as congruent, that is, they are the same inside and out. He states, "A person has integrity when he or she is whole, seamless … there's no gap between intent and behavior." People with integrity will act in perfect harmony with their deepest beliefs and values. If they feel they ought to do something, they make no hesitation – they do it. They're not driven by the opinions of others. "The voice they listen to is the quiet voice of conscience," Covey concludes.

Belief Inspiring

Annette Simmons stated, "Genuine influence goes deeper than getting people to do what you want them to do. It means people pick up where you left off because they believe." Ask yourself this question, "Does my life – who I am, what I do and the manner in which I do it – inspire hope and belief?" When you choose to believe in someone, they may very well start believing in themselves and amplify positive behaviors. Your belief inspires them by sending a shockwave of emotional resonance within their soul. The beauty of being charged and charging people through deep connection and by inspiring them is that our brains literally give emotions the upper hand! They are designed to do this! When we bark off commands, our commands never grace the emotional power of the limbic brain – the part in the back just above the spinal cord that feels. When we breathe inspiration and give someone hope, we allow them to feel it in their soul. *When we truly believe, we emotionally and powerfully inspire!*

Today, more than ever, people need someone to believe in them. Everyone has a story, a background or some past hurt. This is life. Some overcome; others haven't yet. Our belief could be the very thing that changes their paradigm. Four of the most powerful words are, "I believe in you!" Stating these words in a heartfelt way may be the defining moment of change in someone's life! Belief is a powerful thing. It's contagious! It may be as simple as a positive affirmation, yet the flame it lights deep down inside can literally take us from a destructive road and set us on the highway of life's meaning and purpose!

Several have impacted my life in such a way. When I was 12 years old, my mom wrote me a note I've never forgotten. The red ink, white paper and shape of characters are banked in my memory. Her message of belief in me is etched on the walls of my mind! Yet, have you ever been around the person that scrutinizes everybody? How'd they make you feel? Perhaps their own insecurities were being cast on you. These people compare, tear down and don't take time to empathize with others. On the other hand, there are those who believe the best in people. Sometimes they see the good even when you yourself cannot.

Energizers master the art of finding the good side of everyone and building on that. McGinnis writes, "The people who like people and who believe that those they lead have the best of intentions will get the best from them." Are you looking for strengths in people perhaps others have overlooked? Are you able to find the beauty in people? *Can you help people articulate their gifts and inspire them to channel that creative energy into usefulness? This is the art of the Energizer!* When you believe in people, even when others or they themselves don't, you show the deepest care. Purpose today to live your life being a change agent for people by truly caring for them! As long as there is breath in our lungs, we should speak redemption and empowerment to those around us. Accept people for who they are and believe the best in them. See the best even when people themselves can't see it. You'll change someone's life. Energizers care. When analyzing the profound loyalty Colonel Douglas MacArthur received from his men during World War I, William Manchester wrote in his book, *American Ceaser*, " … he shared their discomforts and their danger and they adored him in return." He showed his men that he truly and deeply cared for them! Leaders whose people know they deeply love them will ignite their people's passions like nothing else ever will.

Becoming an Energizer

Energizers accept life exactly as it is today. I may be up, you may be down; tomorrow, you may be up, I may be down. We're all human and our energy condition is just like the batteries in our cell phones. If 100 people were to snapshot their phone screens right now, there wouldn't be 100 snapshots showing battery levels at 100 percent charge; instead, there'd be approximately 100 variations of battery charge levels. Each one of us must make time to recharge – daily. Each of us can look back over the last 3 months, last year, or last 5 years and we can think of times where we were full of energy or empty. So today, think about where you are and think about the Energizer the world is longing for.

Whatever the circumstance or your position or phase of life right now, you're reading this book because you want more out of life. Do you want to maximize your potential? Do you realize and hear the cry for more: more love, more understanding, more peace, more responsibility, more direction, more drive, more passion, more vibrancy? Do you want more out of life? Do you want to make a greater impact? We're not lacking in motivation – this world is full of motivation. What we're lacking is personal energy. Energy is life! Energy allows us to fully thrive – to show up, make huge impact and enormous contribution! Energy to be attractive – abundant, full and overflowing life and energy into others. A lighthouse in our world is what we really want to be. *Deep in every heart is an adventure wanting to be lived, a legacy desiring to be left, and a difference craving to be made!*

Be Energizing

My oldest daughter, Nikki, had this little "press-my-tummy" teddy bear I distinctly remember when she was just a baby. It would sing, "You are my sunshine, my only sunshine, you make me happy when skies are gray." Clouds form in the sky; but, the sun's shining above the clouds and gorgeous! We know the sun's up there, yet how encouraged do we get seeing it break through the gloom of cloudiness or dreary weather! Whose life is full of clouds right now? What if your text message, your phone call, or your visiting them is just the sunshine they so desperately need? Everybody has struggles. Some are facing trials and tests stronger and longer than others. The fact of the matter is, when Mr. or Ms. Sunshine walks in with a sincere word of encouragement, a hug, or even just an encouraging smile, it can make the hurt or pain ease up just a little bit. It's often just enough glimpse of sunshine to renew hope. Think of three people needing a text or phone call today and spread the sunshine of love! Let someone say to you, "You are my sunshine…" Energizers consistently bring the sunshine! Smile! To someone who has gone through their day completely used to the scowls, the frowns, and even people habitually glancing away, your smile can literally be like the sun breaking through the dark clouds on a stormy day. People endure all kinds of pressure: family, relationships, a boss, customers and so on. One smile can spark hope in someone's soul. A deep, genuine smile that quietly communicates, "I love you" or "I believe in you" can literally lift someone over a trial. "A smile costs nothing, but creates so much" like Carnegie penned. "For nobody needs a smile so much as those who have none left to give." When your smile is the overflow of deep, internal joy – the kind the energizer builds and bolsters – it will warm the coldest heart and heal the deepest wound. So, give your enthusiasm for life through your smile – the entire-face kind of smile! Energizers consistently give their smile!

Being the Energizer

Energizers show up full and fully present. They are the calm generators of power. Author of the book, *Getting Things Done*, David Allen states, "… your ability to generate power is directly proportional to your ability to relax." Trying too hard simply sabotages rhythm. You need to arrive where you need to be in your mind first, and then relax into the role of being. Be an Energizer. Don't seek to impress or strive. Work consistently on being whole. Let all your doing add value from an abundant heart. There is no striving. Be fully present – you're already there. Live fully; love deeply – right now.

How do you make people feel? When someone meets you, do you breathe life into them? Do you truly care for others? Do you listen, not for calculated response, but to truly hear, understand and empathize with what they're saying and how they're feeling? When our minds are in a state of uncertainty, fear, competition or comparison, we are not ready to offer hope and grace through encounters with others. John Murphy, in his book, *The WOW Factor*, states, "The intangibles are often mood changing. They can shift a mindset, a mood from lousy to very positive. What's the difference? In a word, it's energy." We can get to the place where our faith is bolstered, our eye is on the future, we compete with only ourselves and fear of others' opinions doesn't haunt us. This is freedom. This is where living to inspire happens! Running this morning, the blooming flowers jumped out at me! They are blooming early due to the exceptionally warm winter we've had, and they just thrilled my spirit! Flowers may just be one of the greatest expressions of grace and hope in creation. We buy and send millions of flowers for the happiest and saddest occasions in life. Flowers give you feelings of love and hope! Flowers say so much; yet, they never say a word. I stopped and considered a few things on Maney Avenue this morning as I equated the feeling flowers gave to those an Energizer gives:

- Flowers are open. They smile at all who walk by. They use open gestures and welcome people and tiny noses in.
- Flowers are there. They are present. They don't say anything at all, yet they say so much!
- Flowers are encouraging! Consistently giving off a feeling of springtime – a feeling of life!
- Flowers are forgiving. They get trampled on, but they're resilient and grow again with the same strength and dignity to offer encouragement once again.
- Flowers are growing. Always soaking in water, rooted in good soil, and drinking in the sunlight. They know without growth and nourishment, they'll wither and cease being able to give.

The list can go on and on. I like how Maya Angelou said, *"People will forget what you did, people will forget what you said, but people will never forget how you make them feel!"* Be a flower and make people feel incredible about life! When you're fully present, you're not stressing people out. You emit a positive vibe. People feel good around you. Sure, they're encouraged to forward action because, as an Energizer, your focused on doing work – getting things done. But, your emotions are flowing positively – powerful and abundant. You're full of life and people feel good around you. You stimulate their emotions to flow positively as well.

I love the word, Energizer, because it means full and filling others all in one. This one word gives the hint that life has greater meaning than mere existence. If life's meaning was simply mere existence, then why not walk through it without a single thought of your effect on others? William Penn said, "I expect to pass through life but once. If, therefore, there be any kindness I can show, or any good thing I can do for any fellow being, let me do it now, and not defer or neglect it, as I shall not pass this way again." But how will you do all this good, unless you can, and unless you have the desire to? *This high frequency of desire to abound is called the Energizer Mindset!* Whole and abundant; full and overflowing! Most of us can trace our successes to people who ignited our energy in some way. They helped us gain momentum in life. Let us never cease to thank them. Who will say this of you and me?

When we think bigger, life becomes bigger than ourselves and everything we do makes life better for someone else. Life becomes much more meaningful! From the time of our creation, we were meant for connection. Connection to our mothers for a good while, then infancy, toddler, adolescent and so on. We were created for connection. Is deep connection happening in your life right now? Are you touching lives? Are you pouring your energy into people? How's your energy? Is your passion red hot? Is your fire and fervor for life blazing? When a life-changing event, or awakening to deeper life happens for you, you won't be able to hide the light or contain the fire! You'll desire connection and making a difference!

Take inventory today. Consider some possible obstacles that are reducing your fire to a few glimmering coals. There's unfathomable treasure lying dormant deep within our souls, and it's time to go mining for it. The time for energy is now! Let's go on a journey together. Let's explore some of the best practices to igniting energy in our lives – constantly! The world needs your fire! You have the potential of being a force for so much good! A force to be reckoned with! Wasting time and energy takes on a whole new weight when understanding the depth of the lifeforce our energy really is. There's no time to waste; no energy to squander! Become an Energizer – there are three solid principles to ground you firmly and carry you into life as a powerful energizer. *Declare with me the "Energy Declaration": I'm done with dead, unexcited, dry life - I will be present today living fully so that I can love deeply!*

INTERLUDE

> *"The combination of perspective, ownership &*
> *accountability forms a trio so dynamic, so powerful,*
> *it simplifies life, harnessing, channeling and*
> *amplifying energy!"*

3 Simple "Musts"

I want to give you three easy-to-remember truths that will undergird every decision you make in life and propel you forward like never before. If you'll get passionate about applying these truths to your energy condition, every area of your life will be reawakened. You'll ignite your deepest energies and fuel a passion for life that's so rich, you'll be unstoppable. It's time we get passionate about our energy – it's our very life force. It determines how fully we enjoy life and the level of positive impact we're able to make on our world!

Let's discover these keys to improving our energy. *These are called the 3 "musts" because, when you realize their power, I believe you will join me in saying, "I must – MUST – implement these in everything I decide to do!"* When we really want something in life, it becomes a non-negotiable – a MUST! These three powerful "musts" are perspective, ownership and accountability!

There's a principle a good friend and client of mine, Ray, shared with me. It's the problem-solving principle of Occam's razor. Simply put, if two explanations for an occurrence exist, the simplest explanation is often the best. Detectives and mathematicians use this principle often. This principle's attributed to one, William of Ockham, who developed it in the early 1300's. I met with my publisher, at the age of 29, with my pile of manuscripts, Post-It notes, self-addressed emails, audio recordings, highlights and notations in over one hundred books, and all the articles I'd read and perused as I studied personal energy for four years. Sifting through, sorting, hypothesising, theorizing and organizing content, everything kept building on these three powerful truths of perspective, ownerhsip and accountability. In fact, these building blocks account for great impact and lasting value in our world; and, so far in my life, the best outcomes are derived from utilizing all three truths in balance. So solid are these principles, and, like the Occam's razor principle, this was the simplest explanation for the lasting legacies that happened when the trio existed in history.

Our perspective on life harnesses our energy, our ownership channels it, and our accountability amplifies it as it flows into others and back into us. The depth of each of these principles in our lives determines the amperage of our energy flow! These three common denominators consistently turned up in slightly over one hundred books, Scriptures, SUCCESS magazines, business journals and medical reports I read. Additionally, four years of putting myself through college and interviewing several hundred business owners, entrepreneurs and professional athletes proved that combining these three principles is foundational for unfettering a deep and lasting energy.

Throughout coaching executives, sales teams, managers, mothers, teachers, students, and raising four kiddos, these three principles constitute fully awakened life. When setbacks happen, one or more were missing. Some people possess a pretty positive mindset but fail to take extreme ownership or adopt accountability. They don't experience unleashed and ignited energy although life is tremendously better with a positive outlook. Some people take extreme ownership, but they are down on themselves and everybody around them hurting people as they plow through life. They don't utilize the lever of abundance and accountability although accomplishment at any level has its rewards. Then, there are those who love being eternally accountable, but they refuse to adopt empowering beliefs or take ownership. They constantly lean on other people without attempting to learn to stand on their own. They miss out on so much progress due to lack of ambition although they enjoy fellowship which always makes life better than none at all.

3-Stranded Cord

What we've found is this. Combining these three, powerful, life-changing truths forms a 3-stranded cord that a proverb calls "not very easily broken". *Perspective is energy transferred to us, ownership is energy transferred through us and accountability is energy invested and transferred back into us*. These three truths help understand how our energy flows and how to simplify life decisions for maximum impact. From these three, powerful truths of perspective, ownership and accountability, we've built some basic action steps and worksheets. We're blessed to host the *Energy4Life Signature Workshop* planting these three powerful seeds and igniting energy across the globe!

These truths are nothing new - all truth is parallel. There's no new thing written, and there'll always be another book. However, I believe this strategic combination forms a trio so dynamic, so powerful, it literally harnesses, channels and amplifies our energy! This combination takes a complicated world of self-help resources and simplifies it into three principles that even a child can understand and implement. The student can become a more engaged pupil, the machinist a more passionate team player and the sales professional a more genuine, enthusiastic connector. An executive becomes a more caring leader. An addict can find recovery, and someone so wounded by a horrific past can find healing and hope. These three truths will set aflame a fervor in your soul for passionate, abundant and vibrant life! These three truths will build and bolster a pure and undefiled energy. It's positive and lasting energy that we're after! Let's look closer at these 3 powerful "musts."

- Perspective – your mind. How virtuous are your beliefs?
- Ownership – your life. How valuable are your behaviors?
- Accountability – your influence. How are you benefitting others?

Virtuous beliefs drive valuable behaviors delivering voluminous benefits to the world! This is what I call the MVB x MVB = MVB formula. The more virtuous your beliefs are, the more valuable your behavior will be, and the more voluminous your benefits to the shareholders in your life! *We're valuable individuals (perspective), created to add value (ownership) that makes this world a better place (accountability).* Some poeple call this karma, others call it purpose, and some call it legacy. We've found that learning and living all three will ignite deep and lasting energy! Perspective is knowing who you are, what you do and why you do it! Ownership is being and doing. Accountability is connecting and creating lasting impact! Read to build and bolster your energy. Maximize your potential. Ignite the energy deep within your soul and you'll never lack passion!

P.O.A.

Now, you can remember these points very simply with the acronym POA. Think of Power Of Attorney:

> "To whom it may concern,
> In the event something happens to my energy … you have
> my permission to ignite my energy condition so that I can
> live fully and love deeply! Signed _____."

Or, if your're a project manager, you can call these the Plan Of Action. For veterans and military personnel, consider this a Plan Of Attack for increasing your capacity to do your life's work. Read this as intently as an epic novel, for it's a manual to ignite your very lifeforce – your energy! Apply these truths daily with the solid reasoning given. Watch them go to work for you! Watch your life become energized as you become an Energizer! Watch your life legacy become more than an epic novel's hero or heroine – watch it become truly meaningful! Use these three steps for daily healing and hope.

Say to yourself often, "POA, POA, POA!" Use this acronym when you lack courage. Use it when you feel stressed. Use it when you feel inadequate or disconnected. Perspective brings calm, ownership builds courage and accountability bolsters connection! Ready to live passionate, abundant and vibrant each day? Ready to let genuine energy drive your enthusiasm and passion to fully engage life? Ok, let's begin! Grab your pen or highlighter and write actions you WILL take as you work through these next three sections.

PERSPECTI

Changing perspective &
gaining a clear & powerful vision
for life. Understanding your worth &
unlocking the ability
to make peace with your past,
plans for your future
so that you can live fully present
today & every day!

How would life change
living with
clarity and confidence,
excited and fully present
every day?

"Make peace with your past, plans for your future, so that you can live fully present, today!"

Birthday Bonus

Soap suds went everywhere, and so did the water. Down the front of the cabinet and all over me. Two things you can count on when I wash the big stuff after dinner: I love doing it, and I inevitably slosh water all over the place. Manipulating big pans in a small sink – daunting task. This evening was extra special. Jen was expecting our third child, Ethan. She had baked a wonderful cake – chocolate cake – for our family and my two older brothers and their families. The occasion was my 25th birthday. Since Valentine's Day comes just before, my birthday likes to sneak up on me. We had a blast celebrating, reminiscing, and pumping each other up like brothers and sisters do. When everyone had left and gone home, Jen and I prayed and sang to Nikki and Jeremy, our two children, and tucked them into bed. Since she was technically supposed to be on bedrest, she retired to the bedroom. "I'll wash up the big stuff," I said.

Standing at the sink, with my hands in the soap suds. I looked at the red-painted wall and picture with yellow lemons that hung over the sink between the dark, cherry wood cabinets. *I pondered*. Life was grand, my career was thriving, and Jen and our two kiddos were happy in our Tennessee, country home.

Bonus

I wasn't completely fulfilled, though. There were holes of addiction in my spirit, wounds of bitterness in my soul, and a lot of doubt and baggage in my mind. With trepidation, my memory slowly took me back to the pain of childhood. I remembered the abuse, the toxicity, the fear – then, out of nowhere, I remembered the night when the chilling, "Ring, ring, ring, ring … ring, ring, ring, ring …" of the telephone sounded through the hallway and up the marble flights of steps startling the family at 3 a.m. Central Europe Time.

The shuffle of Mom hurrying from her bedroom to the hall telephone, her voice answering, "Hello?" … a long pause. Still a long pause. I remember my gut thinking, "something terrible has happened." I don't remember much after that except Mom crying and saying, "Mary, I'm so sorry." Dad's instructions were, "Go back to bed; we'll all talk in the morning." I don't think any of us slept the rest of that night. Mary was my oldest brother, Paul's wife, and in the morning, our fears were confirmed. Paul had been shot and killed.

My mind came rushing back to our Tennessee home as the warm sensation of water splashed all over me. That sensation along with the steam from the sink and the natural warmth of the kitchen after cooking had me sweating. I realized right then that my brother, who had passed eight years prior, was 25. Cold sweats broke out and an eerie feeling came over me – I sensed the hand of death. My mind raced. "This is my year," I thought. I went to the back door and throwing it open, stepped out onto our wooden deck at 11 p.m. The cold, crisp, February air hit me in the face. Looking up at the crispest stars and darkest sky I think I ever remember seeing, I declared, "I will not die this year!" I paused. Tears filled my eyes. Looking back up, I said, *"Paul, I promise to live every single day as a bonus, OK?"*

I stepped back into the house, my mind still racing. What did I want out of life? Move into sales. Start a company. Start exercising. Be an amazing husband and father. Go back to school. Bring my family back together. Make an impact in Murfreesboro. Volunteer at the fire department. Connect deeply with God. Sing. Play the trombone, again. So, that night I made a commitment to go visit my brother's grave for the first time. I also sent an email to John, my second oldest brother, asking him if we could talk websites and business names for a company to "ignite energy for people who wanted to experience life fully awakened!"

My entire life changed that night. It was snatched from blending in and mediocrity to beginning the quest for more fulfillment, greater meaning and deep connection.

Power of Perspective

So why do we start with perspective. Let me tell you why. Wayne Dyer said, "When you change the way you look at things, the things you look at change." ***When you change how you see things, powerful things can happen in your life and the lives of the people around you.*** Your greatest obstacle becomes your opportunity. Your overwhelmed life can immediately become calm. This is what happened for me. I had so much I struggled with in life, so much I wanted to do, so much I didn't know where to start or how to do it. So much hurt, pain, bitterness, addiction, yet so many goals, dreams and endeavors. I had everything going on and making life happen; but, I figured a lot would have to wait. I mean, I'm so busy and stressed. How in the world could I even think about having time for myself, for exercise, or to develop a healthy eating plan. Additionally, I'm drained. My energy's gone after work and my family suffers. We need a family vacation. Time will free up someday. This all shattered around me when I gained the height of clarity that the bonus mentality gave me. One realization, one perspective change, one shift in how I viewed life, one simple thought set me on a life changing course.

Have you heard the proverb, "The dew drop is the ant's flood"? It's all about perspective! Rick Warren states, "Your perspective will influence how you invest your time, spend your money, use your talents, and value your relationships." Perspective is a powerful word! Relative to mindset belief and attitude, your perspective defines your point of view – the way you look at life. "A perspective is like a pair of glasses." as my friend and spiritual instructor, Mike Stroud, puts it.

Changing your perspective can literally change your life! Out walking with the kids yesterday, we were just about to peak a small hill in the road when I shouted, "Grass!" Grass is our code-word for stepping off the asphalt into the grass and waiting for daddy due to an automobile sighting. My son, eager to keep running, steps into the grass and quickly replies, "Daddy, there's no car...may I run again?" As I caught up, we squatted there together in a "wait for it...wait for it" moment. Then, there it was coming over the rise – a car. Why spend the time telling a simple story? Here's why. My five-foot-eleven-inch height versus Jeremy's three-and-half foot height made all the difference when it came to that hill. Similarly, a slight change in perspective can shift your entire purpose and motivation in life.

What would change in how you see things if you were born blind? Everything. If you were born blind, you'd never see anything the same way as your parents. You'd have nothing to compare colors to and in your mind you'd create the picture you wanted. Perhaps this is why the lady who wrote thousands of inspirational hymns, Fanny Crosby, said, "Oh what a happy soul am I although I cannot see, I am resolved that in this world contented I shall be. How many blessings I enjoy that other people don't. To weep and sigh, because I'm blind? I cannot and I won't." The power of perspective is so tremendous I don't know if we'll ever be able to fully grasp its richness and height. I've determined to keep climbing though. Napoleon and Helen Keller are perfect illustrations. Napoleon had everything you could crave, glory, power, riches, and yet he made the statement, "I have never known six happy days in my life." Helen Keller on the other hand said, "Proclaim to the world I have found life so beautiful." Many that can see are indeed very blind, or they open their minds to nothing outside of what they're used to or feel comfortable with.

Perspective is a learned vision. If you were blind, you would not see skin color, and if you were deaf you would not hear criticism. We must become blind and deaf in a way. *We must learn new perspectives. What perspectives do we need to climb and grow in? What perspectives need changed?* Everyone sees things at different perspectives! How is your perspective on life? What meaning, and what purpose do you find in your life? Constantly seek to gain a little better perspective. Welcome different perspectives! Changing your perspective can literally change your entire life dynamic!

A Lear Jet Ride

A plane ride will change your perspective pretty quickly! I love getting in a Lear jet. The thrust, high whine of the engines, the sleek bird lunging above the clouds. Literally within minutes a cloudy day can be sunny again. I went up with my father-in-law recently and within seconds, a runner down below us on the road was lost to sight. Whoa! I've spent 4 hours running a marathon and felt pretty good about that accomplishment. Within three minutes from a 30,000-foot-view of life, it seemed pretty minute.

We spend thousands and millions of dollars on a speck of real estate. All the up-keep, landscape, and so on. Within minutes, it's a tiny speck. Yes, a home, a marathon, and all of the things we do to house and care for our physical bodies are important – extremely. But, consider the eternal people that reside in these homes with us. Many value a piece of real estate more than the mental, spiritual or emotional importance of their family, or the people in their lives. It's all about how you look at things. Life's so much more than impressing people. How quickly the things we value change when we raise our perspective.

The Bonus

What if we woke up each morning knowing that we weren't supposed to, but someone had gifted us an extra day. It's a bonus. The old you – good or bad – died. All the guilt and baggage of the past – gone! All the anxiety about the future – gone. All the stress about the day ended – gone! You've just been gifted a day. It's a bonus. How will you live this bonus? What will you do? I die every single night when I lay down to sleep. I make peace with my past daily. I sleep – and trust me; it's deep – just ask Jen! We symbolize death every time we lay down and close our eyes in sleepy unconsciousness. Then, rising, we experience the miracle of a new day! It's a bonus! Why did my brother have to die at 25 and I've been gifted with life? I may never understand all the reasons, but I do know

I've become aware of life in a greater way! Realizing life's fragility makes you appreciate every new day, not as a guarantee, not as something promised, but as a bonus!

Imagine getting a phone call that a loved one was critically sick, and you needed to be there. A lot that we make a big deal out of – life drama – would vanish. Being completely reverent of life and with all seriousness, I ask you to carefully ponder this. *What would you do differently, right now, if you could be afforded the knowledge that your last day was sometime this year?* What would you change? What could you quickly, easily, and without second thought, shed from your life? What would have to go so that you could have time for the people you deemed direly important. Scribble them here:

_____

_____

_____

_____

_____

_____

What would you like to have done in your life?

_____

_____

_____

_____

_____

_____

Just think. Get life – your life – in perspective. Determine to stop coasting and start charging! Take extreme ownership of your life. Personal responsibility stops asking "What am I getting?" and asks instead, "How much am I giving?" Are you giving every day your all? Right now?

Make Peace with the Past

You know those maps in the tourist places – the ones with the "You

Are Here" star or marker? Remember the sigh of relief when you spotted the map as the gut feeling of being lost or turned around swept over you? Our lives are similar. Things have happened in our past outside of our control, things will happen in the future outside of our control. Bitterness, shame and guilt over past wounds, scars and failures suppress our spirits and swindle our energy. Freely forgiving the wrongs of others and our own failures is the first step to accepting that everything up to this point right now – right now – is past. It can be used to hold you back; or, upon releasing every shred of remorse, it can serve as a bitter ingredient in the sweetest dessert – your life. Everything that's happened to you up to this point makes you strong, and if you let it, makes you perfect. Embrace all of your past – the good, bad and ugly! Learn from our past hurts, implement the lessons, forgive freely and let them go. Learn from past successes, leverage them for future success, and let them go. ***Our past directed us to this point, but it defines us no longer.*** Give full forgiveness for others and yourself and full gratitude for everything you've experienced.

Forgive the Past

Instead of letting go of everything hurtful, many people numb themselves to the pain, the fear, and the baggage of the past. Whether alcohol, prescription drugs, narcotics, binge eating and sleeping, bitterness, or even competition, we numb past voices. David Allen, talks about numbing the past guilt, future anxiety and current stress with some sort of medication or alcohol. "The numb-out solution is temporary at best. The 'stuff' doesn't go away. And, unfortunately when we numb ourselves out, we can't do it selectively – our source of inspiration, enthusiasm, and personal energy also gets numbed." You must allow for healing to happen – not numbing. Full forgiveness of the past, fearless faith for the future and fully flowing into the present is where energy unleashes its fervor! When we resist dealing with the pain and truly healing, we relive the pain and reframe it into every future endeavor and relationship. We also, numb some of us today because we've closed off some feelings of pain and with those, some level of joy. Face the skeletons and make some difficult phone calls if necessary. Don't ask for forgiveness – this is an expectation you shouldn't set up. Instead, have definiteness of purpose and sincerely apologize. If the person casts shame and toxicity over you, then write a letter, or get counselling on the best approach. The goal is not to change a toxic or hurtful person; the goal is to empty yourself of an infectious bitterness. If this seems impossible, please read my personal story in chapter 23. I can assure you, it's very possible. *The power to take a huge step like complete forgiveness not only shores up an underground tide of energy draining from your soul, it heals the wound so beautifully and allows renewed energy of love – love like you never thought possible – to exude from your being and heal people.*

Be careful to forgive without vengeance or expectations. Like acclaimed author, Maxwell Maltz M.D. in his book, *Pyscho-Cybernetics* says, "Forgiveness itself can be used as an effective weapon of revenge. Revengeful forgiveness however is not therapeutic forgiveness. Therapeutic forgiveness cuts out, eradicates, cancels, and makes the wrong as if it has never been." Therapeutic forgiveness is like a healing surgery. Many are not willing to forgive completely and unconditionally, and they rob themselves of so much joy. Granted, there is a certain enjoyment out of nursing our wounds as long as we can condemn another. In a way, it makes us feel superior to them. Neither can one deny a certain distorted satisfaction in feeling sorry for oneself. We all carry a blame card deck into adult life. We can collect cards and add to this deck. In fact, many do. It's insurance in a way. "If you ever wrong me, well! I'll be ready to pull these blame cards out and throw them in your face," we seem to think. We collect them from managers, business leaders, spouses, parents, politicians, and the list goes on. Take your blame card deck and let it go!

Forgive yourself! Oh, how we can be our own worst enemy! Maltz points out, that "remorse and regret are attempts to emotionally live in the past. Excessive guilt is an attempt to make right in the past something we did wrong or thought of as wrong." You cannot control the past. It is futile to hate ourselves for our mistakes. We mustn't allow others hate and condemnation to swindle our energies, either. People with emotional scars who hold grudges live in the past. Bitterness is unforgiveness on steroids; it's cancer untreated and it will swindle positive energy from this present moment leaving only a calloused, empty, negative shell.

The important thing is the present – we control right now. What are you doing right now to make peace with your past? Those refusing to make full peace with their past are banking on future access to excuses, blame and reasons why they couldn't live fully. Maltz shares something so key to understanding how emotional wounds literally clog our energy from flowing freely and abundantly when he writes, "Many people have been hurt or injured by someone in the past. To guard against future injury from that source, they form a spiritual callous on the emotional scar to protect their ego. This scar tissue, however, not only protects them from the individual who originally hurt them, it protects them against all other human beings. An emotional wall is built through which neither friend nor foe can pass."

Epictetus, the stoic philosopher warned that we ought to be more concerned about removing bitter thoughts from the mind then about removing tumors and abscesses from the body. Dale Carnegie shared that even in his day, four out of five patients admitted to John Hopkins Hospital were suffering from conditions brought on in part by emotional hurt and stresses. Montaigne, the French philosopher, said, "a man is not hurt so much by what happens as by his opinion of what happens." *Our opinion is our response. We get to form each opinion.* I love how Covey says, we have the ability to choose our responses – "response-ability." You alone are responsible for your responses and reactions going forward. You don't have to respond at all. "You can remain relaxed and free from injury; no man is hurt but by himself," said Diogenes. "Nothing can cause me damage except myself," said Saint Bernard. The pain sustained by us, we carry around with us – that sort of suffering becomes perpetually self-inflicted.

When we choose to carry pain and bitterness, our real self slowly dies and begins to sink beneath the surface. The good news is, we can heal. With healing comes reawakening – new life! New York Times best-selling author, Lewis Howes, states, "Compassion for self and compassion for others grow together and are connected; this means that people finding and recuperating the lost parts of themselves will heal everyone." Why is making peace with our pasts – all the wounds, hurts and painful incidences – so imperative? Buechner says it like this in *The Sacred Journey*, "To do for yourself the best that you have it in you to do – to grit your teeth and clench your fists in order to survive the world at its harshest and its worst – is, by that very act, to be unable to let something be done for you, and in you, that is more wonderful still. The trouble with steeling yourself against the harshness of reality is that the same steel that secures your life against being destroyed secures your life also against being opened up and transformed." Tommy Newberry, in his book, *Success Is Not an Accident*, states, "Forgive someone including yourself daily. Harboring grudges or hostility toward anyone, including yourself, tends to attract more circumstance to be upset about." Every night we lay to sleep, we're called on to make peace with the day past. For any hurt or wrong done to you today, reframe all of your responses and opinions through forgiveness. Forgive freely – daily!

If anyone's the expert of reframing, it's the man born without arms and legs, Nick Vujicic. In his book, *Life Without Limits*, he states, "While you can't always change your circumstances, you can change the way you look at them." At first you may have to work extra diligently to consciously reframe; yet, with practice, reframing can become automatic. Making peace with your past is a process and at some point, along your journey, you'll experience breakthrough!

Until we make peace with our pasts, we'll allow excuses and blame to stand guard at the tomb of dormant energies within our souls. We'll never know the joy of soaring with the eagles; instead, flying will be the futile flapping of chicken wings. The burden and bondage of the past grows every day if we absorb our energy in it. Left unchecked and unhealed, it will at last bury bitter souls. Let the past go. Forgive and be grateful for everything you learned through it.

Gratitude

Gratitude. Start here – end here. Be thankful for everything. Let your perspective be fueled with gratitude. Perspective's the jet; gratitude's the fuel. Everything up to this point in your life, be thankful for it – embrace it. I made this journal note in 2014, "Tim, STOP thinking about past failures, about other's faults, and about what may go wrong. STOP IT! Good! Now, START being grateful for all the ways God shone through you in the past, be thankful for every person in your life and all their beauty, and press forward full of hope and faith for the future! PRESS ON!" Be grateful for where you came from. Change your perspective from hurt to grateful.

Set a daily time of reflection. Reflection is often best done right before sleeping so that your mind is filled with acknowledgment of blessing past and blessing to come. When is your reflection time? Scribble your time here: _____. Reflect on all the good that happened. Then, freely forgive, giving everyone the benefit of the doubt. Find thanks in everything, and be thankful for what's coming – your next minute, hour and very likely another day. Be grateful for the realization of your goals. If you've written them down and are holding them consistently in your mind; then, taking action toward them is exercising faith. Paul, the apostle states, "Faith is the substance of things hoped for, and the evidence of things not yet seen." When you are grateful now for the realization of your goal in the future, you exercise the greatest form of faith and unleash belief and power in your life. Gratitude keeps you in a mindset of abundance – a bonus mentality – and will change everything!

Bestselling author, Melody Beatti states, "Gratitude unlocks the fullness of life. It turns what we have into enough and more." *Gratitude makes sense of our pasts, creates vision for our futures, and brings peace to the present. Commit to be grateful for this bonus called today!*

Have you ever considered how one trial, test or great adversity can garner two completely different outcomes in people's lives? It's all a matter of perspective and choosing responses. One sees life as a bonus and grateful to be alive. They choose to look outward and upward. Their mindset expands and emotions flow from their bruised heart, yet they experience life and feel the greatest of joy from having experienced the deepest of pain. They become better through the fire and come forth as gold. The other sees life as bondage and becomes disgruntled with it as well as all those who would dare to thrive. They turn inward. Their mindsets shrink and their emotions stagnate as they box their heart in. They exist in life, numb to any feelings of deep joy, and alert to the hurt in everything. They become bitter through the fire and come out brittle.

Gratitude demands we let go of ego and accept blessing. Gratitude is the highest form of faith. Someone said, "A happy life begins on the path of gratitude." Gratitude transcends life circumstances and channels into our very beings the energies of blessings. Gratitude dusts off our receptors as they become intentional in recognizing all the blessings we've received and possess. Excuses and problems vanish in the presence of gratitude. *A grateful heart begins looking for the blessings all around us, and when looking through this perspective, sees the diamonds laying literally at our feet.* Blessings find the grateful heart as the two were designed to coexist. Gratitude is the highest perspective one can acquire and when exercised frequently, this gratitude turns hard hearts soft allowing emotions to flow freely and energizes life within! The grateful soul is an energizing force. I love the poem that goes:

"Remembering our many blessings,
All discouragement will flee.
A grateful heart lives inspired,
And we gain the victory.
We can meet whate'er befalls,
With a smile, and not a whine.
Take heart; beat anxiety,
With gratitude's pow'r divine!"

With courage, let us express our thanks. Have you ever paused sending a text of gratitude? "I wonder what they'll think?" "Will they receive it the right way?" Or, did some other fear hold you back. Speak it! Unplug the fear from that emotional artery and flow. The world is longing for grateful hearts! Express your thanks and gratitude more boldly and more often than ever before. Don't allow fear to hold you back!

It's A Wonderful Life

Do you remember the old movie, "It's A Wonderful Life"? George Bailey experiences trouble after trouble at the old Mortgage and Loan. He's put plan after plan and dream upon dream on hold to save the family business. He has a beautiful wife, wonderful kids and a ton of friends. But the pressures of business and overwhelm of mean people close in on him. One evening, he's home. The noise of piano playing, children shouting, and the phone ringing sets him off. His temper flares, he gives the teacher an earful, yells at his daughter to stop playing the piano, and finally runs from the house. Long story short, he's about to jump off the old bridge, saying, "I wish I'd never been born." Of course, the angel, Clarence Oddbody, is there and jumps first, because as he claims, "I knew you'd jump in to save me, George." The angel gives George his wish and they rush back to town to find a corrupt culture, people fighting, his house abandoned and literally a dump, no wonderful children, and a single depressed woman who doesn't recognize him as her husband. His brother, who in real life George had saved from drowning, isn't alive. Hundreds of men, this brother had saved during a World War II battle, weren't saved. One scenario after another of all the good George had done and all the lives he'd touched played out in front of him. He begs the angel to take him back to life. When he finally wakes from this dream, George rushes back to town. He sees things again as they used to be; but, does he? Not really! He sees them in a whole new light! His perspective has radically changed. He's hugging people. Jumping up and down! He rushes into the house, grabs his wife around the waist, hugs her, kisses her and scooping up the children, hugs them and says, "Play, play!" The discord of the piano is now beautiful music to his ears. He rushes to the banister of the stairs where the wooden knob had consistently fallen off. He picks up the knob and kisses it, crying, "I love you, old rickety knob." ***Nothing changed for George that night except one thing – his perspective.*** Perspective changed everything; perspective is the key!

The "Get-To" Mentality

When we "Have-to" do anything in life it becomes a burden. Imagine changing your perspective on anything in life to a "Get-to". "Have-to" leads to hate; "Get-to" leads to gratitude!" Gratitude accepts that which is outside of one's control; therefore, it requires a humility of heart. "Get-to" mentality can literally take on any task. There is no meaningless labor. There is always something to be thankful for and someone to serve.

A "Get-to" mentality transforms a career into a calling. A "Get-to" mentality transcends mediocrity creating meaning in every moment! A "Get-to" mentality doesn't look for happiness, it creates happiness by choosing an emotional response – a grateful one! This mindset is the signal to the heart. A "Get-to" mentality can only invoke a positive emotional response. This emotional response transforms the lower energies summoned to perform a "Have-to" career into higher energies that perform a "Get-to" calling. Among the most passionate spiritual teachers, the beloved apostle Paul said it like this, "Forgetting those things which are behind, and reaching forth to those things which are before, I press toward the mark for the prize!" I press! I want to. I get to! I'm blessed to! Raise your perspective today! *One shift in perspective is all it takes to unlock the energy within your soul!*

Make Plans for the Future

Here's a quick question. Between proactive and reactive, which do you tend to be? See, proactive people typically have a plan. They have definiteness of purpose in their life. While everything might not be perfectly spelled out, they know action means mobility, and mobility brings flexibility and flow. You won't know everything until you get there, and when you get there, things may have already changed. These people learn and grow because through action, they force themselves to grow. Things will happen, plans go awry, trials and setbacks may come; but, their definiteness of purpose and proactivity give clarity and keeps their journey in perspective. Proactive people never over-react; they take things in stride. They're prudent looking much further ahead than just the here and now or immediate gratification. In contrast, reactive and overreactive people are drifters. They may have an inkling of what they hope happens in their lives, or they don't care at all and have relinquished their life responsibility to someone else, some business, some family member, or society. Perspective seems elusive, and life's lived in a constant fog.

Proper Valuation

Many go through life without a definite plan or purpose. It's as though they're expecting a do-over, or this life is one of many; like it's a video game with a reset, or a cat with nine lives. Where does this frivolity stem from? Some treat their futures like a plague. They're fearful; anxious. They fail to plan for fear they mess something up or get something wrong. So, the fear of wasting life creates a barrier to dreaming and going after something worthwhile and this barrier of fear wastes their life for them. Seth Godin calls anxiety needless as well as imaginary. "It's fear about fear – fear that means nothing," he says. It's the absolute worst kind of fear. "Anxiety looks into an unknown future and imagines possible dangers and threats as though they were real and will really happen," he continues. Anxiety's totally debilitating.

How quickly, though, does our valuation of life change when it's threatened? A tragedy happens; everything screeches to a halt. The real tragedy, then, is when everything's fine and we don't stop to awaken fully to life! When we're still aware of everything around us, we should stop. Stop and sit for a day, or week, and decide exactly what the remainder of this precious life is going to look like! What are we going to experience more of every day? When do we periodically screech to a halt to ponder and consider our course, our direction and initiate more fullness to living, and deepness to loving? We become numb and rhythmic to habits and routines until stimulated by some outside force. *Instead, let the inside force of your emotions and desires to live life to the fullest burst forth from your heart. Break the boredom and squeeze every drop of life out of every moment you live!*

So much of what we do will never have any eternal significance. When we come to the end of life, what will we look back on and say, "That was significant!" It probably won't be the social media presence and all the hours of posting and scrolling through the feeds on our phones. It will instead be the creations we made with our kids, the painting we gave, the service in our community, the ball games we attended, the date nights with our loved ones, time walking the beach hand in hand, travelling the world, spending a week hiking and renewing our spirit, the relationships we built with our co-workers and clients, the big difference we made on this world funding the research of some disease, giving a month to help build clean water wells in Africa, stopping to help the elderly lady unload her groceries, and the list goes on. What stirs your soul deeper than anything else? Why aren't you doing more of that now and some of that every day?

In his TEDx Baltimore talk, Joe Ehrmann pointed out that at the end of life, we're not going to ask about the awards, achievements, applause or what we accumulated. We will ask questions about those dear and close to us – relationship questions. What kind of a dad was I? Husband? Friend? And we'll ask if we made a difference. We'll want to know if we left a mark or imprint. Did we live fully and were we fully here? If you were about to go into a risky surgery right now, who would you want there by your side? What would you want to say to them? What will our family and friends remember about us? We sow things completely toxic to our physical and relational health as though we have a "get-out-of-jail-free" card or restart button to this video game of life. Are you expecting a do-over? Do we act like we're expecting one? *We coast through life with no definite plan as though a do-over is coming.* Brendon Burchard cautions in his *Motivation Manifesto,* "Each day, there are a million divine wonders, acts of human kindness, and beautiful sights. Yet we are too checked out or busy thinking about yesterday or tomorrow to even sense the magic!"

A quick Google search averages our lives for us. For example, if you are 25 years old, you have 18,250 days to live because the average person lives 27,375 days. Let's stop going through life like we have another one coming, or like we can postpone living 'til we make it through this job, or until we save enough money, or until we get enough education, etc. There's never enough. You're enough – right now! One of my friends, Jenna, served in the Airforce and now loves professional barrel racing. She's writing her book called, *Enough.* Her whole theme is this, "When I realized I was enough, right here and right now, my life moved forward." What do you want out of life? There's some small step that you could take right now. Before you even read another line, you could literally reshape the course of your life. It just takes one dream and you planting one small seed – right now. That's all it takes. Your belief doesn't even have to be that great. Jesus said a grain of mustard seed is all you need when it comes to faith, but you must only believe. Write one thing that's possibly stirred in your mind:

_____

_____

_____

Earl Nightingale said, "The mind is a fertile field; what you plant there will grow." What you plant, will grow. But you must plant something. Don't wait.

Created for More

Do you believe you're created for more? Inside the human soul is a cry for more. We know we are capable of so much more. *If we've grown deaf to this cry, we need only look around us at the despair in the faces of anxious and often hopeless people we pass and allow this to stir our soul once more.* What more are you believing for your life, your family's lives, your neighborhood, your community, your city, your state, your country and the world? Do you want it badly enough? When you want it as badly as oxygen, you'll succeed.

Is it going to be easy? It's not easy; it's always worth it and that's always easiest in the end. Life becomes incredibly easier as you build habits of living fully and loving deeply. Many seek comfort out of life; they want an easy road. With this comfort and ease, they're willing to compromise and conform. Is easy all we want? When are we going to fully live? Are we banking this feeling, this power, this amazing sense of deep awakening for some time in the future? Our soul awakened fully is the power we need right now to change everything! "Why sit we here 'til we die?" The future is what you're creating right now. What are you creating? Where do you want to be in 5 years? 20 years?

Living Fully Present, Today

All past hurts, bitterness, ego, fear, shame and baggage would vanish if the universe whispered in our ear, "Today is your last". If we engaged each day like our lives depended on it, and if we prepared for each day like it was the grand finale, we'd make a habit of excellence and adopt the highest standards for ourselves. We'd demand more of life and life would give us more. We'd be living in the bonus and summoning our deepest energies to live in fullness and abundance! We'd seize the day – today! It's our bonus!

Think of your first day at a new job, in your marriage or at school. Remember the excitement? Then, over time, if we're not careful, the excitement turns to boredom. Quickly, familiarity breeds contempt. How do we shake this complacency? How do we overcome this boredom? Here's how. *Live every day as if it were your last; treat every day as if it were your first; experience every day as if it were a BONUS!* It's high time we died to the past, died to the future and died to all anxious worries and stressful drains. What would happen if we truly engaged everything in this one day with everything we have?

Squeeze today for every last drop; for, today is a bonus! There's no other day like it, this day wasn't ever promised, and neither is tomorrow. Mark Van Doren said it like this, "There is one thing we can do, and the happiest people are those who can do it to the best of their ability. We can be completely present. We can be all here. We can give all our attention to the opportunity before us!" Are you showing up at this very moment all in? Is your mind someplace else, or are you engaging all your mental faculties in reading, imagining and stimulating thoughts of application?

Living in The Bonus

What are you doing with your life? Your bonus – right now? We aren't promised tomorrow. Live everyday as if it were your bonus. Let me tell you from personal experience and from overwhelming evidence, when you carry the weight of past wounds and experience anxiety about the future, you miss out on a good portion of today. The vicious cycle continues. A piece of you literally never experiences the fullness and abundance of today. Albert Schweitzer said, "The tragedy of life is what dies inside a man while he lives." When you daily adopt a bonus mentality, you can't even consider hatred, judgement, pride, or complaining, you have today – today – to fully live and to deeply love. Each morning is a fresh start allowing only peace and an open heart to experience life fully - no carry over; no baggage allowed! *Make peace with your past, plans for your future, so that you can live fully present today!* Every day is a new day. Days are simple promises, years are empty guarantees. Live fully today! You get one shot at today; take your best one. There are always obstacles, troubles, and issues. The one waiting for the perfect moment will never find it and waste away their energies saving for that perfect moment. Energizers makes perfect every moment they're handed. Always finding the joy, even in the things we dread could actually turn to delight us.

"Carpe diem!" That's a fancy, Latin way of saying "Seize the day!" I want to love life and everyone in it! I want to live in peace and I declare today that I will live every moment fully present! Technology's a tool so I can properly plan for the future and better plan to be fully present. When it acts as a distraction then it is robbing me of my very life and my peace! I indict fatigued, anxious, stressed and tense living! I choose passionate, abundant, vibrant and energized engagement in every moment of life! I will cease **FAST** living:

> **F** – Fatigue
> **A** – Anxious
> **S** – Stressed
> **T** – Tense

And, I will **PAVE** the way to a new future:

> **P** – Passionate
> **A** – Abundant
> **V** – Vibrant
> **E** – Energized

I love what Martha Graham said, "There is a vitality, a lifeforce, an energy, a quickening, that is translated through you into action; and, because there is only one you in all time, this expression is unique." If you block or limit your energy's expression, it will never happen through any other medium and is essentially lost. We block our energy by living in the past or fretting over the future. Wake up to life, today! Engage fully present, now! The only way to create history is in the present time and with the opportunities just before us! Whose sparkling eyes haven't you gazed into recently just communicating, "I love you" to them? Whose wrinkled hand haven't you held; what unique individual haven't you paid attention to along your path? Here's the **BONUS** of life that I can't and WILL NOT waste:

B – Blame cards gone – make peace with the past.
O – Overwhelm gone – make plans for your future.
N – Now is the time for action – all in; fully present right now.
U – Unleash my reserves of energy – live fully; love deeply.
S – Serve others – accountable and responsible; only creating value.

When you daily adopt a bonus mentality, you realize you no longer have any excuses, just one powerful reason – thriving! When you look at the big picture of life and live in the perspective of "The BONUS," you will reduce stress, increase your satisfaction because you will have a definiteness of purpose about you – you're living in the bonus of today. Stress, anxiety and worry are our attempts to control what we shouldn't – the outcomes. We can only control our actions and be fully present today! It's interesting. The person so bold as to point their finger to the mountain top and say, "I'm going there," has the same boldness to choose the attitudes and beliefs to get them there. The people who have big-picture, BONUS perspectives and decide to live fully present, today, experience deep peace and joy and radiate this to others! Decisions are so much easier for the BONUS-thinker. They look at today as another blessing along this wonderful journey – our wonderful life!

Commit to the BONUS by proclaiming with me,
"Every day I live – every moment I live – I will live as if it were a bonus!"
Now, proclaim it again, only this time, say it with all the passion you can,
"Every day I live – every moment I live – I will live as if it were a bonus!"
Now, stand up and shout it with me for the world to hear,
"Every day I live – every moment I live – I will live as if it were a bonus!"
Consider signing this page and dating it. You may even have a loved
one, like my brother, you'd like to dedicate this as a pledge to. They
weren't afforded the opportunity of life past a certain point; therefore, the
joy of life and the opportunity of the bonus mentality is pledged in their
honor:

On this day: _____

By: _____

Dedicated to: _____

Defining moments in our lives bring with them tremendous clarity.
Right now, consider what's really important to you. The BONUS
mentality is a powerful perspective and can keep our priorities straight in
a confusing world. *With clarity on life's calling and the courage to
consistently carry it out comes a confident calm and compelling cause!*
Every day you wake up, you have a cause and it compels you like
nothing else. It's the bonus mentality. This day wasn't promised to you
and tomorrow's no guarantee. Forget the past, have faith your future's
going to reveal greater things than you can imagine, and today – TODAY
– engage with a bonus mentality. Pour everything you have into
everything you choose to do and everyone you decide to do it with. No
playing it small! Take courage. Show up! BONUS mentality! You don't
have a minute to waste.

CHAPTER 7
LEGEND YOU
you're worth more than you think

*"We travel the world to marvel at man's handiworks;
yet we pass by our own mirrors and miss God's."*

Scared Kid

"TIMOTHY!" That was the most dreaded sound I heard growing up. It was a loud, unnerving voice that would send fear and anxiety through me. Sure, I messed up – a lot it seemed. But, after a short while into life, I simply couldn't do anything right – it seemed. I was too young to remember when it first started, but when my name was shouted by my dad, or when another male authority figure would get angry, fear would shoot through my body. My gut would wrench. I'd tremble and quake; and, trying as hard as my 4-year-old legs could squeeze together, nothing would help. I'd wet my pants. Not until I was a teenager did I overcome this. Walking around, constantly scared. About a mile from our house was this waterfall where'd I'd run away to as fast as I could. I'd shout, scream, and I'd even punch the gnarly bark of a large maple tree's trunk with all my might until my knuckles bled. I felt so timid inside; so, I'd try to bring myself to toughness. *There's nothing more unnerving to a person than feeling intimidated, and nothing more exhausting than feeling unworthy.* The safe and loving place a father was meant to provide his children rarely existed. The worth and value that he was meant to pour into them, wasn't mentioned. Young men and women grow up and search to find strength and genuine love in all sorts of ways. Young people become grownups who never feel worthy, valued or appreciated.

We're trying to feel worthy; we're trying to feel valued by this world. We're untrusting and timid around authority in our lives. We feel somehow that everyone is looking at us – devaluing us. We avoid conflict and suffer from the disease to please because we fear pulling back the emotional scars of someone being upset at us. We leave relationships sometimes, too. Not because we don't care, but because we're fearful of the other person getting angry with us, or letting them down. We apologize for everything and walk into every environment of life feeling unworthy. We over compensate in our workouts to show our strength. We run over relationships in business because we must prevail. All the way down in our deepest soul, locked away in his room, is this beautiful, vibrant, sparkling-eyed little kid – scared.

Your Appraisal

What if someone asked you how much are you worth? It's a powerful question; one I feel most haven't considered. So, let me ask you. How valuable are you? What price tag would you put on yourself. What value could you demand for the uniqueness of your DNA; the stunning formation of molecules called, you; the sum of all your days here – your life; all the beauty you've created; all the people you've connected with; and all the lives you've touched?

Knowing your value means getting to know yourself. *This is a journey – to know ourselves better so we can awaken all of ourselves and subsequently, others as well.* I began writing this book because, so many people told me they wanted my energy. My original purpose was to capture what it was that drove me each day with vigor and passion. I would package this stuff into a book and sell it to the world. While there was a good bit of healthy drive, much of it was fear-based and attitude of undeserving. So many of my preconceived ideas about energy, drive and passion were misconceptions as they tied nowhere to the emotions of who we truly are as humans. I was being driven in life by competition, past wounds and scars. Hopes and desires for a bright future weren't mixed with faith. I didn't feel deserving at all. Much of my drive came from so many outer forces and inner, ugly voices. Not knowing who we are and not feeling a good sense of self-worth can swindle so much life from us – our very energy. Hanging around good mentors who valued me as a person, I noticed something. Most were calm and powerful people. I realized some simple, basic truths about self-worth. Your worth starts with knowing yourself and having congruence between that identity and all its behavior. Solomon said, "a good name is rather to be chosen than great riches." A good name! Does that mean someone else is giving you a good name or can you look at yourself in the mirror and say, "I have a good name." One of the oldest admonishments of the ancient philosopher is this, "Man, know thyself!" Let's boil this down to a two-word journey, "Know Thyself." Wow! Know thyself. Who are you? What experiences do you create? How do you feel? What unique features do you have unlike any other? What do you love? What's your divine purpose on this earth? What is it you want out of life? What do you want to do? What would you love to become? What could you get out of bed for without an alarm clock? *Until we're willing to be still and know ourselves, we'll rush through life marching to everyone else's drum, seeking praise, listening for every acknowledgement, hoping for recognition, needing approval and never feeling worthy.* We can only understand our worth when we finally quiet ourselves, be still, and get to know ourselves deeply.

We live in a noisy world and from a very early age up into adolescence and adulthood we have a lot of ideas, formats, templates and blueprints prescribed for us by wonderful people, parents, teachers, mentors and good-meaning leaders. Some of these see natural gifts and abilities and help us craft a life plan. Some, however, pressure us or simply help us craft a typical, socially-acceptable plan. Most of the time, however, crafting our plan (or what's left of it) falls squarely on our shoulders. We listen to all the voices and try to fit in. We don't consider who we are, what we would like to do, or what we were uniquely gifted and designed to be in life. What invigorates us? What awakens us? What is it we get so passionate about? So, on this journey of knowing yourself and learning to see yourself worthy, it may surprise you that most of us have a pretty good idea of who we are, but we simply won't believe it. After all, society has said something completely different. Because of conformity and fear we've settled for something far less, or we're too scared to share what we think we'd really like to do – living authentically. Who's defined your worth to you? What are you believing? What are you finding value in becoming and doing?

Many check the ticker of WOTOM (what others think of me) every day and place their life investment in this poor performance, risky and fluctuating stock. Whose standard of self-worth are you buying into? Most live enslaved to someone else's estimation of their worth. So, ask yourself, "How much am I worth?" Instead of "know thyself", we're looking around at what everyone else says about us. *Instead of claiming a higher perspective of our worth, we buy-in to what we think others think of us.* Instead of believing and tapping into a Creator's amazing knowledge of us, we simply settle for what society says they know of us.

Barriers

We learn at a very young age what's acceptable and what's not. Unfortunately, for many of us, our worth was tied to our behavior. We learned to value ourselves based on our behavior. For many, their behavior was never good enough; therefore, they've never felt good enough. At this moment in time, while the mountain of past devaluation may seem insurmountable, you get to choose the standard of your worth. Most won't because of the greatest barrier known to man – fear! "The price of our vitality is the sum of our fears," says David Whyte. President Kennedy said, "The only thing we have to fear is fear itself." Are you afraid to claim your worth? Is it easier to perform at a lower standard because that matches what you think you're worth? Fear of redefining our value because of what others will think of us causes us to live trapped by insecurity. We fight others in our minds, our thoughts and our actions because every scenario of life we walk into, we're trying to place and find our worth. We're living with past negative inputs. We compound these negative inputs when we live in insecurity, judgment, comparison, competition and condemnation. Furthermore, many people self-sabotage. They really don't mean to; it's simply imbedded dialogue they seemingly can't get away from. Psychological roadblocks will decrease your capacity to live fully. The mental and emotional scars are just as debilitating and much farther reaching than perhaps their physical counterparts inflicted in the past. Physical hurts often heal with time while emotional and mental wounds compound. Analyze the inputs and the voices – your beliefs. Do they ring true to your inner conscience? If not, why, do you think? What voices are in your mind right this second starting up negative dialogue as you read these lines?

Past inputs aren't your fault. Your mind was an open book as a child and not everything taught, nor name you were called, nor way you may have suffered pain, nor abuse was your fault. The problem now is that these negative inputs take up space in our brains and run rampant in our subconscious. Until we face them, and name them, they hold power over us and retain lodging in our minds. They swindle our energy. We're called to do great things, but we fear what someone's said. I was told I'd do nothing more than swing a hammer. In fact, my first year away from home, I did exactly that – swung a hammer. There's nothing wrong with swinging a hammer. In fact, there's an amazingly efficient and proper technique to swinging a hammer that will make you feel like a million bucks mastering. The point here is imbedded dialogue exists. Negative inputs become self-fulfilling prophecies. We succumb to them. We fear facing them. Face them we must! Not only face them, but in faith and full assurance that we were created for more, and that our worth is priceless, we must replace these negative inputs. Yes, replace them! Focus your energy, not on fighting the old negative inputs, but on building pure, powerful and positive replacements. Positive inputs you will assign in place of the previous negative ones. The original inputs weren't our fault; leaving them there is totally our fault.

No matter where we're at in life, if we want to grow or change our legacy, you will face criticism. The nail that sticks up gets hammered down. This inherent fear – the fear of others' opinions ranks highest among humanity's fears. This fear alone claims more lost legacies than anything else. *This fear blatantly robs people of ambition, advertises the status quo, and turns them from being critical thinkers into drifters – wandering generalities in a world that is dying for someone to lead the way to greatness.* Fear of others' opinions has stopped more people from stepping up to the plate when it could've counted for society. Fear of others' opinions has buried more achievements on the campuses of our high schools and universities than all fears put together. Its twin of peer-pressure and distant kin of conformity raise wanderers and strip young people of purity, intellect and passion. Fear of others' opinions shackle church members to their pews, fearful of stirring too much or praising too loudly. Fear of others' opinions cause couples to hide truth from one another and start down the slippery slope of relational ruin. Fear of what others think bars away, in the deepest dungeons of our hearts, the energy that could flow and would flow if we'd only open up and be real, authentic and vulnerable. Fear of what others think instructs its students to impress one another binding people in debt, tradition and pride. Fear of what others think blinds people with insecurity. *Fear of what others think prohibits us from making peace with our past, or plans for our future; nor will it grant us the freedom to be fully present, fully alive and fully loving everywhere we go today.* It demands us to be reserved, undelighted, unhappy and masked. It forces us to cower in constant analysis and paralysis. Fear of what others thinks is the biggest dream killer of our day. Fear of what others think is the greatest barrier to reclaiming our worth.

Crabs, Monkeys & Fleas

Breaking free of the barriers is tough. There are people who bank on us feeling inferior, unworthy and undervalued. There are many fighting the same barriers, and should we escape, it may not look good for them. Zoologists are amazing people and I'm thankful they know how to keep ferocious animals well fed, happy, and locked up securely. One animal they don't have to lock up, though, is the crab. That is, as long as two are placed in the same bucket. If one tries to climb out and enjoy freedom, the other will pull it back down. They'll never escape. The admonishment not to be crabby takes on a whole new meaning here. Have you heard about the caged monkeys? They put two monkeys in a cage with a cluster of ripe, yellow bananas at the top of a tree. When the first monkey climbed up to get the bananas, a blast of cold water was released from a pre-arranged spigot, hitting the poor fellow in the face upon which, he quickly scampered down. Repeated behavior brought the same result. When the second monkey, tried to climb up, the first monkey made such a racket about it, and still, the second monkey climbed and experienced the same cold blast. This time, though, one cold blast along with the other monkey's admonishment did the trick. They took the first climber out and replaced him with a new monkey. The second climber who was still in the cage communicated with this monkey and this monkey never even tried to climb. Again, switching the second climber out for a brand-new monkey resulted in no takers. Monkey after monkey kept communicating of the danger of cold blasts for any monkey who'd attempt reaching for the yellow banana cluster. I remember hearing Zig Ziglar talk about training fleas. You take a jar and fill it full of fleas. Sealing it with a lid, you'll hear the ping, ping, ping of fleas jumping and hitting that lid. Before long, however, the noise stops and you can literally take the lid off. Those fleas have been trained on how high they're allowed to jump.

Understanding these phenomena can help us in life. Surround yourself with value-creating people. These are the people who believe the best, see the best, and bring out the best in you. People who will affirm your worth. People who will help you replace the negative, fear-based voices with positive, faith-filled affirmations instead! ***Until we replace inner dialogue with the truth that our worth is priceless, we continue taking stock in the negative voices, judgement, self-righteousness, blame and holding onto excuses.*** Maxwell Maltz states, "Since you were engineered for success and happiness, then the old picture of yourself as 'unworthy of happiness' and a person who was meant to fail must be in error." Let go of the fear of what others are going to say when you change your self-talk; it's only natural they may not like it. Avoid giving any attention to their dislike. You continue right on, by faith, reclaiming your inner self-talk! When I realized that the emotion called "fear of what others think" was literally channeling and draining my energy – my life – away, I decided to cast it off. Perfectionism – fear of making a mistake – distorted my inner conscience. I allowed this to hold me back. My own dialogue was limiting me; and, I projected this dialogue onto others, perhaps limiting them. Feelings of undeserving may come up for you due to excessive and harsh criticism you experienced in your youth. Unfair, excessive, or abusive punishment may have created emotions of distrust for authority figures in your life. I don't know exactly what negative dialogue might be there, but we live in an imperfect world where negativity exists. I do know that most have inner struggles, despairs, hurts and negative dialogues to overcome. Maltz says "such a distorted and unrealistic conscience does indeed make cowards of us all as we become overly sensitive and too carefully concerned with whether we have a right to succeed in even a worthwhile endeavor." We become too carefully concerned about whether we deserve success or not. Many people with an inhibited conscience will hold back or take a back seat in any kind of endeavor – even a profoundly good and noble one. Join me and claim courage, today. Courage to face those fears and reclaim your amazing value!

Reclaim Your Value

If a symbol of resolute courage existed, it did so in the embodiment of Winston Churchill. He declared, "There comes a special moment in everyone's life, a moment for which that person was born. That special opportunity, when he seizes it, will fulfil his mission – a mission for which he is uniquely qualified. In that moment, he finds greatness. It's his finest hour." When we take our value back, we realize just how valuable our life is. We gasp at what fake and empty threats the paper giants of our inner negative dialogue really were. We stop allowing our energy to be swindled. Every individual gets to decide how valuable they are at this very moment. *The fact is, when you don't value you, you won't value your ideas, your dreams and your goals.* Many are playing it safe because of fear or limiting beliefs. Why play it safe? Why blend in with the multitudes playing it safe when you were born to be a star who shines brightly? In overwhelming love, I implore us today to think bigger than ourselves, for there's a world needing fully awakened and thriving people!

Scared Kid vs. Mighty Warrior

There's a Scriptural account of a young man who was hiding out by the winepress – it's one of my favorite stories. Sneaking around scorched fields, he gathered what grain he could and hid it. Why? An oppressive group of people had conquered his nation. There wasn't any strong leadership and the people capitulated. All of the land that should have been bountiful, lay barren. They scrimped and scraped for the food they needed so desperately. They were literally bargaining with life for a penny instead of living in the abundance of their land. On this particular day, this young man's life was transformed as an angel appeared to him and said, "Greetings, mighty man of valor!" Gideon, this scared kid, must have looked around him to find who the angel was greeting. Finding no one but himself, he realized the angel was referring to him. What? Gideon, the man who would end up leading his people to freedom received his calling that day and began a journey of claiming the mighty warrior he was created to be. It didn't happen overnight, but the initial greeting was so affirmative – so powerful and positive – it literally reshaped a scared kid's destiny! How do you see yourself? Have you considered changing your paradigm? Change everything by thinking only of the person you wish to become! Change your perspective. *Stop trying and failing. Instead, start being, and living as the person you were created, destined and called to be.* I remember watching this sharp teenager whose family Jen and I knew pretty well. We watched him grow up, finish college, marry this amazing lady, have kids and make something of himself. He shared something his dad would say every time he left the house. He'd say, "Remember your name." It wasn't "don't do this," and "don't do that," although I'm sure some fatherly counsel took place. The most prominent piece of admonition was this simple statement, "Remember your name – you're a Russell." Wow! How about living in a legacy like this! What's your name? Scared kid, or mighty warrior? You may say, my father failed me; or, I grew up without a mom. We may not have a lineage or family legacy we're thrilled about. Then my friend, never has the time been better, and never has the need been more compelling than right now. Let us right now, square our shoulders back, lift our faces toward Heaven and boldly claim a new name – a changed legacy! Many of us think a happy, abundant and legendary existence is reserved for a select few like celebrities, politicians, world leaders, or global businessmen of renown. Why? That's the news we listen to. Someone right now is looking at you as their celebrity – guaranteed. Ask yourself. Does your life hold any less worth than the superstar's? Start seeing yourself as priceless and you change everything! Raise your perspective, reclaim you worth, and change your life legacy into the priceless treasure you are!

Snowflakes

See, our worth really can't be dictated by anyone but ourselves. We raise and lower our standard of worth based on life circumstances, our environments, accomplishments or failures and others' appraisals. What if we changed our perspective; and instead, started with a bold statement of value? How valuable are you? Where do you get your worth? Questions like these cause us to take personal inventory, not just of our titles, riches, status' and tangible wealth, but our lives, our whole unique experience of mind, spirit, soul and body, our relationships and connections – our entire legacy. Truth of the matter is, there's no one like you and me. Like the snowflakes that fall and grace the earth, each of us are different and engineered, designed and created specifically for a definite purpose. Place your hand over your heart. Feel that? That's an amazing heart pumping, beating, making a rhythm throughout your whole being. Take a deep, deep breath in. Hold it … one, two, three … exhale. Feel that? Oxygen just saturated your entire body and ignited your energy within. Amazing or what?! Wow! You are priceless, my friend! Embracing our uniqueness and living in our authenticity is attractive. ***When we conform, we blend in and short circuit the energy that only our DNA can create and radiate to others.*** Hans Selye, a great psychologist and one who was referenced by Carnegie said it much like this, "As much as we thirst for approval, we dread condemnation." Many of us remain frozen; scared to live differently – fully! We adopt a cookie -cutter mentality – trying to fit the mold of others' expectations. What if we set abundant expectations for ourselves? We don't because we're seeking someone's approval, and we're scared of another's disapproval. You're magical and miraculous, everything about you is unique; why try to be someone else? Live in your uniqueness! Be a courageous snowflake!

Value vs. Pride

Sometimes, we have the tendency to confuse confidence with pride, or a proper valuation of self as haughty. We've let others define how we should feel about ourselves. Let's keep it very plain and simple. Pride is an inflated ego. Conceitedness can inflate one's ego to crave position and power, just as hurt can inflate one's ego to settle for entitlement. Certainly, self-righteousness and high-mindedness are the clothes pride wears. Pride gets defensive when someone offers counsel or criticism. Pride doesn't always dominate, however; pride, can cause us to hold back just the same. Pride can't imagine giving up a title, ranking, position or credit, but pride can also keep one from accepting it. Pride stems from an elevated sense of one's position just as it stems from fear of what others think. John Wooden, maybe one of the best basketball coaches in NCAA history put it like this, "Talent is God-given; be humble. Fame is man-given; be thankful. Conceit is self-given; be careful!"

What then is humility? Humility is nothing more than a proper valuation of one's worth. Humility esteems all as equal. Humility is fair with a willingness to serve our fellow man. Humility won't discount anyone's value. *Humility isn't thinking less of yourself, it's simply thinking in terms of others worth with a willingness to let someone else have right-of-way.* Neither is self-abasement or speaking negatively of ourselves humility at all. I know a father who withheld any form of praise from his daughters. Fearing that looking beautiful would make them prideful, he simply refrained from any sort of acknowledgement. Well, the first young man that came along and gave a daughter words of affirmation snatched her heart and used this very thing as leverage to get what he wanted in the relationship. Had this daughter a healthy respect of her value and genuine affirmation that she was beautiful (wholly beautiful), perhaps a young man's cheap lines wouldn't have captured her craving heart so. Pride may be an inflated estimation of one's position, and self-abasement or viewing oneself in a negative light leaves a vacuum of self-pity, comparison and fear of others' opinions resulting in the same pride. I like how Tony Evans writes, "God is not opposed to greatness; God is opposed to pride." In fact, we won't properly esteem others when we first can't value ourselves. Instead, this vacuum looks for and points out the flaws in others, and in so doing, we get some sort of better feeling about ourselves. When we have a false sense of humility and resort to self-abasement, we don't speak up for our beliefs. We stop living our truth and alter our conscience. We become infected with the disease to please. Inwardly, we churn with chagrin for a leader's request, instead of possessing the confidence to stand on our belief, and with a proper self-respect and valuation, question something in a respectful way. How do you look at others? What we project on others is usually the deeply-rooted beliefs about ourselves. We look at others exactly how we look at ourselves.

When we realize we're better than no one else, but we're all called to be the best version of who we can be, we inspire more from ourselves and others. ***Nobody is better than anybody, but everybody is encouraged to be better by somebody giving their best!*** It's what I love about running. You are in your lane. You are competing against your last best time – if you want to. Or, you're simply running to stay fit and inspire healthy living. No competition. No comparison. And if ever we are to compare, let it be only that form of comparing, not proving we're better, but realizing how much better we really have it. With this realization, let us all be grateful for the amazing life we live and we are. Those trapped in the wheel of comparison are missing out on becoming invaluable.

For humble souls, no task is too small; they don't seek fame; they stay in touch – they're fully present! Insecurity and humility cannot coexist. Maxwell Maltz states, "You must know yourself, both your strengths and your weaknesses, and be honest with yourself concerning both. Your self-image must be a reasonable approximation of you, being neither more than you are nor less than you are." When your identity and value – your self-image – are intact and secure you feel good, confident and ready to engage life. When it's threatened, you feel anxious and insecure. When your self-image is one you can wholesomely be proud of, you feel confident, you feel free to be yourself, and you express yourself as you function at peak performance.

Visualize the Person

Breaking free of the barriers will not happen fighting the things you or others don't like about you. ***Breaking free will happen when you step into living like the pricelessness you are!*** You will become a life-giving force in this world. The world is waiting to see something awesome. They won't ask you necessarily, and they may not even like you at first for climbing out of the bucket, grabbing that banana cluster, or jumping from the jar. Stepping into your pricelessness, however, empowers you to do priceless things. Brendon Burchard shares that greatness is found by those who "rarely seek permission from the world, because they know the masses bound by mediocrity will never approve of anything that breaks convention or speaks of boldness and magic." Let me tell you what's truly amazing. Someone breaking free of the fear of others' opinions. Someone breaking free to live in their gifts and calling. Someone breaking free from living a lie and instead, living their authenticity. Shad Helmstetter Ph.D., stated, "Your subconscious mind is working right now, day and night, to make sure you become precisely the person you unconsciously describe yourself to be." What are you describing yourself to be – way down deep in your soul? What are you visualizing for yourself? What kind of a person do you envision operating at peak performance? What experience are you bringing to this world? Take a moment to think of seven things that the world could experience because of you living fully energized? Jot them down. Let them stretch your capacity and maximize your amazing potential:

_____

_____

_____

_____

_____

_____

_____

Are you visualizing who you were created to be? Helmstetter again beautifully writes, "The God-given birthright with which all of us were born and deserve to retrieve, embrace, enjoy and possess for the rest of our lives is one that restores us and builds us up. It structures our character, sustains our strength, reinforces our courage. It is internal substance of self-belief; it's the self-talk of self-esteem."

I highly recommend, in this journey of "knowing thyself", you take some sort of gifts, talents, or strength-finders test. Simply, see what your strengths are. These reports give you that starting point. Commit to knowing and living in your strengths and your gifts – maximize these. My favorites are the well-known "DISC profile" and Sally Hogshead's "Fascination Advantage". One is how you see the world and the other is how the world sees you. Both of which are linked on my site at timehooper.com. Empower yourself with the knowledge of who you are and where you create the most value – know yourself. I'd highly recommend if you're married that you take your spouse through the report as well. Jen and I did these together, and the insights we gained are invaluable! The more we learned how different we were, what drove us, and how best to operate and live in our gifts, the better we related and communicated with each other, and the better our marriage has been.

You're Priceless

You're priceless! Yet, at the gates of our minds there are enemies gathered. This world is full of negativity and if we aren't affirming what Zig Ziglar called the pure, the powerful, and the positive, we will succumb to the naysaying, numbing and negative thoughts that permeate our news feeds and fill our airwaves. Why make such a big to do about our minds and thoughts? Because the thoughts of our minds literally create our reality. *Therefore, decide today to wage war on any negative thought until it is eradicated. Dwell only on the positive.* Many of us go through life never taking inventory of what we're thinking about all day long. Some start the journey and turn back thinking it's unrealistic. It's a journey, and building a powerful mindset takes time – it takes faith. I love how Jesus, the great teacher from Galilee, said, "If you will only believe, so shall it be done unto you." Our minds form our beliefs which our souls embrace and live out. Our minds are so powerful, yet because they were given as gifts to us, we often take them for granted. Much like our very lives, familiarity breeds contempt, and we neglect to exercise our minds to their greatest and highest capacity of faith and belief. Like Earl Nightingale stated, "Our minds came to us as standard equipment, and we don't fully realize what we have until it's taken from us." In the matter of the thoughts of our minds, we've conformed. We've simply checked into everyone else's opinion, mainstream ideas, and negativity. In fact, negativity is so rampant, we actually believe it has to form at least a part of our mental structure.

We've stopped exercising our minds. Think with me. What set time to you have every day to simply think? To quiet all the noise and to think. Not even reading a great book, or listening to a great podcast. I mean, absolute quiet and meditative thought. A close analysis of your mind and the thought traffic contained within. A determination of focus on that which you are holding in front of your mind as your life vision and your definite purpose. A close inventory of the progress you are making towards its attainment. An arrest of the distractions that must go. An acknowledgment of the resources you must call upon to aid you in your quest. *This daily exercise of our minds is paramount.* Without thinking, many go to prayer with no definite purpose. We talk aimlessly instead of boldly stating our desire and asking for the plan. It would be as if my son came to me and said "Dad, I need an answer for this problem on my math homework." If he hadn't given any thought, or if I didn't see some sort of chicken scratch on the side with an attempt to solve, do you think I'd take him seriously. When I did help him, do you think I'd simply give him the answer, or give him the plan, the process or the steps to attain that which he asked. I find that engaging my deepest mental thought in prayer creates the greatest form of active faith and with the activation of thought, a plan usually comes into view.

Auto-Suggestion

Have you realized that the importance of analyzing our thought patterns and replacing them with empowerment contains more than meets the eye? It's the vast world of thought called our subconscious mind. Napoleon Hill, in his notable work, *Think And Grow Rich*, stated, "the subconscious mind is our chemical laboratory which combines all thought impulses making them ready to translate into physical reality." This laboratory – our subconscious mind – makes up 90 percent of our mind and makes no distinction between constructive or destructive thought impulses. It simply fulfills the proverb that says, "As a man thinks, so he becomes." Our subconscious mind works with whatever material we feed it. The problem is, many of us allow our minds to run on auto-pilot; therefore, our subconscious chews up everything it sees, hears, senses and attracts. *We simply don't make the time to do inventory on the major thoughts of our minds – constructive and destructive.* Empowering beliefs or limiting ones. Voices of positivity and faith, or voices of negativity and fear. Many of these thoughts, beliefs and voices were little weeds planted by someone else in our youth; they've grown up into deep-rooted shrubs. They've become deeply carved pathways.

Hill calls these pathways whereby our thought patterns operate the law of auto-suggestion. He states, "Auto-suggestion happens in your mind whether you exercise it or not. It is simple. Take an addict from his addiction and environment without replacing the auto-suggested thoughts from his brain, he will return to his addiction." The underlying and largest addiction known to mankind is the addiction of self-validation. We're consumed in finding our identity and value, or seeking to prove our worth. Living in insecurity has adverse affects which result in competition, comparison and condemnation. These mindsets can't stand for anyone to be better, and views every relationship positionally. It's limited and withholding. In fact, many will serve out of fear or an undeserving mentality. Yet inwardly, the voices planted in our minds aren't silenced. We constantly come up short. Forming addictions is simply an outward reflections of deep, internal hurt – feeling devalued. It's why some people look at someone addicted to drugs and think,"How could you do this to yourself?" The person addicted knows they're doing it to themselves, and feels in some way, that they are less deserving of abundant life, or can't attain abundant life. Different mindsets; different valuations. The law of auto-suggestion is simply telling someone over and over, on auto-pilot, what they're worth, and what they need in order to feel better. Instead of seeking to gain a proper self-valuation, we addict ourselves to all sorts of things, and we cope. Humility – a false kind – is touted by some of the most insecure people, and life is lived walking on egg-shells and never seeking to thrive. We're fearful of finding too much enjoyment in life. We fear someone might envy us or be jealous of us. We fear what others think of us, so we level off to blend in. We're worth more and are created for so much more. Until we, by faith, see ourselves from our Creator's perspective, we won't value ourselves the way we should. *Until we value ourselves, we won't exercise our spirits, our minds, our souls and our bodies the way we could, and should, to enhance life and maximize our potential – stretching and strengthening our capacity to do life's work.* You're amazing! You're beautiful! Sure, we have flaws; we all do.

I'm a carpenter by hobby, not by trade. When I finish a piece of furniture, only I know where the flaws are. Do you think it's any less valuable, any less useful? Usually, we think everyone sees us like we see ourselves. Most of the time, someone's opinion of us means more to us than our opinion of ourselves. Many times, their appraisal is much higher than our own. Many times, their appraisal goes unspoken because you already look perfect to them and they're insecure in stating the beauty they see. More than likely, the people around us see a beautiful life and hope the best for us. They want us to succeed. It takes me, the carpenter, to point out the flaw I made in the furniture, and all those admiring my work consistently will say, "You'd never know! Ha! It actually looks like the design or adds to the piece." Let me tell you friend! You are valuable. We spend billions to travel the world to marvel at the handiworks of man; yet, we'll walk right past our own mirrors and miss God's!

Have you ever been running late for work, burnt supper, spilled the bowl of cereal all over the table, or done something that caused you to give yourself a good chiding? Have you ever called yourself names? Somehow, we thought the other party would do the same, and when they didn't and the heat's off, we get back on good terms with ourselves. We thought calling ourselves names and beating ourselves up would some-how make the situation better or help us act differently next time. It's a myth. Maltz states, "It's necessary to the happiness of man that he be mentally faithful to himself. Infidelity does not consist in believing or in disbelieving; it consists in professing to believe what he does not believe." Deep down, our subconscious knows when we don't value and respect ourselves, and this is why we can lose our tempers at ourselves! Deep down, many are upset at themselves for something they did or are doing.

They feel undeserving and although we cover this up externally, we feel inadequate and insecure deep down. Sometimes these limiting beliefs and voices were put there early on in our lives, and we continue the rhetoric. Navy Seal, Mark Divine states, "Deeply hidden beliefs can cause your subconscious mind to work against your conscious desires in direct and indirect ways." These limiting beliefs, he states, "can sabotage your confidence in your own intuition and decision-making, especially when things are tense and chaotic."

Why do we belabor this point of thought intentionality? Why set aside daily times of meditation and understanding what's happening in our auto-suggested subconscious minds? Because, until we replace the negative inputs with positive ones, we remain stuck and unable to thrive let alone empower others. What we must do is intentionally reclaim and restate who we are and imbed this into our subconscious minds. *We must reprogram our minds with empowering beliefs and focus our energy into positive and faith-filled reinforcement.* We must call to attention the 10 percent of conscious mind that acts as the instructor to our subconscious. We must consciously reclaim our value over and over. Our Creator already did; it's time we yield to His redeeming perspective of us. "You become what you think about all day long," said Earl Nightingale, and Napoleon Hill claims, "Every man is what he is, because of the dominating thoughts which he permits to occupy his mind." All impulses of thought will eventually clothe themselves in a matching physical reality. So, how do we consciously speak to our subconscious mind – this machine that never sleeps? Our subconscious mind is most activated and also highly susceptible to thoughts that are mixed with feeling or emotion according to science. Those thoughts originating solely in the reasoning sectors of our minds pale in comparison. Theory states that only emotionalized thoughts will influence our subconscious mind to take action. This is why most people are ruled by their feelings and emotions. Your mentality, your attitude and everything else about you is influenced and controlled by what you plant in your subconscious mind. Zig Ziglar states, "You are what you are, and where you are, because of what has gone into your mind. You change what you are, and where you are, by what goes into your mind." Let's discuss placing into our minds statements of the priceless treasures we are!

Affirming Your Value

Selling is a human function and we all sell every moment of every day. Mothers sell their children on broccoli, husbands sell their wives on why they need a motorcycle, boat, or other contraption, coworkers sell each other on ideas, kids sell each other on each other's toys when a trade is desired, and the list goes on. Understanding your own value, and knowing what you have to offer is valuable, makes you a passionate sales person. Do you really believe in your value? Do you really believe in your product or service? Do you really believe it will add value to those you're promoting it to? When you're energized, you realize your value, and with clarity, confidence and courage, you name your price. For instance, if you're dating, you're not discounting yourself to win the affection of a boyfriend. *Many are walking themselves down to the pawn shop of life and putting themselves on display like some off-brand purse. You're not a cheap purse – you're a Gucci GG Marmont!* Don't discount yourself; you're priceless! I love how Tommy Newberry states, "You are an original masterpiece. Your DNA proves it. There has never been anyone just like you, and there will never be anyone just like you."

Have you ever considered that nothing would be the same if you didn't exist! A lot would be different! A lot of people's lives wouldn't have been blessed by your touch! Consciously, you are shaking your head in agreement with me; deep down, though, you've identified some negative dialogue. Great job! Name it. Let's move into building some faith-filled positive affirmations to replace the fear-based negative voices. Every morning, I make a case for my energy usage. That's right! Our energy starts with the thoughts of our minds. The more empowering my thoughts, the more energy I can channel into everything I do! This *C.A.S.E.* is my *"channeling and affirming statement of energy"* and has become a small, second book I'm working on. This affirmation is praticed, restated and reinforced throughout my day. Doing an activity such as affirmations has been knocked by some. That's to be expected. It's a negative world, and how could something so simple as an affirmation stated every morning become so empowering? Let me tell you how. Faith is often simple. Not easy; simple. Faith takes on a higher perspective that values ourselves. Faith dumps all doubt. It must only be faith. Faith that my perseverance in a certain action will reap a certain result. Doubt and fear can't coexist with faith and herein lies the reason most won't affirm their priceless value. Will you choose, by faith, to see yourself as the legend, as the priceless creation, as the unique, one-of-a-kind, beautiful whole person you are? When you see yourself as legendary, as amazing, as beautiful, as the priceless treasure you are, you will only be able to conceive one thing a valuable creation would do – create value. Anything less stems from fear. It takes faith to accept the opposite of what men for thousands of years have tried to regulate – the value of a person. Our entire society is set up on a value system – spoken or unspoken, discrimination happens. The soul of every person cries out and longs for identity. The person who thrives and abounds is the one who breaks out of this system and accepts the value that's been gifted to them by their Creator, for only a Creator (like my carpentry example) has the ultimate right of assigning value. The only way people know how to assign value is through the usefulness of the creation. Sure, we should seek to be useful in our world. Our level of usefulness, however, will level off somewhere. Or, it may fluctuate with our environment – useful to the level of societal demands. *Abounding in life, going above and beyond, constantly reaching to maximize your potential and raise your expectations stem directly from our perspective regarding our worth.* Finally realizing how priceless we are will break us through all limiting fear and we'll abound to the highest level of living fully and loving deeply!

Accepting a Creator's standard of worth is a simple matter of faith. Here's what the powerful thinker, Napoleon Hill, says about faith. "The sum and substance of the teachings and achievements of Christ were nothing more nor less than faith." The apostle Paul stated, "That which is not of faith is sin." What is so necessary about faith? Faith is power. Faith calls upon the unseen. The smallest portion of faith elevates one to the highest perspective. Akin to faith is love, for without faith, we choose lesser responses than love – fear based responses. Faith chooses to love without proof of a result believing that love will win. Faith operates one way and is consistent. At the turn of the twentieth century, Hill pointed at Gandhi as evidence to modern civilization of what power lies in faith. He stated, "Ghandi wields more potential power than any man living at this time, and this, despite the fact that he has none of the orthodox tools of power, such as money, battle ships, soldiers and materials of warfare. Ghandi has no money, no home, and he doesn't own a suit of clothes, but he does have power! Ghandi has accomplished, through the influence of faith, that which the strongest military on earth could not, nor ever will ... he has accomplished the astounding feat of influencing two hundred million minds to coalesce and move in unison, as a single mind. What other force on earth, except faith could do as much?" And one must not confuse faith with religion, for many of the teachings of religion distort faith as something we can boast to having. A man-made distortion of faith will always exhibit itself in fear – the very opposite of faith. You must have faith to love yourself and love others. *Faith operates at the highest frequency and performs the greatest acts. Faith overcomes all obstacles, for only fear produces obstacles.* Is this discussion on human valuation necessary? Let's ask ourselves, "How valuable am I?" There's only one answer based on faith – priceless. All other answers are physical, tangible or fear-based and all are limiting. Every human problem stems from a valuation error. Every war, every conflict and yes, every argument can be attributed to an improper valuation of humanity. One person putting down the value of another person. Writing it out and reading it may sound so trivial. How could anyone put down someone else's value? Herein lies the problem with self-righteousness – distorted valuation of self and other people. Faith, however, starts in our minds and quickens our spirit! Faith accepts an eternal spirit, a beautiful soul, a unique mind and perfect body and attributes priceless value to every amazing molecular arrangement known as a human person!

The mental energy created by faith unleashes a spiritual awareness and emotional depth of love unknown to mortal man. This sort of combination mixes to inspire the souls of men everywhere with hope. The greatest forces on earth are faith, love and hope. Paul, the great apostle and perhaps most energized man to stand before commoners and kings alike, said the greatest of these three forces is love! Oh, friend! The energy of love – true love – will propel you further than life itself ever could. Jesus said, "Love your neighbor as yourself!" The problem. Most of us don't value and love ourselves like our Creator does, so we'll only value and love others up to a certain level.

Emotionally, many don't know how to truly love, or experience being loved. It's very ritualistic and even saying, "I love you" seems rote. Love's

not genuine when it speaks through the perspective of materialism, positionalism, or a distorted, political or religious view of the value of humanity. We wear all sorts of glasses; perhaps that's all we know. By faith, today, accept the legendary force you are! You – a legend! Yes! And by faith, define what this legend is! I am _____.
What desired behavior, outcome, or experience do you want to create? Write it with extreme clarity. Auto-suggestion can be relearned and today is when we start! I used to be called a "clutz" and without even trying, I tripped and "clutzed" my way through life. I was a self-fulfilling prophecy. It's when I formed empowering beliefs and daily – through faith – claimed these affirmations that I realized the focus of energy shift to creating positive outcomes and, even more powerfully, aligning with and attracting them into my life. This was the beautiful part. *Far exceeding my own expectations and beliefs of my own capability and possibility, a little bit of faith of what I could be transferred to me the energy to live, to thrive and to persevere no matter what!*

Affirmations can become your best friends. If you practice them daily – they will become your best friends. Helmstetter gives us some wonderful examples. I will list here what he has written before me. We can see that affirmations can be written for any desired behavior. Here are a few of his:

- "I choose my thoughts. No thought, at any time, can dwell in my mind without my permission."
- "It's true that there really is no one else like me in the entire world, there never was another me before, and there will never be another me again."
- "I am unique from the top of my head to the bottom of my feet. In some ways I may look the same as others, but I am not them I am me."
- "I have many beautiful qualities about me. I have talent and skills and abilities. I even have talents that I don't even know about yet, and I am discovering new talents inside myself all the time."

Affirmations – 4 Things to Remember

Affirmations are powerful in several ways. Not only do they affirm something – like their name indicates, they can also be used to overcome fear and past hurts, replace negative voices or limiting self-talk, and stretch one's faith and vision! Affirmations are fun to create and can be uniquely customized around what you're going to conquer for the day. Remember four important aspects as you train your mind to affirm your vision and goals:

- Positive – always write in a positive tone. Instead of writing "There is too much negative in the world, I'll try not to be negative today," you can write it like, "Today, I'm turning up the light; my positive vibes are attracting positive people and things." *The absence of negative in your affirmation is teaching your mind what to focus on and what to shut out.*

- Personal – keep them personal. Say them in the first person; they are your affirmations and not just general statements or quotes. Your subconscious mind will listen up when you address yourself.

- Present – write them and say them in the present tense. That's right. Put your mind on the lookout for them right away. Also, watch how you start turning doubt to faith. When you say, "I am going to do…" your mind is waiting for a date and time. Without this, there's no decision. When you state, "I am doing…" your mind says, "Oh, I am? … Sure, let me start right away on that…" "Today," is also a great starter word for an affirmation.

- Passionate – when you say your affirmation, proclaim it! Jump up, stand, act it out, make a move, believe it, say it with courage and full faith. This will compel emotion and get your heart behind it. Say it passionately! This may be the most important point in changing your mind's auto-suggestion! Hill states, "Plain, unemotional words do not influence the subconscious mind. You will not get appreciable results until you learn to reach your subconscious mind with thoughts, or spoken words which have been well emotionalized with belief!" This takes practice so don't give up. Keep speaking and casting your vision until your psyche catches on and your soul is invigorated. Sometime, we've told ourselves enough lies and given enough excuses that a simple affirmation feels like more of the same to our subconscious mind. Persevere in faith and reframe your mindset. Passionately claim your affirmation – retrain your powerful subconscious mind!

Your affirmations don't have to be perfect and no one is grading you on this, so let go of those fears. Just start and you'll get better and bolder as time goes on. What do you have to lose? Take a minute to create one, now. Here's mine for today:

> "Today, I'm planting good seeds! Every thought, prayer and action WILL be reaped – sometimes immediately; most times at a future date. I WILL reap if I simply keep planting."

Affirming Others' Value

We will never properly value others as the priceless treasures and imperfectly perfect creations they are until we value ourselves the same way. *Many are longing for others to like them because they don't like themselves. Get to like yourself. You're unique and special!* Everyone is unique in their very own way and a special creation! Instead of trying to get people to like you, start helping them like themselves becoming more of the beauty you see in them. When you recognize and live as a priceless human being, you will value everyone and they feel valued around you. You literally lift people to their best selves.

One stark devaluation that happens over and over in society is the disparity of men earning more than women. Tony Evans points out, "To undervalue the woman in your life is one of the gravest mistakes you could ever make." We have a society that places value on people through position, prestige, fame, beauty, strength or IQ. It's time we cast off our impoverished ways of thinking and blaze the trail for real and genuine equality. Women, in fact, put in more emotional labor and build strong relationships. Not to label this as solely a "mothering" quality, but women have incredible ability. Why, then, are we still debating valuation? I'm a male business leader who takes full responsibility in calling on other male business leaders, men in all walks of life, husbands and dads to elevate the women in our lives and businesses to the priceless valuation that all humanity deserves. Paul, the great apostle stated, "submitting ourselves one to another." David penned, "Dwell together in unity," and Solomon in his wisdom, dedicated an entire chapter of Proverbs to women. We need not look far to realize we all were birthed into this world by a woman. *The faster we can learn from mistakes of history and begin appreciating every human being with the priceless worth their Creator gave them, the sooner agendas of discriminations against gender, race and creeds will cease.*

Have you ever wondered why emotional hurts run so deep and in what were once the closest relationships? It's because those closest to us tend to hurt us deepest. We see abuse happen in marriages all the time. How many police officers have lost their lives in domestic violence cases simply because of deep emotional hurt, resentment, hate, anger and rage? It all started with devaluation. As kids, as lovers or as friends, we expect a nurturing relationship. Too often, proper valuation isn't given. People attest feeling unappreciated. Criticism isn't constructive like it can be. We attack in the harshest tones the ones we're most comfortable with. Consider the sad irony of this situation. People we fall in love with, marry, and the little kiddos we raise all live with us – we're close to each other. Perhaps it's a good friend we've become emotionally open with. In these relationships, people literally lower all walls of defense and, very naturally, become the most vulnerable with their most honest feelings and emotions – because they can, right? Why emotions are hurt the worst in marriages and friendships is because a harsh attack, or a snarky criticism violates the emotional trust we placed in the other person's hands. The attacker simply devalued the other person and stomped on the emotions laid open before them. This may be the most important note in this entire book – cherish close relationships and be the guard of the emotional trust given you – whether implicitly or explicitly given. Energizers live fully, why? So that they can love deeply! Be a tender healer and an emotional haven for those you love. Military, boot-camp-style, drill sergeant should not be the MO of a father. It's the most emotional devastating experience and devaluing existence you will place upon a child. War and military -style training are ugly; they're created to harden mental capacities to withstand the grueling horrors of war – they are not designed to implement into relationships. If ever our attitude is, "get over it" or "buck up," chances are, we're disregarding the sacred emotional trust given us by our lovers, our kids and our friends. Cherish and build trust. Commit to doing the hard work of valuing every human as priceless so you can see their emotions as priceless treasures, too! *Value your people! Value your wife, husband, your kids, your friends, your business relationships! Affirm their value to them and for them!*

Legacy You're Leaving

What legacy will we leave? What will people remember us for? What will people remember us as? What do we want them to have known us as? The life legacy we leave is the life we live – right now. Let's write a life legacy that defines, not who you are right now, but who you are by faith. You will be remembered; how you're remembered is completely up to you. Here's why we're going to write a "Legend You" life legacy. Covey states, "Just as breathing exercises help integrate body and mind, writing is a kind of pyscho-neural muscular activity which helps bridge and integrate the conscious and subconscious minds. Writing distills, crystallizes, and clarifies thought and helps break the whole into parts." From this "Legend You" life legacy, you can take small snippets and turn them into your affirmations. Start with the end in mind. What do you desire to be? Visualize what this person and the space you create looks like. Visualize the results you create for yourself and all those in your life. Imagine how it makes you feel? What do you desire to do? It's pretty basic and taking into consideration the four P's of affirmations, let's fill in the following, starting with, "I am." After the words, "I am," define what you are. Here's my "father role" statement:

> "I am a proactive father pouring love into my kids and nurturing them with powerful beliefs and responsible, virtuous actions. I am

role modelling these beliefs to them. I am intentional in my time with them, dating them, playing with them and being fully present with them. My kids are my biggest fans and I'm their biggest cheerleader!"

Write yours for every role you find yourself responsible for at this moment in life. Print a form from our website and fill it out. Frame it. Put it on your bulletin board at work. Review it daily. Live in it and affirm it. Focus all your energy, not on fighting the old fears, but on creating what you affirm in faith. Legend You – yes, you! Avoid thinking legends are reserved for the rich, famous, celebrity and elite people in the world. It's all a mindset. Now, accept that you're legendary and start doing legendary things! *Draw a line in the sand today and step into living legendarily.* Your story is waiting to be told around future campfires … if people still tell stories around campfire a century from now. Some people call this a personal legacy statement, a personal mission statement or some other name. The name doesn't matter. For this book we're calling it, "Legend You." A great sales leader, and powerful mentor of mine, Jeffrey Gitomer shares a few considerations as you write:

- Define yourself: Who are you? What are your roles?
- What's your vision for your life?
- What are you committed to creating in life, in your relationships at work, etc.? You may start with a few of your most inspiring words and build out a short sentence around each.
- Define your commitment to grow.
- Define your commitment to inspire others: The examples that you set. The emotions you encourage.
- Define how you will achieve your vision.

What affirmations can you create out of this "Legend You" life legacy to use every day?

Legend You

I am

_____

_____

_____

I am

_____

_____

_____

I am

_____

_____

_____

I am

_____

_____

_____

I am

_____

_____

_____

Blessings to you, Energizer, as you create your Legend You life legacy! Now, post it where you can see it every single day you wake up, and commit to live it fully every single day! **Be legendary because you are!**

Linda Ellis' "The Dash"

There's a poem I read by an amazing poet, Ms. Linda Ellis. It incredibly sums up this mindset that "the legacy you leave is the one you're living right now!" Imagine if today were the last day in your dash. I'd highly recommend going online and buying this poem to post somewhere to remind you of this powerful thought:

> I read of a man who stood to speak
> at the funeral of a friend.
> He referred to the dates on the tombstone
> from the beginning…to the end.
>
> He noted that first came the date of birth
> and spoke of the following date with tears,
> but he said what mattered most of all
> was the dash between those years.
>
> For that dash represents all the time
> that they spent alive on earth.
> And now only those who loved them
> know what that little line is worth.
>
> For it matters not, how much we own,
> the cars…the house…the cash.
> What matters is how we live and love
> and how we spend our dash.
>
> So, think about this long and hard.
> Are there things you'd like to change?
> For you never know how much time is left
> that can still be rearranged.
>
> If we could just slow down enough
> to consider what's true and real
> and always try to understand
> the way other people feel.
>
> And be less quick to anger
> and show appreciation more
> and love the people in our lives
> like we've never loved before.

If we treat each other with respect
and more often wear a smile,
remembering that this special dash
might only last a little while.

So, when your eulogy is being read,
with your life's actions to rehash…
would you be proud of the things they say
about how you spent YOUR dash?

This poem is powerful – *we get to define our dash!* A question we can ask ourselves is this, "If my eulogy were to be read, what would my wife, my kids, my loved ones, my colleagues, and my community read? Above is our opportunity to define that. To write the legacy we will bequeath to those coming after us! To live now as "Legend You!"

CHAPTER 8
VISIONART

simply, start painting your picture

"Dream lofty dreams, and as you dream, so you shall become. Your vision is the promise of what you shall one day be; your ideal is the prophecy of what you shall at last unveil." – James Allen

Miracle Poster Board

It was "Dream Board Night." Stacks of magazines, construction paper, glue sticks, scissors and poster boards decorated a break room full of tables. Joy, our receptionist had ordered pizza. The families of Turner Machine Company gathered on this special night. "What was this night all about?" you may be asking.

We planned a fun-filled night putting Dream boards together. A simple Dream board. Who thought you could have so much fun flipping through magazines and clipping out pictures that struck your fancy. Whatever the magazines lacked, we'd jump on a laptop, Google the picture, and print it off. Gluing those pictures to poster boards, everyone left with a Dream board. **Sound too simple**? Some of us at the time thought it was, too; but, we went along with it anyway. Most of us had a lot of fun. The results, however, speak for themselves. Jen and my boards were completely different. She put five, big things on her board. I put about fifty on mine. Hers were a sewing business, a van (indicating she wanted to grow our family of two kids), a picture of four kids and girl-friends holding hands (three, deep friendships). Three years later, we had a beautiful van in the garage and paid for, four healthy kids, and Jen had grown herself exponentially to find the ladies she was going to deeply connect with. This was no small ordeal for Jen who's an introvert and very much polar -opposite from my personality. She learned about herself, amplified her strengths of deep communication and forming trust, and not only did she form these friendships, every other relationship in her life benefitted. My company name had been formed, so I put a speaker's face in the center of my dream board, a best-selling book, connecting with business leaders, going back to school to get my degree, making a bigger impact globally with a pic of kids from Africa, a loving marriage, 4 smiling kids, building a go-cart with my son, singing, and running a marathon. I didn't run at the time, yet within a year, I ran my first 5K and a year later, completed my first St. Jude marathon. Today, I'm on a quest to run a marathon in all fifty states by 40 raising awareness and funds for childhood cancer, I began singing shortly after, of course the kids happened, the book miraculously appeared, and I began speaking more with my inner-city kids' outreach, and then to a sales team in Nashville, and then over 20 times professionally. I went back to school to earn my degree in communications, and began coaching executive teams connecting with business leaders like crazy. While Jeremy and I haven't built our go-cart yet, we've put robots and birdhouses together and my intentionality with my kids skyrocketed. Was there magic in the poster boards we used that night? No. The key is this. *We planted some seeds that night in the most fertile soil this universe possesses – the soil of our minds.* We painted a vision for our lives that night. We raised our perspective and heightened our frequency by holding our vision constantly before our minds. Have you cast a vision for your life? Have you painted yours?

Visionary

Being a visionary and casting a vision comes first. Writing it and making it plain and clear needs to be a quick followup. Think about Dr. Martin Luther King Jr. Here was a man who decided his vision was worth everything and gave everything to delineate a plan! What a notable visionary & champion he was! Visionaries see life clearly. They've raised their perspectives to imagine what the future could look like, and the destination is crystal clear in their minds! In his book, *Kingdom Man*, Tony Evans called this perspective, "the long-range view of life." Visionaries are filled with hope & belief! This hope & belief compels them to action! It drives them, guides them & energizes them! They are contagious because they offer hope & belief to others! Are you a visionary? Do you envision your life & what could be? Here's a simple definition, "a person with original ideas about what the future will or could be like." We have one life, only one! What will it be? What will we make of it? Reserve a small slice (a tiny fraction of your life) to unplug completely and think about your life. Ponder what's in your heart. What vision do you have for the future? Why settle into the rhythm of life without ever stimulating thought, dreams and faith? Someone once said that if we did all the things we are capable of, we'd astound ourselves. Dream & envision your future today! Imagine if Leonardo da Vinci had left Mona Lisa in his mind, no one would have known; and, we'd have never known. *Where there is no vision, creativity is left dormant, passion is wasted, stagnation occurs, and energy is stifled.* I love how Brendon Burchard says, "By deeply contemplating higher aims, we energize ourselves to pursue them" Purpose to become a visionary for you, for your family, for your kids, for your colleagues, for your clients and for your community. A visionary is one who can see the future and further, convince people to see that future collectively. They think and dream complexly, yet they speak and define it simply. They can bring clarity to confusion. They innovate and think outside the box. They imagine. They start with a blank sheet and begin to put definition on 1, 5 and 20 years down the road. Are you a visionary – an artist of a compelling future? Visionaries are fearless, for fear would seal their lips and never allow them to utter their vision – sometimes as unrealistic as it seems. I like how someone said about a company's vision, "It must be slightly between unrealistic and impossible." Cherie Carter Scott said, "Ordinary people believe only in the possible. Extraordinary people visualize not what is possible or probable, but rather what's impossible, and by visualizing the impossible, they begin to see it as possible." Create your vision today. Great visionaries started with a personal vision that went viral. Hope & believe in your vision! It will motivate & energize you! In doing this, you may just be that contagious spark to offer hope to someone else!

World Changers

Great visionaries do not only have a long-range view of their lives, but of others' lives as well. Think of world-changers for a moment. What good world-changers throughout human history come to your mind? People who made a huge impact. People who blessed others with their lives. People who inspired and did incredible things. They were kids once. They grew up. Some vision captured their heart. Did they possess something in common? Were they born with titles, or did they get lucky? Did they win the popularity contest or have an easy life? That must be it: easy life, popularity, titles and luck! These come nowhere close. In fact, most world-changers overcame incredible odds and perhaps never possessed a title. Most were scoffed as if they were childish! To many, world-changers' dreams seemed so outlandish! Take George Washington who Congress almost replaced as general of the Continental Army. His resolve, perseverance, and nothing short of Divine intervention is why we call ourselves Americans today. Winston Churchill was almost pronounced a political failure before stepping out of a flawed past to be the unbreakable backbone against horrid Nazism. The list could go on. Anne Frank being among this noteworthy tribe said, "How wonderful it is that nobody need wait a single moment before improving the world!" Seriously? This unwavering belief from a girl who was killed at the hands of her Nazi captors? This is the one thing world-changers have in common – unwavering belief. *They believed they had a purpose in this world, so they made their life count for others.* Their life visions encompassed more than themselves. They raised their perspectives and in doing so, multitudes raised theirs as well! Trials beset them, yet with faith and endurance, they resolved to get stronger through the struggles. Their unwavering belief that they could change the world drove them to action. We know from some of their journals and history, that they prepared, learned, tried and failed often, but they always got back up! These people made a difference. They made the same difference one-on-one as they did for millions. Making history was never their intent; making a difference was! Are you making a difference for somebody today? That's all it takes. A heart to change this world one person at a time. You can start changing the world today and indeed, it's a wonderful thought! *Be a world-changer; but, you cannot truly change the world until you change your world.*

Declaration

Let's put ourselves back in time for a moment and visit a defining moment for thirteen colonies that would later become the United States of America. The treacherous assignment of drafting a declaration of independence not only saw furious retribution from a mother country, it tried the very soul and resolve of the founders of the United States. People were tired of oppression. The imagination of opportunity and hope of liberty lay simmering deep within. The honorable JT Headley beautifully sets his pen to paper in his famous book, *The Life of Washington*. I include a larger portion below to help us imagine what hope being invigorated in people's souls looks and feels like:

"When the day arrived, the declaration was taken up and debated article by article. The discussion continued for three days and was characterized by great excitement. The next day, July 4th, 1776, was appointed for final action. It was soon known throughout the city, and in the morning, before Congress assembled, the streets were filled with excited people, some gathered in groups engaged in eager discussion, and others moving toward the State House. All business was forgotten in the momentous crisis the country had now reached. No sooner had the members taken their seats, than the multitude gathered in a dense mass around the entrance. The old bell-man mounted to the belfry, to be ready to proclaim the joyful tidings of freedom so soon as the final vote had passed. A bright-eyed boy was stationed below to give the signal. Around that bell, brought from England, had been cast more than twenty years before the prophetic sentence, 'PROCLAIM LIBERTY

Chapter 8

THROUGHOUT ALL THE LAND UNTO ALL THE INHABITANTS THEREOF.' Although its loud clang had often sounded over the city, the proclamation engraved on its iron lip had never yet been spoken aloud. It was expected that the final vote would be taken without any delay, but hour after hour wore on and no report came from that mysterious hall, where the fate of a continent was being settled. The multitude grew impatient – the old bell-man leaned over the railing, straining his eyes downward, till his heart misgave him and hope yielded to fear. But at length, at two o'clock, the door of the hall opened, and a voice exclaimed, 'It has passed!' *The word leaped like lightning from lip to lip, followed by huzas that shook the building.* The boy-sentinel turned to the belfry, clapped his hands, and shouted, "Ring – ring!" The desponding bell-man, electrified into life by the joyful news, seized the iron tongue and hurled it backward and forward, with a clang that startled every heart in Philadelphia like a bugle blast. "Clang – clang!" it resounded on, even higher and clearer and more joyous, blending in its deep and thrilling vibrations, and proclaiming in long and loud accents over all the land the glorious motto that encircled it. Glad messengers caught the tidings as it floated out on the air and sped off and every direction, to bear it onward. When the news reached New York, the bells were set ringing, and the excited multitude surging hither and thither at length gathered around the Bowling Green, and seizing the leaden equestrian statue of George III which stood there, tore it into fragments. When the declaration arrived in Boston, the people gathered to Faneuil Hall to hear it read, and as the last sentence fell from the lips of the reader, a loud shout went up, and soon from every fortified height and every battery the thunder of cannon reechoed the joy. Washington drew up his army and had the declaration read to each brigade in turn. The acclamations with which it was received showed how thoroughly the troops were penetrated with the principle of Liberty."

Think of the power of this vision. A vision that would carry a young nation through a daunting and impossible war. This vision would not only see a Constitution ratified and stepping stones for true equality and freedom established, this powerful and prophetic vision – The Declaration of Independence – would light the way for nations to follow for well over two centuries.

Your Declaration

What's your empowering vision? What does your life in 1, 3 and 20 years look like? When will you make your declaration? The business of life robs us the time for vision. Why wait for crisis to reframe and restructure our life vision? Coasting through life looks appealing; yet, it's the biggest Ponzi scheme out there. Fear grips our heart, and we delay imagining and believing a life of abundant joy can be ours. *The most powerful voice for you is yours; too often we're speaking in the past tense with negative tone!* Dreams and hopes lay simmering deep within hearts around you. When your life's bell begins to ring, you not only realize new life, you inspire the same for your fellowman! When you dream it, think it, write it, and speak it. When you prophesy it, it will manifest itself. Speak it! Declare it! Speak your vision loudly! Your vision is your WHY of living! Your vision is the imagined realization of your life purpose! Simon Sinek says, "Dr. King didn't change America by himself." He wasn't a legislator, yet legislation was created to give all people equal rights. It wasn't Dr. King who did this, it was millions of others whom he inspired. The vision of the leader – their charisma – will attract. Like Sinek says, the innovators and early adopters turn what was once just a dream into a provable and tangible reality, and "when that happens, a tipping point is reached, and things really start happening." Do you have the faith to declare your dream and the perseverance to keep right on proclaiming and striving for it until it becomes a reality?

A Kid's Imagination

    Go back to when you were a kid. Remember your mindset? You were fearless and the further you go back, the more fearless you become. Remember dreaming as you looked through a toy magazine. Remember the LEGO commercials, the G.I. Joe advertisements? Remember the life vocation you planned out – the scientist, astronaut, nurse or president? Anything was possible. John Eldrige, in his book, *Wild At Heart*, states, "Most men think they are simply here on earth to kill time – and it's killing them. The secret longing of your heart whether it's to build a boat and sail it, to write a symphony and play it, to plant a field and care for it – those desires are the things you were made to do … explore, build, conquer – you don't have to tell a boy to do those things for the simple reason that it's his purpose!" We learn fear as we grow up and many don't escape the trap of conformity. Perhaps we told someone our dream and they laughed at us. We became the joke at school. Painful to remember? Well, take this into account that if they laughed, it means we were on the right track of wanting more out of life! Don't hold it against them, forgive them, love them, and believe in your dreams – let the energy of those empowering dreams give you a powerful drive back into your life. There is vast energy transmitted through thought, and like Jon Gordon wrote in *The Energy Bus*, "when you identify what you desire and write down your vision, you begin the process of mobilizing the energy to create the life you want." Vision: the proverb goes, "Where there is no vision, the people perish…" Write a vision for your life. For startup businesses, writing a vision statement is imperative. It helps them navigate in uncertainty & stay focused on the plan! *Your life is your business. Write your vision! Know what you do & why you do it!* Reflect on this often! Too often, we don't dare to dream big dreams because they'll sound ridiculous to our friends and we risk being laughed at. Easy to imagine big things, but we quickly retreat to reality never daring to breathe a word to anyone. Another reason we dreamed and imagined big things growing up is because we weren't busily rushing through life trying to keep up. We had the bandwidth to think and a vivid imagination. Believe it or not, we've put our own constraints on ourselves, and because we don't truly believe in the power of our thoughts – the power of every thought – we simply don't make thinking a priority. We'd rather adopt what the thought leaders and the imaginators are coming up with. Start by making 10 minutes each day to do nothing but think! When is your time? Go ahead and pick a time that you will make work each day: _____. Think, dream, imagine your life as you'd like it. Do it consistently enough and you'll see patterns form, you'll start to get in touch with your thought-traffic and be better equipped to harness that power. *To the one brave enough to be a kid again, to think – to really think and imagine – to dream again, to speak that dream into vision and to create the reality of that vision; to the one courageous enough to boldly, and full of faith, claim the impossible as possible, to this one opens endless possibilities!* The deep thinkers from all past ages as well as the more practical of men have all recognize the fact that imagination has power. Napoleon said, "imagination rules the world;" Glen Clark said, "imagination, of all man's faculties, is the most God-like." "The faculty of imagination is the great spring of human activity and the principal source of human improvement," said the famous, Scottish philosopher, Dugald Stewart.

What's to say that what you write down on your Vision Board won't become the best that ever was of its kind. Might there not arise a greater life than all the greats who've already passed this way? What's to say the greatest classics aren't yet to be written, or the greatest symphonies yet to be composed? Are the best inventions, cures, businesses, marriages and communities in the past? I say, they don't have to be. Until we start envisioning, declaring and writing our vision, we can almost assuredly say, perhaps the best has already come and gone. Yet at the moment you grasp that pen and stroke the first mark envisioning a great life before you, and by faith, continue to simply paint your life's picture, you will join me and millions in shouting to the universe, The best days are yet to come – it is we who will go create them! So, dream my friend! Dream! Why is creative imagination difficult? It takes faith. "Faith is the element which transforms the ordinary vibration of thought created by the finite mind of man into the spiritual equivalent," said Hill. How many times throughout history can it be said that one kid, one woman, or one man imagined one idea that changed everything. That's where it starts. Heaven and earth align behind the one willing to exhibit faith to imagine, envision and speak into existence that which once was not.

Purpose

From creative imagination comes vision. From vision comes purpose. Discover your purpose. "A man without a purpose is like a ship without a rudder," said Thomas Carlyle. Most are purposeless on account of having no vision. What gets you fired up and keeps you driven to achieving great things in your life? Discover your core motivation. What do you want out of life? Who's it for? What impact do you want to leave? What's important to you? What's your desire? Ask questions like these to find out what inspires you deeply and inwardly. What squeezes your heart? *It's when the mind, soul and spirit align into what our purpose is that we experience an uprising of the deepest energies lying dormant inside.* Committing to living fully in our purpose will ignite deep internal energy that wells up and over driving you to your best self! Your life's too precious to squander, too priceless to waste, and too powerful to live any other way than energized.

Believe

When you commit to anything in life, change will occur. Commitment is a powerful thing. How committed are you to your beliefs? To your dreams? Too many times, we dream and that dream sparks the magic of belief and life inside of us. Then, someone comes along and tells us how it will never work, it's not possible, or how they failed at it. We quiver inside. We doubt ourselves. We subscribe to their beliefs. Many of us look for validation of our beliefs. You see this everywhere in society. We want people to see things our way and if they don't, we question our own beliefs to see if they're too far out there. Maybe not right at first, but eventually. We then either waver or continue believing. Not saying at times our beliefs are off and we should consider adopting a more empowering belief. However, our seeking validation traps us. We place more legitimacy in what others believe about our beliefs. Here's the key. If our beliefs are virtuous, if they will drive valuable behavior, and deliver a benefit to our world, then we can have confidence they're solid. You're a world-changer needing to mix a bit of courage into your life to charge!

Find people to bounce your dreams off of, and accept guidance in forming your beliefs. We discuss this in greater depth in the "Scrum Time" chapter. These people must be dreamers, believers, doers and achievers. These people need to be powerful sources of life that you thrive when surrounded by. Filter your mind against small talk and short-sightedness. Believe! Don't let anyone steal your dream! I love how Les Brown states, "Our dreams were given to us." Your dreams make magic happen inside of your mind. Your beliefs (of what's possible) will either stimulate or stifle your mental energy. The fight for empowering beliefs is the fight to release energy into everything you do! *A solid vision and a firm belief for where you're going will be a bridge over many waters!*

Vision Board - Your Life's Canvas

There are plentiful stories of people who arrived at the end of their life with regret and remorse. Many of these had plenty of fame and fortune. What happened? They left fully living and deeply loving on the table. They allowed what others thought they should do be the brush strokes on their canvas, or they spent their life painting someone else's canvas because theirs had a tear or blemish. They couldn't go stand in front of their easel, face the wound and dipping the brush of healing into paint of forgiveness, blot out the blemish. What would become of the bitterness that consumes them? Why give it up? Others spend their colors on the canvas of addiction and leave a pale, yellowing and empty canvas as the only heirloom their family will have for remembrance – wasted legacy. Friend, what is planned for your canvas? For what purpose was your beautiful life created? Have you considered painting your picture? Have you considered what it is you want out of life? Have you allowed your mind to dream, to imagine, to envision what impossibility you could make possible? Have you dared to be a day-dreamer? It's your canvas; it's your life. Knowing who you are, and what's important to you – the purpose you find in life – are the two foremost keys to unleashing a powerful vision for your life! Ask yourself, "Who am I?" and "What's my purpose in life? The answers don't need to be perfect. Perfection isn't the goal; starting to proclaim your vision is the goal. Your vision will become clearer as you state it. The fact of the matter is, most people have some idea of what they want, or they may know who they are; but most haven't put the two together. What's more, many of us haven't stated any sort of faith-filled vision for our lives. Most people have never declared what it is they wish to become. Most don't take the time. After all, why should we? The majority don't, and many just don't know where to start. We've stated our vision with a smidge of confidence and we're laughed at or scorned. We decide to fold up any vision we had, or thought we had. We stash the one dream that made our soul come alive and live blending in with society. We numb ourselves with the frolic and fun while we walk down life's path amusing ourselves with mediocre results. We never rise to our greatest potential, powerfully and purposefully claiming our destiny. Friend, this moment, right now, is your moment! Will you paint your picture? Simply, start! Claim a powerful vision for your life!

Visionart

Art! Who loved this subject? I always thought art was amazing, and while I'd probably be considered an abstract artist as opposed to a classical, I learned that no matter what piece the art, every artist has their style, and there are certain characteristics that critics look for to classify art as good. How do we go about taking the vison that's floating around in our head and begin painting our powerful life picture? Artists are awesome! They take a canvas and with deliberate strokes create art! They spend a lot of time mixing colors, preparing the canvas, and envisioning the painting. Is it all just for a painting? The answer is yes. Artists love creating! They love the intricacies of the process. The masterpiece comes years after daily growth! *Believe it or not, we're all artists! We've been given the greatest canvas – it's called life. Some have painted on this canvas in beautiful ways, and some have perhaps marred the canvas. What's past is past, but today your actions are the paint. Paint-overs are possible because grace and mercy are abundant!* Today is a fresh start! Will you pick up the brush and paint? Have you envisioned what you want out of life? Wipe the slate clean so to speak, and let envisioning what could be, motivate and energize you! The definition of envision is "to picture mentally, especially some future event or events: to envision a bright future." Are you afraid of envisioning? Some are. Be courageous and envision! Dream! Start painting small strokes. Love painting and paint every day! Be intentional! The masterpiece comes slowly by getting better and better, but YOU have to start!

Simply

We've been talking about thinking, imagining, dreaming, declaring and painting. Now, let's get the sparks that are happening in our mind out onto paper. We've all heard the **K.I.S.S.** acronym – *Keep It Simple, Superstar*! Well, let's do just that. There's no need to reinvent Steven Covey's mastery of the four parts of self. Let's break our lives down into these quadrants as he defined before us:

- Body – need to live (house, car, what you eat, exercise, finances, tangibles).
- Mind – need to learn (intellectual, reading, college degree, new skill).
- Soul – need to love (family, kids, people, connection, relationships, emotions, feelings, love).
- Spirit – need to leave a legacy (impact on the world, making a difference, cause, world hunger, faith, hope).

Vision Board

Vision board or dream board, call it whatever; having one's the important part. Vision literally ignites energy deep in your soul. A dream board is one of the simplest, exciting and straight-up fun creations to add to your life, and the effects on your life will be the most profound! Guaranteed! Here's why. Take out a sheet of paper and draw a line vertically through the center of the paper. Now draw a line horizontally through the center. The intersection is the center of the paper and represents you. Write body, mind, soul and spirit in each quadrant. Pause right now. Take two solid intentional minutes to think – think deeply – about each category. Change your perspective. Climb on that Lear jet again and climb to 30,000 feet. Where could you be in 20 years? In 3? What would you have to go do this year to get there, and what's a small step you can take right now? Now, according to the definitions of body, mind, soul and spirit, write three things in each quadrant that you'd like to do, create, or become. Scratch some things down in this book. It's all good. It's all faith. Isn't it amazing how a pen and paper can literally change the world? *One faint line of vision put to paper is greater than ninety-five percent of humanity can boast ever doing; and, on that line stands your destiny ready and waiting to come into view.* Now, your mind is going to begin formulating some small steps to set in motion the start of progression towards realizing this dream. It's that simple. Let your vision board be the story board of your life! NOTE: Vision boards aren't just for physical things, but emotional as well. Put emotional goals down in writing. Visualize yourself succeeding emotionally. This way, when you're in the real-life situation, you have something in the limbic brain that can get going for you! Therefore, visualization and affirmation are so vital as they invoke our emotions and get positive habits entrenched. As you write, consider grabbing a poster board and find the expression of what you write down in some form of a picture. Go search the internet or a magazine and clip the picture out of the thing you've envisioned. Don't settle for anything, but get as close a representation or draw a picture – if you can. Why? Well, let's look at the RAS effect.

RAS Filter

Did you know we have this amazing filter in our brains that keeps us from going crazy? It's called our Reticular Activating System – RAS Filter. We're bombarded with so much stimuli that our brain couldn't process it all at once, and certain situations call for different reactions. In new spaces, our RAS is on high alert, and we take in only what our RAS deems we need to know. On the other hand, we let our guard down in familiar spaces because our RAS has already processed the data here. Here's something about your RAS filter. Once you begin visualizing, you're pinging the RAS system to let it know it's safe to open your mind to the things that will make this certain thing, idea, behavior happen. Visualization opens the RAS filter. Your limbic mind begins this journey and is at first, reactively suspicious of your visualizations and affirmations. They're new. With enough faith and perseverance though, your RAS begins accepting, and then becomes your greatest ally expecting the materialization of that which you're visualizing. Not magic, just how your RAS, conscious mind and subconscious mind work together. *Visualization and affirmations hand over to your subconscious mind a picture so clearly defined that allow faith and persistence to step in. This unleashes an energy so real, it will literally astound you.* Hill states, "Your subconscious mind works continuously while you are awake and while you are asleep."

Visualization

Here's how our RAS filters and our Dream Boards go together. If you can take a picture of what you envision and continually hold it before your mind, your RAS Filter will start opening when you come in touch with the resources needed to accomplish the dream. That's why the people who commit their dreams to writing, and take consistent actions to make those dreams happen, see them come to reality. They're holding the vision before them. This is the map. The map delivers to the mind the first step and then the next. When progress is happening, you know it deep down inside and there is a stirring of your entire being. You simply stay excited about your dreams, and your mind attracts and picks up on the resources needed to make it happen. Here are a couple examples. A friend of mine's daughter put a horse on her dreamboard. He had no idea she'd ever wanted a horse. Within a week, he overheard someone talking about needing to pay someone to take care of their horse living at this equestrian center. While the immediate answer didn't give her a horse, it gave her every chance to ride, to learn and to care for a horse and they loved the arrangement for many years. Another lady absorbed herself into a diet to lose weight. She put a swimsuit model on her dream board; it became essentially easier as she held this picture in her mind on a daily basis. Visualization can take place without pictures through concentrated thinking and clearly articulating in your mind what this looks like as if it's already been attained. You can create by simply believing, envisioning and then living in that belief. Our minds create our reality, and a picture will make it easier and hold it more consistently in front of us. I always remember Zig Ziglar sharing his story about the "man in the Jockey Shorts." That was his vision. He started jogging, and over time began running. Little by little, slowly, then faster, he ran. Years later at 65, he was running as fast as the Dallas Cowboy's wide receiver. And, in incredible shape!

There's no telling what your vision board will do for you, but by imagining the picture of what you want out of life, through faith visualizing its existence, and mixing in the persistence needed for your desire to become reality, you will achieve far greater than what could ever happen by waiting on happenstance. Like Jack Daly says, "If it's meant to be, it's up to me." What are you visualizing? Your small steps of going to the craft store, picking up the poster board, printing picture or cutting them from a magazine, gluing them to this vision board, and looking at this vision board daily in full faith of its realization are steps of faith. The simple first step of walking into the craft store will align you with a greater power and energy of thought. Try it. Walk in. Feel weird? Like, what am I doing this for? That's the climatic point of the novel. That, my friend, is where faith comes to the rescue! And not only that, when you persist through that same faith, you will receive the plans and attract the resources to you. There's nothing magical about it. It's the law of faith. *Those who exercise faith live on a higher frequency.* Faith, hope and love coexist. You won't pressure anything. You won't force any action. Your actions will always create more value and your mindset will be that of giving out love, giving of your resources and energies into others' visions that align with you. It's an interconnectedness and alliance of energies where no selfish ambition can stand to exist. The silliness that one flimsy dream board could change and reshape your entire life turns out not to be silly after all. The magic isn't in the dream board at all, but in the thoughts that you will now hold continually in the forefront of your mind! Maltz states, "Visualizing – creative mental picturing – is no more difficult than what you do when you remember some scene out of the past or worry about the future. Acting out new action patterns is no more difficult than deciding, then following through on tying your shoes in a new and different manner each morning, instead of continuing to tie them in your old habitual way without thought or decision."

Other things that once devoured your mental capacities and energies will become trivial and you'll chuckle as you quickly let arguments, busyness, laziness or any other mental plague go. You'll realize that nothing can stand in the way of a little clarity and definiteness of purpose! So, start painting your picture, today! Become a visionary! It's not easy, but it's very simple! So simple, most won't grab a sheet of paper right now and start on it. The ones who do will look back in a couple of years completely astounded. I also recommend updating yearly or every couple of years. This may be simply adding to it, writing on it, or renewing it entirely. You start to become more aware of who you want to become and what it is you want when and only when you decide to become more aware. Reflection through journaling are also important because you can gage whether you moved closer to your vision, or at least in its direction. It also provides an organization of ideas and can help you capture and categorize random ideas, lingering thoughts and predominant beliefs of your mind. Hill powerfully states, "Ideas are the beginning points of all fortunes. Ideas are products of the imagination." Take time to reflect, visualize and affirm. This fits the model of making peace with the past (reflect), plans for the future (visualize), so that you can live fully present today (affirm). Perform the most magical ability of humanity. The calling into being that which is not yet. Write your vision and make it so plain so that you can get excited first thing each morning!

Value Creation & Dream Job

I asked Annie, a fellow Middle Tennessee State University student, "What's your dream job?" Not only is this a great conversation starter, you'll be surprised by many of the answers. The answers that require some form of personal growth – stretching – inspire me! Annie wants to be top-level film director at Time Warner! Yes sir! The focus and passion she had in studying tells me she's going to get there! I asked her not to forget me when she does. Do you see the magic in dreams? By having a powerful dream – this vision – ever before her, her studying was more engaged, her participation was more passionate, and you know what else, she kind of walked and talked like a film director. Kudos to the faithful people working right now where they're planted, even if it's not their dream job! Contentment is a virtue! If you're dreaming about something bigger, or you feel passionate about making a difference somewhere else, here are a couple considerations:

- Love what you do now! Yes, love it! It's more a mindset than anything else and the first thing to change before a career is ourselves – our mindsets.
- Determine to bring 200% every day and be a giver, right now where you work.
- Take small steps to learn all you can about your dream job.
- Grow by doing a little something of your dream job (you'll find out if it's really your passion or just "greener-grass"). This may be after hours, on weekends, shadowing someone already doing this kind of work, etc.
- Seek counsel from multiple trusted advisors in your life.

Take these small steps consistently and you'll be amazed at what will happen. Your mindset will change to looking far down the road and small adjustments to life's steering wheel now will get you to your destination. I'll bet Annie and you are working, no, pursuing your passion one day, soon! It's the same law of the vision board, the law of giving, and the law of faith combined. *Give more of yourself than ever before, plant a seed in fertile soil, nurture it through persistent action and one day, you'll sit under the branches of your oak tree.*

Daily Energy for Life

Vision is powerful! Vision infuses your mindset with positivity and faith. Unwavering belief invokes tenacity for the work of bringing the vision to reality. The power of positive thinking demands we face reality and then, in all its grit and grime of daily action and hard work, we choose to believe in the power of positive and faith-filled thinking regardless. *Impractical and superficial positivity is lazy; whereas, realistic and genuine positivity is faith-filled and tenacious.* There's a difference. Superficial positivity slams the door after an argument; then, putting on the "Mr. Nice Guy" look and acting like the argument didn't exist, it forces ingenuine relationships to form. Genuine positivity embraces the Energizer principle of "being, then doing," so the "act" of positivity will never work. Genuine positivity goes back, opens the slammed door, accepts responsibility and asking forgiveness, it makes up. Bottom line, positivity is either realistic or impractical. One is genuine and guided; the other is lying and lazy. Knowing the difference is key to be a truly energized person. They accept work as part of the equation. They expect setbacks and prepare their emotions for them. They are super-heroes who understand kryptonite exists. They know what to do and where to go when it strikes. They face the reality and positively make a difference by creating value in their worlds – their lives, homes, workplaces, communities, relationships, and literally everywhere they go!

What will you do? Will you start envisioning what could be? Will you start dreaming big dreams? Will you face your fears and speak into existence what once may have seemed impossible? It starts with painting your picture. This process lifts your perspective and your perspective installs empowering beliefs. Your beliefs about your worth, your vision and your purpose – getting to serve; getting to contribute – ignite your mental energy. Energy starts in the mind. What the mind can conceive it can achieve. Believing negative thoughts puts you on the defensive and your energy is flowing backward. Negative energy isn't creating true value; instead, it's a trampling on, tearing down, competing, striving, stressed, anxious, bitter and constantly defending ourselves. *Believing powerful, pure and positive thoughts releases creative energy and flows from you. Your mindset is abundant, your methods are passionate, your mission is vibrant. Your energy is flowing forward and attracting every resource needed to accomplish your life's noble purpose.* Our virtuous beliefs are driving valuable behavior and delivering victorious benefit to all humanity!

So, my dear friend, dream dreams and set out pursuing them at once!

Speak them in faith and never stop speaking them. Proclaim your vision until the laughs cease, and faces turn to blank stares then to grins as you realize your vision. With courage and boldness – dream! And like Will Smith told his son in the movie, "Pursuit of Happiness", "Don't let me … don't let anyone – anyone – ever take your dream from you!" Energy starts in your mind – there's magic in dreams.

Definiteness of Purpose

Napoleon Hill coined this; it's what every book on goal setting seeks to teach – knowing what you want to become and do, defining the plan for its achievement, and persevering until it's achieved. It's so simple; we overcomplicate it. Most don't know what they want. Perhaps stemming from a sense of undeserving, they fear wanting anything. So, they wander through life fitting into the group. Settling. Looking to others for the plan instead of unleashing the magic of creative imagination and faith. Many will go through life as Zig Ziglar put it, "wandering generalities instead of meaningful specifics." When you zoom in on what it is you definitely want, it will require zooming in on some definite thinking. Through purity of heart to care for the needs of others, articulating a solution, integrity of character and being true to yourself and carrying yourself in a definiteness of purpose, you will attract success to you.

Faithfulness to proclaim and press toward your dream will bring to fruition your prophesied destiny! This faithfulness is perseverance toward a worthwhile goal or ideal! This faithfulness is perseverance and it realizes results. This definiteness of purpose is paramount! Covey tells the story to one of my favorite songs, "The Impossible Dream!" The song comes from the musical, "Man of La Mancha". It's the redemptive story of a medieval knight who met a woman of the streets. Through her choice of life-style, she found validation by men taking advantage of her. "But," Covey shares, "this poet knight sees something else in her, something beautiful and lovely. He sees her virtue, and he affirms it over and over again! He gives her a new name – Dulcinea – a new name associated with a new paradigm." Covey continues, "At first, she utterly denies it; her old scripts are overpowering. She writes him off as a wild-eyed fantasizer.

But he is persistent. He makes continual deposits of unconditional love and gradually it penetrates her scripting. It goes down into her true nature, her potential, and she starts to respond. Little by little, she begins to change her lifestyle. *She believes it and she acts from her new paradigm*, to the initial dismay of everyone else in her life. Later, when she begins to revert to her old paradigm, he calls her to his deathbed and sings her, 'The Impossible Dream.' Looking into her eyes, the noble knight whispers, 'Never forget, you are, Dulcinea!" Consider the definiteness of purpose of this story and the persistent faithfulness of this song:

> To dream the impossible dream
> To fight the unbeatable foe
> To bear with unbearable sorrow
> To run where the brave dare not go
>
> To right the unrightable wrong
> To love pure and chaste from afar
> To try when your arms are too weary
> To reach the unreachable star
>
> This is my quest
> To follow that star
> No matter how hopeless
> No matter how far
>
> To fight for the right
> Without question or pause
> To be willing to march into Hell
> For a heavenly cause
>
> And I know if I'll only be true
> To this glorious quest
> That my heart will lie peaceful and calm
> When I'm laid to my rest
>
> And the world will be better for this
> That one man, scorned and covered with scars
> Still strove with his last ounce of courage
> To reach the unreachable star

This impossible dream was the only hope this lady had. Similarly, your dream will be the wind beneath your very sails when the going gets tough, when people scoff, and when hurts, disappointments and setbacks come. When you feel like throwing in the towel and giving up, the power of your dream will inspire and encourage you! Many don't realize this power of dreams because they're afraid to dream powerful dreams. See, here's the secret! A powerful dream will never let you go! It will carry you through everything! But, a powerful dream takes courage and boldness! Powerful dreams do not – cannot – reside in a cowardly soul! So, heed these words, and then dream! Dream a dream that will change your life for the better, that will propel your family to healing and victory, that will uplift your community, your city, your state, your country, your world. *A dream so bold and powerful that everyone you meet is touched in some way.* A dream to cure a disease, build a company, serve in a greater way, accomplish a seemingly impossible goal, become an intentional father, or a deep and listening friend. Dream a powerful dream, state it, write it down, repeat it over and over, be consumed by it and let it change you!

Dream Big, Goal Smart & Action Small

Zig Ziglar used to say, "Everyone has goals." We're either aiming for something great in life, or we're aimlessly just settling to try and make it through; but, both aiming and aimless are goals. The one to create something great; the other to just get through. "We don't see things as they are, we see things as we are," said Anais Nin. Life is exactly what we make of it. And our life is the sum total of all of our thoughts? What are you thinking about right now? What's internal? What is swindling your very life away, right now? What's your dream? What are you powerfully envisioning for your life? Have you painted your picture? Are you courageously going after it?

You're much more likely to achieve your goals if they're set properly in the first place. I find that most people struggle setting goals because they haven't done the hard work of dreaming and deeply thinking what it is they want out of life. It's as if we fear painting our vision – setting something down definitely. We might get it wrong and waste our life, so we don't put anything down and sadly, we spend our life on far less than what was possible. Let me encourage you to envision what is it you want and even if it's not perfect, you will get into the habit of definiteness of purpose, clarity of decisions, and focus of actions. The moving car is easier to steer. Once you're going, course corrections will come easier to you. The top of the mountain will never be yours until you take the first step upward. In this book, I want us to empower ourselves and ignite our dormant energies by dreaming and envisioning the life of our dreams. Avoid getting bogged down setting the perfect goal, however. Goal setting comes easiest to those with definiteness of purpose and life's picture painted. A quick, Google search can give you charts, tools, the SMART acronym and anything else you need in actually writing out a goal. However, let's sum it up like this: write down specifically what you WILL accomplish this year to get you closer to your vision; now go one step farther and break that down to quarters and weeks and now you have your targets to hit week to week.

I like to say dream big, goal smart, action small. These actions form your daily targets. They're bite-sized for daily achievement and momentum. *Goals will always work, and the goal setting will naturally force its hand when the vision is yours!* On the other hand, goals won't last, you'll make endless excuses, or it'll take constant heavy-handed supervision to attain the goal when you don't have, understand or believe in the vision. The majority of people who won't believe in a vision never dreamed and believed their own. This is why you must envision your life and paint your picture. Start with your vision! Your energies will be unleashed when you do. From your vision, you will align all energies behind your desire and with persistence, your dreams will be yours. Your 20, 3, and 1-year plans will not be difficult for they will derive themselves from your vision board. The beautiful thing about vision boards is their ability to capture both "by the end of my life" dreams and next year dreams.

Here's what happens for your goals. With this life-long perspective – this powerful vision – continually in front of you. You'll be thinking daily of your life direction so that, naturally, all the little components either easily align or glare back at you, stopping and asking, "Now why are we doing this?" Alvin Toffer said, "You've got to think about the big things while you're doing the small things, so that all the small things go in the right direction." Review your vision daily to deepen the belief and inspire faith. Set specific goals with deadlines for the dreams you've captured here. Be specific and definite, and begin them immediately. But, don't get hung up on perfection. Add to your vision board as valuable thoughts manifest themselves into great ideas. I like how Joe Vitale said, "A goal should scare you a little and excite you a lot," Goals must align with your vision – what you really want out of life. This is the greatest secret of goals. Some people don't write any goals down and go farther and are happier because they're honest about what they really desire and go after that in everything they do. Others write goals down and struggle because they really don't have a deep desire that will naturally stem from a powerful life vision! Sure, it might be a coach's desire for you to do a certain thing, or a friend's belief that you should. Until you get clear about your life vision – what you want out of life – goals are a forced formality! *You should have goals; but you must first have a vision! This is so key! Then, the secret sauce is writing down those goals that are aligned with your vision.* When you write your goals down (not typed) you have 47 percent better chance of getting them done. Keeping them in front of you daily increases this exponentially. Get your business goals infused into your life vision! Your employer will be best served when you figure out how to align your work with your vision. If part of your life vision is becoming a kinder person, use every interaction at work to help you. If it's increasing revenue in your life, let your leadership know. Ask how you can grow and add more value to gain promotion. Align your business and personal goals with your life vision! Because you entered someone else's employee does not mean you stopped being you. Many turn a lot of themselves off at work and that's why 80% of people hate their jobs. Turn it all on! Our workplaces crave authentic, real people. Be a person with a powerful life vision. Align all goals with this vision! You will be the cream that rises to the top!

Did you know that the happiest people aren't those with a lot of stuff, but are the people who are happy with the things they have. It's interesting to ask people why they belong to the club, why they own the boat, why they have this or that. I've heard so many former boat owners say owning a boat was a money-drain or ended up being a negative experience; they seemed completely disgruntled! Many, on the other hand, truly enjoy boat ownership and rejoice when the sunset and water meet at the horizon; love when the water claps from the splash of the bass on the end of the line; and allows the experience of deep connection and relationship with a business partner or fishing friend. Many will get the boat, buy the truck, over-extend themselves, and live above their means simply to live out someone else's vision. They want people to think well of them.

Here's the key. Fear, not vision, is driving them. You want the best guidance? Paint your picture with everything in it right now. Will it serve or distract from your vision? This is the litmus test! It's guided me so well we've been able to launch two businesses debt free. Just recently we've mapped out the dream home as well as one for my mom and every square foot serves the vision of Jen's and my life as we raise our four kiddos and serve our clients. Paint your picture. Be a visionary today. I've seen the guy get up and haul the metal boat and outboard motor to the lake with his son and really enjoy the boat. I've helped my father-in-law sand and Bondo his. ***It's a fun thing to have because it brings you a source of energy in your life, or it's a burden because it swindles your energy.*** We can't fool ourselves, though we try. When we operate out of fear, all the stuff in the world will drain us. When we operate from vision, it's fun and satisfying. Vision takes faith. Faith says take a step, now. Will you? Set meaningful goals to achieve what matters to your life!

This doesn't mean easy goals. Who do you want to become? Set some lofty, personal-improvement goals. Avoid choosing easy; but, definitely choose meaningful. Meaningful means they align with your life vision. You can do anything! What our minds conceive, and our hearts believe, we WILL achieve! I like how someone said, "Set a goal so high you have to grow into the person capable of achieving it!" When you define your goals, you give your brain something new to look for and focus on. It's as if you're giving your mind a new set of eyes from which to see all the people, circumstances, conversations, resources, ideas and creativity surrounding you. With this raised perspective of vision, your mind begins matching up on the outside what you want most on the inside – your goal. It's that simple. Darren Hardy states, "The difference in how you experience the world and draw ideas, people, and opportunities into your life after you have clearly defined your goals is profound!" He couldn't have summarized the Energizer's WHY of goal setting any better. *Goal setting lets you know what to be before you go and do. The being first; then doing second.* The doing is just as important. It's knowing you CAN make a difference and doing something about it. A person with no goals is like a car with no place to go. Albert Schweitzer said, "The number one reason people don't set goals is that they have not yet accepted personal responsibility for their lives." Accept responsibility, dream big, goal smart and action small. Shad Helmstetter wrote, "If you want to achieve your goals, give yourself the right direction (visualization) and the right words (affirmation) – take advantage of your own mind's natural dedication to do for you what you tell it most." Notice, "what you tell it most." I want your vison to be the fire burning in your soul, the light radiating from your spirit and the drive that propels you forward to your greatness! Your level of perspective – your frequency – is a daily choice! Reset! Recharge! Check in with your Vision board daily!

CHAPTER 9
SUNRISE

how to wake up giddy

*"It's not how you feel; it's how you choose to feel.
Choosing to go to sleep means you're choosing to feel
giddy about the fast approaching miracle of a new day!"*

Numb Extremity

"Beep, beep, beep, beep ...." The alarm clock is going off, across the master-bedroom in the bathroom where I've positioned it safely out of reach. Dashing out from under the covers, I step onto what I thought was a solid leg .... Nothing! Crash! To the floor I go. Numb leg! Ever do that? Listen, I know what it's like getting up in a cold sweat, looking for my glasses, realizing my contact lenses are still in resulting in the almost glued-shut eyelids, ultra-blurry vision and yes, additional frustration. I had collapsed in exhaustion the night before. Further, I failed to plug in my phone, which I'd taken to bed with me to catch up on some work. Now, I'm running this piece of technology – the most critical known to man – on empty. Any of this sound familiar? Millions of people face this struggle, and it's understandable. What happens? ***Busy life and not valuing sleep.*** For me, it was the seven years of having children. That is, seven years of Jen having our four children and me trying to help, or sleeping right through the little ones crawling up on top of us in the middle of the night causing the aforementioned extremity to go numb. Or the middle of the night wake-up where you take the kid back to bed and fall asleep in the rocker, on the floor, or half-way slumped over their bed. You startle awake just in time to dash out the door. OK, so this is life and as our precious bundles of joy grow up and sleep terrors become a thing of the past, it's amazing how much rest you get in the same amount of sleep or less. Life phases change. We need to insulate and protect our sleep as much as possible. Over the years, I've had a coach call me if I didn't ping him first, had a friend pick me up and rideshare, and most recently placing the alarm clock in the bathroom across the room and out of reach. I'd even place my washcloth on top of the alarm as my signal to cleanse my face. OK, creativity can continue, but it's all stemmed from one root cause – refusing to acknowledge my need and get enough sleep.

Are there times when we can get plenty of sleep and just aren't enthused about getting out of bed? Sure, there are times we get off. Some stay off for a very long time and dread getting up. Their morning is so dead. I want to help you change your morning ritual – and your evening ritual. I want this chapter to harness the underlying principle that you need a powerful night's sleep just as you need a powerful life vision! It's being; then doing. The two must coexist to be an energizer, and in order to wake up giddy. This chapter is very much about getting excited about life and life still includes our mornings. Can you wake up giddy? Can you truly bound out of bed excited? Yes, you can. It takes work, commitment and trusting the process. If you have a documented sleeping disorder, then consult with your physician; *but, for many, we simply need to reinvent our morning and evening rituals.*

Something every one of seven billion people are blessed to do each day is wake up. So, if we know we are going to wake up, why go through the exercise five times every morning? That's right. Think about how many times we silence our alarms before crawling out of bed. I've lived through times of mastery and failure in this area and what I know is this. If you don't control your day, your day will control you. However, before you can be the sunrise, you must be the sunset. Fighting to go to bed, and how you go to bed, means less fighting to wake up. There are a ton of books written on sleep, finding REM, the perfect morning rituals, quality of sleep, sleep position, etc. While all of these techniques are important, I firmly believe, like me, most people simply try to skimp on sleep. We don't value a good night's sleep enough! We have too much going on. Let me say that again. We have too much going on! We don't value a great night's sleep. Please avoid looking at this chapter as a fix all! I want you to simply stop and reconsider the importance of sleep and then apply the **"5-GETS of GIDDY"**:

- Get Excited,
- Get Some Rituals,
- Get to Sleep,
- Get Up, and
- Get Giddy!

Get Excited

Prepare yourself to be excisted. Set the next morning up for success. Pack your gym bag, layout your reading, set the coffee pot, etc. *Whatever gets you winning early, get it bumped and set so that you can jump up out of bed and spike!* Each night, take some time for reflection. Write down wins and key takeaways from your day. Perhaps you can jot a thank-you note to someone. If you have a notebook, or journal, this is an ideal time for its use. Recalling the days positive choices and how they made us feel allows us to relive the feelings (because feelings are banked in our brains), and it allows our brains to carve better channels to choose positive again and again. Don't miss the "how did it make you feel" part. Invoke your emotional brain and ask, "How did I feel overall today?" Break this down and consider the elements that made you feel one way or another. Ask, "How did my emotions flow today?" "Did I express gratitude, or was I critical?" Ask, "What energized me today?" Pause to reflect, reminisce and journal. If you were a store manager, you'd close the store every day and get ready for customers early the next morning. Friend, your life, your days, your time and moments are much more valuable than a hundred stores. Why not close the store every night? Journaling is closing the books for the day past and prepping for the next. One benefit we offer our clients through *Energy4Execs* coachinbg is a sounding board. We listen to ideas, thoughts and feelings. Often, big ideas come about as a result of intentional journaling. The goal then is to find and implement the ideas that align with your vision. Thinking – powerful, intentional thinking – is crucial to an energized life! Empower yourself and think back over your day and leverage what was learned for all future days.

The difference is being dragged out of bed by an alarm clock or being driven from within by the opportunity to thrive. *We should rename alarm clocks, ignition clocks, for it sounds at the exact time we're to ignite and unleash our deepest energies and stretch and reach our greatest potential!* What's your drive? Do you check in with your life vision – your dream – before you go to sleep? Are you fanning the excitement over the contribution you get to make? Sleeping-in indicates one of two things: not getting enough sleep, or not having a big enough vision. I love how T.E. Lawrence brilliantly stated, "All men dream, but not equally. Those who dream by night in the dusty recesses of their minds, wake in the day to find that it was vanity: but the dreamers of the day are dangerous men, for they may act on their dreams with open eyes, to make them possible." Checking in with your dream and purposing to do everything in your power to make that dream a reality builds the drive that'll push you from the bed. "Although vision tells people where they need to go, purpose tells them why they should go," says John Maxwell. What do you get out of bed before the alarm clock for? Is your vision zeroed down to a purpose? Do you have a compelling WHY? And better yet, is that WHY triggered immediately as the ignition clock sounds? Are you getting excited about the next day before you go to sleep?

Get Some Rituals

I almost wrote routines, but ritual has a more sacred sound to it. I like that! Hold your spaces of morning awakening and evening reflection as sacred times. These are important! Do you have a morning ritual? An evening one? Formulate a simple one and work to make it the most empowering of your life! Just read through the suggestions I list below and pick some that work for you! Come up with some on your own. Avoid trying them all at once, and some may not work at all. These are some simple, tried and true suggestions. Work hard to prune your morning and evening rituals until clarity reigns and excitement flows! I like how Joel Osteen says, "Life begins each morning!" High achievers like Oprah Winfrey, Tony Robbins, Brendon Burchard, Darren Hardy and others emphasize the importance of an energizing morning routine! The main question is, "Do you have one?" Is it too cumbersome and hard to keep, or is it lightweight and energizing? I will caution. Avoid trying to cram everything into your morning routine. Some people want reading, meditation, and this and that – all packed in their morning. Do the physical, first, if you can, as fully waking up your body will stimulate and invigorate everything else – mind, soul and spirit. Then, meditate, read, pray, visualize, affirm, or maybe listen to something great on the way to work. Perhaps you record your affirmations like I did; you can play them during your commute. *The KEY: pick and implement the things that give you a lightweight morning and energize YOU as a whole person!*

... Evening Rituals

- Let eating at dinner time be it. Excessive snacking or heavier foods keep the metabolism going longer and cut into the efficiency of your sleep.

- Drink something soothing like tea an hour or two before lights out.

- After dinner, set the next day up for success. If it's a presentation, review it. A paper, outline it. A plane ride, pack it. A meeting, email the agenda. Going to the gym, have your gym bag ready and your set of clothes loaded in the car. Whatever you can take 5-10 minutes doing - lightweight your morning.

- Do something fun for your soul. For me, it's playing with the kids when home or maybe a short jog or swim while travelling. Maybe it's a walk after dinner, but stay mobile and awake until it's time to sleep.

- A glass of water a couple hours before lights out to stay hydrated while sleeping, or sip a quarter or half glass depending on your restroom needs and life phase. I drink a whole glass before bed and it wakes me up in the morning.

- Stretch before sleeping; sleeping loose is best.

- Adopt proper form and use correct pillows. My best nights I have a roll under my neck, a small pillow in the small of my back, and a larger pillow under my knees for natural bend. Three pillows have been scientifically proven to improve sleep posture. I love travelling and piling the pillows on.

- If you're going to catch the news, do it in the morning after you've inputted YOUR routine of affirmations. Why put a majority of negative news in your brain anyway, especially right before you sleep? What you put in your brain just before you go to sleep will be processed in your subconscious thought as you sleep.

- If you're going to watch a movie, be cautious what heightened sense of drama, negativity or brutality comes with its consumption. Again, the subconscious mind must process this. Imagine, instead, having goals and dreams of our lives or a great book dancing in our minds instead of Hollywood.

- Some humor can be a great relief. I've found from personal experience that the happier I can fall asleep, the better I sleep, so Barney Fife might not be a bad idea. TV shows are often humorous, and the episodes are shorter which could help taper off of greater amounts of media consumption.

- Secure 30 minutes of quiet and calm. This will transform your life. Journal. Journaling forces reflection and is one of the best insurance policies of living fully present. Our *Energy4Execs* clients rave about our customized, daily journaling. It's invaluable to the Energizer!

- Practice reflection: gratitude for blessings past, and those to come; forgiveness for all hurts or failures, of others and yourself, and faith of what will be – Jen and I claim these in prayer.

- Set or review your top three priorities for the next day. I write my top three priorities down and state WHY I cannot wait to jump out of bed to crush them! I once heard Jim Rohn say, "Never start your day until you've finished it on paper!" State these priorities aloud with heartfelt emotion. Psyche yourself up about the next day. Mornings mean leaving the comfort of cozy; and a powerful WHY will help awaken the warrior – you!

- Read something positive, I save my deeper readings for the morning and shorter readings for the evening.

- Electronics away from the bed; plugged in across the room or out of the room.

- Ignition clock set in the bathroom with wash cloth on top.

- If you have a hard time getting up, practice. I've done this, and it works. Practice laying in bed the night before. Set your alarm for two minutes ahead. Get as comfortable and relaxed as possible, and then, when the alarm goes off, get up immediately and imagine it's 5 am. Reset the alarm clock and repeat this process several times each night. You'll help get a new pathway of immediate rising in place. If 80 percent of success is found in getting out of bed, why not practice the art? I read this a long time ago on a blogsite and it worked for me.

- Perhaps some technology – CPAP machine if you have allergies or other conditions that this would aid in better sleep. Consider a sleep study; consult with your doctor if you struggle.

... Morning Rituals

- Set physical defaults like a glass of water by the bed, a book propped open, your running shoes by the chair, etc. Have your first thing cued up.

- When the ignition clock sounds, getting up as opposed to reaching is best – place your clock near the sink with the washcloths so naturally you can visualize splashing refreshing water in your face.

- Have a glass of water by the sink or your bed to sip and drink within the first 5 minutes of waking up and getting ready. This starts your engine like nothing else can.

- Make a move. Your mind is foggy in the morning. Go make a move first. Move your body, stimulate your mind, invigorate your soul and awaken your spirit. This move may be stretching on a mat in your living room, going on a jog around your neighborhood, running, walking the dog, cycling or aerobic machine at the gym. What we know is that regular exercise has absolutely solid health benefits and proven to get your heart rate up, opens your lungs and gets energy flowing.

- Eat a powerful, nutritious protein shake post-workout and then eat light breakfast and/or mid-morning snack. You need replacement for your workout and fuel for your day. Plan your morning fueling well. Josh Axe has some wonderful counsel in this arena. Check out his website: www.draxe.com.

- As soon as you're done making a move, it's best to read or stimulate your mind. You may also listen to a podcast or audio-book on your run. While I save my morning run for worship and prayer – my time of centeredness – I know many who are learning something or simply enjoying some music during exercise. Whatever it is, use the surge of blood flow to awaken the mind and thought either during or right afterwards.

- Right after my move, I'm sitting quietly to meditate and think for 10 minutes. Focusing on my breathing and watching my thought patterns. Then, visualizing what I'm becoming and how this day will be used to grow, to thrive and to love. You may do this in your club's sauna, in the shower, or sitting still in a quiet place. Powerful thinking is so important.

- Revisit your top three things and give a "Whooop!" and charge into your day!

Everyone's different. But, here's what we know. We are bombarded with technology, TV and a constant virtual window into the lives of people we care about via social media. We have past hurts that eat at us and anxiety of what lies ahead of us. We stress internally and because it's unidentified, we ease it with habits such as snacking or surfing social media right before bed – both are fun and addictive. Both are not setting us up to maximize the next day – to be the sunrise. Instead, shorten the time of social surfing and allow something more meaningful to be the last mental exercise before drifting off to sleep. Back the ice cream up closer to dinner time (still working on this one). Take back some calm, quiet thought before sleeping and when you sleep – sleep.

Get to Sleep

Be the sunset! Go to sleep. In the olden days, night meant sleep. Nowadays, shifts of work, red-eye flights, 24/7, non-stop industry and a very fast-pace, require all sorts of bedtimes. Have a time when you go to sleep. Value a good night's sleep. How you go to bed is more important than how you get up. It's the leading indicator as opposed to the lagging indicator of trying to get up in the morning. It's the coach of evening clarity over the coach of early-morning cloudiness. Don't fight to get up; fight to get to bed! Unless you're an amazing dairy farmer, you don't have cows to milk before breakfast. Most of us don't have a rooster crowing at the crack of dawn either. We rely on our ignition clocks to get out of bed. I burned the candle on both ends working three jobs and putting myself through school as a young, married man and dad. Sleepwalking and sleep apnea plagued my childhood, and, with this deprivation, it showed up again. I'd dream as clear as day: getting up, showering, driving to work, and getting about my day only to wake up startled in utter disgust at myself for "sleeping in." So, I worked on my morning motivation. I took Zig Ziglar's advice as a young guy and started calling my alarm clock an opportunity clock. I built a little box with a lid and latch. I called it my opportunity box. Later, I used to go to bed watching TV and eating an ice cream sandwich or snack and drinking a cup of coffee or tea. It was a comfort thing; a reward for a hard day of work I'd tell myself. In reality, it was an addiction I used to cope with the business of life – the stress. What I wasn't realizing, was that these habits stimulated my metabolism and took energy away from replenishing my body to digesting food and inflating my heart rate with caffeine which altered my depth of sleep. *The most empowering realization is that in order to have an epically power-ful morning, you have to control what you can control – your evening.*

A powerful evening sets up an equally powerful morning. You have to be the sunset before you can be the sunrise. Work to narrow your evening ritual down to fit your life phase and fight for meaningful moments of evening clarity to initiate your excitement about the next day! Benjamin Franklin famously said, "Early to bed, early to rise, makes a man healthy, wealthy and wise." After all these years, there's still a lot of truth to that! David Niven PhD, says that people are happiest who limit their thinking to one subject before they lay down to sleep. *Gratitude for the day past or the miracle coming is a great mindset in which to sail away into the land of Nod!* Niven goes on to say, "Don't skimp on sleep. A full night's rest is fuel – energy – for the following day. Rested people are proven to feel better about their work and more comfortable when the day is over." Pilcher and Ott published this statistic in 1998 and I don't believe technology's made it any better. They said, "For those who sleep less than eight hours, every hour of sleep sacrificed results approximately in an 8 percent less positive feeling about their day."

Get Up

Be the sunrise! Be as big as life itself! How do you jumpstart your day? How do you wake up giddy? How you wake up determines a lot about how your day goes. Having some very basic programmed responses that wake you up is key. First thing waking up, you're going to have cobwebs. What's an empowering thought, reminder, quote, statement, or perspective shifter for you? What gets you excited about contributing? Find someone you can text that needs encouragement (my favorite), or find someone to text you if you need some. Build a choice-changer for you. It's not how you feel; it's how you choose to feel. Choosing to go to sleep means you're choosing to feel giddy about this miracle of a new day! Get up and do something first thing in the morning to get yourself excited about what's possible! Drink in the exhilaration of the morning's stillness; burst forth as the brilliance and awe of the horizon's sunlight arrayed in glory. Small business coach, Mark LeBlanc says, "Wake up expecting a miracle!" Some of the greatest ideas are born in quiet stillness; why miss them for the rush? Proclaim something like, "7 billion people are counting on me!" You say, Tim, you're crazy. Well let me ask you. Is anyone less important than the other? Someone is counting on you!

... Pick A Time

The time you wake up is irrelevant. Some people pride themselves on how early they wake up. Some recommend getting up with the sunrise, before the sunrise, and for some, the sunrise is when they go to bed. That's why we say, whenever you wake up, be the sunrise! How you get up is extremely important! Create a super warrior mindset line, word, or chant; one which you'll jump up and rehearse! Be the sunrise and get up giddy. Considering the different shifts and wildly different lifestyles, there is no "right" time to getting up. So, providing you have a strong enough WHY to get out of bed, pick a time that's going to allow for your ritual, and give you time for getting off to a good pace. Not too slow; not too rushed. Have a morning ritual so simple you can do it anytime you wake up. Eventually, the same time helps, but you have to purpose to go to sleep. Say NO to whatever is keeping you up, so you can say YES to getting up. *The powerful morning of exercise and routine is ten times more productive than the worn-out evening of TV consumption.* What's your WHY for getting up? Shakespeare said it like this, "To business that we love, we rise betime, and go to it with delight!" The greatest battle of the morning is clearing the cobwebs and sorting through the feelings you have of not wanting to get out of bed. They're feelings of fear – stagnation; lifelessness. We have this thing inside our great big brain called "negativity bias." It keeps us alive by looking for every possible bad thing that could happen and putting us on high alert. That's why you walk into a room and are drawn to five toys out of place on the floor instead of the dozens of pictures in place on the wall. This negatively-biased voice is at its peak in the morning. All of what could go wrong, and all the opposition before us is thrown at us. Living fully wouldn't dare lay there another moment. The face of morning resembles death symbolic of a distant night; therefore, when the eyes open and conscious mind realizes its first breath, cast off the warmth of immobility, stretch every fiber to its fullest capacity, cleanse the scales of night from your face so that you may radiate and glow as warm and bright as the sunrise. Unless you're a bear in hibernation, you have to wake up each morning. Why do it five plus times each day with the help of the energy swindler called "Snooze"? Snooze is mediocrity's bait! If we woke up envisioning all the good we could do - all the good we will do - we'd grin from ear to ear with a sense of giddiness coming over us!

Get Giddy

Someone may say to you, "do you really wake up happy?" Really happy or not, I'm reprogramming my perspective to see the good in everything, so my choice is based on my ability to choose a higher and better response. Then, when I see the joy that my faith-filled choice brings, I receive ultimate happiness. Morning's can be tough. Our joints creek, backs are stiff, and life can get heavy. If we'll get excited about our life vision, if we'll get some powerful, easy-to-repeat rituals, get to sleep so we can get up, then we will experience a higher rate of giddiness about our life and days. Mark Baterson, in his book, *In A Pit With A Lion on A Snowy Day*, said, "The most important choice you make every day is your attitude. Your internal attitudes are far more important than your external circumstances. Joy is mind over matter" Mark Sanborn asks, "Did you wake up this morning intending to change the world?" To admit this, he agrees, sounds a bit grandiose and even delusional, but Mark continues, "I believe that you do change the world every day, whether you intend to or not. Often it only takes a small act to make a big difference." I love Og Mandino's intentionality to choose positive responses and *I think every morning we must first exercise our mental energies of thought to pull to us the thoughts of gladness, joy, gratitude, abundance and faith that today will be the best day of our lives!* Og says:

> If I feel depressed, I will sing
> If I feel sad I will laugh
> If I feel ill I will double my labor
> If I feel fear I will plunge ahead
> If I feel inferior I will wear new garments

If I feel uncertain I will raise my voice
If I feel poverty I will think of wealth to come
If I feel incompetent I will remember past success
If I feel insignificant I will remember my goals
Today, I will be master of my emotions.

Fact: our emotions and feelings get out of whack. Fact: this usually happens when we first wake up and the subconscious is handing the reigns back to your conscious mind. Fact: we must check our emotions immediately, lest they throw us off the tracks of our empowering and energizing ritual and swindle our energy.

... Good Choice

Is life a "bed of roses"? Is it free of struggles and challenges? Do we smile simply because it's a popular thing to do? Do positive thoughts just happen on their own? Some may have a more "happy-go-lucky" disposition than others, but happiness and finding the good in life are clearly a choice. Why make the choice? We've all met those who "got up on the wrong side of the bed." I've jumped out on that side several times. It's easy and often tempting to stay there; however, the long term isn't worth it! Chances are we're reacting to life instead of realizing its meaning. Victor Frankl, Austrian neurologist, psychiatrist and Holocaust survivor, promoted the philosophy that happiness comes through finding life's meaning in every situation. *Every morning looking in the mirror, it's a choice to believe that YOUR life has significant meaning! This belief produces positive energy!* Your body will move to achieve what your mind chooses to believe. The choice to find the good – life's meaning – kept Frankl alive in the horrid concentration camps. If he could choose good there, how much more should we today!

Seize this day! Breathe deeply! Start finding your meaning even in difficult, painful and challenging situations. Don't react. Look for ways to do good. Make the daily choice to find the good!

... Good Finders

Just like focusing is difficult, finding good isn't as easy as it sounds. Like the speck on my clean, pressed shirt, the 99 percent good pales as our eye focuses in on that one speck. Think about it. That negative political post comes across the news feed and it's so tempting to hit the share button. It's easy to subscribe to negativity in the workplace. Coworkers are talking about the boss, so why not share your two-cents-worth? The details of the couple breaking up often fly too quickly over the airwaves of Messenger, text and phone conversations. What if instead, we stopped and prayed for someone? When's the last time you CHOSE to overlook someone's shortcomings and focus on everything they're doing right? This is love. This is the awesome power in choosing to find the good! This thinking would transform husband-wife, parent-child and employer-employee relationships. *The beauty is, that as you choose to find the good in others, you'll feel good and also realize the good in you.* It's going to take work. I challenge you to take out a piece of paper and write down everything your spouse does right. Write down everything your boss does right. Write down everything your church does right. Write down everything your daughter or son does right. Don't write anything but the good. Now, start praising the good. FOCUS on the good! Watch it expand! BOOM! This is the magic! This is *The Juice!* Nothing worthwhile comes easily. You have to choose to be a good finder. Work at it! Complaining and griping would cease if we chose to be good finders! Energy would increase enormously! Getting up giddy and staying giddy throughout the day means that you're making the choice for good and finding good.

Sunrise

The key is this. Getting up giddy means you are eager about getting after your day! Excitement is a state of mind. To initiate excitement, you think – yes, think – about what you're going to get excited about. That's why vacation is always easier to wake up for. Ralph Waldo Emerson said it like this, "The day is always his who works with serenity and great aims! Waking up giddy means your excited about achieving a result and getting closer to your goals. You're expecting a miracle; no fear. You're ready to charge into the day with all of your gusto. Here's how to **CHARGE:**

> **C** – Commit to love today,
> **H** – Humor to laugh at yourself,
> **A** – Action defined,
> **R** – Remember, you "get to" change the world,
> **G** – Give today your all, and
> **E** – Expect a miracle.

Charge out of bed; 7 billion people are counting on you! Getting up and reconnecting with your why – your perspective on life – gives you a giddy sense of elation. *With a powerful, divine perspective comes extreme clarity eliminating energy-zapping drama!* This is the focus, centeredness and clarity you need to propel you through your day. Join our online group under *Time4Energy's* Facebook page – click and join the group "Sunrise." We'll share ideas and ask questions, so members can add value to each other and help us all raise the bar on how to wake up giddy!

OWNERSHIP

*The thrill & acceleration of living
wholly, fully and abundantly!
Consistently building and bolstering
your energy as YOU decide
where to spend it
passionately & wholeheartedly!*

What would more passion for your work, unstoppable momentum & more peace along the way mean for you?

CHAPTER 10
ENERGY MAPPING
fullness: sources, swindlers and switches

"You cannot give what you do not have." – Andy Bailey

Water Everywhere

"Jen! Jen! I'm a fireman!" I remember coming home from my first volunteer meeting. I was elated! I wanted to help our small city out and this was just the thing. Signing up wasn't that difficult, and before long, I'd driven the truck, blasted the siren, and done a bit of radio training. I felt like big stuff. Listening to the radio day and night, I couldn't wait for the call to come. Finally, it did. Big brush fire – all hands on deck! I was elated. Shouldn't have been, but I was. I race down to the firehouse, park my Toyota, Yaris next to the Chevy and Ford trucks in the gravel parking lot, and jump out to begin suiting up. "Pull your pants out of your boots," said the chief. "You don't want coals to fall down in your boots." Good call. Now, I'm ready to drive the truck, I thought. "We're not taking the truck," said the chief. "It'll get stuck in the field; taking brush trucks." Brush trucks? These pickups had vats of water on the back with small, generator pumps. OK, well at least I'll get to run one of these I thought. No. "Tim, here's a rake." A rake? Yes. "Turn over as much of the burned parts of the brush as you can … that fire can spread under the brush and we've got to make sure we get it all put out." Three grueling, hot hours later and we had the fire put out. I'm glad they knew what they were doing I thought. There was more to firefighting than met my eye. Phew! We pulled up to the front of the field where all the volunteers had gathered. A large engine from the city was parked on the street with hoses pulled all the way out. "What are these hoses for," I asked the chief. "He's going to refill the brush trucks … always put them away full," he said. Oh, ok. I waved toward the city fireman up on the street, motioning as though I were picking up the hose and climbing up on the pickup to fill the vat. He nodded in understanding. Shoving the hose into the vat, I gave the thumbs-up to go ahead with turning the water on. Now, I grew up on a horse farm. Those water hoses were a tenth of the size of these, and they gave some kick when the horse barn's spigot was fully opened. Sizing up this hose against my muscles, physics told me to shove as much of this hose into the vat as possible for extra leverage – the only hope my muscles had of even standing a chance. "OK, turn it on," I hollered. The slight twinge of the grin on the seasoned fireman's face told my gut something was up, but I paid no mind. That hose got stiff so fast, I literally braced my body over it for all I was worth. "You good?" he hollered. "Gooooooood," I grunted looking anxiously in his direction. I wasn't about to say I didn't know how to be a fireman. To my dismay, his hand went back to the lever that was at the halfway point, and he slid it over to full. The rest felt like slow motion. The hose expanded even further and the little kink in the hose holding it in the vat stiffened straight out. *Out of the vat shot the hose-end with force – wild and free!* It shot straight up into the air – me riding it! As it made its ascent, it not only soaked the chief who had his back to me, but it hit the chief from the city south of us who'd joined in to help. Several of the volunteers got splashed; then, as if to signal the grand finale, I nailed the open door of the minivan in which sat our volunteer reporter. Inside of the van soaked, reports soaked, then … BOOM! I hit the ground with a thud as water pressure was cut off. Both chiefs, my team, and the city's seasoned fireman came running over. "You ok?" was said in unanimity. "Yeeeesss," I stuttered getting to my feet. The seasoned fireman pointed toward the "Rookie" triangle on my helmet, and said, "Chief, you might want to teach this kid about a nozzle."

I hadn't even thought about a nozzle, but what a novel idea. You mean I could regulate all that power? Yes! Two lessons I've learned from that story. First, the water in the hose is like the energy in our life. Powerful, and plenteous when tapped into a great source like the huge fire engine parked up on the street. And, second, without a map defining into who and what we're to transfer our energy, we find it being drained and swindled from us into highly unproductive areas. Just like the water flying from the hose with no direction and leaving water literally everywhere, without a nozzle or switch, we too have little control over our energy.

Before we discuss our energy and building a map for transferring that energy for maximum effect, let's discuss this powerful concept of ownership – the second must to igniting our energy! *The hard work is owning our energy, because it means speaking your vision consistently in faith leaving no other direction for the flow of your energy but the direction that's positive, upward and overflowing.* This compels us to tap into positive sources and channel all energy into great assets. There are a lot of actions, issues and relationships we dump a ton of our lifeforce into with no return on our energy. The hard work that truly owning our energy will be is totally worth it! You're worth it! When a liability comes knocking, think of the asset that'll suffer! Invest your energy into assets. Choose powerful and positive sources that transfer thought energies into your mind, energies of health into your body, energies of love into your heart and energies of hope and faith into your spirit! Choose to install positive switches to shut off the flow of your energy into toxic liabilities and only flow into worthwhile assets.

Ownership

Ownership means owning something and signifies you're in control of, or possess something. In our day, we lease, rent to own, finance our real estate through a mortgage, and leverage finances in many ways. We're truly blessed to have so many options available to us. These things make the principle of ownership just bit harder to grasp, though. Back in the day, you pioneered, you built a log cabin, a homestead, a farm, passed that farm down to your children and thus the empire was built. In the industrial age, men found an opportunity, risked everything, shared the vision and built empires. With the technological age, everything is sped up. An application may go viral instantaneously, and it can also be replaced quickly. What once took years can seemingly happen overnight. But, can it? The infrastructure and relationships that once were built over a lifetime aren't there. The depth of ownership is tough to grasp. Take the internet for example. It's become a tool that all of us share, but no one owns. Because we have instant access to an audio book, articles, and research on the internet, deep reading and comprehension has dropped off. We feel like we "own" the internet. Like we're carrying around our own library with us at all times – in a way, we are. But, here's the problem. Our minds know what's out there and that it's out there, but we've not given the advantage of processing this data through reading, or even through writing something ourselves. Speed reading courses sell like crazy because we want to skim information. We really don't own it. So, we know a lot of good ideas, but we really don't deeply believe these ideas. Belief comes through deep investigation and critical thinking. Home ownership feels great. We settle in to paying the mortgage off and only a small percentage figure out how to save hundreds of thousands by paying it off early and truly owning a home.

Complete possession whether of our home, a book's knowledge, or our life – our energy – has become foreign to us. ***Ownership realizes that we are the only ones who can decide where our energy goes.*** We are in complete control. Complete ownership is not a crazy concept, just foreign to our way of thinking. When you realize the freedom extreme ownership brings, you realize that if you truly want to change something, you CAN change it – right now. Brandon Burchard sums it up beautifully when he declares, "A great maturity opens in the human psyche when we accept that we can control our impulses by conditioning our thoughts, and that we alone are responsible for our emotions and reactions in life." Many times, when we dig down deep, we find that our mind has built obstacles. We're waiting on the right conditions or waiting on somebody. We must come to the realization that no one else owns our life, our time, our energy and our responses, except each of us individually. The ownership-rich mentalities are the movers and shakers of this world! They own it!

Definition

Ownership is "The act or art of possessing or owning something." Ownership forms the basis for all beliefs that small steps taken, and small seeds sown yield huge dividends! Ownership accepts full responsibility, takes immediate and determined action, and enjoys the rewards. Ownership mentality doesn't only speak, it speaks and does. Ownership mentality in a sales professional doesn't skim a website and blast off a quick email. Instead, they research, define a fit and customize the email.

Ownership understands that the work done in secret (the quiet hours of thankless toil, the strategic thinking, planning and charting, the brainstorming, the digging deep to learn a new system, a new skill, or reading a book that will help you improve) is the most important work. ***Ownership realizes the principle, "You cannot give what you do not have."*** It's the hard workout that makes me stronger for my family. Just doing the work that you know will build you and make you stronger should be rewarding enough. We can take satisfaction knowing that our capacity is enhanced and increased. Ownership decides to keep energy high in life. Ownership asks, "What's putting a drag on my energy?" "Am I conserving my energy for priorities?" "Am I running life efficiently?" "Am I whole as a person and fortifying my energy?" Ownership asks, "What energizes me?" When you identify this, do more of it! Avoid being stagnant in life. Stay in motion, build momentum, keep growing! This is your life. Own your areas of weakness – that dreaded kryptonite! Overcome by thriving in your strengths, redefining your inner dialogue and having a plan of accountability. Ownership reflects on life's vision often to stay inspired. Ownership stays in motion – stays energized!

Ownership takes full responsibility. Ownership understands that this is my life, no one is coming with a magic wand to save me. Cinderella stories are great, but in reality, most of us can make a change in diet, exercise, mindset, or career any second we decide to own it! Ownership understands that we're to blame for our own choices, but it moves past blame to acceptance and improvement. I like how Hal Elrod defines it, "Blame determines who's at fault; responsibility determines who's committed to improving things." Shad Helmstetter Ph.D. wrote,

"Personal responsibility is at the root of everything we think, do, conceive, fail at, or achieve in our lives. Personal responsibility is the bedrock of all individual action. Responsibility doesn't mean duty or burden; it's the basis of our individual determination to accept life and to fulfill ourselves within it."

Map It

Commit to saving your energy. Transfer your precious lifeforce – your energy – into pure and powerful assets. Avoid transferring your precious resource and very lifeforce into mediocre, toxic and debilitating liabilities. Liabilities give you literally no return on energy. Water in the vat was worthwhile for the fire department, on the ground, it was wasted. Such is the story of our energy when we transfer it into every little argument, disagreement, or poor activity that comes along. We're simply swindled – energy wasted.

Sometimes, great sources like a great workout, healthy food and relationships take time and, since we're so busy, we take shortcuts. Soon, we become stagnant. We feel tired. We feel sluggish, or we feel bored, unexcited, or burned-out in life. *Most people share their biggest hold ups, obstacles and energy swindlers are these: entrenched habits, being too busy and discord among relationships.* Things worthwhile take time; we simply haven't taken the time to map our energy. Just by clarifying and naming the swindlers, we can reframe and overcome them. Let's map our energy and talk about sources, switches and swindlers. If we map out our energy sources and swindlers without an honest assessment of how they ultimately leave us feeling, we'll miss a powerful concept – our energy flow and how we feel. We must think of our energy as a flow – our emotions; energy in motion. Which way is our energy flowing and why? What caused this flow? When do we feel at our best and why? What caused this feeling? This is both a map of realities and vision. The way things are – reality. The way things should be – vision.

Remember back to when you were a kid, or perhaps you have kids. My four kids don't need an alarm clock, always know right when to eat, and they thrive when they have a place to play or activities to do. It's when they're hungry, thirsty, cooped up, have no clearly defined boundaries or get yelled at that their little energized selves get sideways. Little kids especially have all sorts of drive. How do we become this honest with ourselves, again? Evidence shows we learn most of our fears and debilitating habits as we grow up. It's then that we conform. We decide it's easier to fit in and in fact, it becomes the hardest thing we've ever done. Many societal norms are not healthy and life giving, but we go with the flow to make others happy, or we fear seeming contrary. Fear brings with it a great trap, and the ensuing mental battles drain our energy.

Think now about a time you felt fully awakened, fully alive, fully aware and happy. A beach? A mountaintop? A good meal or favorite restaurant? A long evening stroll? A good book? Maybe time with a loved one or dear friend? What's changed? The point is this. There are things that increase and decrease our capacity. *The things that decrease or deplete our capacity (swindlers) seem easier to come by, the things that increase or fill our capacity (sources) are harder to plug into and thus, we must create habits (install switches) to turn on the sources of power for our energy and turn off the swindlers.* If you can understand this, you master mapping. You'll soon be living fully aware to your energy flow. Let's discuss sources, switches and swindlers of energy. What sources are you plugged into for energy, how are you switching on these sources, what things are swindling you of your energy, and how are you switching these off? These won't be exhaustive lists but will include some very key areas we've found through research and interviews that have some of the greatest effects on our energy. Highlight and jot down your ideas along the way. Commit today to journey with me to renew your energy and learn to protect and fortify it. Your energy is your life, and you're worth it!

Sources

Think of a power plant. Its purpose – supply power. Power lines stretch millions of miles and provide connection from the power plant to businesses, homes, street lamps and so on. What if you missed an electric bill payment one month and the power was switched off? You'd pay your bill and tap back into the power, as soon as possible, correct? Well, what energy source or power has been disconnected from your life? You know if you'll just go back there, you will draw renewal into your being. Is it that workout, does it mean losing weight, going back to school, improving your marriage, travelling, listening, making time for prayer, connecting with God and others? What must change to plug you back into the source? Like the battery on our phone, or the fuel tank in our car, so our level of energy determines how far we can go. When we're empty, we need a filling. How's your battery? Full, drained or dead? Where's the plug? How do you get plugged in?

Pre-Y2K, my brothers built an entire room of train batteries, backup generators, power inverters and solar panels. Like many, we considered our energy sources should a large-scale power outage happen. Power outages happen in life, too. We wake up sick or just feel off-kilter some days. Perhaps a super-busy, stressful stage of life pulls more energy than we're used to expending. Considering your sources of energy is critical because there are healthy and unhealthy sources. 5-Hour Energy shots are not a great choice, unfortunately. Not knocking them, Monster or Red Bull per se. Grandma always said, "If it comes easy, it's probably not worth it."

Quick fixes aren't going to give lasting energy. When the power outage strikes, we could light the house by setting it aflame. Light and warmth would result – for a short time. Lasting energy, however, must start with the right sources. A great source will fill you; you'll feel energized in a calm way. A great source may be a person, place, object, activity or idea. A great source is a consistent source of energy. The purer the source the more positive the energy.

Recharging

Recharging means you're constantly renewing your sources. Don't run out. Fill your cabinets with only good sources; make no room for swindlers. Plan your time productively so that you're not tempted by idleness. It must be intentional idleness and even then, let it be turned to inner renewal of rest, meditation or creative thought. When we think sources of energy for our mindsets, we must perform an environmental analysis of where our minds have been and where we want to go. Our minds are created to think, so when we don't have an energizing plan for them, the vacuum is filled with whatever information is presented: TV, miscellaneous reading, social surfing – no real plan. Analyzing mental needs for where you're going can help you identify education, reading materials and wholesome sources of energy for your mind that will help you overcome an obstacle or enhance a skill.

Recharging means plugging into quiet power. People say time and time again, "I want your energy," or "I need more energy!" All the while, we're scrolling our networks and social feeds. We're plugged into email, to instant messaging, to the internet, to several podcasts and to our TVs at home. We're checking in on everyone else's lives. In fact, we've allowed technology to push notifications into our pockets, purses, or hands (where our devices reside a good majority of the time). Hyper-social appeal sets in and undermines a sense of peace – peace of who we are and where we are. According to the *Boston Herald*, technology is hurting our very ability to breathe properly. Taking satisfaction in quiet accomplishment has become foreign to the norm. Marketing agencies have targets on our backs; advertisements filled with instant gratification and quick fixes seem to be everywhere we turn. We've started half a dozen self-help books, fad diets, and perhaps jumped into a get-rich-quick program or two. Nothing seems to pan out in the few weeks or months we try it.

Recharging means understanding your desires and controlling them. Understand your desires. They're healthy and usually come from a lack – an emptiness. Often, we identify the wrong emptiness and plug it into the wrong source. This is called "Runaway Desires." Democritus said, "It's hard to fight desire, but to be able to control it is a sign of a reasonable person." Desires are good. If you feel a desire to do something, it stems from a good desire. A desire to steal stems from a desire to possess things. This desire to steal is a runaway desire and doesn't create value for anyone. It's not valuable behavior driven by virtuous beliefs of love and peace. It's a desire out of bounds and hurtful. When we talk about energy mapping, we must understand and accept desires. "Ignore what a man desires, and you ignore the very source of his power!" Desires are legitimate but either in bounds or out of bounds. We short circuit the recharge of our energy when we have corrosive forces at work in our hearts. We all have superheroes in our lives. People on top of the world. People who make a difference in the world. People we look up to. People we follow! Truth is, they're human just like the rest of us, and they'd admit they have areas of weakness in their lives. What keeps them focused on their life mission? How do they avoid the kryptonite that's sure to cripple men and women of steel? *Being fortified with an empowering vision, they know where and when to recharge – they're plugged in to powerful sources!* Let's look now at powerful sources for the four dimensions of self. As you read through these questions, let them challenge you. Let them go to work for you by adding them, or a variation of them to your life. As you read and other thoughts or ideas are stirred in your mind, jot them in these pages.

Mental

- Thinking – When is your daily time to think about your life, your impact and your desires? Do you have a systematic process to think through what's going on and what best possible solutions there might be. Do you have a tool in place to capture other random thoughts that are floating around taking up bandwidth in your brain? David Allen sums this up when he says, "You increase your productivity and creativity exponentially when you think about the right things at the right time and have the tools to capture this value-added thinking."

- Imagining – Do you carve out time with a blank paper and pen to simple creatively imagine plans to move forward, idea generations, brainstorming solutions? *The majority of energy is transferred into our life by the source of thoughts.* Our thoughts rule us. To understand the airwaves in simple terms and the origination of thought, let's listen to Napoleon Hill's description of vibration of thought. "The ether ... carries at all times, vibrations of fear, poverty, disease, failure, misery; and vibrations of prosperity, health, success, and happiness, just as surely as it carries the sound of hundreds of orchestrations of music, and hundreds of human voices, all of which maintain their own individuality, and means of identification transmitted over radio" (and nowadays, the internet, TV, etc). From this great storehouse of thought, the mind is attracting vibrations that harmonize with its dominating thoughts. Therefore, ideas of value creation will come to the prosperous-thinking mind, but ideas of holding back and calculation to the poverty-thinking and fearful mind. You will attract more of the same thoughts of your mind.

- Reflection – do you pause at the end of the day to gauge how you're progressing toward your vision, how focused you were, and how you feel? Reflecting (whether you journal, pray or just sit quietly before bed) on your day allows your brain to defrag and cognitively think through how you did. Quiet time, journaling, mindfulness (experts recommend at least 10 minutes per day), grateful thoughts, prayer time and meditation are all forms of reflecting.

- Positive Mindset – How do you reset your perspective through-out the day to stay positive, peaceful and calm? What does peace of mind mean to you? What past hurt keeps coming up for you? What future anxiety is stressing you? Perspective, or a state of mind "is something that one assumes. It cannot be purchased. It must be created," Hill states. *Your state of mind – your perspective – that you choose to operate from every single day can be your greatest source of energy when it's faith-filled and empowering, or it can be your greatest swindler when it's fear-based and limiting.*

- Powerful thoughts – Do you think, cultivate and inspire positive, pure and powerful thoughts? Og Mandino said, "Every thought-seed sown or allowed to fall into the mind, and to take root there, produces its own, blossoming sooner or later into action and earing its own harvest of opportunity and circumstance. Good thoughts bear good fruit, bad thoughts, bad fruit."

- Vision – Do you have an empowering life vision spelled out in written form?

- Purpose – Have you derived an everyday purpose from your life vision?

- Values – What are your values? The foundation that your life and the experience you create are based on?

- Focus – How focused do you feel every day in general? Focus increases decisiveness. Focus on the end goal means fewer decisions as you're enabled to put basic decisions and repetitive tasks on autopilot by forming routines and habits. *Do you prioritize tasks based on the highest and best use of your time? When vision leads you, it's much easier to determine what's aligned and what's not.* Prioritization of tasks is key and focus yields results. Making time to plan and write down goals keeps you centered on what's important to work on in the present. You'll take only focused actions that move you forward. Dump everything else out onto a "miscellaneous / to-do-maybe-at-some-point-in-the-future" list. This way you've captured random thoughts but haven't derailed your entire day. Stay focused on your daily, top-three priorities.

- Reading – Are you actively reading or listening to powerful sources that inspire the best in you? Reading engages the mind. Mind generates thoughts which pull energy into your life. Think. Stimulate great thoughts through powerful reading! Build your intellect fully with knowledge and the "how to" of application.

- Learning – Are you approaching learning opportunities with intention to learn something new or sharpen your skill?

- Music – Do you listen to the right kinds of music at the right times? David Niven PhD says, "Music excites our mind, whether we are one, forty-one, or a hundred and one." Positive lyrics and rhythms are both important. We should listen to what emotions are stimulated by different types of music. Humans love music and music invokes feelings!

Spiritual

Our spirits have a need to leave a legacy. We call this our impact, or the difference we made on this world. This world is made up of people. Are you looking up and out from your own set of circumstances to touch and empower others? Whose lives are you touching? As you think, consider your face, your smile, your words, your touch, your feet that take you to connect with others. Are you connecting wholly? How are your thoughts towards them? Empowering and loving or calculating and distrustful? Consider some sources:

- Faith – Are you hopeful and confident about the future? Have you envisioned the future you're going to create? Do you have an overarching definiteness of purpose for life and every day persevere towards it? William James when he was professor of philosophy at Harvard said, "of course the Sovereign cure for worry is faith." Are you decisive? Can you quickly align your decisions with your values?

- Dreaming – Do you dream intentionally about what might be possible. Something big, scary and exciting? Something that stirs your emotions so deeply it blows upon the coals found in your spirit? Les Brown says dreams are given to us for a reason. Don't let anyone swindle your dream! Dreams are one of the greatest sources of spiritual energy!

- Prayer – Do you utilize prayers of faith? In fact, Tony Evans states, "Prayer is the most underused tool in our arsenal." Because of this, we simply aren't igniting the energies of faith in our lives and we live below the high calling of the fullness of our destiny as fathers, businesswomen and men, friends, community leaders and so on! Prayer can be the greatest source of energy. It demands we lift ourselves out of the physical state. It requires a gratitude for that which we may not understand and a humility of heart to realize we need a spiritual awakening and connection to live for something greater. *Prayer transcends turmoil and brings peace; for, even the act of prayer moves one to believe.* Through prayer, one learns to give up doubt and live in faith. Faith surpasses our own reasoning allowing a greater force to go to work on our behalf. Prayer and faith demand we do our part. Some would argue that prayer is simply a state of mind. However, I believe prayer's very essence is connection with a loving Creator. I believe prayer taps us into a divine and spiritual energy when we live in a constant frame of faith. I like how financial guru and leading voice on living debt-free, Dave Ramsey, states in his life-changing book, *Complete Guide to Money*, "I'm not a preacher or theologian; I'm just a regular guy. But ... I know for a fact that prayer changes things. I'm not saying God will make you a millionaire; I just want you to 'call home' and talk to your heavenly Father about what's going on ... He loves you like crazy." Whether you pray r eligiously or simply state an affirmation in the morning like a prayer; or, whether you pray deeply with heartfelt supplications for others, true whole-being prayer demands we act in faith and humility. Prayer accepts our spiritual essence and calls out to a Higher Intelligence. I like how one spiritual leader said, "When we work, we work; but when we pray, God works." Prayer demands an openness and genuine heart; for, if we accept, even in the smallest measure of faith, that a Higher Power exists, we also accept this Higher Power knows our heart and motivations. Prayer calls into the courtroom our motivations, our intentions, and our determination. Without prayer, our intensions are countless while our determination is rare. This is the same reason we often wait to pray until we're in a very determining situation of our lives. Those times where we absolutely must have an answer or a "miracle," we pray. The times we are unsure if we really want something, or we are simply going to try something, we avoid prayer, or forget to pray. Genuine prayer requires faith and definiteness of purpose. Prayer demands we do something. You can pray without believing in God, absolutely; but, you cannot pray without faith. Sincere, heartfelt prayer opens our minds to Divine Power. If there is a God, and your prayer is mixed with the smallest measure of faith and humility, wouldn't it seem like He'd reveal Himself to you? Prayer is the Energizer's go-to, not last resort. *Prayer calms you in faith, centers you in humility, and gives confidence through determination.* The insincere prayer will feel rote and a waste of time; the sincere, whole-person prayer will transcend life itself and be a moment so sacred and divine. The Energizer makes prayer their greatest source of energy. Prayer lifts us past temporal wants and illuminates eternal purpose. Prayer taps us into Infinite Power.

Power to forgive, power to heal emotionally, mentally and even physically. Prayer raises us to a higher frequency and resonates in every action, conversation and connection. Prayer connects strangers and is love's quickest transport. Praying will be for you exactly what you put into it. I like how Dr. Mike Norris says, "We must stop saying our prayers and start praying our prayers!" When you invoke your soul into your prayers, when you posture yourself physically into your prayers, when you focus your whole mind steadfastly on prayer and enter by faith into the spiritual realm of help, you set into motion the answer. The same faith by which you enter wholeheartedly carries you through your physical surroundings. You transcend worry, you eliminate anxiety and you claim peace. You slay procrastination as faith gives you the victory. It's interesting we call people of prayer "Prayer Warriors." Energizers realize prayer's importance and tap into this Divine Wisdom first and often.

- Service – Do you look around for ways to help a stranger or friend? Did the people in your influence feel your desire to serve and were they encouraged to do the same? Have you ever volunteered? Taking time to help others (even a simple smile, calling a waitress by name, paying it forward or giving a hug will crank up the generator inside of you). *How are you creating or adding value to lives around you through service?*

- Gratefulness – Did you express your gratitude to someone in a specific way today?

- Love – Did you show unconditional love to someone? Did you show your appreciation of another human being today? Did you lift someone up, give an encouraging word, or perform some small act of kindness?

- Giving – Do you exercise the abundance of giving? Are you creating value so that you can give more? Are you working through all five-levels to be an abundant giver?

Emotional

While our souls, our emotional makeup, tie each of the four parts of self together, think through this part of self. We have emotions which generate feelings for a reason. The greater the feeling, the greater chance a habit will form (switches). Analyze your emotions. ***Which sources of energy in your life garner the greatest emotions?*** E-motion is energy in motion. Does the ocean stir your soul in a great way, the mountains, spending time with a friend, performing acts of service? Understanding and opening our emotional arteries will ignite our energy.

- Feelings – How do you feel on a consistent basis – stressed, drained, anxious or charged, ready and enthusiastic?

- Emotions – Do you feel emotionally intelligent? Do you understand the most powerful emotions? The top seven are faith, love, hope, desire, romance, sex, and enthusiasm, as researched by Hill. Can you clearly identify how they're affecting your and other's life experiences? These are among the most powerful positive emotions and tied to all actions of value creation and addition. These emotions ignite the deepest energies within us. Can you identify emotions and why you feel a certain way? Are you able to stay calm and seek to understand in any situation?

- Healthy Relationships – Do you feel deeply connected in loving relationships?

- Love – Are you dating your people? Wife, kids, friends, and close connections need our time and attention. When we water our relationships, we ourselves are watered. Do you make it a point to proactively invest into them? Do you spend time with them – fully present? Do you operate with high integrity, nurture trust and touch empoweringly?

- Nature – Do you go spend time in nature for calmness, clarity and centering? Go barefoot. Ground energy is absorbed through the soles of the feet. It happens automatically and unconsciously. A rock has mass and therefore contains energy. Sitting on a rock can transfer a sense of balance and groundedness, to you. A natural rock is full and still. Why do people love the mountains? They radiate with energy, they are full, massive, awe inspiring and comforting.

- Beauty – When's the last time you sat to watch the sun rise or set?

- Slowing Down – When was the last time you stopped to pick a wildflower or smell the blossoms on a beautiful rose bush? *Technology is no longer scarce; nature and peace have gone missing.* John Muir stated, "Climb the mountains and get their good tidings. Nature's peace will flow into you as sunshine flows into trees ... while cares will drop off like falling leaves."

- Smell – Have you freshened up the aroma in your environment, office or in the fragrance you wear. How are the smells in your life? Have you ever aired out your home in the spring? How'd the fresh air and freshness make you feel? Have you ever brought flowers home and their fragrance livened up the kitchen and perhaps your relationship with your wife? Make your spaces smell nice and people will appreciate you. You feel a little better about everything when it smells nice. Good smells awaken the senses and feelings can arouse positive emotions!

- Pets and animals – Taking a dog for a wall. Consider dogs, cats, birds and other pets. Why do we call pets, "man's best friend?" Why can they bring us so much joy petting them? They have energy about them! Wagging their tail, wiggling around, so happy to see us. Get around some good pet energy from time to time.

Physical

- Breathing – are you fully absorbing air into your lungs through proper breathing?

- Humans can agree to disagree on many things, but one common interest is we all must breathe. Oxygen is life. We may not all run. I cannot prescribe a standard list of activities, but what I can promise you is this – running, walking, swimming will require you to prioritize learning how to properly breathe. *Take deep breaths and practice breathing properly.* Exercise daily in some way to increase heart rate and lung expansion.

- Sunlight – Are you able to get proper amounts of sunlight (while wearing proper sunscreen)?

- Solar energy – sunlight – is invigorating and promotes good health through sunbathing, approximately 20 minutes a day (research recommends before 11 a.m. and after 3 p.m.).

- Sleep – Are you getting a good night's sleep every night; do you feel rested when you wake up? Proper amount of rest (different for everyone). Saying no to TV and not staying up too late pay huge dividends.

- Healthy Nutrition – Is your nutrition planned; is it proper? Do you budget your calories and plan the day or week before to know exactly what this looks like, where you're going to eat, etc.? Have you considered local farmer's markets, local honey for organic benefits? How about homemade, oatmeal cookies? One of my favorites. Do you eat fruit as a snack? This is nature's sweetness and since we naturally crave sweets, we can avoid turning to the energy-swindling, man-made manufactured kind that are proven to have negative outcomes. Fruit's cheap, requires little prep and statistics show is beneficial in so many ways for you!

- Water – Do you consume 64 or more ounces of water each day? We consist primarily of water! Approximately 14 gallons to be exact! That's 60 to 70 percent of water walking around in the form of you! According to *National Geographic*, losing just one quart of water results in lost cognitive function. High fructose corn syrup and carbonated drinks don't hydrate; they deplete water in order to digest. Drinking a lot of water is the solution! It's a must for healthy living. One of my clients' goals is drinking 64 ounces daily. It's that important for him he wants to commit it to habit! 64 ounces consistent with the famous 8×8 Rule of eight 8-ounce glasses of water per day. Perhaps you carry a 16- ounce Gatorade bottle and drink four of these daily. Do what works for you, but whatever you do, make drinking water a HUGE priority! The simplest trick to energy (both mentally and physically) is proper hydration! Let's get the water power going today! Measure it and get a water accountabuddy! Drink up!

- Exercise – Are you exercising daily? Are you incorporating a mix of strengthening exercises; stretching exercises; shorter, intense aerobic exercises; and longer endurance exercises in your week? *Exercise increases blood flow to the brain, strengthens your lungs and heart and releases natural feel-good chemicals in your body.* Physical exercise stretches and expands your capacity. Exercise, in any of the four parts of self, expands your capacity – exercise equals energy enhancement!

- Clean Environment – How's your environment – home, office, car, etc. – is it clean, orderly and energizing?

- Recharging Recreation – What do you have planned for recreation?

- Simply a time to be unplugged and recharging, fun with friends, or travelling, etc. Do you have a favorite hobby and make time to incorporate it into your life?

- Flow State – Defined as, "the state of operation in which a person performing an activity is fully immersed in a feeling of energized focus, full involvement, and enjoyment in the process of the activity." How do you stay loose, in flow and moving at home, at work, school, etc.? Clutter happens in life and we can get stagnant. We often stop finding full enjoyment in life's activities. We were made to move – do what works for you, but make a move. Are you stiff, sore or hurting? Consider some form of shiatsu massage, a *HoMedics* system for loosening up the tight muscles in your back, a yoga class or reflexology (techniques of hand and foot pressure application). Stay loose and make a move.

What are some other sources you can think of? Write them down. Focus energy implementing energy-giving sources in your life.

Swindlers

The definition of swindler compelled me to use this word over others that come to mind like energy drain, energy vampire, energy thief, etc. The dictionary defines being swindled as, "cheated (a person, business, etc.) out of money or other assets." A swindler will "put forward plausible schemes or use unscrupulous trickery to defraud others." Swindler matches what happens to our energy best because most of the times, we know we're being swindled, we just can't figure out exactly how. If we do know how, then it's often difficult to stop the swindler. Negative influences and toxic relationships are difficult to guard our energies against. Fears imbedded in our minds swindle the largest share of energy. Actions we know are debilitating swindle our energy, yet society and marketers have painted them as "fun." They continue to beset us through habitual use. ***The best way to stop being swindled is to stop hanging out with swindlers.*** The trick? Stop guilting ourselves over past failures, build a powerful life vision and begin hanging out with great sources! When you plug into good sources of energy and experience the feeling of being fully awakened, you'll expel the swindlers without second thought. Let's not complicate it - some things are worth your energy, some aren't. Focus all your energy on the source; don't give any attention, let alone your invaluable lifeforce of energy, to the swindlers!

When Jen and I bought our second home, we were elated. It was a short sale and needed a few touch-ups but nothing too major. The electric bills seemed higher than necessary, and it took the home inspector's report to remind me about the crawlspace that was in deplorable condition. Leaking of heat in winter and conditioned air in summer are examples of swindled energy. Until I braved the nasty crawl space, cleared out garbage, and replaced the old, tattered moisture barrier, I wasn't able to see all of the areas amidst the joists where insulation had fallen out. Replacing these areas made a world of difference for not only the electric bill, but drafty floors as well. There are plenty of areas in life where energy's being swindled from us. We can insulate these areas and save valuable energy. It starts with mindfulness and being honest with ourselves. It's so easy to waste energy on swindlers because in life, they come dressed as fun-loving distractions. We've got to identify and label the swindlers. We've got to shine the light into the crawl spaces of our lives and expose them for what and who they are so that we can implement a replacing source!

Replacing

The trick in life is to figure out the past noise that keeps haunting you and the future worries that keep stressing you and eliminate them. Research shows, however, that elimination doesn't work out as well by fighting the swindlers. That's right. You might actually reinforce them by focusing on them. What we must do, instead, is redefine how we're going to think about something, and spell out the replacing energy source – thought, action, relationship, etc. *Now, focus all your time and energy with the sources, and give no time or energy to the swindler.* At my first job, the company kept a huge room full of old inventory – ancient parts that were best categorized as miscellaneous. We spent so much time counting and reorganizing slow, stagnant parts; and we hardly incorporated any of these parts into new projects. Finally, I contacted this salvage company and went back and forth until I felt their cash offer was a deal. Approaching the CEO and leadership team, I asked, "What could we do with twenty-thousand dollars? I could have you a check by the end of this week?"

"From who? From where?" they responded.

"All that old inventory we're wasting so much time with." I replied. "Done."

Cut the swindlers you're spending so much time and energy hanging on to, but make sure you put an energizing source – like twenty thousand dollars – in its place! Leverage the knowledge you gained from the swindler, do better, improve and grow. We have to identify what is draining our energy and replace the swindler with a source. It may mean better friends, another association, a different job, replacing addiction with a healthier habit, and the list goes on. Let's take a look at some swindlers. Again, this is nowhere near an exhaustive list; so, as ideas and thoughts come to mind while you read through these, jot down a note or two; or, highlight one or two you could replace.

Mental

- Negative Thoughts – fear based, limited, impoverished thinking. There are negative thoughts emitted, and stated, by people all around us. Napoleon Hill states, "Every human being has the ability to completely control his own mind, and with this control, every person may open their mind to the stray thought impulses which are being released by other minds, or close the doors tightly and admit only thought impulses of his own choice." Since all thought has the tendency to clothe itself in the exact physical equivalent, the thoughts allowed to permeate one's mind garner greater bandwidth in the subconscious mind until the force is strong enough to initiate action. If these thoughts are fearful, limited and impoverished, they'll never be translated into courage, abundance and creating value! People driven by faith instead of fear are principled people. They choose their thoughts instead of reacting to emotional impulses; and, by choosing their thoughts, visualizations and affirmations, they replace old emotional generators with new and empowering ones!

- Limited Mindset – bargaining with life instead of owning life and demanding more from it. I like how Hill contrasts this mindset of abundance with how many live life " … *bargaining with life for a penny, instead of demanding prosperity, opulence (wealth, affluence, abundance), riches, contentment and happiness.* Planning what to do if and when overtaken by failure instead of burning all bridges and making retreat impossible. Expecting poverty instead of demanding riches." With an abundant mindset, you are thinking value. Every thought, every action and every relationship is built on value. You become satisfied with life because of the value you're creating, and your mindset is wealthy. The mindset of not being satisfied is a swindler and many will rush off to work their entire lifetime postponing their own spiritual, mental, emotional and physical wellbeing to go make more money. They are slowly killing the goose that's laying the golden egg - themselves They're not thriving; therefore, they don't truly know how to give their best because they're not living at their fullest and best. They're willing to exchange mediocre for mediocre, resulting in more mediocrity. Instead, what if we changed our perspective to gratitude and were thankful for everything you already have. With this gratitude, you could dismiss the need for anything more. By changing your mindset from barely having to already having enough, you quickly become content and full. This doesn't mean leveling off. In fact, the hardest work is finding contentment because you must overcome the fear of poverty, fear of criticism, and other swindlers. When you do the hard work now of finding contentment, then you gain freedom and now you can ask yourself, not "What do I need," but "What do I really want and desire?" "What am I going to demand out of life because I can?" Most of us would have to admit our needs are already taken care of. And peradventure hard times hit, had you been in a lifestyle of gratitude prior to hard times, you'd have been thankful for every relationship. The joy and abundance of a grateful heart would have nourished those relationships so much so that a friend or relative would quickly share a roof with this abundant soul known as you. Gratitude has everything it needs and never fears being without. It's abundant and attracts everything necessary. Because you're doing the real work of living abundantly – gratefully – you never settle down or levels off. You have no limit; you're limitless. Gratitude abounds, and the grateful heart is content and abounding – full and overflowing. You're grateful for life and take care of yourself as a whole person, you stay full and content, driven and charged! ***Needing more, versus demanding more, are two completely different mindsets. One's limited and fearful, the other is abundant and full of faith.*** Which mindset are you? Eliminate limited mindsets and adopt gratitude, contentment and abundance!

- Addiction – the basis for most addiction is coping. We are unwilling to go all the way back to when the pain happened the first time, uncover the fear behind it, and begin replacing with faith-filled thoughts. Often, by abusing ourselves, we feel some sort of vengeance over the one who first set us down the addictive path. Addictions are not only mentally addictive; but they also feel good – numbing – and bring some sort of physical, short-term pleasure. This swindler must be eradicated by first reclaiming your value. *Valuable people do valuable things.* Addiction swindles our value. We bargain with it for as much value as we think society demands us to have; instead of demanding our full value and delivering ourselves from what we know will end in ruin.

- Distracted – difficulty focusing on activities that deliver results. Or, not being aware of distractions in the first place.

- Uncontrollable Situations – those over which we have little/no control. Avoid giving your energy to these. Things like memes, political posts and sensationalized global or personal news tempts us to share. Think about how many others' energy will be wasted as they analyze the same shared uncontrollable content. This doesn't solve anything. A letter or phone call to your political representative, a prayer for a friend, or a more inspirational post would be much more beneficial.

- Indecision – too many decisions to make, or too many options. Seek clarity. Know your desired outcome and make the best one.

- Procrastination – fear based stalling, over-analysis and perfectionism. This can drain our mental and emotional energy so fast. Not only do you end up thinking about the task over and over; but, by not taking a small action step and getting started, delay forms a pattern of delay and makes starting even harder. Every time you get an assignment or take on a task, complete a small action item immediately. Then spell out the next small step so you can stay engaged and keep forward motion.

- Excessive Gaming – limiting our connection to reality. Gaming is a big deal. Video games aren't natural when we consider they put our minds into cognitive overload with intense adrenalin of limbic emotion. These heightened emotions lack any direct physical connection or relationship. It seems very possible this could lead, through excessive use, to shallow emotional connection in real relationships. The fantasy and stimulation of a virtual world is also highly addictive. The same amount of stimulation in the physical world is non-existent; therefore, our brains are trained to slumber in our natural habitats waiting to be reawakened in the virtual space. Not to mention the lack of mobility gaming brings, the addictive nature, and often excess of violence. If life is about investing our amazing cognitive ability into a game-roster's leaderboard, then let us consider how we're robbing the world of some creative idea that could potentially deter hunger, cure disease, inspire action, help some charity, stimulate growth, bring value to others, etc. If you play a game as a healthy past time, or building a relationship with a friend, then more power to you. The highly addictive nature of video games and virtual media should be named for what they are – cognitive swindlers.

- Overconsuming Television – saying, "No" to something better. One psychologist said it this way, "TV robs our time and never gives it back." David Niven PhD states, "Without TV, you can do something actively fun instead of something passively distracting!" What if we shut off the TV, went to bed early and rediscovered the great feeling of getting up early again? Realize that TV is biased. Everything we see has some sort of frame. We don't get the full picture. Limit this. One statistic by Jeffres and Dobos states, ***"TV changes our view of the world, and can encourage us to develop highly unrealistic and often damaging conclusions that serve to reduce our life satisfaction by up to 50 percent."*** What do you think makes the most news? Good events or bad? Bad. Good is supposed to happen, so it takes the bad happening to make news. If you're not careful, you'll think and begin living more fearful and reserved simply by the news you consume. Impure, or excessively stimulating TV robs our mental, spiritual, emotional and, unless the TV's mounted to the top of the treadmill, our physical energies as well!

- Excessive Social Media – feeling the urge to check every notification. Massive amounts of cognitive energies are spent endlessly scrolling social media and processing a disproportionate amount of data. Limit your consumption and be purposeful. Setting calendar times for social media just like DVR-ing a TV show can save tons of mental energy!

Spiritual

- Wounded Spirit – dry or dead to love, hope and faith. Solomon states, "A wounded spirit dries the bones." *Many have suffered so much hurt and pain in life that they stopped believing. They stopped dreaming. They formed spiritual callouses.* The sparkle in their eyes has dimmed. The emotions of bitterness and unforgiveness have flooded their boiler rooms. Their spiritual engines have ceased propelling their life's ship forward in faith. Dr. Paul Chappell in his book, *Stewarding Life*, states, "As vital as physical and mental rest is, there is a deeper rest available and necessary ... no amount of sleep, no abundance of recreation, no weeks of vacation can give sufficient rest to the person who's overloaded with envy, bitterness, unresolved conflict, or guilt."

- Worry – lack of faith about the future; focus on negative possibilities. Stemming from procrastination, lack of purpose, and undeserving voices. Rick Warren states, "If you know how to worry, then you already know how to meditate. Worry is simply focused thinking on something negative."

- Anxiety – this is the cognitive and repetitious processing of emotional fear. Debilitating! Exhausting! Anxiety is often due to the lack of "know-how" in starting a new behavior or exercise. Often, gym memberships are under-utilized due to uncertainty of speeds, reps, weight, etc.; or, it's caused by the "out-of-place" mentality one feels surrounded by fit athletes. Perhaps the thought of everyone else sitting indoors, while you're the only one jogging your neighborhood streets, stops you. Whatever is causing the anxiety must be dealt with head on. Chances are, you begin to run and find out there are more people out there running than you imagined. Or, you get to the gym, start small and work out for a short period of time; and then, looking up, you realize a bunch of us aren't as fit as the brain originally told you. Gyms are meant to get healthy – not for comparison. Own whatever it is you need and go after it! Fear not – take courage! No anxiety - charge!

Emotional

- Fear – manifested and falsified evidence appearing real. We were only born with two fears. The fear of loud noises and the fear of falling. All other fears were taught and learned as we grow up. It's then that we conform. We decide it's easier to fit in and in fact, it becomes the hardest thing we've ever done. Many societal norms are not healthy and life-giving, but we go with the flow to make people happy and not stir any waves. Fear brings with it a great trap, and the ensuing mental battles drain our energy. We fear what people think if we act or look different, if we try something different, if we fail, if we succeed, or if we get more excited about life than what is typical. *This great swindler stifles our energy, muzzles our shout, erodes our joy, and asks us to pander to expectation of others – legitimate or not; stated or implied.* However, if fears are learned, then this means fears can be unlearned and replaced with faith and empowerment. Brendon Burchard states it this way, "Fear was given to us as a motive to avoid physical harm and death … we are the ones who have perverted it into a tool for the ego's protection." Carnegie shares "Emotions of fear, hate, jealousy and envy are driven by primeval vigor and the negative energy of the jungle. Such emotions are so violent that they tend to drive out of our minds all peaceful happy thoughts and emotions." Take inventory of your fears. Like many who have faced their fears and courageously achieved great levels of personal growth, unfettered their emotions and who live empowered lives, you too will discover most of our fears today have nothing to do with physical threats at all! To move forward takes courage, and courage is identifying the fear to do something and then doing it anyway. Courage is action in the face of fear. Courage is a muscle that when exercised produces greater courage. Brendon continues, "We are afraid of being rejected, isolated, or abandoned – not of being eaten alive … these kinds of social fears can be overcome by willful practice." Fear swindles our energy. It drains our very drive to progress forward and realize our dreams. It prevents us from rising to our highest potential and making our greatest impact. We calculate everything through the frightful filter of fear. We transfer a hundred times the energy calculating the level of possible failure than it would take to create a positive outcome. We paralyze ourselves focusing on fear; instead, let us empower ourselves choosing only faith. *Dogs bark on the low frequency of fear, while angels sing on the highest frequency of faith!* And what are these fears in particular? Hill spells them out perfectly. He compiled the 6 greatest fears after years of research. He calls them "the ghosts of six fears because they only exist in the mind." Zig Ziglar said of fear that it's simply "false evidence appearing real." Ask yourself which of these fears drive you? The energies of faith, hope and love will never be fully realized as long as they're syphoned off and swindled by these fears. In fact, these are listed in their order of the most common appearance:

1. Fear of poverty
2. Fear of criticism
3. Fear of ill health
4. Fear of losing the love of someone
5. Fear of old age
6. Fear of death

There are a lot of little fearful relatives, too. Most stem from these top six. Some of the fears in my life I consistently must replace with faith and courage are: perfectionism, undeserving and people-pleasing.

- Emotionally Unintelligent – not understanding the most powerful negative emotions can leave us trying to satisfy the lowest drives known to man. We become quick tempered, irritable, relationally poor, and lonely. The top seven strongest negative emotions are fear, jealousy, hatred, revenge, greed, superstition and anger, as defined by Hill. We must form habits to install and use positive emotions instead. We must take ownership – extreme ownership – or we'll be run by our emotions and lead unproductive lives and experience most unfruitful relationships. Build, practice and strengthen positive emotional generators. The positives will slowly but surely supersede the negatives.

- Emotional Imbalance – emotional imbalance and emotional instability are real. Suffering from years of stress, some form of abuse or hormonal imbalance can cause emotional imbalance and drastically affect our energy. Take ownership by first getting super vulnerable and honest with some trusted coaches and spiritual advisors in your life; then, seek professional or medical guidance if necessary.

- Catching Up – the feeling or need to carry over unfulfilled expectations or tasks from yesterday.

- Perfectionism – trying to be perfect.

- Undeserving – saying, "I'm sorry," when you didn't do anything wrong. Sign of calculative, looking-over-the-shoulder kind of fear.

- Disease to Please – saying yes to everyone for fear of "letting someone down." The disease to please everybody is deadly. *This swindler causes us to say "Yes" before analyzing alignment with our goals.* This ties closely to fear of what others think.

- Unforgiveness – unwilling to let your guilt or another's wrong doing go.

- Gossip – sowing discord, feeling the compulsive urge to share how you've been wronged.

- Guilt – unnatural, fear-based guilt that threatens to crush us. We should ask forgiveness when natural guilt gives us a heart squeeze, but are we stuck in past, unproductive guilt? Paul Tournier wrote in, *Guilt and Grace*, "Legitimate guilt is that which stems from the knowledge that we have erred, and which leads to correcting our course. Neurotic guilt is that which lingers long after any corrective measure have been taken and is crippling rather than constructive." We must let go of guilt! Guilt from our internal conscience is what Covey calls a great teacher, but he also states, "Most guilt many of us carry with us is from the social conscience. It doesn't teach at all but impedes our progress." Guilt can literally swindle our energy, and it's one of the most danger-ous swindlers. It's the thought of that person you let down in the past. It's the hurt you caused in the past that you keep reliving in the present. It's the new year's resolution to call that distant relative that you've failed to do. Guilt is the baggage of yesterday's defeat. Guilt holds yesterday's unfinished business over your head while tying today's noose. Notate yesterday's defeats into a mental pad, learn from them, and then delete the note. *Clear the slate every night and be ready to start writing successes each morning.* Denis Waitley says it perfectly, "Failure should be our teacher, not our undertaker. Failure is delay, not defeat. It is a temporary detour, not a dead end."

- Triggers – events, places or thoughts that set off a conglomeration of uncontrolled emotions.

- Toxic Relationships – calculating, untrusting, fear-based and abusive. These energy swindling relationships can come back over and over if you don't make peace with them. Write the forgiving letter, make the phone call or "break up" with someone from your past who continually tries to pull you down, or back into an unhealthy lifestyle.

Physical

- Poor Health – lack of attention, or desire to stay healthy and feeling fit. Poor health swindles many people's energy. Out of respect to those who suffer, we understand poor health is sometimes unavoidable. But most times, we can take ownership and enhance our health and ignite physical energy through four simple steps: choosing better nutrition options, begin consistently exercising – the key is being consistent, drinking more water, and getting the proper amount of sleep.

- Empty Calories – whether we realize it or not, empty calories and highly-processed foods limit our capacity to show up in abundance. When we nonchalantly skip a workout, let our health go, fill ourselves with empty calories, we're not maximizing today.

Not saying don't enjoy some ice-cream or a sweet treat; the point is, there are healthy boundaries and much richer sources to bolster our physical energy!

- No Exercise

- Addictive Medications/Drugs – opioid epidemic has just been announced. Are you struggling with drugs or prescription drugs. Friend, know this! You can rid yourself of these. I believe in you! ***You can replace these swindlers; you deserve to thrive!***

- Toxic Environment – emotional or mental barriers and anchors.

- Poor habits – we all have our nemesis. This is the habit sheer will-power has proven insufficient against, time and time again. Know this! By focusing our time and energy on the replacing source and building and bolstering healthy emotions, we can overcome. Mark Divine concurs with Tony Robbins, "The best approach is not to focus on eliminating unwanted behaviors but to replace them with new habits and drown the old out." Get vulnerable with someone, now. Ask someone for help. Be accountable, and take steps to replace poor swindlers for rich sources.

What's another swindler you're thinking of. Name it. Get it out in the open. Denial and belittling what's swindling our energy are both perfectly natural tendencies. After all, we have expectations that others have placed on us and we don't want to let them down. Friend, when you're not full, when you're not deeply at peace, when your capacity is drained and your energy condition is deteriorated, you can never live fully. Operating half-full is letting ourselves down. Take time and energy away from swindlers and put into sources. Imagine returning home from vacation. Pulling into the drive, you see several orange extension cords stretched across the lawn from the neighbors' houses and plugged into every external outlet of your house. They figured while you were out of town they'd put your electricity to good use for you. We'd be perfectly ok with this, right? Wrong. We'd probably be a little peeved at the thievery. Now, this may be unlikely to happen in reality, but it happens to our energy every day by the swindlers we allow into our spirits, minds, emotions and actions.

Switches

A great switch is a habit-forming-mechanism designed to overcome poor energy-swindling habits. Switches help us create rich energy-sourcing habits. Creating a new mental pathway happens best with added redundancy, so use a couple techniques and always include your WHY! A Post-It note to overcome smoking might read, "I'm breathing in wonderful, life-giving oxygen today so that I have life to give and to play with my precious children!" A Post-It note or even a 3x5 card to carry around in your pocket is so old fashioned, yet so effective! Move them or rewrite them from time to time. ***Read them aloud, with confidence, faith and feeling to passionately reinforce what you're doing.*** See yourself doing the activity every time you see the note. Put yourself there! As if you're already experiencing this solid, wonderful, high-energy yielding action. If it's time to think, put this note in your lunch box, or on your night stand. If it's journaling, put the pad, or journal next to your bed. Jeffrey Gitomer wrote an entire chapter in his book, *The Sales Bible*, titled "Post-It Note Your Way to Success." Sometimes we're too busy looking for a sophisticated plan to change something when a simple commitment placed on a Post-It note for constant reminder and accountability would do wonders! Go install some switches!

Remember buying the new home. The strip of light switches was harder to memorize than the names of a hundred strangers. You had the light, the fan, the outside lights – plural, the hallway light, the stairway light, and then there's that strip in the kitchen for table lights, recessed lights and, the garbage disposal. That was a bear. You go to quietly grab a glass of milk before bed and startle yourself switching on what should have been a dim light; but, instead, the growling, churning motor of the garbage disposal. Not only do you have the difficulty of getting in the habit of flipping the right switch, there is also another issue. Other humans. Kids! They love turning on all the switches – what fun! Teaching kids how to save electricity has been a generational theme since Edison. Similarly, in life, we know where to go to ignite our energy – healthy relationships, prayer, gym, forgiveness, nature, focus, and so on. Getting in these habits can be tough when there are other, older, opposing habits. Our habits in life determine where we transfer energy to and from. Other humans enter life and flip our switches, too, don't they? Yes. Unlike a wall switch, these are switches in our minds. Emotional switches are flipped, feelings are generated, and mental energies can become quickly exhausted. We can quickly spring into action, whether aligned with our life's vision or not, based on switches being flipped by others.

For great switches to be effective, though, they must be switched! Switches are choices, and every choice fortifies a rich or a poor habit. The rich and poor habits we develop then repeat and embed themselves in our minds. It takes work, but any poor habit can be relearned – just like a switch can be replaced. Don't give up simply because an old habit is deeply entrenched. I like how Will Rogers eloquently stated, "When you find yourself in a hole, stop digging!" You know, it was a year after we moved in when I finally mastered which switch was the garbage disposal. Jen got a lot of laughs watching me jump half startled across the kitchen. There are choices in life we've made – switches we've flipped – for a long time, the wrong way. They swindle our energy. *We can relearn habits by replacing them with better, more productive habits. But, you must bring attention to them. You may label the switches.* Or, you may have to pull an electrician's trick out of your hat and put duct-tape over the switch that's NOT to be flipped. In life, if the toxic person continues reaching for the "gossip switch", and you're determined to exercise the newly installed "grateful switch" (grateful for all the good you can find in someone), then you may need to have a heart to heart conversation, so they can support you in your new direction. In fact, Solomon talks about someone who gossips, sows discord and runs around with every latest "hot" social topic. A kind but firm statement may have to be given to stop toxic people from flipping a negative switch. Use the duct-tape sparingly, but when you need to – do! Don't flip the switch for swindlers. Similarly, replacing hangouts, friends, activities and thought processes with healthier, productive events, friends, actions and thoughts may be what it takes. If you've allowed free reign of your switches, make sure to have meaningful conversations with those flipping them. "I'm going in a different direction, if you'd like to hang out, let's do it on my run, or with my new study group." Chances are, they won't unless they, too, are ready to change.

Get ready to do the hard work of FLIPPING powerful and pure energy -sourcing switches! The hard work is always worth it! The source is never hard to identify, just like the swindler is never hard to identify. The hard part is installing positive switches and FLIPPING them consistently to tap into positive, powerful and pure sources of energy! The hard part is replacing the negative switches and staying true to your vision with a consistent positive dialogue even when old thought patterns and people try to get your negative energy flowing. The hard part is allowing good people to flip your positive switches for you – hold you accountable. The hard part is kindly asking your loved-one not to keep bringing up a toxic subject that's already been dealt with. Brendon Burchard says, choosing not to listen to swindlers is especially hard for those of us who are good listeners and empathetic friends. It takes "true personal power!" He states, "We must be discerning with those we hold close … it's possible to listen lovingly while being careful about what energy we absorb!" A great mechanism is asking a topic-changing question or letting your loved ones know what you love to talk about. Switches are completely in our control. They may get flipped when someone brings the gossip to you, you can point to gratitude's switch instead – you've intentionally labeled it! The garbage disposal uselessly grinding, just like the fire-hose spraying water everywhere, is unchanneled, wasted, swindled energy! ***FLIPPING an energy-rich switch is the valuable behavior that follows a virtuous belief. The action of FLIPPING the switch is hard work. Self-mastery is hard work.*** However, we must employ ourselves first and foremost in this line of work; for, without self-mastery, one can only hope to control his energy let alone ignite the energy of those they lead. Hill states, "If you do not conquer self, you will be conquered by self." You may see two people when you walk in front of a mirror – your best friend and worst enemy. Feed the best friend and starve the worst enemy! Be mindful to absorb energy from virtuous beliefs and invest it in valuable behavior. Your banks of benefits will literally be full and overflowing back into your life – guaranteed!

You change your life when you change something you do every single day. Your energy is no different and is the micro-economics of your life. We must change certain emotional sources, physical sources and enhance spiritual and mental sources daily for the lifeforce – called energy – to change your life and amplify everything you do and everybody you touch! Assess all of your habits in life – your mental attitudes and the beliefs forming them; your feelings and the emotions driving them. Take inventory of all habits – good and bad. Which are working well for you and which are not? ***Routines are powerful. They decrease stress of life by making our actions automatic and much more effective!*** I remember a business coach giving the example of putting on our socks and shoes. He asked, "Is it sock, sock, shoe, shoe?" "Or, is it sock, shoe, sock, shoe?" Unless you go back through the process in your mind, chances are you were running on auto-pilot. Forming great habits will take work, but imagine yourself running on autopilot soon with the new, warrior-like, super-hero, energy-enhancing habits! "What you do once in a while doesn't matter as much as those things you consistently do on a daily basis," said Jim Rohn. Someone else said, "Losing is a habit; so is winning!" Get a few powerful switches working for your energy! Avoid installing too many all at once. Take it one at a time. You've got this! I believe in you! Get in the habit of winning because you're a WINNER!

Here are just some examples of switches that can help build and bolster great habits. Think of your environment, relationships, place of business, office, home, car, and especially personal energy. What are some simple, fool-proof, physical reminders that make it more likely for you to TAKE ACTION. Physical paths – to help form mental ones:

- Write your top three yearly goals down daily to form the habit of alignment. My friend, Andy Bailey, writes his down every day of the year to keep them before his mind.

- Water cup filled by your bed gets you in the habit of drinking first thing in the morning and easier to keep up all day long.

- Walking/running shoes by the door and gym bag in the car puts your mental state in forward motion when the ignition clock sounds.

- Coffee pot on auto-brew helps form the habit of getting up to enjoy a quiet morning routine

- Phone charger away from bed bolsters the habit of unplugging for sleep.

- An alarm set on your phone saying something like, "Plug me in, and go to bed," forms the habit of intentionally going to sleep.

- Book marker for your book and laying the book where you are going to sit the next day and read helps form a routine of learning.

- Some pictorial reminders/cues of your goals attached to your purse, backpack, or in your briefcase; or, a screensaver collage on your phone – sort of like a mini-dream board – builds the habit of visualization.

- Post-It notes on your mirror with what YOU wrote to be important habits and WHY help you build accountability and consistency. *Carve new neurological pathways in your brain by keeping your goals – sources of mental energy – in front of your eyeballs.* Gitomer states, "You have several goals you want to achieve, but they're not written down in plain sight, they just sit on a piece of paper in a drawer or pop up in your head every once in a while – only to be buried in a black hole of procrastination, excuses, and guilt."

- Small, simple and repeatable steps (needs to be simple) helps build the habit of making habit building fun.

- Environmental help like going somewhere for certain important tasks. Gym or greenway for exercise, coffee shop to read, or a quiet nook in town for creating. Limiting or getting away from other mental anchors can help form habits of focus.

- Triggers can be effective switches just as much as they can be ineffective when setting off unwanted emotions. Tie an important priority to each of your daily fun routines. Let's say you love to grab a coffee each morning but you struggle following up with clients; then, create a wonderful coffee experience while knocking out emailing clients and prospects. You might even get creative and say something like, "hope you've got your coffee and ready for an epic day!" You may be surprised what happens when you incorporate something fun into what your brain previously found boring and unexciting. Say you like to run but hate pushups. Run one mile, then knock out ten – yes, right there on the sidewalk. Continue for your run's duration. Get creative and you can build fun, focused, forward-motion activity-based switches in your life.

- "Touch-It-Once" is a great mental memorization serving as a switch to build the habit of decisiveness. When it's in your hand, or on your phone screen, deal with it if you're pretty sure you know what to do and can knock it out in a minute or two.

Know temptations exist & have a game plan for when they're the strongest. Donuts? Coke? Old habit? Either avoid the place or replace the habit with a better option. Example: I've always enjoyed coffee in the evening, but as I get older, tea with honey is a much better choice. Can you do me a favor right now? THINK. What's a great habit you'd love to form? Jot this habit down on a Post-It note and stick it to your bathroom mirror, the inside of the coffee filter cabinet, or wherever you WILL see it just before this habit is to be performed (here on this page is fine if you don't have a Post-It note on you right now). NEW HABIT I WILL FORM:

_____

_____

You can set an alert on your cell phone, too. Set it for the time the new habit is to take place and repeat it daily. Here's a great example of a cell phone alert: "10 minutes to THINK because my mind is an amazing tool."

Reframing Habits

You can reframe the painstaking discipline required to form a new habit! Reframe by repeating your WHY over and over. Know WHY you're installing this switch that will form this new powerful habit! *Reframe by realizing all the benefit you and others will receive because of this new habit!* Reframe by making the process fun! Get crazy excited about this new habit! In her book, *This Year I Will*, M.J. Ryan writes, "because of the way our brains are structured, the most powerful thing your can do is to engage your emotional brain in a way that makes it fun, new, and different." To make any change, she shares, you must have the desire, intent and persistence. James Allen says, "Our life is what our thoughts make it. A man will find that as he alters his thoughts toward things and other people, things and other people will alter towards him." Reframe everything! Make it exciting by keeping the beautiful destination front of mind! Our brain has the tendency to habituate which means we sleep-walk a lot. That's why new things excite us – for a while. Shake up your routine a bit, keep it fun and engaging and ignite energy around it constantly! Remind yourself of your WHY every day! Get creative in constant pursuit of your goal. Like someone said, "Be firm with your goals, flexible with your methods." Engage your emotions into changing! WHY do you want to change? Turn any sort of fear-based WHY into a positive one. For instance, if you're afraid that "obesity will make me sick", then reframe to "being fit allows me to feel so alive and energetic!" State your WHY and write it with your goal. *Ignite all your energies of the mind, spirit, soul and body so that all your emotions go to work for you and stimulate positive feeling!* Tough goals like running or exercising are already working for you releasing all sorts of feel-good hormones into your blood stream. Remember, every day you keep going, your new emotional generators are signaling stronger and stronger; your new mental pathways are getting deeper and deeper! There's a Chinese proverb that says, "Habits are cobwebs at first; cables at last!"

Rewiring Feelings

Feelings are a great indicator of our energy condition, as our emotions (energy in motion) create our feelings. Feelings are the wiring back of the switches we install. To effectively form any new habit, we must understand our feelings. Feelings are tricky. Often, what we feel initially is not the feeling that lasts the longest. The initial feeling often stems from peer-pressure at first and then habitualized activity. The lasting feeling is often more trustworthy and should be analyzed on the front end. Have you ever been tricked by the urge to do something that you know isn't good for you? Maybe an addiction or other poor habit. How about the urge to not do something? Perhaps skip a workout, a phone call, etc. We might say, "Oh, I crave, the feeling of nicotine," or, "I don't feel like running." What we have to consider is the feeling afterward. This feeling is designed to reinforce good decisions by letting us know our energy is flowing. When you have a feeling of regret or remorse afterward, chances are, the urge or feeling to do or not do something was habitualized excitement and not positive energy. When you workout, it's tough, when you run, you must push through, when you relate – truly and deeply relate – with your partner, it takes time. Going for a walk takes time. *These activities might cause some feelings of pause right at first, but in the long run, they deliver a feeling of release, contentment, opportunity to breathe, a chance to be quiet, or to think.* Too often, we'll cave to the fear-based "feeling" of being behind and muddle through another task on our never-ending to-do list. With this fear-based, energy-swindling mind-set, we'll always feel behind. Consider this. When we feel overwhelmed, should we speed the treadmill up? These are actually the best times to STOP, breathe and think. Often, there is something so powerfully life changing we could do to change everything if we'd just take the time – MAKE the time – to think. As we build our "Energy Maps" think of all aspects of life when you felt renewal, recharge, fullness, peace and an overflowing sense of joy for living. Think of the feeling afterward! The feeling upon exit from the activity; not the feeling when you considered entry. Were you stimulated to live more fully and to love more deeply? Did the feeling bless you because you were a blessing to others? Start with the exiting-feeling, and soon, the entry-feeling will align. Don't always trust your feeling "urge" beforehand. Discern between entry and exit feelings based on the facts of the activity, the thought, the idea, the person, the place, and what follows. Here's the formula to help us process and remember our **FEELING**s:

> **F** – stands for feeling.
> **E** – stands for entry feeling (tricky test)
> **E** – stands for exit feeling (truer test)
> **LING** – means trust the feeling that LINGERS long afterward forming an energizing habit.

When I began in the workforce as janitor, I soon began wiring electrical panels. I'll never forget Rob O. The most patient, kind mentor of a panel builder. Rob taught me about reading a wiring schematic and knowing how electricity would flow. "These little things that look like a door-way on an architect's drawing – these are switches," he told me. "They change direction of electricity." Wow! That simple example and lesson that tremendous amounts of power could flow all the way up to a switch I installed, and then could be stopped instantaneously by a switch not being flipped. This literally could mean stopping a massive press or robot that this small panel of wires would control. Incredible! Our emotions are the electricity in our body. As stated before, our emotions are our energy in motion. We must map out our schematic. *We're all wired differently, beautifully and wonderfully. Installing some simple switches in our life can control our energy and turn on tremendous power in our daily lives.* We've got to map it out if we are to enjoy rich energy sources and avoid poor energy swindlers. Energy is stored up waiting to be tapped into – to be switched on. We can read all the motivation and know exactly what we should be doing to grow in life, but until we make the choice to make a move – to FLIP THE SWITCH – we lie dormant.

I've watched team members trudge in to work on Monday, but as soon as Friday arrived, they were charging for the door. Energy switched "ON" at 4 p.m. Friday! Yes, our corporations are filled with people showing up, but not truly engaging. Many powerful warriors sit on the sidelines of their homes, their churches and their communities for various reasons. Perhaps they truly lack physical energy. Maybe the thought of what will happen (success or failure) paralyzes them. Maybe they think their leadership role isn't that important or has a significant impact on others. Maybe they don't know how or where to begin and "elephant-sized" anxiety overwhelms them.

To switch energy and passion on in our lives, we have to make a mental choice to activate. Attend the meeting and sit on the edge of your seat. Take ownership of a task. Take notes. Give feedback. Engage. Pick up the phone and call someone just to say, "I love you." Smile. High five some random person. Make energy happen inside so it can flow outside. Ignite your energy and show up with your best! Give your best! When you get home for the evening, take five minutes to write your notes, finish social posts or call a client back. But baby, when you step in that door, get yourself a big glass of water and switch that energy right back on for your best clients – that wife and kid(s). Play, cheer them on, listen to them recount their day, ooh-and-aah over their homework and be fully present. This is FLIPPING the switch to energy-rich sources of relationship. Alas, we don't always "FEEL" like it, do we? However, just like pushing ourselves in the gym, we're often surprised at how much more power lies just behind one great switch. Start asking more of your energy reserves by turning off the swindlers and turning on the powerful, energy-rich switches in your life. You'll be surprised how much engagement and passion is stored up inside! *Believe that by switching OFF poor swindlers and switching ON rich sources, you're able to show up full of energy – fully present for your people and ready to make a lasting impact!* FLIP THE SWITCH – let the energy fill and overflow your life!

CHAPTER 11
ENERGY EQUATION
a 4,000-year-old secret

"Whatever your hand finds to do, do it with all your might!" – King Solomon

Algebraic Epiphany

BOOM! Crash! From upstairs in our house came the commotion – it was my brother's laboratory/invention room – and something had just blown up. John and Stephen were inventing and testing something again. They were twin brothers. In fact, we called them, "The Twins." They built a light-bulb, deconstructed motors, studied Einstein, principles of relativity, and loved experimenting with cause and effect! Later, they went on to obtain their electrical and mechanical engineering degrees. One of the biggest impacts they made on me is when Mom sent me to sit under their tutelage, as I struggled with my entrance into Algebra. I can't say I remember everything they shared, but one thing stuck with me and really helped me understand a lot about Algebra and its practical twin of Physical Science that followed shortly. They told me one day in very scholarly wisdom, *"Tim, always remember this one key: both sides of the equal sign must equal! Therefore, whatever operation is done on the right, must be done on the left."* I never forgot this and in case you're a middle-schooler reading this, hear me well. Mastering Algebra – knowing how to solve for the unknown – is a skill that will allow you to excel in every phase of life. It's so very practical! One day, on one of my runs, this epiphany happened for me that I call the **"Energy Equation."** Come to find out, it's a 4,000-year-old secret.

4,000-Year-Old Secret

Why is the Energy Equation a 4,000-year-old secret? I remember studying and memorizing Solomon's words as a kid, but not until the middle of my career was the secret unlocked to me. With this ancient secret, we begin our journey of intense ownership of life. Are you ready? King Solomon was known in his day as the wisest king – the wisest man – that ever lived and ever will live. He created wealth like no other empire. His was a kingdom so vast and at peace with all surrounding kingdoms there's not been an era like it since. Buried in his proverbs is this golden-nugget that will carry a young person to the top in business, a kid from Chicago to the Presidency and a regular person to super-hero status. The proverb goes like this, *"Whatever your hand finds to do, do it with all your might."* At first glance, we hear the quote come to mind, "Do it with passion, or not at all." This gets us super close to the secret. But, here's where ownership comes in and makes this one of the greatest keys I've ever been handed. Here's the secret from an ownership perspective:

Whatever I decide to do = I will do with all my might

I own my hand; therefore, I choose what I do. Whatever my hand finds to do, I will do with everything I've got. If I cannot, I will stop finding that half-hearted thing to do. The equation must equal. Must equal! What's done on one side must be done on the other side of the equation. It seems so simple, and it is. Sometimes it's the simple truths we overlook for a more complicated way. Simple doesn't mean easy, however. We must work at being all in! We've heard the saying spoken in jest, "He's all heart," meaning he really isn't. It's used to depict stingy, holding-back and lack of engagement. If you're truly all heart, you put all your zeal and emotion into your work. When your emotions are flowing freely and in the right direction this exudes positive energy. Remember, emotions are simply your energy in motion. When you're truly all heart, you're brimming with energy and it overflows in what's known as enthusiasm. In her book, *The Spirit of the Teacher*, Flora Plummer writes, "There is no adequate substitute for enthusiasm." Half-hearted effort means defeat; wholehearted effort means success and victory. As I'm sitting here writing this book, my seven-year-old daughter Nikki walks up and shares this poem she learned in school. Coincidence? I don't think so. It goes, "be the labor great or small, do it well or not at all." If I can't give it my all, my absolute best, then I must give it my "no". The principle of energy trans-ference equated for us four thousand years ago is so **KEY**:

Whatever I decide to do = I'm engaging all of my energies into!

Engage Everything

You've already decided on everything you're currently in. Further, one side of the equation is a constant – all your might. That factor never changes. Therefore, if you can't give all your might, why? Consider why you're not engaging everything that's in your life with everything you have. *"All your might" signifies every last ounce of spiritual, mental, emotional and physical energy into your life work and relationships!* The word "might" is defined as, "great and impressive power or strength, especially of a nation, large organization, or natural force!" Might's synonyms consist of words like force, power, vigor and energy! All of our energies – focused and fervent (a passionate intensity)! In order to engage everything, we must start by eliminating some things. That's right! GIVE SOMETHING UP! When I began practicing this equation, it's funny how easily gossiping by the coffee pot at work dropped off. It simply seemed so unworthy of my everything, and I could never truly give it my full engagement. It was always lowered voice, or looking over a shoulder. After elimination, let's consider the roles we've committed ourselves to such as career or family. Do you engage your work and relationships with everything you've got? William James said, "On any given day, there are energies slumbering in everyone which the incitements of that day do not call forth ... compared with what we ought to be, we are only half awake. Our fires are dimmed, our drafts are checked. We are making use of only a small part of our possible mental and physical resources ... stating things broadly, the human individual thus lives far within his limits; he possesses powers of various sorts he habitually fails to use. It's evident that our organism has stored-up reserves of energy that are ordinarily not called upon – deeper and deeper strata of ignitable material, ready for use by anyone who probes so deep." The question here is evident. Are we calling upon all our energies to engage everything to which we put our hand? Or have we, by habit, learned to play it safe? To stretch jobs and tasks out. To overthink and underperform; or, simply adapt to the status quo? In engaging everything with our everything, there are three things that will prevent us from doing so:

- We can't give our all because all or more is taken. We're maxed out.
- We can't give our all because the outcome isn't aligned with our beliefs (we don't really care).
- We can't get give our all because we're allowing the swindlers of distractions.

Who are the ones who'll unleash all of their might – all of the energies – in their workplaces, behind the counters of our coffee shops, in the halls of our governments, in the classrooms of our schools, and in the living rooms of our abodes? What will your friends, coworkers and kids remember of you?

Equation's Insurance

Another reason the energy equation is so vitally important, it is our insurance policy against energy swindlers. How many things in life do we do half way? Think about it. Consider speeding. Can your whole being get in on this? No. Our conscience is on the lookout for blue lights. Condemning the waitress for a mess up? We're not sure how much anger is too little, or too much. The insurance, if we're applying the equation, will cause us to stop right away. It will lead us to invest our energies into that which we know we should do – and can do wholeheartedly! This insurance takes the guess work out of decision making. Have you ever found yourself saying, "I knew I should've said no." Of course, we have. With the equation, swindlers must go – you KNOW you can't go all in. Poor habits that would cause us to cover our tracks, or hide, simply can't measure up to Energy's Equation. *Energy's equation gives us the legitimacy to guard sources. You KNOW you love going all in on the sources. You feel great, whole, renewed and refreshed when you do.* Even the wholesomely good-kind of exhaustion brings fulfillment, but it's hard to carve out the time for energy-rich source engagement. Swindlers called distractions see to it! The equation puts a priority of positive switches – they simply must be installed under the policy of this insurance. This is the preparation to win. These switches form reminders, accountability mechanisms, and formation of neurological pathways to imbed whole-hearted action in the right activities. These switches may be quotes, mantras, or powerfully stating your WHY, and hereby reminding yourself to show up to everything with everything!

Clarity Brings Confidence

Knowing yourself and having a powerful life vision mapped out brings clarity. Seeking to constantly raise your perspective brings clarity to every moment. Knowing your one thing, what it is you do best, the experience you create, the gifts and strengths you were designed with and what energizes you is paramount to moving through life with energetic confidence. At this point, your conscience is at peace, your very DNA and all your energy can be unleashed. What's your secret sauce? What's something about you that you can add uniquely no matter where you are? For some it's encouragement, strategy, leadership, support, strength, inspiration, connecting, analytics, relatability, promotion, giving, and the list goes on. Of course, all of us have different, valuable perspectives. "Clarity precedes mastery and the clearer you can get on what you want to create in life, the more focused you will be in your daily behaviors," says Robin Sharma.

Analyze

Analyze your life for alignment. Seek to gain clarity. Ask deep questions that probe whether you're truly living fully and loving deeply – engaging your everything into everything you decide to do. Who do I love? Do the people in my life, close relationships and those I spend the most time with, feel that I'm all in? Do I have these prioritized? Wife, kids, colleagues, friends, etc.? Analyze all activities and habits of life.

Are you stuck? Perhaps addicted? Apply this equation! There were past relationships in my life that I knew would turn toxic, yet runaway desires led me down some dangerous, emotional paths. This Energy Equation saved my family from irreversible hurt. I could neither fully engage myself deeply in the toxic relationship, nor was I wholly myself in the healthy ones. Not surprising, I began feeling the healthy relationships dwindle while the toxic ones choked me. I became guarded and powerless. *Freedom was mine when I had a moment of analyzation, I gained clarity on who I was, sought emotional healing and realigned my actions to what I knew I could and should do with ALL of myself – my whole being!* To gain this clarity, we must first think, remember our vision and who we're called to be, and then operate wholly aligned with it.

Take education. I firmly believe college education is pushed too early nowadays. Young people are pushed to make life decisions before they really KNOW who they are. They lack engagement in college, and many finish with a degree they feel isn't useful. A college education is priceless; yet, there's nothing futile with exploring a career, an entrepreneurial endeavor or travel before attending. Instead of following the crowd, seek clarity, or attending college may end up taking you down paths other than growth.

In sales, it's grossly important that we be "picky" and choose only the prospects we KNOW we can help. Perhaps we have a pretty good gut about them and with prompt discovery we confirm they're a fit. Ask tough questions so that you don't waste a lot of your or the prospect's time. There's nothing worse than a perceived relationship with disjointed objectives and no clarity on how it's to be mutually beneficial. On the other hand, there's nothing better than a strategic fit, where both parties know how they benefit each other. Clarity brings confidence into all activities, endeavors and relationships. Lee Iacocca said, "If you want to make good use of your time, you have to know what's MOST important and then give it all you've got!" I love how Lincoln said, "Whatever you are, be a good one." Clarity fills you with confidence and arms you with courage!

Freeing up RAM

Give your energy demands a cleanup. Free up some RAM. Start engaging everything and eliminate complexity that comes with uncertainty and procrastination. We have super creative minds – they're amazing and beautiful. Often, though, we overcomplicate simple "yes" and "no" answers. Ask yourself. "Can I get my heart completely on board with this?" If not, ask, "Why not?" If that why not is true and proves misalignment with your goals, then it's an easy "no." Most appreciate an employee or staff member who just obeys and carries out commands, right? However, One of the best questions anyone can ask a manager, employer or leader is, "Why are we doing this?" Too often, a WHY question is seen as a threat and a retort is given without really answering and instilling the same belief and insight from the leaders' heart into those following. Great leaders, encourage WHY questions. This is quickest and surest way to inspire enthusiasm in your team and garner their conviction! Of course, this demands a thorough understanding and belief of the WHY ourselves. When we don't make time to distill and instill the reason – our WHY – we miss the truest nugget of gold any leader really possesses. Clear utterance of our WHY demands the hard work of thought and clarity. *Leaders who adopts the Energy Equation and put all their might into their work of instilling the WHY will in turn enable their followers to throw all their heart and might into achieving it.*

Free up RAM by dumping what you're half-heartedly believing in; invest all your energies into those things in which you believe whole-heartedly in. Regarding stray thoughts and ideas, have a standard operating procedure for getting them off your mind so you can stay focused. I have this practice of texting myself great ideas and going back through at the end of the week to see if anything stuck, resonates or is something I should apply or follow-up on. Text, email, write, chicken-scratch, Evernote, or voice-record it so that you can data-dump and keep RAM freed up. Then, have a routine time to reflect and journal. Your mind will understand, and will begin loving your habit and ease up on you. When your mind knows you will make the time to listen to it, it will settle down a little bit for you. Have this routine so that you're less stressed and can attack what you're working on with everything you've got!

Courage Beats Cowardice

Goethe said, "Whatever you dream you can, begin it." Take bold and powerful action. McGinnis writes, "Boldness has genius, power and magic in it." Therefore, to operate within Energy's Equation, one must move with courage and boldness.

- We hold back when cowardice sets in – fear.
- We're all in when boldness lets out – faith.

Be courageous and whatever you find to do, do it with everything you've got. Stir up all your energies for the magical work you're about to perform. Jump up, dance, sing, get excited, make a big deal out of every deal and knock everything you do out of the ballpark!

Outcome – Know It

How many times have you had generalities, or big bulky tasks stay on your to-do list (or lists) seemingly forever? Sure. We all have. Often, procrastination is simply lacking the clarity of what the outcome looks like. One of my professors in college wrote in big and bold words across the syllabus, "PLEASE READ," and told us that most of his students wouldn't read the syllabus. He knew this how? By all the questions he fielded that were answered right within the four-page document. Here's a better way to complete everything on time or ahead of schedule. Engage all of your energies into the very first part of any task – thinking! Og Mandino said, "Mind power is today the sole measure of mastery. Resolve that your own brain shall be made to work for you with all its might!" *Think through the real demands of the project, break apart its components, define resources needed, action steps necessary; then, take the first step of starting on it. It takes mental energy, sure, but it's worth defining at the very beginning of taking on any task.* Confucius said, "A wise man can carry out whatever he can specify." Get specific about what it is you're going to do, today and even more specific about the outcome you desire. "Until you know what the next physical action is, there's still more thinking required before anything can happen," says personal productivity guru, David Allen. Take this advice to heart. Seek clarity first. Know the outcome and action items so that you can unleash all your might on accomplishing and driving for the goal. Don't settle by wallowing in uncertainty. KNOW the outcome of your day before you begin the day and your energy will be a focused investment. You will exhibit the stealth of the special forces. You'll get-in and get-out completing the mission. Live as an elite warrior by getting super focused on specific results you will achieve each day! Avoid letting an elephant sneak onto your to-do list. Take one bite and put that on your to-do list. Don't worry. The big elephant-sized project isn't going anywhere, but it'll be achieved much faster if you'll think bite-sized, actionable specifics.

Procrastination – Overcome It

The reason most don't put their whole heart into anything is because they're unsure. They've not bought in, or they're holding back because of doubt. That's why clarity is so vitally important! It's also why this simple formula works so well. If you do it, do it with all your heart! Flora Plummer states, "The secret of true enthusiasm lies in loyalty to an objective." Remember the story of the Hernan Cortez who burned the ships? It's nothing but taking the first step and never looking back. Solomon said it like this, "Talk with no action leads to poverty." Walt Disney said, "The way to get started is to quit talking and begin doing."

Someone else said, "After all is said and done, a lot more will have been said than done." You don't need another protocol, complex system, committee, etc. – you need life! You know what to do; do it, now! *Time is now! Indecision will swindle your energy every time.* Great leaders attest to making decisions quickly and changing them slowly. Henry Ford popularized this saying, but it's been modelled all throughout history, "Successful people make decisions quickly (as soon as all the facts are available) and change them very slowly (if ever). Unsuccessful people make decisions very slowly, and change them often and quickly." Decisiveness alone unleashes energy that lies dormant. "If you can't decide, you procrastinate." Says coach Zoe McKey in her book, *Daily Routine Makover*. When people don't know what decision to make, or their waiting on the chain-of-command, energy flow is stifled, and things come to a screeching halt. In fact, great organizations empower their people with decision-making ability. Decisiveness in your personal life just as in business is imperative. Empower yourself and make the simple decisions quickly and change them slowly. Often, we do just the opposite. We take all year thinking about something we know we should do, we slowly decide to do it, and then, at the first sign of trouble, we turn back. Energizers know the value of staying in high productivity state – getting work done – and they make decisions quickly and throw their "souls fresh, glowing ardor" back onto the field of battle!

Understand every time procrastination begins setting itself up. What about when we agree to too much? That's the start of overwhelm and procrastination setting in. Because many of us are overachievers, we have the disease to please. Notice when you shake your head slowly with uncertainty walking out of the next meeting. You're not exactly sure what it is you're supposed to go start on, or the outcome is unclear. Don't go! Stay and ask. Don't spend your energy floundering around and frustrating yourself; it's achieving the result that we need to give all of our might and power to. When you can't figure something out. Ask for help. Procrastination stifles our energy every time. Here's how to over-come procrastination in **3 STEPS**:

- Speak it – knowing how to definitely state the outcome unleashing energies of thought and the plan is already being formulated.
- Share it – embrace accountability and be willing to ask for help.
- Start it – sow something small to get the ball rolling; then, take

the project past the point of no return as quickly as you can, while mapping out a powerful plan for its completion!

Simply getting started is 51 % of the battle. In sales, the way to apply the Energy Equation and give everything you've got is being fully present with your client and following up to add value to their lives. Let your prospects and clients know you've heard them and you care enough to help. To keep relationships long-lasting and energetic, this equation must endure. Therefore, if you're not the company that's right for their needs long-term, you refer them to the company that is. Very few things scream "I care about YOU" louder than giving up a sale for their greater long-term good. *Nothing screams "I care about YOU" louder than you engaging them with everything you've got for the entirety of the relationship.*

Start – Decide To

Whatever you say "yes" to, frame it in terms of your vision and goals. Believe whole heartedly that by putting your all into something, you'll move closer to your goals. You may work what you feel is a terrible job. Reframe. Know that you're earning a living and learning skills every chance you get to move you closer to your vision. Reframe by seeing people at the same job that you can inspire, encourage and support. Pour everything into your work through a reframed perspective. If you're going to invest any energy into a problem, it must be both important and improvable. If not, move on. Don't choose it. Make all decisions with confidence and calmness. The quote, "You don't have to be great to start, but you have to start to be great" is compelling! How many goals set dormant & how many dreams are stashed away because we simply fail to start? Conditions will never be perfect. In fact, perfection often leads to procrastination which is the greatest enemy of start! Starting is half the battle. Starting will teach you lessons you couldn't have learned any other way. Starting will energize & excite you! Starting will kickstart mometum in your life! Be an initiator! Be a starter! Starters change the world!

Starters set things in motion! Starters experience the thrill of accomplishment & achievement! It may be the smallest step; just start! Do something right now to get you closer to your goal. What's some small step you've had on your mind for a while? Dump it here in commitment that you're going to start on it – take one tiny step – as soon as you lay this book down:

It's the "thrashing early" that Seth Godin talks about in his book *Linchpin.* This thrashing may be setting out your shoes or gym bag the night before so you're that much more prepared for success. Listing what action items will accomplish a priority and then starting! Yes, get started – Go!
You may say, "Tim, I want to run a 5K but I've never run before." OK, for the next week, walk one mile after dinner, or in the morning, whatever works best. Would you go start on this action right away? Most people won't. They begin analyzing, overcomplicate it, and fail to ever take any action. I heard one business leader call it the paralysis of analysis. Sometimes, we over analyze and thus, stop dead in our tracks – no forward motion. I've begun this practice. As soon as a meeting is over, I will take all of the easy, small action items and for ten intentionally, focused minutes, I'll pause, pull out my iPad, and send the email, or schedule the event, or text and ask the client if we can chat in a few. BOOM! Ball rolling immediately. Obviously, some tasks may require some further brainstorming, etc. But, knock the small stuff out, and get clear on the big stuff enough to take the first step. *Always KNOW THE FIRST STEP SO YOU CAN START!* The more time we think about something, the more chance our brain has to build up fear about taking action. Simple things become mountains, and we sweat the small stuff. The fear our brain manufactures is what Zig Ziglar calls "false evidence appearing real – F.E.A.R." Now sure, we should think through our actions, but what better time to start then when the subject is being discussed. We've all heard that our actions speak louder than words. So, let's get clear, get courage, and get crankin'!

Saying Yes

Know the start, what the outcome looks like, and the requirements and resources you'll need. It may take a bit of faith to see the resources that aren't yet in place, but by saying "yes", you know you're going to go after those resources, exceed the requirements and drive for the desired outcome so you can win. You know, that by saying "yes", this work or relationship fits and aligns with your gifts. You know you will give it everything you have. Work thoroughly, hug tightly, handshake firmly, walk boldly, give freely, smile radiantly, and the list never ends so long as you said "yes". "Yes" in both your voice and heart takes full responsibility – extreme ownership; on the other hand, "yes" in your voice alone, not in your heart, makes excuses. By diminishing your input, you diminish the task or the possible outcome. Make decisions based on the equation for both your sakes. Poor engagement means they get a poorer product than they should have. If you say "yes" to a project, yet you're not willing to throw all of yourself into it and give it your best – all in – then, you should've said no! The equation doesn't equal.

Saying No

Do you struggle saying no? Someone once said, "It's easy to say 'no' when there's a greater 'yes' burning inside." We're wired to be productive and we like a sense of accomplishment. For those who fail to plan, they plan to say "yes" to anything. Or, we simply don't have any real dreams or goals in our own life. We lack direction. We lack the power of dreams; therefore, we simply say "yes" to every sparkling opportunity that comes along and looks exciting. This is a good way at the end of the day to do what sparklers are best known for doing – fizzling out. Do we say "yes" because of the disease to please? Sometimes we say "yes" to please someone, but we really don't mean "yes". Our hearts are saying no. This is a real struggle for many and ensnares our energy. We're only half-way in and it shows. *Say "no" so you can say "yes" and throw all your vigor and might into the work that aligns with your gifts, your vision and your calling.* You can practice graciously and tactfully say "no". Working with my Asian clients, I had to learn that phrases such as "that could be very difficult," or "no, maybe," meant "no". My further attempts to convince them were fruitless. Master negotiator, Charles L. Karrass claims that "most cultures are more comfortable saying 'no' than Americans." Do you feel bad saying "no"? Try these approaches:

- "I'd love to take part because I love you and believe in what you're doing, but it doesn't align with my goals right now.
- "I'm already committed over here, but have you thought about asking _____." Think of someone (not to pawn them off) whose goals this task may align with, and who'd love to take part. If you believe in what they're doing give a minute of cognitive value to connect them or warmly introduce them to someone who can help.
- Or a simple, "Not at this time" is completely ok.

Commit to Complete

True energy and enthusiasm is rooted in belief. Belief in the outcome! Belief enough to see a task to completion. Therefore, one word can help detect phony enthusiasm every time. It denotes work. The word is preparation. Preparation is just as necessary as enthusiastic execution of a plan. *Authentic enthusiasm will be as deep in the preparation process as it is in the delivery.* Leaders, look for those who will either get excited about the details of a plan, or leave and immediately follow up with action. The one enthusiastic about the party – the celebration – but giving little cognitive focus to the plan or execution may be phony. It's the countless hours of practice, the tiring work of study and research to which genuine enthusiasm brings joy. Are you engaging the preparation process with just as much enthusiasm as you are the action? Planting the seed and pulling the weeds is wearisome to the mind of him who doesn't envision and visualize the sweet and yellow corn, the green and glistening peppers or the bright, red tomatoes. The excitement displayed by the one who passes by seeing the beautiful and lush garden will never equal the enthusiasm possessed by the gardener who has patiently and faithfully labored long. He will joyously reap the results The gardener believes in and trusts the process. He doesn't rush the process, and the harvest time brings satisfaction, not surprise. Conviction is deeply rooted belief. When conviction is present, passion abounds, commitment to complete is evident, and enthusiasm overflows!

... Commitment

Conviction drives commitment. Remember a couple weeks into the new year? The rush of goal setting & freshness of the new begins to dwindle. Commitment is a daily mentality! Someone put it like this, "Commitment means staying loyal to what you said you were going to do long after the mood in which you said it, has left!" Commitment takes discipline. It takes a reminder of why you committed in the first place. Rewarding yourself by celebrating milestones is a great way to gain some extra jazz along the way! Commitment doesn't always mean easy; however, the benefits are huge! Staying committed gives you internal peace, builds perseverance & energizes you for the next step! Stay focused and committed to whatever you say you will do! *What you do is exponentially more important than what you say!* Whatever your hand finds to do, commit to doing it with all your might.

... Completion

What creative idea do you have that will change your world and the world of those you care about? We can change the world by first changing our world. Proactively changing from the inside-out and working in our center of influence should excite us. Here's why. We own this space. We don't have anything holding us back. We can maximize our capacity, influence and engage everything we have!

Changing ourselves is manageable and has huge ripple effects! Believe you can, start on it and you're half-way there! There's still the other half, though and if we fail to formulate a plan of completion, we can get stuck in a creative process with no clear finish line. Our energies can be bogged down enormously with big tasks and projects hanging open. William James stated, "Nothing is so fatiguing as the hanging on of an uncompleted task." We were created with a desire to create. That's right. From birth we've been busy putting things together: blocks, trains, Legos, ABCs, words, sentences, relationships, life, etc. Figuring out how to put together our basic needs comes most naturally. The dreams of life, the passions of our hearts, better life conditions and higher ambitions can present completion challenges, especially if we're pioneering a new way. We're curious about doing something. We think maybe the diet will help us, maybe going for a daily walk will increase our clarity, or perhaps prayer time will reach the hurting friend. Our creativity kicks in and we start considering, ruminating and thinking. We put ideas together in our minds, we build the house in our minds, we start the diet in our minds, we make the career change in our minds, and then – we shelve the idea. We begin it in our mind, believe it will add value to our life or those around us, but we fail to take an initial step to get the ball rolling. David Niven PhD states, "Nothing kills progress or deadens enthusiasm more than someone who talks but never follows through." *The energy enhancement when we start creating and then finish that creation is incredible. It literally expands our creative capacity and strengthens the muscles of follow though.* We limit ourselves and shrink our muscles when we fail to implement. We go through life being great idea generators and talkers – that's it. We must move past fear and procrastination, decide to start creating and unleash all our energies to complete it.

Making the leap from creativity to actual creation is key! Like Mr. Incredible says in the great Pixar movie, "It's show time!" Take a step of faith. You've planned, and you KNOW you can make a difference! Like my three-year-old son said, "Dad, I gonna a build train." With six foam blocks and a minute later, "Dad, look! I builded a train!" Do this! Write below, then text a trusted friend:

I'm going to create: _____

Say it. Say it over and over. Create it! Change the world! Energizers create and complete by taking daily action – no matter how small – and throwing everything into it!

Heightened Frequency

When we put our entire being into one thing, we call an invisible and powerful force into our ranks which allies with us pulling in opportunities we didn't see before, attracting talent we thought inconceivable, charging through barriers we thought impenetrable and summoning strength we didn't know existed. It's the law of heightened frequency. We rise above the clutter, we harness our energy through clarity and we literally attract anything lacking. Heightened frequency is a vision so clear you speak it and it resonates louder and longer than it used to. *The more of us we put into something, and the fuller our capacity is, the higher frequency we generate.* A former CEO of mine would say, "What you focus on will expand." He's right! Why do we get the most done the last day of anything? We simply must do it! We create unparalleled urgency and a muscle called "will" flexes itself. We rarely flex this muscle until it's an absolute necessity. The person who will flex the muscle of "will" daily, will perform at much higher levels than the average person They create urgency for themselves to do what may not be necessary, but they deem the highest necessity for the highest rate of return! They ignite energy at deeper levels, operate with fuller engagement, and rise to the highest levels. We get the most done the last day of anything because we must and so we do! The old saying goes, "Where there's a will, there's a way." It's so true. What would happen if we lived every day with this same amount of urgency? This will cause our will to be exercised! Whatever our hand finds to do indicates our agreement to do something. Doing a thing with all our might indicates we know we must recharge so we can go at it again with all our might! Understand this and you'll rarely miss a good night's rest, you'll dismiss busyness, distraction, and mindless mediocre endeavor. Understand this and you will thrive in life as a powerful energizer. When you have a definiteness of purpose and clarity on that which you desire, you must apply everything within you, all your energy and give all your focus to make it reality. The heightened frequency says, "I must," and "I will!"

Tired Is Good.

Do you engage your workplace with everything you've got, and are you able to sustain that engagement? We should tire, but it should not force our energy to flow in negative directions. If it does, then we may not be aligned in our gifts and calling. Tired is one thing, but stress, overwhelm and burnout are another. When I speak, I tire, but I gain fulfillment and satisfaction from connection with the beautiful souls in the audience. Am I tired, yes. Any less energized, no. I'm flowing, and passion is going through the roof. Writing does the same for me. What's your gift that you get tired while doing without shrinking capacity. Like muscles, properly exercising your gift is like time under tension – your capacity will expand. Tired is good, it's an important indicator. Tired means you left everything out on the field. Physical exhaustion and feeling tired are good signs. Follow your body's call for rest so it can recharge. Tired means your physical and mental energies need renewal and recharge. The energy transference will take place as you sleep.

Whatever you're doing in life should not stress you out. That may be a sign of inadequate feelings prompting a deeper look at what emotions are signaling hurt or need repaired. Overwhelmed and anxious people struggle sleeping; tired people don't. Knowing when you're tired is equally important – recognizing the feeling so you can choose your response to it. A good night's sleep may be one of the most powerful tricks to physical energy; and really, it's no trick at all. Whatever your hand finds to do, do it with everything you've got – all your energies – and sleep like a baby at night!

Deep Fulfillment

Whatever we decide to do must equal doing it with all of our might if we are to experience living fully and loving deeply. This equation will save us from half-hearting anything, and allow us to experience the joy of passionate living, full contribution and deep fulfillment. I remember as a kid, there were days I'd dilly-dally cleaning my room. I'd feel worn out. My lack of engagement stifled my energy – I had no drive. I'd feel sluggish. I'd be restless that night, not feeling the deep fulfillment of total contribution. Then, there were days when something else exciting was about to go down. The stipulation was stated by Mom. Clean your room BEFORE you go ride horses, "and don't stuff things in the closet." Bummer. I was counting on the closet. Oh well. Even without stuffing, doing a pretty good job organizing my desk and folding the clothes and hanging the shirts with the first button buttoned (we weren't allowed to just drape them over the hanger), I could have the room marine-tight in an hour. Our careers and our lives can be much the same way. We can psych ourselves out the same way in life feeling like we did a lot, but we simply stretched out an hour task into days because of lack of focus, discipline, etc. We feel restless and unfulfilled. If you go a step further, this happens even in the corporate world. Our lack of productivity can go unnoticed for a long time. Literally. Or you just outperform someone who's less productive. We collect our paycheck and feel ok about ourselves. *We literally fail to tap into the tremendous joy of full contribution when we don't give each objective – and every day – our all.* Why hold back? "Whatsoever" means everything. Do everything you do with everything you have, or don't do it at all. What a life saver! Tap into the abundance and deep fulfillment of giving your all! Why do we hold back? Fear of what others think instead of faith of what could happen? Are we ruled by fear? Do we shrink back into the shadows? Does perfectionism stop us? Do feelings of undeserving or fear of accolades scare us? Why? If we're confident in who we are, then we didn't do it for accolades, but simply because our belief is to do everything we choose to do with everything we've got! Avoid lowering yourself to accolades. Competition and comparison thrive on accolades. When you thrive in the virtuous belief of giving your all, then credit can go to anyone and you're joyful. Competitive and comparative fevers have been eradicated and you feel the health of being whole hearted in everything you do. You give your all and do your best! Deep fulfillment is immediately yours and that's enough. You become a team-playing, synergistic cheerleader! Whatever you choose to do, you do it with all of your might!

CHAPTER 12
TIME MACHINE
creation and redemption formula

"It's not the shortage of time that should worry us, but the tendency for the majority of time to be spent in low-quality ways." – Richard Koch

Backpack's Proof

Crash! Papers flew everywhere! I had slung my backpack down from my shoulder in an attempt to grab one form – one simple piece of paper – I needed an advisor to sign. Everything was so tightly packed together, that, when I finally gripped and yanked this one form out, everything else gave way. Going back to school amidst launching a business and raising four kids with Jennifer, my wife, who was also launching a business was invigorating – to say the least. We had to prioritize! Talk about backlog like crazy if one day got off kilter, though. Well, this morning was that one day. I'd slept in, missed my run, literally stuffed two, three-ring binders, a stack of business paperwork, some thank-you notes, my client's coaching folder, power cords, my laptop, iPad for class, a sales coaching platform I was working on, sponsor package I needed to scan, two brown legal-size envelopes for the Post Office, an apple and some turkey/spinach wraps into my backpack and scurried out the door. Now, there's no way I could have or should have worked on all of that this particular day. *The problem. I hadn't planned what would be priority that day.* When I prioritize, the backpack load is much lighter, the plan is efficient, the priorities move forward, focus is easier, and the day actually feels more fulfilled – not to mention the backpack's weight! Besides, I have time to look up and breathe on the days I planned my priorities. When I didn't plan, I didn't know what I may or may not need that day and I'd take it all just in case. I'd start and stop things a dozen times, feel unorganized, and simply work so inefficiently. We get up off kilter in life, lose sight of our vision and are catapulted into a busy rush. *Getting off kilter is always the greatest opportunity to slow down and pause just long enough to touch back in with your vision.* When you do, light-weighting happens. You can see clearly and make priority-based decisions. And, you carry a much lighter, more efficient and focused load. You won't experience "Crash" on the campus of Middle Tennessee State University. You may experience increased joy along the way, instead. *Time4Energy* was born because so many of us treat time and energy as scarcities. I don't have the time and energy for _____. Now if you're making that statement on a regular basis, chances are, like me, you like to stay busy. Did you know having a busy mentality is addictive? Movement feels like achievement and our brains get lulled into a false sense of accomplishment. Instead, let's figure out the keys to transcend time. Would you like to know the secret to creating and redeeming time?

Creation Formula

I like how someone said, "Time is a quality of nature that keeps events from happening all at once. Lately, it doesn't seem to be working." Time is valuable; time is life. Energy is valuable; energy is life. When you ignite all your energy into all your time, life is lived to the fullest. We've discussed energy, how to ignite ours and measuring where we invest it. But, what about time? How do we spend ours? Know this! We are all given the same amount of time. Every year, month, week, day, hour, minute and second is a sliver of our very lives. How are we investing our time? Since the nature of the universe is abundant, we have all the time we need. Like energy, our time is usually poorly invested and isn't maximized. We look at time as flat instead of leverageable. We can actually gain the ability to create time. Journey with me through this mindset. Creating time should be the very first thing we think of as we walk into work, into our homes, or into our day. These five points form the acronym **LOBBY** for ease of memory:

- Light-Weighting
- Opportunity Cost
- Busy Mindset
- Build Machine
- Your Vision

Let's look at each a little closer and lobby for the creation of time, shall we?

Light-Weighting

If we're feeling overwhelmed, perhaps the best thing that could happen is for our to-do list to disappear and your email to crash. I'm kidding here a little bit, but here's a long story short. It happened to me. My email crashed. Magically, everything important came back. I could remember the important things by simply grabbing a scratch pad and data-dumping from my brain. Everything else was useless or didn't really matter. This is key! Think of email for a minute. Try moving everything to another folder called SORT, begin spamming or unsubscribing from the senseless, daily bombardment that we've grown addicted to thinking we need. Then write down goals for the day. Anything not aligning with the goal gets a quick email stating, "I received your email and will work to align with my goals." *Too often, clutter besets us and literally destroys our time just scanning it, re-analyzing it and thinking a dozen times of the response we should send. We straighten and organize ridiculous amounts of clutter on our desks. We start and stop tasks countless times due to interruption, email alerts, social media vibrations, or unfocused-anxiousness* that calls us to go for a walk to the break room.

Our lives simply have too much going on. Say "no", or eliminate something. Light-weighting must take place if we are to experience effectiveness, focus, peace and alignment This is where one must narrow what it is they will complete, make it a priority and then focus on that! Have you ever gone through a day where you accomplished a ton of busy work – just not the priorities you really needed to complete that day? We all have countless things vying for our attention. **KEY**: dump everything onto a yellow pad, or make a data-dump in Evernote. Now, pick two or three of the most important items and go to work on number one until complete, then number two and so on. Focusing on two or three priorities will keep the important things at the forefront of our minds and it may just be you have to say "no" to something to keep your commitment to accomplishing the priority you're working on. *Experience the peace and alignment this freedom brings. Own your life; own your time. You're not evil for saying "no", you're wise.* The burden is on the requesting party to find alignment with your vision and goals. Do the high value activities that you know align with your vision and goals. Here's how to light-weight and get your energy to **LAST** all day:

> **L** – Lightweight. Dump all the stuff you "have" to do.
> **A** – Ask for help. There are resources you need to tap into.
> **S** – Stop it. Any distractions – stop them!
> **T** – Top Priorities. And, the freedom to say, "It's not on my list" for all the things that aren't on your list.

Now that we've cleared the clutter, we find the golden nugget – opportunity cost.

Opportunity Cost

What could I be doing instead that's of higher value? This is the Time Creator's question. This is the Energizer's mindset as they seek to live life to the fullest and leverage as much time as they can to touch lives and love deeply. Ridiculous protocols, senseless traditions, mental clutter and toxic environments are anchors to the ship called "Opportunity". When I studied accounting, I learned about something called opportunity cost. It's a concept that took some getting used to, but basically, if we spend a certain amount of money over here, what other opportunities did we miss out on and what did those opportunities cost us? Say you buy a $4.49 green-tea Frappuccino with strawberry drizzle. That's wonderful, but had you invested the same amount, you could have earned approximately $250 by the end of your life at a decent rate of return. Your opportunity cost is $250. It cost you this amount to spend $4.49 today. It's gut wrenching when I'm privy to a negative conversation or find myself speaking negatively about somebody. That time in conversation cost me, and it's wasted. While I may have only spent 10 minutes, how many more lives will waste their valuable time once my story or gossip hits the rumor mill? Had I used the time speaking positive, life-giving words, might that have changed a life and mine forever? Understanding this concept is paramount to capturing the opportunity cost mindset. You and I must count the opportunity cost of our time and energy when we spend it. *Negativity is an expenditure yielding no return except an inflated ego. Investment into a better set of pure, powerful and positive activities will literally create time. Every thought, action, call or keystroke creates value!* Thinking about this principle of opportunity cost, when we let things overwhelm us and we freeze, dazed by inability and begin to feel stuck, we are wasting the very time that could have been used bettering the situation. John Maxwell, in his book, *Talent Is Never Enough*, says "Your focus needs to remain in the one area where you have some control – today. What's ironic is that if you focus on today, you get a better tomorrow." This is the Time Creator's stuff right here!

Make plans for creating value with your time in every future relationship, engagement, activity, or project you decide to do. When you create value, you create time. Value appreciates. You don't have time for gossiping, criticizing or jealousy. Investing your time in these liabilities would be a complete waste. The opportunity cost is even greater as the investment into the assets of priorities and people will have lost time germinating and yielding eternal fruit! Mahatma Gandhi stated, "You may never know what results come from your actions. But if you take no action; there will be no results." The closest we'll get to creating time is stop spending it on the actions we KNOW won't garner a result. At this point – when you stop a fruitless action – you just created time.

Busy Mindset

Someone said, "Busy is a mindset," and they're right. It's neither natural, healthy nor energetic to be busy. Energy's definition is "the capacity to do work," and work means something happened – a result was achieved. We must understand why we feel this desire to be busy. What emotion is driving this sensation? Busy is the uncontrolled treadmill of life. Sometimes it feels we're sprinting on this treadmill of life. We have so much being thrown at us we simply put our heads down and respond with a "it is what it is" mentality and never really feel like we can thrive. Or worse, we stay up later, get up earlier and cut out social interaction and relationships to conquer the ever-growing to-do list. Maybe we feel it will warrant a promotion, a raise, or accolades. Question is, do we gain these at the sacrifice of other important things. The treadmill only promises to get faster as technology, artificial intelligence, and Internet of Things advances. *This is our life, and how we spend our time is completely up to us. One choice can literally create time through investment, or waste it through expenditure.* Let's call busyness for what it is. Busyness is a state of mind, an addiction, a drug for minds not at peace. It's a swindler of our very energy.

I was managing a multi-million-dollar budget for my organization as purchasing manager. I loved my job. It was a highly active position and a lot of different tasks which my multi-tasking, busy personality loved. One awesome feature, I was able to touch every department. Everybody needed something from me. Since I love people, this worked out perfectly. Through negotiation training, I learned to love having crucial conversations and handling expectations. The handling expectations wasn't mastered, but I had the textbook stating how powerful this truth was. The interaction with everyone meant the most traversed lane was to my office. When the workday ended, there were many nights I called Jen stating, "I've barely touched my top priorities due to meetings and putting out fires all day, I'm going to have to stay and wrap up." And, because the UPS labels didn't get processed on time, I got to haul the boxes to the hub. I didn't mind, and Jen was always gracious. Problem was that the constant interruptions I allowed caused me to look up from my screen far too many times in a day. Every time I reengaged the task, it took me a good fifteen minutes on average to get back into the terms I was reviewing, email I was crafting, etc. As the kiddos came and grew older, and after a life-changing moment on my 25th birthday, I began taking extreme ownership of my time and energy – my life. One evening, Jen and I were discussing our days and she told me how the kids would constantly come and go needing something. While she loved being a mom, she implemented "Quiet Times" where everyone was quiet, and left each other alone for an hour. "This way I can have time for the important things like exercise and time to sit, think, meditate and pray," she stated. BOOM! The light came on. I went back to work and began implementing "Quiet Time." I created a system for order requests that had to funnel to managers and then established time for the managers to visit my office right before lunch. It kept the meetings very on-point as lunch time was held very sacred by most. From 8 am until 10 am, however, the receptionist banked my calls, I checked out of email, unless my priority happened to be working in or on crafting an email, and I'd work on my top three priorities. Would you believe, many days, I'd at least get the first two completed, get up, grab a coffee, grab any messages from the front, return calls for 30 minutes, answer emails, and then close it down for managers visits.

Lunch time would hit, I'd go run, eat and think through conquering that last priority. My days became fun, and I literally felt as though time had been created. Running, or exercise, doesn't steal any time – it creates time because the swindler called "worry of being unhealthy" is replaced with the source called "a 30- minute run a day" and BOOM! Done. Worry gone. Bonus is you feel great, AND invested thirty minutes of quiet, focused thought. My friend Randy Boyd, who ran 537.3 miles across Tennessee as he ran for governor, and who's completed over 50 marathons, calls his running time, "My time of centering; a time to gather my thoughts and prioritize." Some people spend their entire day trying to find just one priority among their busyness. Maybe it's a walk for you, but here's the deal about time creation. ***Busyness won't allow us the chance to slow down for the important things.*** Doing important things like exercise behooves us to charge back into life to conquer more important things so that we can go back to important things like exercise. It's the first things first principle. Being, then doing as opposed to busy-ness. It's "Aha" moments like these that cause Tim Ferris to write, *The*

4-Hour Work Week. It's "Aha" moments like these that we realize, life's not as complex or as busy as we make it look. In his phenomenal book, *The 80/20 Rule*, Richard Koch states, "There is thus a natural tendency for business, like life in general to be overcomplex. All organizations, especially large and complex ones, are inherently inefficient and wasteful. They don't focus on what they should be doing – creating value for their clients and potential clients." These "Aha" moments cause us to realize how many of our actions don't really create value, but are simply unproductive. We get what we allow. That's right. **We GET *what* WE allow.** Let's stop being victimized; it's our life. Let's start figuring out how we can do more with less. Remember these two acronyms when asking yourself:

- HBUT – "Is this the highest and best use of my time?"
- HVA – "Is this a high value activity?"

Ask and answer these questions truthfully and you'll join a rare breed of Time Creators!

Build Machine

Let's build a time machine. Lao Tzu said it like this, "Time is a created thing. To say, 'I don't have time' is to say, 'I don't want to.'" As we build our time machine, realize how many things we say, "I don't have time for that." It's not always because we don't want to work out, run, go on an afternoon drive, have a spontaneous date with our spouse, surprise the kids by getting home early to throw the ball, and the list goes on. It could very well be that we just don't want to offend a boss or manager. It could be that we are lacking the focus to conquer our priorities as we're pulled into this and pulled into that. Ah!!! Talk about stress as your conscience is screaming to do those all-important things, but you can't find the time! Let's look at four ways to literally put more time back into your life so that you can put more life back into your time.

First, be Columbus! He discovered a whole new world and reshaped an entire planet's perspective simply by raising expectations – he wanted to find a faster way of sailing to India. You too can discover a whole new world of time and reshape the "flatness" most of us operate under by simply raising your expectations. Purpose to do more with less time. People believed the world was flat. Columbus had to cut through the noise of squabbling, fighting, whining and complaining sailors to get "far enough out there" to prove it wasn't. Low expectations never pull us far enough out there. They don't call on our noblest and best energies. We lie dormant spending time like it grows on trees. Raise your expectations of yourself and you'll create time by leveraging it, unleashing mental energies to figure out better ways and kindly questioning, "Why?" You'll take people to a higher dimension and like a Lear Jet, the trip to arrive at a destination is cut in third and you can get on creating value and time much faster. Like Columbus, rejoice, sing and by faith envision a better way, a raised expectation, a higher paradigm. *You literally see the vastness of the ocean, not closing in on you to gobble you up, but stretching out beckoning you to sail on!* We need some modern day Columbuses in our organizations today. Raise the level of expectation and create time by thinking of better ways to leverage the present time!

Second, be effective. Time creation ties to effectiveness. The more effective you are, the more time you free up – create. Brian Tracy says, "Your main goal at work is for you to increasingly develop your personal and corporate effectiveness. The more effective, efficient and productive you are, the better you feel – FEEL - and the more successful you'll be." This is the central focus of Time Power. And efficient, effective and productive work is exactly what truly energized people look to accomplish.

Time Power = EEP (effective, efficient and productive)

Third, think simpler by leveraging what's already learned and buiding from it. Create ways to share lessons learned so you can cut waste and unnecessary steps for others on your team and in your life. When you fail, open up about it and share your lesson learned. You can create time by taking all of the past – the lessons and skills learned, and the mistakes made – and leveraging it to enhance the present and maximize the future. Leverage the best of your past into a focused and value-creating present. Invest it into your future vision! This is time creation! Leveraging the past to invest in the future! Celebrate failures with an application. Leveraging the past means looking for the simplest explanation – constantly simplifying. It's why technology has grown smaller and smaller. Think and learn how to simplify the past to leverage it!

Finally, take extreme ownership of your time! Let's sum these four things up in building the **BEST** time machine:

> **B** – better. Find better ways; raise expectations.
> **E** – effective. Time power; learn how to be most effective.
> **S** – simpler. Think simpler; leverage the past for present results.
> **T** – take extreme ownership. This is your life; it's your time.

Your Vision

Busy is the enemy of thinking. John Maxwell attests that, "a minute of thinking is often more valuable than an hour of talk or unplanned work." When do you think? Have you developed an empowering vision? Not many people have empowered themselves with a life vision. *Many under estimate the value of their thoughts, their lives, or what a vision would mean to them.* M. Scott Peck states, "Until you value yourself, you won't value your time." Your time is part of you. You waste or invest some of you every single day. When we stop and think about this, we're compelled to develop our vision. This vision becomes our WHY for everything we are and do. This vision saves us so much time today which compounds over time – literally creating time! I was sitting with my financial planner, Peachtree Financial, and even in financial goals, they start with your vision – your WHY. Start with vision; create time. Infuse your vision into your day, every day!

I'd encourage you to envision what's possible for every arena of your life. Whether you're a middle-schooler, college student, young entrepreneur, mother, father, corporate CEO or factory worker, and the list goes on. Your vision will empower your beliefs and define your mission in life. You will act in alignment with our vision. You won't fall into the great trap of no direction. You become more powerful than a host of time management specialists. Sure, you can use the tool of time management to categorize tasks, but too often this tool becomes the cart before the horse. Without a vision, categorization is difficult. You wander about which way to go on many of the issues that come up. Your mental energy is exasperated constantly making these decisions on equally good tasks. A vision gives powerful direction and aligns tasks. This is the horse now pulling the cart. You must have a vision. You must know where you're going. All of us are going someplace; most of us just don't know definitely where. We've not dreamed and defined. Dream and define for determined direction! My friend, Jack Daly, calls this "Life by Design"! BOOM!

As a person, team member, business owner or entrepreneur having a vision is crucial to your success. A vision will keep the energy high and magic happening. A clearly defined vision will serve as a guidance system for every decision. It will literally create time for everyone working towards it. If you're the CEO, the power of your vision will directly correlate to how your people value their time. Yet, visions mustn't be reserved for only the CEO. Everyone deserves the empower-ment and thrill of vision. If you work for an organization, ensure your vision can align with corporate goals. Even a janitor, empowered by a vision, will infuse his signature of sparkle into everything he touches! Time is richer and fuller for those infusing vision into it!
Grasp your vision; become a Time Creator!

Redemption Formula

Something must be lost, before it can be redeemed. Redemption means regaining possession of something. If we were to intentionally ponder all the possible outcomes of spent time, would we spend it any differently? *Making plans for the future means that we've mind-traveled to a distant year, envisioned what wasted or spent time looks like, and returned to the present, we're bound and determined to maximize it as an investment instead.* We don't wander; we're specific and know where we're going. We're buying back time – redeeming it! Let's look at what I call "The **4 P's** of Redemption."

Priorities

Do we really have time for time management? What is time management? Can we manage time? We've heard of the four master quadrants of time management:

- Urgent & Important – emergencies.
- Nonurgent & Important – planning, prevention, improvement.
- Urgent & Nonimportant – interruptions.
- Nonurgent & Nonimportant – time wasters.

While these quadrants offer great guidance on categorizing task importance, without vision you have no direction; without direction, it's difficult to know what's important – let alone stay enthused about it. Isn't time management subjective? What's important to someone may be completely non-important to you. In fact, time management consumes so much time! Time was created as a tool. It's a powerful tool, yet many feel its constraints and stress beneath its load. Time also tricks us. It never stops, so we think it's going to keep on going. Buddha said it like this, "The trouble is, you think you have time." *Time isn't the greatest tool, as it doesn't inspire us to transcend it! Yes, we can transcend time. Vision is the greatest tool. It allows us to transcend and yes, redeem time!* With vision comes priorities. Think about blinking, breathing, eating and sleeping. You didn't have to schedule these things, and order of importance was figured out for you. You may have to remind yourself to eat, but are you reminding yourself to breathe. Breathing obviously takes the immediate importance. Priority management, not time management, redeems time. Priorities make goals out of visions. Goals that never burn out for they're fueled by vision. Priorities take us farther faster. It takes time to manage time; and, time management often views time as one linear movement. It doesn't require vision let alone crafting priorities. How useless the visions that never translate into definite plans – smart goals that bring the dreams into reality. Dream big; goal smart; action small! With priority management we shift from a complex four quadrant mentality to a lightweight version of top priorities. Much simpler, more aligned, and it requires – REQUIRES – us to be dreaming big and goaling smart. We save mental energy; we redeem time. With success clearly mapped out through clearly stated goals, every task, wish, hope and desire can quickly be prioritized. You can figure out what needs done first to move the company or your life forward in a big way. The trick then, is to not have too many priorities at once, to build some flexibility around them, and learn to delegate and empower others. Priority management sees time as a leverageable and compoundable resource. Transcend time with dreams. If it's important to you, you'll go for it and work your hardest on it no matter how long it takes and no matter what the sacrifices. Les Brown says, "Go after your dream until it's yours."

Avoid wasting time managing time – how many times have we managed that perfectly and not charged forward in life? Build repeating tasks into a routine, then, manage your priorities! *The people and tasks that align with your vision will align with your priorities; the ones that don't, won't.* Stephen Covey says, "Time is a limited resource, but we aren't. As we create synergy among the roles of our lives, there's more of us to put into the time we have." For example, taking a mental break to come back with renewal may actually redeem time for you instead of pushing through with waning mental focus, or fatigued. Capture this and you quickly become an important versus an urgent thinker! This is Energizer thinking! This is being priority driven – vision aligned! This is time redemption! Ask tough questions of yourself and how you waste, spend or invest your time?

What are the top level most high paying activities you do?
Write the top three that come to mind:

_____

_____

_____

What are the most wasteful, frustrating and seemingly little-to-no value creation? Write the top three that come to mind:

_____

_____

_____

Make these lists. Go to your manager, employer or leader. Let her/him know I asked you to come chat about what's on your heart and mind. Get their valuable opinion and see if they may agree and help you eliminate or delegate something that doesn't align with your highest and best use of time. Redeem time by being priority aligned! Only invest your time in people, in planning and in priorities!

Planning

If we could buy more time, how much would we buy? Well, we can't; but, we can plan to stop losing so much! I like how Orna Drawas, in her book, *Perform Like A Rockstar and Still Have Time For Lunch*, depicts time, "Each of you has a bank, only instead of money, it credits you with time, exactly 1,440 minutes each day and every day. Every night it writes off what you failed to invest." So, how do you buy back time? Figuratively speaking, travel to the future. What do you see? What do you want to see? What habits of time-use will not help you get there? Now, come back and spend it in a better way – right here, right now. This is planning. Be fully present in everything and with everyone you decide to spend your time with today. ***Maximize your impact by planning your spent time before you spend it.*** I've watched sales people spend half a day with a prospect that wouldn't fit; but, in desperation, or to ease the pain of rejection, they logged hours of time investing into nothingness. Be up-front with people, describe a perfect fit, and ask powerful questions so you can determine a fit or not. Create time by stopping its waste. "Yesterday's history, tomorrow's a mystery, but today is a gift," Drawas continues. Don't waste the gift. And what if we re-worded our thinking from how we "spend" our time, to how we invest our time. Time Redeemers plan on how to **INVEST** their time. Time's invested when it's poured into priorities that bring vision into reality. Do you want your kid to do well in school? Then helping her/him with homework instead of surfing the internet is an investment. Do you want to grow in your career? Then taking a course or reading a book is an investment. Investments yield dividends down the road. When you meet with some-one, are you impressing them, or are you helping them? Spending versus investing time! Time Redeemers invest their time!

Consider redemptive thoughts. We become what our thoughts are. So then, our thoughts are the first seedlings of how we invest our time and lives. How are our subconscious thoughts? We've discussed affirmations and mindfully channeling our energies of thought in the morning and reflecting each evening. During the day, however, we are bombarded with stimuli often triggering negative thought patterns. We must think ahead of these usual or possible triggers, and have redemptive triggers at the ready. This is proactivity. This is the formula for replacing negative thoughts that are easily triggered and dwelt upon. How many times do we use our thoughts to look for faults in others instead of training our minds to look for the good? Sometimes replacing old triggers means we must forgive the person or event causing them, which, if we're not willing to do, will continue the negative triggers. Therefore, we MUST forgive and stop fighting the old triggers, and we must redemptively create empowering triggers for the future – redeem the time!

Redemptive responses also require planning. Our responses can get us into a lot of trouble if we're not careful. Think through your responses. *What response is going to create value and what response is going to exhaust time and energy? Often, the necessary response – the energy igniting response – means listening, understanding people's emotions, and crafting a wise solution. The necessary and responsible response takes time. Alas! We're rushed as it is.* Flying off the handle, raising our voice and demanding things works so much faster – but does it really, in the long-run? Think of the work we've just created for ourselves. Yes, we created something alright, but was it valuable? No. We didn't create value. We only created more work and caused emotional wounds which literally evaporate positive energy in our teams and families. The only redemption now would be learning from it and sincerely apologizing to the people we emotionally hurt: our coworkers, associates, wives, kids, etc. We didn't "have the time," responded in a rash way thinking we were saving time, and instead took a loan against banks of future time. Yes, this future time will be spent fixing emotional hurts. Or, unfortunately, in many situations, the future time is spent excusing and explaining why we act certain ways and never taking responsibility for our responses. We simply aren't redeeming the time and we go further and further into debt with time we don't have and aren't guaranteed. Many have come to the end of their physical lives full of regret over wasted time. Redeem the time by planning redemptive responses!

Planning how to spend your time, how you're going to think, and what your responses will be are all forms of redeeming time. This planning brings definiteness of purpose. You aren't distracted and lulled into arguments, squabbles and time-drains. You're sharp, on point and moving through life creating value and generating results. This doesn't mean you can't have fun. Crack up and have fun! Life's fun! Especially when you're intentionally positive and finding the good! A lot of time will be spent sharing laughs. Your emotions are flowing positively and you're not holding back. But, having fun on purpose and with definiteness of purpose is much different than having fun because you're lost, trying to soothe emotions, or addicted to having fun. You've planned what moving toward your vision looks like and you're flowing. You're sharp and focused and producing results. There's a time and place for being casual, relaxing and hanging out with friends. I like how Covey talks about being efficient with time, not with people. Time isn't eternal; people are. Therefore; we must be efficient with our time and gracious with people. When we find ourselves in a wasteful situation, we have the power to graciously excuse ourselves. This is your life. Own it. I've been on visits with clients where I left realizing I gathered nothing that would tell me how we could help each other. It was just a social call. Again, nothing wrong with just being social, but redeeming time means you're buying it back. We must agree that in much of what we do, we don't hold ourselves accountable to being specific and speaking with definiteness of purpose. What's to come from a meeting isn't outlined. We're ok leaving, only to struggle through finding an outcome instead of stating one boldly beforehand. We try things in our families, our communities and groups that we hope pan out, but we never really commit to. Many times, we lack definiteness of purpose until stimulated by an outside event. Think about it. When a firing or layoff occurs, performance naturally increases. Our psyche – fear – goes to work. We get active and try to get healthy usually when what? A doctor's report looks off or ugly. It's our lack of definiteness of purpose that causes indecisiveness in our lives. Instead, let's grab a powerful vision, put together a simple plan, and move with definiteness of purpose to redeem time! Let's redeem time by going back to the future and mapping our way from here to there! This is planning. This is definiteness of purpose. This is being a Time Redeemer!

Preparing

"Always clean the kitchen before bed, Tim!" My Mom's motto was "Don't wake up at a loss." Remember this, plant one **KEY** ingredient today that'll build momentum for tomorrow! Tie up loose ends. Prep for the next day to always start on top. Prepare to win the day, the day before. Zig says, "You were born to win, but, in order to win, you must plan to win, and prepare to win!" As a teen, someone called me "Preppy". I thought it meant I was prepared. We didn't grow up with TV so the "Saved by the Bell" TV-series correlation took place years later. The term technically implies a prep school student clad in certain garb (possibly monogrammed), put together & usually of class. Perhaps Slater's snarky, "Hey Preppy", to Zach Morris, comes to mind. However, Slater's term "Preppy" for the guy who "made it to the corner just in time to see the bus fly by," doesn't correlate to preparation at all. OK, getting past the re-runs occurring in our minds, let's think about preparation for a minute. Preparation is **KEY** to winning at your plan & accomplishing your goals. You must plan to win and prepare to win! Remember that big interview? The night before you laid everything out, shined your shoes, touched up and printed off a crisp resume, studied up on the company, etc. Why? To be ready, confident – prepared! *Is your vision powerful enough to demand the same intention? Do your goals get the same devotion? Do you prepare to win on your plan? Winning at the game of life takes preparation!* It's evening, and you're worn out. Laying out your gym bag, or making that shake can wait 'til morning. Come on, we've all been here, right? Well, it's time for energy! That's right! Remember your commitment to win and WHY it's so important to you! Splash some water on your face! Grab that bag, stuff some clothes in it, blend a shake (better yet, a couple to store in the refrigerator while you're at it), and place a glass of water next to your bed to kick start your engine when the "ignition clock" goes off! Build preparation into your routine! Win at preparation and you win at life! Redeem time by preparing to win the day!

People

Our bodies are bound by time and space; our minds and spirits aren't. Our minds can travel; our spirits can connect. This is the secret sauce of redeeming time. When we change our perspective, we begin deciphering between non-eternal and eternal things. When we change our perspective, and begin to take ownership of life – our whole life – we transcend time and space. *At the end of life, what is it we really have to account for? Relationships. Wow! The other humans we shared this great big ball called Earth with. The other people we were supposed to get along with, and if by any chance we broke past the norm, we may have formed some deep, loving and eternal relationships with.* Yet, we find that we spend much less than 80 percent with the few relationships that make up 80 percent of "relationship value" to us Richard Koch points out in his book. Why not invest our emotional energies building and growing the relationships most important? We engage in more time management activities than we do relationship enhancing activities. We pack a day to the max and pride ourselves on our efficiency instead of making one big, earth-shaking visit or relational investment. Time comes and goes; relationships last forever. Create time by spending what time you have in eternal things. We are so enamored nowadays with fads, trends and the things that simply don't and won't last. We move in and out of relationships, yet these are the eternal things that last. We spend more time on our phones' apps walking through society than we do connecting our eyes with others human's eyes. Strange? Yes, very strange. What has become of human connection – deep connection?

Imagine ten visits with a client, ten dates with a friend, ten evenings with your family, or ten discussions with a team member. You'd think that after that amount of time, you'd get to know them pretty well and magic of relationships would begin to happen. Yes, it should. Now, imagine the redemption of time if you took time before the very first client visit to research them, develop three powerful questions (customized to them to gain the maximum knowledge how your relationship can grow) show up fully engaged, all ears, all social media and phone calls turned off and invest fully into them? What would change? Being fully present in our time with people would be ten times more effective and memorable! We'd do more in the first visit if people felt our depth of engagement – being fully present with them! As a young father, I'd find myself correcting one of my children at one moment and turning around correcting another child all the while being plugged into my phone, some work I took home, etc. The times I said, "Enough," unplugged from everything, and went out in the yard to be intentionally fully plugged into play with them, the whining and issues simply vanished. Inevitably, at bedtime prayers, one of them would say something like this with folded hands and squinted eyes, "Dank oo dat daddy pway wif us." Tear-jerker moment? Yes, and you know what? *I went from fighting issues and barely able to focus, to fully present and harmoniously playing. Temporal to eternal!*

I used to walk into a client visit fearful of missing every little detail. I wrote kids' names, spouses' names, their names, coworkers' names and every problem they were facing. Over ambitious? A little bit of disease to please? Slightly nervous, fresh, green-behind-the-ears salesman? Yes to all. What's worse, I'd take notes while we talked. I finally learned that a notepad in the pocket or Evernote on the phone was enough to capture critical points if necessary. When I began simply pouring my full attention into them and developing a relationship, we connected much better and at deeper levels. Then in the car, what stuck out in my mind as I debriefed myself was what needed to be captured. My recollection and intuition were both exercised and increased as I simply purposed not to be so perfect, but instead, connect deeply. Ask what they love, what's important to them, etc. Inspire, believe and encourage them. Send them a snapshot of your time together, highlight the important things that stood out to you and how you believe you can add value to their life. Create this proposal and send them a Thank-You in the mail as soon as you finish the visit. Let them come back to you for more deep connection.

With my family, I can stress and rush everyone out the door, probably get on a bad nerve and stifle someone's emotions depleting their energy and spend a lot of time and energy later apologizing and healing wounds. Or, I can intentionally plan better by adjusting departure time, not making unrealistic commitments, or – a novel idea – get myself ready earlier and help get the family out the door. At coffee, I can glance at my phone a dozen times, or turn it over and focus in on the needs of the human sitting across from me. This takes thinking ahead about how you're going to spend your time. At work, I can be distracted by all the projects I have going on, the calls I haven't yet made, and the rush of business, or I can calmly sit or stand, and energetically engage my mind and focus on the discussion at hand. Not only will the meeting go better, but you may just be the one to craft the million-dollar solution, plant a powerful question that launches the win-win outcome, or think of the fourth option no one else has thought of. Think of how you will spend your time and maximize every moment to create value. Consider our interactions with other humans: our families, coworkers, neighbors, community or church members, friends or complete strangers. Not only could my mind imagine or create some sort of value for them if I'd simply be fully present and give my mind a chance, but the person would notice and feel loved and cared for. This fully present visit over coffee would equal a dozen of less than fully present visits. By the way, you try this nowadays and you will stand out even more. We've simply grown accustomed to allowing distracted, shallow connection. We excuse each other's lack of full presence in business, in society and on our couches at home. Being fully present in the life that you're in, right now, is the biggest redemption of time! ***Make every visit with family, a friend or business colleague worth a dozen by simply showing up in force as a force – be fully present!***

CHAPTER 13
ENERGY BUDGET
a focused investment

"A successful warrior is an ordinary man with laser-like focus!" – Bruce Lee

Squirrel

"Squirrel!" one of my kiddos shouts! He's quickly joined at the front window by three others. Not to mention a parent (me) who's determined to capture this Kodak moment! It's always priceless seeing four heads crammed into one window space, shades raised, noses pressed against the glass, and the excitement and commotion that's aroused. While this simple illustration created a fun memory, squirrels in life aren't as funny. Squirrels of life manifest themselves through distractions, be it technology, people, busyness, or just difficulty focusing. Working in manufacturing 10 years, we would light-heartedly shout, "Squirrel!" in leadership meetings when someone jumped off topic. Like the dogs' collars in the Pixar movie, UP, life is full of squirrels, or exciting things that sound like "squirrel." **Distractions are after our energy like squirrels are after nuts!** Staying focused on our goals and on the plan sustains our energy! Squirrels are busy darting here and there; and similarly, the distractions of life do the same. Distractions WILL happen. We can count on it. "The average American has fifty interruptions a day, of which 70 percent have nothing to do with work." says W. Edwards Deming. Our minds like to jump in with the distractions to try and complicate things and run a million miles to make us feel accomplished. Focus looks past the distractions to the goal. Success cuts a busy mindset. Success defines between priorities and a "to-do list". *Success lives each day as a focused investment.* This simple energy budget is so basic, you can let go of your anxious mindset. Successful people simplify to save energy!

Power of Simplification

You say, I'm going there, so I have to get on this road, turn left onto the interstate, and then exit onto this road to arrive at my destination. Detours will come up, but you find the quickest way around. We input our destination into Google Maps, Ways or a navigation app before driving (hopefully before driving). Why not map out your definiteness of purpose – your destination – before starting your day? Even the night before to help lift you out of bed? Standardize your wake and sleep times as much as possible and stay consistent. What if your only rule was wake with the sunrise and turn in for the evening with the sunset? That's what used to happen. SIMPLIFY. The point here is simplifying. Unclutter your brain. I've been guilty of setting three morning alarms. The first alarm was the time I desired to get up, the second was when I'd probably first hear the alarm, and the third was the absolute latest I could afford getting up. What's setting three alarms telling our subconscious? It's ok to catch one or the other. Someone said, "No man who chases two rabbits will catch either." Steve Jobs said, "Simple can be harder than complex: You have to work hard to get your thinking clean to make it simple. But, it's worth it in the end because once you get there, you can move mountains." Simplify. You say, Tim, this is too simple. I ask you. If you wrote your top three priorities down and took a month to complete them, would you feel pretty good? Well, you'd be ahead of the majority of people. Not competing here, but the statistic of people waiting to be told what to do is astounding. Many are simply plugged into every distraction and are plotting no definiteness of purpose for their lives. A great practice is to sit quietly, Sunday perhaps, and reflect on your goals and life vision. What needs to happen this next week to move you forward? Write these things down as they come to you.

_____

_____

_____

_____

This is not to get it perfect. This is simply tapping back into the context of your life. I review visits I've scheduled, and I reach out to confirm scheduled events. I make sure my goals have the reserved time needed to complete them. Simply, look over your weeks in context of your life. I like how Tommy Newberry says, "Complexity is negative; simplicity is positive! Go for simplicity!" Determine to simplify your day. With this determination and mindset, you can move into setting fewer, more powerful, and higher priorities!

Power of Top 3 Priorities

At first, in my Energy Budget, I'd write down all of what I felt was important in my life, family and work. It all needed to get done, right? I felt rushed. It was all important. Most days, after writing everything down, I'd get sidetracked here or there; disappointed with little progress made; and then, the day would get crazy. Many times, these priorities were nothing more than a glorified "to-do list". How do you define a priority? Here's the deal. Zig Ziglar said, "Don't count the things you do, do the things that count!" Have fewer goals; get more DONE! I'd rather plow and care for one garden and have squash at the end of the year, than start 20 gardens and abandon the project half way through when the weeds and life get the better of me. Have you ever started a garden? It's fun – for the first week. *Dreams, goals, and planning can be equally as enchanting. The hard work of daily execution is the tough part.* Successful people realize that certain to-do list items must occur and they place these on auto-pilot. If it's not aligned with a goal, and it's something that must occur, put it in autopilot somehow. Dentist appointments, dry cleaning, mowing the lawn, paying bills and shopping for standard items are among some very basic, auto-pilot activities. I know super successful people who still mail a check to the utility company, but one time a week, they have a couple hours reserved to do these "auto-pilot" tasks. These must get done, so whether it's auto-draft, calendar slot, errand day, or delegating, they get done without any wasted thought. This is the key: free your metal faculties for top vision-aligned priorities. The difference between successful and average is the ability to prioritize. Priorities are the activities that move your life, family or organization forward. Priorities align with your goals and dreams. Don't jump onto a last-minute trip because it looks fun unless it's in the plan, or unless one of your goals is becoming more spontaneous. If you have "be more spontaneous in my love life" as a relational goal, then maybe you do snatch a last-minute trip. The point is this, invest your energy into priorities that move you forward. Priorities are tied to goals that add value. Good priorities must revolve around the assets of your life and business. To-do list activities often revolve around liabilities of life. Like Robert Kiyosaki talks about in his book, *Rich Dad Poor Dad*, "Cash flow tells the story of how a person handles money." Similarly, priorities tell the story of how a person handles energy." When we max out our to-do lists and get so distracted accomplishing little, we pour our energies into busyness instead of the assets of priorities. *When you invest your energy into the assets of powerful priorities, that energy is banked; when you invest your energy into the liabilities of busyness, that energy is wasted and usually demands interest.* Priorities achieve the finish line and complete tasks. Priorities deliver results or get you closer. Priorities create value. With this mindset, we drop busyness and become super intentional with what priority we choose to work on. Not saying this doesn't get interrupted from time to time. However, the more definite we are in our priority management, the more powerful our focus and the faster our progress will be! Goethe said, "Things which matter most must never be at the mercy of things which matter least." I remember, as a young guy, reading and listening to, *The Rockefeller Habits*, by Verne Harnish. Jen and I had just been married, and I'd listen to audiobooks on my night-time drive down to Chattanooga delivering pharmaceuticals for my second job. Verne told the story, "Charles Schwab, CEO of Bethlehem Steel, asked management consultant Ivy Lee to show him how to get more done. Lee asked Schwab to write down and prioritize his six most important tasks to complete the next business day." He told

Schwab not to be concerned if he only completed two or three, or even one as you'll be confident you're working on the most important one – the others will have to wait. The story goes that Lee asked Schwab to go two weeks, share the practice with his executives, and, "send me a check for what it's worth to you." Two weeks later, Lee received a $25,000 check which was "a king's ransom" in those days. Schwab's note said this was the most profitable lesson he'd ever learned. To keep your priorities in front of you, look at these FIVE steps:

- State your **big dream** and share it for accountability.
- Write your **smart goals** that move the dream toward reality.
- Clearly define your **small actions** that achieve your goals.
- Know your next **top-three priorities** at all times.
- Focus on your **first prioirty** until completed.

Have your next two priorities written at all times. If you get stuck on priority one, move to number two until one can be resolved. Keep moving forward at all times.

Busy can't even come close to comparing with the productivity of a priority-focused mind. In fact, busyness is exposed for what it is, and stress begins to be an ancient memory. *You live requiring results of yourself; not simply filling time. Everything changes. Own life; it's yours!* Eliminate all distractions and work hard to find simple solutions. Prioritize your day and the actions you take by the highest valued activities. Bestselling author, David Allen, says it this way, "Our sense of anxiety and guilt is the automatic result of breaking agreements with ourselves." When we're too busy, we set ourselves up to break agreements with ourselves. We then carry these broken agreements as baggage and add them to our busy agenda and compound this sense of anxiety day to day until fatigue and burnout set in. With fewer priorities, we set ourselves up to complete, gain a result, finish something and win! Plan to win by planning your work and working your plan. Make a simple and focused investment commitment for the day. Unleash your wholeness, show up in fullness and abundantly knock out priorities 1, 2 and 3!

Power of Budgeting

First quarter, second quarter, third quarter and finally the fourth quarter, still no change. In fact, I felt like I'd worsened the situation. I had identified focus as a very weak point in my life and set out to change it. Really, I hadn't worsened the situation at all. I just became more aware of what was going on. My energy budget wasn't created. My day happened to me instead of me happening to my day. Problematic with many journals, planners, etc., they are simply too clumsy. When we allow our day to happen to us, it's an inefficient expenditure of energy at best; or, it's completely wasted on liabilities. What's the difference between an expenditure and a waste? An expenditure is trading energy for activities that don't move life forward (typically maintaining or busy activities); whereas, a waste is trading our energy for liabilities that move our life backward (these actions come back to haunt us). How do we channel our energy, instead, into a focused investment? *Here's the secret sauce. An investment yields a return. When we invest, we trade energy for actions that move us forward.*

One of my mentors, Dave Ramsey, says budgeting money is naming every dollar before the month starts. I started evaluating everywhere I spent my energy. I realized I spent a lot of energy where I didn't intend to spend it. Unplanned expenditures leave less capacity for what we know is important. By simply changing some habits, some expectations others had of me, and fighting the "disease to please," I stopped spending my energy on those things I didn't budget at the start of my day. By kindly asking others if we could curtail a negative conversation, or not talk about the employer a certain way, or structure a meeting in a more efficient way, or setting clear expectations for my team, or taking the complex email or customer concerns and thinking through them on a run to map out a clear solution, I began budgeting my energy investment – being intentional with investing it!

Power of Investing

There is spending, and there is investing. I would rather have something to show for my energy transference, wouldn't you? This principle of investing my energy caused me to realize and change my clumsy meeting patterns as a manager. This same mindset helped me identify a limited resource of time and energy every CEO and leader faces. We led our sales team to email something like this, "May I get three minutes of your time?" What sales person says they're coming by and only want three minutes? I had more CEOs meet with our team because they thought I was crazy and some even pushed it to see if we really meant it. What I was subliminally saying was, I respect your time and energy and don't want to waste it if we discover we're not a fit."

I realized that in life, especially when you're energized, many things – good things – will pull on you. You can always give something, even if it's a word of encouragement, but if I'm going to get involved with something, it must enhance my energy in some way and be focused and aligned with my life vision. This helps you rule out so many distractions – good and bad. It must be an investment. Wealth guru, Robert Kiyosaki, again says that rich people allocate money to their asset column before paying expenses. *People rich in energy will allocate their energy to their asset column – value creation priorities – before ever paying expenses – urgent to-do's.* Invest your energy first and foremost into high value activities. Are you becoming more intellectually savvy, learning a new role, getting better at your current role, helping promote your company, giving extra time when and where it counts, helping coworkers grow, encouraging them, creating harmony. You can invest your energy to add value to your organization and your team! Ask yourself if you're intentional about adding value to your organization, to your family, to your church, to your social club, organization, place of volunteering, etc. Are you an asset or liability? Be honest and change what you don't like and do more of what you do like! I like how Jack Daly puts it, "As an entrepreneur, I believe that there are no such things as expenses in business. There are only investments." Your time every day must be a focused investment, and an investment for which you gauge the return! Your focused investment must be results driven. Know that your investment will bear fruit. Results build credibility which amplify your wholeness. Trustworthiness is a huge part of being whole. It's your very integrity. So, if you're content to make noise and look busy without driving something across the finish line, then your branches aren't producing fruit – you're simply wasting time. KNOW what activities are fruit bearing activities. Then focus your investment of time and energy on producing a result, for this is what the "work" in energy's definition requires – producing something. Investing money builds wealth; investing energy builds wholeness!

Power of Focus

When I was a kid, my older brother and I went out to the woods. He took a magnifying glass and told me he could light a leaf on fire by simply holding the angle of the small most powerful lens towards the sun. This ball of energy's rays shine across the universe, scatter light all over our globe, yet captured in one small, three-quarters-of-an-inch circle, can light a fire? I didn't believe him. Thankfully, he didn't light a fire in the woods, but blackening and burning a hole right through that leaf taught me a valuable lesson. When I focus my energy, in time, powerful things will happen! *Focused energy produces results!* Focus is powerful. Mark LeBlanc states, "You only need a sliver of focus to move mountains," and "the difference between an ordinary person and success-ful warrior is laser-like focus," says Bruce Lee. Tim works at this. I am a people person and creative mind. I can jump tracks easily and effortlessly and be perfectly happy doing it. It's all part of the adventure. When I work, I can easily follow one task and then get a great idea, go to write it down, think of something else which prompts a text message and you know the rest of the story. This is why naming top three priorities and reviewing these over and over is so key. If you want to move the ball forward in life, know the play and run the play. Harness your mental energy. Practice focusing. Concentrated effort = focus! When I passionately state my affirmations in the morning, I close my eyes and hold in my mind the visualization of the affirmation for at least one solid minute. If it's speaking vibrantly on stage, I will focus powerfully on this carefully guarding my thoughts for that minute of visualization. Practice makes perfect; therefore, simply practice focused mindfulness. Exercises in focus are so great for us and the discipline can be transferred to creative thinking, task completion, exercise, conversations, listening, greater attention to detail, etc. Ask, "Have I allowed any energy to be swindled today through lack of focus on my priorities?" Avoid burnout; focus your energy. Even the sun has a peak performance and then sets.

Power of Process

What's your process? Is it working for you? The famous coach of Alabama State, and leading the charge known as "Roll Tide," Nick Saban is truly an inspiration. A neighbor to Saban said he could set his alarm clock by the legendary coach. His daily morning ritual is consistent, not to mention chicken salad for lunch every day, because he doesn't want to "waste time thinking about it!" Saban has a process and he's consistent with it. The process is his deep, inner belief that preparing on a "methodical, daily basis is key to success." He states, "It's about committing yourself to being the best you can be on that particular day … improvement is a steady march and you have to be committed to it." Consistent preparation is required to achieve the result you want. Ask, "What's my daily process?" Does it march you toward your goals? Does it make preparation a necessity? *Does your daily process keep you focused? If not, what does a focus-enhancing process look like for you?* Saban is obviously winning at football; are we winning at life? A process should be set up so that you can focus on putting more life into your time. A process shouldn't take a lot of thought ever, except on the front end when you're establishing it. When I run, I want to track my activity and measure my results; therefore, I wear my *Garmin Forerunner 235*. While I had to spend some time setting up the activity and screen preferences, I now push one button and am free to run, knowing the stats and data are captured for me. It moves me towards my goals. It allows me to focus on the run. Form processes around the important things in life.

Processes are simplified complexities. Processes are the small bite-sized pieces of the elephant – and, process wins! What we must do is form simple, repeatable and fun processes around everything important to us and our success. That's right. Keep your processes fun to keep your emotions working for you; and when an old emotional generator throws a fit of "being bored", you challenge it with your creative imagination! Speak your invigorating vision over it! The immediate feeling of boredom pales when compared with the bounty and beauty of what your steady process is creating! Use this same mindset to envision the next sales call becoming a lifelong relationship. Imagine the next run being your best, the next date forming deeper connection, the next gift sparking so much joy, the next patient's life being changed forever. *Systems should be in place to track progress and measure results so that you can GO ALL IN on the activity that counts!* The process allows you to efficiently do more of the activity! Utilize the power of process in your life to save energy!

Myth of Multi-Tasking

Some of us are expert jugglers. Have you ever opened one internet tab? Then, clicking link after link, and "Oh, I don't want to forget this site", and "Oh my, that will be a great resource", and "Oh, I'd like to catch that article" … thirty plus tabs later, you don't dare close any – you need them. A mentor of mine calls multi-tasking switch tasking. He's completely right. Regaining focus between tasks drains insurmountable amounts of energy. Author of, *The One Thing*, Gary Keller says that "multitasking leads to more mistakes due to the mental tendency to favor new information over old; a distorted sense of time, taking far longer than necessary to accomplish the important things; and, lost time as you bounce back and forth between tasks." This equals approximately 28 percent of your workday lost! Multi-tasking is a way to cope with the addiction to busyness. Fight to focus on one powerful priority at a time. In his book, *The Greatest Mystery in the World*, Og Mandino compels us to concentrate our efforts upon a single thing. "Many persons spread their energies over too wide a field … and in the end, fail to obtain their hoped-for success."

When you focus on meaningful work, creating, changing and effecting something, your soul experiences the gratifying nature that work was designed to give. Perhaps from a negative upbringing, limiting beliefs, a toxic work environment, being hurt by a manager in the past, or simply the habit of doing it for so long that looking busy is the best policy. By emphasizing being perceived as accomplishing something, they sacrifice their emotional well-being. ***When we worry ourselves with appearance, we forfeit the clarity of focusing on effectual labor.*** When we habitually work to look busy and barely get-by with objectives and tasks, we rob ourselves the emotionally and psychological release of a task completed start to finish. Why take on the emotional burden of looking over your shoulder? Realize you're amazing. Your chain-of command is not out to get you. And what better way to ensure this than to KNOW you're consistently, calmly and confidently delivering results! With a focused investment to eliminate all uncertainty by gaining clarity on what needs to happen, making something happen, and achieving the result, you open the channel for work to flow back into you as you realize accomplishment. Leaders take note, especially for ongoing and recurring tasks. Set benchmarks your people can daily drive towards and achieve. Finishing something is set into a human's psyche and is the essence of good work – achieving a result. Tasks that carry on and on, just like court cases, negative news and drama, are wearisome and draining. Know what the outcome looks like and drive for the finish.

Multi-tasking gives false sense of fulfillment – a temporary buzz and high of activity, business and juggling. Sure, some jobs seem to require multitasking; however, whether you're a mother, teacher or dispatcher, you actually have to put one child on hold, or one call on hold, for sake of another. Single tasking and focused requires less hyper activity in your brain. You may not get the immediate neurological buzz that busyness gives us; however, you free up bandwidth to focus all of your energies in effecting change – driving for a result – and finishing a project! To overcome switch tasking, use my **PDF Method**:

P - Pick one project.
D - Decide one date.
F - Focus and finish.

This allows energy to be channeled, knocking one out, then moving the entire force and unleashing its power on the next task.

Something we can learn from manufacturing is called takt time – which means one-piece flowing at a time. Takt is a German word for rhythm. Japanese, automotive manufacturers pioneered the just-in-time mentality getting away from building massive inventories of parts. Instead, they'd build parts at the exact rate they're needed on the assembly lines. This means they work on something right when it's needing to be worked on, not rushing ahead and not lagging behind. When we focus on priorities instead of all the stuff we stress about having to do, we can decide which priority is the most important and work on it fully driving it to completion. We too can work at takt time, or "one-priority flow". A manager from my past and leader who I highly respected, Randy, walked into my office and taught me the "touch it once" principle. "Everything has a place and everything in its place" saves so much time trying to find things that didn't make it back. Touch it once implies putting it back when you're finished as opposed to leaving it lying around for the need of a second touch. *Again, single tasking or single touching versus multi-tasking or multi-touching.*

Poor operation of your mental focus is like a motor running without a load. It'll race and threaten to burn out. Mental energy when unfocused is exhausting. You're heating up mental bearings when you're racing in all different directions. Rich operation of your mental focus will be completely occupied in one priority moving it forward and keeping mental energy engaged and ignited. When you're out of fuel you stop, refuel, and then continue the drive. This is constructive mental energy. It's focused, efficient, and gets results. If you want to ignite your energy and allow it to flow into your work through your emotions, then pick one thing to focus on. It's a proven fact, our emotional brains like simple! Pick one thing at a time! Josh Billings gives us a great metaphor when he states, "Be like a postage stamp, stick to one thing 'til you get there." **FOCUS** someone said is:

F – Following
O – one
C – course
U – until
S – successful

Focus! Engage with one priority fully. 100 percent. Fully present. You will be astounded at how you transform from an average person to the successful warrior Bruce Lee talks about!

Day-tight Compartments

Why do we fall into the trap of runaway to-do lists? We carry baggage day to day. It's a perfectly human tendency. Someone said stress is simply unfinished work. That's right. Every day, at the end of the day, reflect. How'd you do? Now, pick your top three priorities and be ready to start the next day fresh! Baggage can really slow us down and even stop us. Feeling the need to "catch up" signals stress about unfinished business. What's done is done. Start today on what you said was important. *With a "catch up" mentality, we haul around invisible to-do lists swindling our energy and feeling apologetic.* Drive forward and if you miss something, simply be ok with missing it or do it in the next time slot. Live in day-tight compartments. No catch-up! No baggage; no anxiety.

- **Make peace with your past – for your Energy Budget**, means you don't bog your life down with perfecting your to-do list, carrying tasks day to day, nor allowing the feelings of "behind" or "catching up" to plague you. Dump everything from time to time onto a pad and review for alignment with goals or put on auto-pilot as a to-do. Question: Do you ever feel behind? If so, imagaine not feeling behind. Imagine feeling totally caught up. Describe in a word or short sentence what this would do for your mood?

  _____

  _____

- **Make plans for your future – for your Energy Budget**, means budgeting only priorities aligned with life vision and investing in them. Transfer your energy into lasting investments. Expenditures will happen from time to time – know this. Avoid liabilities. Invest, invest, invest. Question: What are some big things you're planning to do in your life? Jot them down and analyze as you do. Jot an "E" next to any that seem more like an expenditure, and jot an "I" next to each big priority coming up in the future that you feel is truly an investment.

_____

_____

_____

_____

- **Fully present today – for your Energy Budget**, means fighting deadly distraction and focusing on one powerful priority at a time. Question: What's the top distraction that happens for you when you're trying to focus on someone or some task? Write what you're going to do with that distraction.

_____

_____

Energy Boost: Go to www.timehooper.com, watch the module and fill out your Energy Budget. Put it to work, today! Simplify; focus!

CHAPTER 14
ENERGY ZONE

cubicles, surfing and intervals

"Do more of what you love!" – Oprah Winfrey

Bouncing Balls

Why in the world sub-title this chapter "cubicles, intervals and surfing"? We'll build a common denominator through the following sections and see why. We want to create Energy Zones in the environments of our workplaces and lives! One of our corporate sponsors, TwelveStone Health Partners, in Murfreesboro, Tennessee, has seen exponential growth. **Team members possess a great sense of thriving, and happiness at work ranks high.** Touring their state-of-the-art facilities, I was overjoyed to learn about the Energy Zones they've encouraged workspaces to become. Large fitness balls are more than decoration, having replaced several cubicle chairs of the pharmacy's 150-person staff. One registered dietician reported her workflow, focus and fitness all increased because of the mobility and slight bounce she enjoys balancing on her fitness ball. Another team member, who works in the billing department, enriches her day with an *"Under Desk Elliptical"* from FitDesk. She shared that "staying strong to fully engage work and then go home with energy for my two sons" is important to her. She said moving and investing in her health significantly impacts how she feels about her

contribution at work and in life. TwelveStone is a sponsor of our global
"Got Energy?" campaign – a campaign to transform business cultures into
passionate, abundant, vibrant and enthusiastic environments – Energy
Zones! Encouraging small changes like those exemplified at TwelveStone,
we witness satisfaction and happiness at work dramatically increase! We
were made to move; when we move our bodies, we stimulate our minds,
invigorate our souls and awaken our spirits! A visitor to TwelveStone will
find gym bags lying in team members' offices. Staff members give cold,
17-ounze water bottles to visitors and patients. CEO, Shane Reeves, has
labelled these, "living water." Additionally, chief pharmacy officer, Lee,
who miraculously fought and rehabbed from a raging illness, was
supplied a height-adjustable standing desk upon his return to
TwelveStone. Leaders set the example as avid members of the city's
athletic club and running community. TwelveStone sponsors local 5K
races, paying registration for team members to encourage health. They're
not just hype; they truly encourage and invest in the well-being, fitness
and energy of their people. *When an organization truly invests in team
members' wholeness, team members wholly invest into their
organizations.* The resulting culture is attractive! Potential clients, future
team members and investors are attracted to a business that's driven by
leadership's clear vision, a sound business plan, and an energized,
enthusiastic and engaged team of people to carry out that plan and propel
the business forward!

An Energy Zone stocks energy; it's there waiting to be transferred to
you. We can change a lot about our environments and how we interact
with our surroundings to make them more energized. We're looking for
movement and flow – no stagnation. For our lives, we must start thinking
in terms of our energy – add things that enhance it and cut things that
diminish it! We want to **"Get in the zone; Energy Zone!"** We want to
stock our shelves with sources of energy. We can, and we must create our
own Energy Zone!

Do you have fun at work? What would make your work fun? One of
my friends told me about her first day at Pinnacle Bank. The team literally
helped her climb a wall and pull herself over the pinnacle as their symbol
of teamwork and growth. The culture there is very active and puts on a
5K run every year among other things. Organizations that know how to
have fun will enchant their clients. People like to have fun. People like to

laugh. These three ideas of cubicles, surfing and intervals all tie together to keep you in the flow of having fun while working hard! Yes! Energetically driving for and achieving results. Additionally, we'll discuss R&R – rhythm and rewards that'll keep cubicles, surfing and intervals flowing! Finally, we'll brainstorm an Energy Zone that can apply to much more than just our workspaces – our homes and lives as well!

Enthusiastic Engagement

I don't know if there's anything more pitiable than giving up so much of our life in our places of work with the little to no enthusiasm that plagues our factories, our offices, our churches, our schools and many other venues of work and labor. An intense "want-to" stimulates enthusiasm. Think of anything you really want to do. It naturally pulls an abundance of enthusiasm from you. Enthusiasm is contagious. It's the overflow of ignited energy! Enthusiasm is apparent, and it's attractive. Never is anything less attractive than the bored worker – the sense of "I could care less." As a team member or leader, why not voice more of what would make us jump up and down to come to work? Why don't more employers listen? Why don't employers ask? The transforming cultures are asking and more importantly, they're listening! The progressive companies understand we no longer work in the 1940's, and the abuse of industrialization on the human body have taken their toll. We must adjust our work spaces, our chairs and our cubicles. *We must exchange mindless boredom for productive and creative labor.* We should begin in the class rooms and allow more play time, creative time, adjust learning to the needs of each pupil, and make learning fun. It must be fun. It should always be promoting a "want-to" environment. Energy is unlocked from deep within and capacity expanded when we tap into "want-to". To stimulate "want-to", we can build an Energy Zone. How does your team get into "The Zone" – their Energy Zone? Where and how can they be the most productive, creative and energized? As a team member, we must draw a line in the sand purposing that we'll no longer arrive at our places of work to plug in and simply get through the day. Our best lives aren't lived this way. We must demand more of ourselves while making this level of high-engagement fun and continuous. This is your life and it's worth so much more than even the money you're willing to trade it for through employment. When we get to the end of our lives, will the big chunk, or several big chunks of time we gave to an employer or to our jobs be worth a body racked in pain and stressed because of the environment into which we subjected ourselves? We have the availability, especially in this technologically-advanced age, to restructure our work spaces and work places significantly. What will add a little more mental energy to your work? This transformation starts when we decide we won't go to work and partially stop living; but instead, we decide to charge into work and thrive! Paint this picture! What does your dream office look like? Dream it, state it, share it with your employer and start on it. Make it happen. What would give your career a higher rate of satisfaction? Have you asked yourself and thought about what you can do? Simple things like an exercise ball or a balance board can make a huge difference.

When I led purchasing, I took up a short run before eating lunch. I'd put my running shoes in the car, t-shirt under my button-up, and running shorts under my slacks. Simple. My productivity went way up, my energy and enthusiasm was contagious, and I found I had more encouragement and love ready to give. My emotional state was bettered and more flowing. *I found a higher rate of satisfaction in my work environment. I had a better frame of mind. Little trifles didn't upset me.* In fact, I attended some heated conversations in which I found a calm I didn't know I possessed. Getting outside away from everything, I could focus my mind solely on my largest challenge. Perhaps a perplexing email to which I needed to respond, or a supplier negotiation I was stumped on. Time and time again, I'd step out and away from all the anchors, the environment and go run. I'd move my body which stimulated my mind and invigorated my soul. My spirit would think of a more virtuous response than the response I may have at first felt appropriate. Many conflicts died, many relationships went deeper simply for getting away and thinking clearer and bigger. Great leaders have places they go to think and things they do to help center them and keep them operating wholly! It's their Energy Zone. Our Energy Zones must take care of your body, your mind, your soul. Why? Because enthusiasm can't be feigned. It's either genuine or not. The enthusiasm a leader tries to conjure up in his team may last a short while, but it'll soon pop like a balloon on hot asphalt if it's not grounded in the wholeness of team members. When our Energy Zones take care of our minds, bodies and souls, our spirits know! The awakened spirit unleashing a "want-to" in whatever it is you're doing. A "want-to" that sets forth an enthusiasm so wondrous, your work will show more completeness, more thoroughness and more sincerity. Your enthusiasm will make your work better and a happier experience!

Team Leader

We could call Henry Ford's assembly line the capstone of industrial revolution. We invented shifts to produce more goods. We run, run and run. Non-stop! Growing up in Germany, curfew was 10 p.m. every night. Everything closed. Families sat around the verandas with their citronella candles, talked and connected. Here in the U.S., it's a culture shock! Sure, our economy is booming; but, are we? Many team members and workers feel like they're simply part of an assembly line, and work – their opportunity to contribute – becomes nothing more than collecting a paycheck. Assembly lines can be exactly what we make of them and there's nothing wrong with this process. I've visited hundreds of manufacturing plants and have seen them run at their best and worst. *Question is, does your team feel like more than a number? Every industry demands different conditions. Simple shifts and small steps can often increase your culture's energy drastically.* We set up the "perfect" office spaces, but do we consult with our team? I encourage you to ask them candid questions of what would energize them more in their work? Where would they like to work; how would they like to work? New studies are coming out all the time as we've learned from the industrial age, been through the communication and technological revolutions, and are about to entering what appears to be a biomedical revolution. What work spaces and places look like will drastically change. Company culture dynamics will wildly change. Working remotely, on beaches, from soft green turfs and other places will replace the traditional cubicle. Sitting cross legged on a Yoga block may define a power hour making phone calls for the next generation of workers. Why not start thinking energy? Why not start asking basic questions of your people with this mindset? What would increase my team's capacity to do work? Think about very modular, active/fitness inducing work-spaces. When I lived in Germany, it wasn't uncommon to see a banker in Birkenstocks – a very tailored prestigious sandal known for breathability. Successful leaders allow creative space, critical thinking and problem solving. Work should be a safe zone of presenting ideas and being praised for doing it. Work should encourage people to know how they best create, add and deliver value. Your culture should equip them to do it and do it to the best of their ability. If your people feel like they have to look over their shoulder, walk on egg shells around you, or your presence stresses them out, chances are, their energy is flowing in the wrong direction. They don't feel listened to or heard (there's a difference). Start asking, listening and hearing them today. Ask the unaskable questions. Inspire them to think through more energizing work places and spaces.

Team Member

Be patient if you work in an environment that's unenergized and sluggish. They exist, I know. It may take you being the light and example for a while before things catch on. That's ok. Avoid succumbing to complaining or being ugly about things that don't or won't change. Think through the solution and who's the best person to present the idea to. Do it in a positive and professional way. On the other hand, you may be content sitting in your chair all day, in your cubicle, working hard on the tasks at hand. To keep blood flowing and to unleash your energy, move about from time to time, stretch and don't sacrifice your well-being and health to the detriments of immobilization. We were made to move. *There is release of energy inside of us when we move.* We will discuss making small changes that could have a drastic effect on your health, your livelihood and your lifeforce – your energy. You'll definitely feel better and more enthusiastic by creating an Energy Zone out of your work environment! Invest in you so that you can feel better and continue to invest in your organization. This is your home away from home. The majority of people spend more time with their work families than they do with their own kin. Keep it fun and never let working – making meaningful contribution – be a drag!

Cubicles

We won't depict cubicles as evil. They serve as work stations, for sure. We're able to have a place to call home. In fact, this is our home away from home. Pictures of the family hang on the walls and we hunker in for the day. Problem is, many times, these man-made, invented walls meant to create focus, instead take the needed emotion and connection out of our work. Teamwork, camaraderie and connection deteriorates, and accountability is lost. Anchors can quickly form in our cubicles and offices as well. Cubicles may be more conducive for the type of work you're doing; and, you may prefer solitude depending on your personality type. This is all very understandable. The principle is this. What space, what environment and what experience keeps you in peak mental condition all day? What keeps you in flow physically? What invigorates your emotional engagement into your work and team? What awakens your spirit to look much higher than the typical "drudgery" work feels like to most people. Physical cubicles aren't the problem, per se. Let's instead get an anti-cubicle mentality. *Instead of a boxed space where we can hide away, sit for hours and allow clutter to happen, let's transform whatever space we occupy to be inspiring, invigorating, planned, one project at a time, focused, fresh, clean and crisp!*

My friend and successful entrepreneur and businessman, Randy Boyd, personifies this mentality personally and professionally. He founded Radio Systems Corp., home of the invisible fence, in the early 1990's, and it's grown exponentially. The culture, though, is amazing! Not only are pets allowed at work, but the work space is completely open. With ear buds and technology nowadays, many organizations are going "coffee-shop style" where you arrive, dock around a common work space and conquer objectives for the day. Production plants are making improvements for the ergonomics of the human body. Work spaces even in the most dirt-slinging tasks can become energy igniting. In sales, I found I could check in the office first thing, define the objectives with my team, handle housekeeping, enter data in the company software and attend team meetings; then, for an hour and half before lunch, I could streamline phone calls walking the greenway at the park just down the road. I love walking and talking. Then, lunch and visits after and I'd stay fully engaged and enthusiastic all day long! There's no one-size-fits-all here. *But do everything in your power to resist slipping into the immobile, sluggish, boring-work mentality joining the 80 percent who hate their jobs.* Someone said, "Flat-butt-syndrome permeates our workplaces." Avoid this! Move! Garmin reminds us to do this every hour or so by buzzing, "Move!" We were made to move. You may get some raised eyebrows if you move around; but, if you'll bring the energy and stay engaged, then watch your results speak for themselves! Keep energy flowing by staying in flow state!

Carnegie made a simple suggestion for creating an energy zone in your office! Realize, this is almost century-old advice and yet cluttered workspaces and mental distractions still plague us! Here's his four simple steps for shaking the anchor of cubicle-mentality:

- "Clear your desk of all papers except those relating to the immediate problem at hand.
- Do things in the order of their importance.
- When you face a problem solve it then and there if you have the facts necessary to make a decision don't keep putting off decisions.
- Learn to organize, deputize and supervise."

Many workplaces and spaces are boring, cluttered, anchoring, and stagnant. We think, "There's too much to do; I don't have time to hang this picture, write that inspiring quote or clean my office." Stop and do it now. Nothing will put you in a better mood than working in a lively and flowing workspace. There's a proverb that claims, "Clutter drains your energy; you never realize it until it's gone!" Work on one project at a time and close your internet tabs when you're done with them. The habits that most of us (myself included) have of leaving a dozen plus internet-page tabs open on our devices, or piling up paperwork on our desks, is evidence of the low priority we place on flow, focus and finish! Light-weight and work on one thing at a time. You'll stay more aware, connective, fully present and focused!

Surfing

Surfing – a high! What gives you a natural high? Pushups? Sending a spontaneous email just because? Think about surfers. What are they waiting for? A large wave and when they get it, they ride that thing for all it's worth. Your energy flows, and you can create, and ride waves all day long! Yes, you sure can! I work out in the morning. Working out may take some physical energy, but the mental clarity it produces, and the release of dopamine and good feelings creates this mental and emotional surge. Right after my workout, I'll sit for a while to recoup. While my brain is firing on all cylinders, I'm emailing and messaging to connect with prospects. Within an hour, I'm done with my targeted connections. I grab my shake, shower and head to the office. My physical energy from my shake is kicking in and I'm able to charge in. When I worked an office job, I'd run around lunch time. I'd create another wave. Then, later in the day, I'd stand at my desk, or sit on my fitness ball – constantly moving hips, or slowly bouncing up and down. I'd use a snack during another dip and save a walk around the facility for another dip. Maybe bust a little dance on your trek to the copier, or do some jumping jacks. Perhaps you can get a fitness ball (very inexpensive) or use a balance ball or board to create movement and circulation! Each of these ideas, along with the ideas going through your mind right now, gets you moving and energy flowing.
 Think of energy like one of those liquid sparkle tubes you had when you were a kid. You had to shake it and invigorate it to get the sparkle happening! *You've got energy, you just have to trigger and stimulate it – ignite it – to get energy happening!*
I don't know what works best for you but think it through. When do you hit your lows, what could you do to shake things up and create a wave to surf? Socrates and the great philosophers would walk hours around the amphitheaters as they taught their pupils. They walked and taught. Wow! What a concept! Some of us work our physical frames more than others. Some of us mostly work our minds. Let's think about whatever part of self we work heavily, and develop a plan to give the

other parts a chance to work while the exhausted part rests. For instance, if I exert myself throwing 100 bales of hay into the barn loft, I may sit at the end of the wagon with a cold glass of water and exert some mental exercise on the next task at hand. Analyzing the best course of action, my mind's working so my body can recoup. Those who sit in a negotiation for hours should excuse themselves, take a walk while they let their brain rest and cool down. ***Stay in a flow state working wholly all day long!*** Interestingly enough, the psalmist mentions praying morning, noon and night. Might this be indicative of inviting the spiritual part of our being to take active role in our lives and our work? I was coaching a client in our local coffee shop not too long ago. In walked my running coaches, Rod and Jenny. They'd been coaching all morning long and stopped for lunch. Walking up to the counter, they reached behind and pulled out the game of Scrabble. I chuckled inwardly, but here was a prime example of Energy Zone creation. Choosing intentionally to work the mental faculties while allowing the body to rest. Here's a good rule of thumb, if you start to feel stagnant, get up and move! Avoid thinking you have to have the perfect this or the ideal that! If you can move – make a move. Stay flowing so you can stay focused. Increase circulation – awaken all dimensions of yourself! Stay at your peak performance creating value and completing priorities! Enthusiastically drive for finishing and delivering results! Energy is the capacity to do work – creating results! Create your wave and ride it for all it's worth! Surf's up!

Your Flow

A revolutionary moment happened for me, when one day, I sat as an employee of an organization and was challenged by our business coach to "paint my perfect day." I had ideas that I knew would never fly. We all have these unstated wishes, right? Well, his instruction, paint YOUR perfect day – everything goes. So, I painted it. Drew it out. Envisioned where my energy would flow best. How I would choreograph my morning for maximum effectiveness. Who I would ban from my office – kidding ... a little bit. Here's the life changer. As I "painted my picture" in my mind of what my perfect day looked like, the unrealistic vision, that once absorbed a lot of my mental energy wishing things were a certain way, now became a little more realistic. While this particular exercise didn't see immediate results, it wasn't long after that the thought of running at lunch time came flooding back and I said, "Why not?" Some of the answers – for the more difficult emails – came to me on my run. It was so effective that I repeated this often. Another instance was implementing "Quiet Time". Yes, from 8 a.m. – 10 a.m.

When we get tired of being tired, and tired of stagnant or unenthusiastic engagement, then we envision greater, more meaningful contribution. *When you create vision in your life - visions of raising your kids, launching a campaign, serving in your community, and living the life of your dreams, you'll raise your frequency in everything you do!* That includes your contribution at work! When you infuse your vision into your career, your career becomes a calling! You simply no longer have any time to waste, or energy to lose. like how Brendon Burchard stated in his book, *High Performance Habits*, that high performers "raise the necessity to win in their lives". That's right. My vision grew, and I painted my picture. What seemed unrealistic was now clarified and started coming into view. Before long, such a simple idea as "Quiet Time" was a raving success and implemented company-wide.

One of my favorite current flows happens on the days that I get up early for a brisk run, return home or to the gym for a cold shower, then even before leaving the gym – when I'm feeling pretty stoked and amped – I'll email a huge prospect, write a love note or text, do a little surprise like getting coffee stuff set out for Jen, and then have time for reading, answering emails and posting an inspirational quote all before the first visit with a client or team member. It's absolutely a way to shake the toxic cubicle-mentality and surf! Do something daunting right after the amping activity! These flows change from time to time depending on life phase, work space, preferences, etc. The key is being aware of your flow. If you're feeling antsy, notice it. If you're feeling super-creative, notice it. If you can't sleep, notice it. If you feel tired, notice it. What is your body needing? What are your emotions feeling? How awakened are your mind and spirit? "Spontaneity is positive," says author and small business coach, Mark Leblanc. Make sure it can occur within a defined framework for your business. Plan your spontaneity. This is Energy Zone stuff! One of my sales guys would make 10 calls and then go run the stairs, grab a water and give kudos to someone; then, he'd be back to his next priority. Leblanc states, "When your fun meter's on max, your stress meter's on min." Work can be fun! I remember as a kid going to the dentist. Dr. Giebl would hum and sing as he drilled on you! What?! He actually helped me relax and took some of the stress out of it – for me the tiny client. How? By the appearance and expression of enjoying himself at his work! Notice and think about what an amazing flow might look like for you!

Intervals

Intervals are short bursts of intense focus and hard work followed by a short rest. Get something finished, then rest. Intervals take intense focus. The good news is that interval training creates better focus! The elusive "work/life balance" is simply a mindset that can be limiting. Most people who are seeking this mirage have, in reality, a hard time saying "no" or establishing healthy boundaries. We work when we're supposed to be home, and then our mind is at home – usually thinking through an argument because we weren't fully present while there – when it should be at work and the vicious cycle continues. When you envelop your life into relationships and transform your career into your calling, then you move into a superwoman and superman state. You can transform in a moment's notice. When you work, you work! All in! Gazelle intensity! Focused on completing something! *Limit what you do so you can complete something! Huge key here! Completing something, just like an intense lap around the track, will surge your energy!* Physically drained, emotionally charged! Then, rest. Take a short break to breathe, stretch, close your eyes, think, pray, smile, chill, walk, take in the beauty around you, grab some water, sing, dance, hug, love, imagine or recharge in some way. Work intensely; rest intentionally! Here's the bottom line, your client will know if you're in the Energy Zone while you're working or not! Your coworkers can tell and even your finished product will exhibit it. A manufacturing leader told me once to always check the VIN number of a vehicle before I bought it. The number has the day of assembly in it. "If it was assembled on Monday or Friday," he told me, "don't buy it." Focus on those days was simply someplace else than fully engaged at work.

While he made this statement with a bit of humor, we know that many a truth is spoken in jest. Whether you engage in interval training or not, it will show up long term. Focus on work when you work; focus on rest when you rest. Be superwoman and superman when it's time – you'll save the day. But, to work hard non-stop isn't any more productive than it is harmful for you. Your posture over time will be resilient or slumped based on whether you worked with interval-mindset or struggled through.

Your Work

Let's look a little closer at hard work. You know, when I train for fast runs, it's called interval work. The demand you place on your body is great, but it's for a shorter amount of time. It takes extreme focus! In fact, you count breaths sometimes just to tune out everything else. 1,2,1,2,1,2,1,2 …. Until the 400, 800, 1200 or 1600 meters is completed. Then you canter at a recovery pace for a short time to catch your breath. These intervals build greater speed, but you must take that break to recover. Intervals are important for great work, because you can demand great, laser-like focus of yourself and train your mind to tune everything else out. You're also conditioning your mind for high performance. For instance, you may have sales calls to make for 2 hours. Pull your script up, dial the first number, stand up … ring, ring … voicemail … leave one, hang up, log your call, next … work solid, no distraction for 10 minutes. Then, walk to the end of the hall quickly returning, clear your mind, sip your water bottle, and then, 10 more intense minutes! You can even compete with yourself or start a friendly competition with a coworker. *Make working fun!* Train your mind to enjoy making these calls. Oh yes! Side note. Reframe cold-calling by calling it something much better and emotionally invigorating – like "visit-setting". Start with the end in mind, work intense intervals, and make work fun! Move around. Stay engaged. You don't have to just make calls. You get to engage in the visit setting process, get some exercise, and increase focus all at the same time. Act like some macho dude you saw in the movies or make your calls in front of a mirror. Crack yourself up. Laugh; have fun! You may surprise yourself with an increase in conversion rate. If you're already a super-focused individual and you tend to zone out for hours into one project, I encourage you to get up and move around as well. You need the mental break. Go outside. Breathe deeply, get some water to increase and fortify continuity of your brain. Stretch. Stay in motion. Stay in flow.

Your Rest

Have you ever thought about your heart resting? Yes! It rests. Right after every beat. It works hard pumping life-giving blood filled with wonderful nutrients and oxygen to every part of your brain and body; then, it rests. The might of this organ – it's power – comes from the principle of intervals. All in! Focus all energies upon one task! Then, take a second. Move around. Rest your mind. Working in intervals is the combination of motion and rest. The evidence is overwhelming that hard work by itself seldom causes fatigue which cannot be cured by a good night's sleep or rest. What causes fatigue? Worry, being tense and becoming upset emotionally are the leading causes of fatigue. We may think physical or mental work is the cause of fatigue. It's not. Exercising muscles doesn't fatigue them, it builds them. Working them constantly, without rest, will fatigue, stress and injure them. ***Remember this. A tense muscle is working. Loosen up, stretch and flow. Save your energy for important tasks.*** I used to furrow my brow when thinking because I wanted my employer to know beyond a shadow of doubt that I was engaged. Show your engagement by the questions you ask and the solutions you provide. Avoid overworking your face. Relax. When you stand, learn to stand properly so that you can relax while standing. When you run, there's a proper way to run. Learn how to do things properly and relax in your work. Work only the muscles you need to at the time. Enjoy working your muscles; enjoy working your mind. Avoid causing needless tension through worry and allowing your emotions to run you. Practice choosing positive emotional responses. It's not only better for everyone else, it's better on you in that it lessens fatigue. Another big one is breathing. Many times, situational tension can cause us to hold our breath. That's right! Let it all out instead. Then, concentrate on sucking air deeply into your stomach cavity. Keep your chest at rest – it shouldn't rise when breathing properly. Breathe deeply; practice controlling your breathing and you jump ahead in relaxing while engaging!

Stop right now. Analyze your life. Carnegie says, "I find that the chief obstacle is the almost universal belief that hard work requires a feeling of effort else it is not well done." We hunch our shoulders through poor posture; we work muscles that have nothing to do with the work at hand; we distract ourselves instead of focusing which works our mental faculties a dozen times more than necessary; and, we simply fear not looking busy. Learn to relax while you are doing your work! Live in the Energy Zone. Transform the cubicle-mentality, create your surfs, and intensely work then intentionally rest! BOOM!

Rewards

When you succeed at a new habit, reward yourself. When your kids succeed by overcoming a challenge celebrate and reward them. When your team succeeds celebrate and reward them. Especially when creating new habits! Build in emotional excitement at every completion! It doesn't have to be elaborate but get excited about overcoming challenges and growth! *Even if it means shouting a simple "Whooohoooo!" Rewards come after intervals! Rewards can be the rest you take, or something a little bit bigger than a simple pause.*

Just Love

I love working at a coffee shop like one of my local favorites, Just Love! The aroma, the bustling background noise, the friendly staff, and the open, cheerful atmosphere. Here's a trick, though. I'll go there and open my laptop getting to work on the toughest project for the day. I'll conquer it with intensity before getting my coffee. Why? I use the coffee as a reward for intense focus. Simple trick and can easily be duplicated.

Technology

Text message dings in. You're in the middle of something. Do you pick it up and look at it? If you're in the middle of something (funny thing … my cell phone and then Garmin watch just buzzed in sequence), you do not owe it to anyone to look at a text message, Facebook notification or Instagram message. Even LinkedIn can wait although it might be business. I've had to work at and practice not looking at my phone when I'm in the middle of something. It CAN wait. Always remember, if it's urgent, anyone can call. Stop fearing every notification, every ding. Technology is a great tool, as well as a great drain of focus. Technology can literally swindle our energy! It's addictive. Someone has said something, and I've got to see what it is. Fear of missing out (**FOMO**) is real! Let's name it for what it is. Social media is a virtual mirage! We feel connected, but we haven't looked at long range, lasting feelings. Are we really connecting? *The length of our friends list doesn't eradicate our depth of loneliness. When's the last time, you sat across the table from someone and looked deep into their eyes, connected with their spirit, and inspired their soul?* We scroll our feeds trying to be a part of everyone's life and it only "feeds the beast." We feed the fear of missing out. We encourage distracted, unfocused, partially present existence. The likes, comments and shares are how we gage our impact. Really? Is this connection? In a way, but it's not the purest and richest form, and in all fairness, we feel compelled by social channels to share more and more. Nothing wrong with sharing; but, why? Have we asked ourselves "Why"? We spend a lot of cognitive energy sharing our food, everything that happened to us each day and our opinions on emotionally stimulating subjects that come along. Oftentimes, these are reactionary and not really adding or creating value – if we are honest with ourselves. "Will it matter at the end of my life?" is a great question. Think of the human beings we brush shoulders with who need encouragement all the while our light and our face is fused to our phone. I only want to encourage us to think here. Think "Why". What if we scheduled a couple times for social media per day, and redeem our time – buy back our very lives? What would happen if we pocketed our technology, looked up and didn't miss the landscape of beautiful people around us in the Starbucks' line, on the elevator, or in the terminal? What if we quieted everything and gave our minds the greatest gift – thinking, dreaming and growing? Especially while we move about during our day. Why waste our mental bandwidth flooding it with messages of hundreds while scrolling a social channel? Why include technology under rewards? Well, think about it. What if you used it as a reward. Focus for 15 - 30 minutes straight before checking your phone. Designate a maximum amount of time to be on, be super intentional while you're on, seek to learn something, connect with someone, and add value through every post, share or comment. Learn to shut technology down to focus on creating something or completing a task that will last and actually matter at the end of your day – or life. Avoid feeling the need to be plugged in at all times. You're giving away your energy. Unplug, then, plug in intentionally when your energy is full and you're ready to impact somebody or post something life-giving. Wean yourself from technological dependency. Think about if all the "friends" you're connected with walked into the Starbucks where you were working. Would you throw everything aside to stand, greet and carry on a dozen conversations? Probably not. Then why tolerate it on your mobile device? Use technology as the connective tool it was meant to be, and to curb its addictive power, use it as a reward.

Rhythm

Let's look at the power of rhythm. Rhythm can be found in nature all around us, and its power has been harnessed into production. Its power can be utilized in our day to day lives. *Imagine systematically implementing your vision into your daily life and continuously improving on it over time – this is rhythm.* Thinking in terms of rhythm, how much power could we infuse into our workflows? Imagine allowing only high value activities to constitute our surge, and then maintaining activities and reflection would constitute our rest. Rhythm is the systematic combination of surge, rest, surge, rest, surge, rest. It allows for standardized motion, teamwork and continuous improvement. It can be found in business as meet, plan, coordinate, action; meet, plan, coordinate, action; and so on. On the production floors of our globe, rhythm is a powerful, predictive and sustaining component. The Toyota Production System, and others like it, champions rhythm with systems like one-piece flow, JIT, 5-S and Lean. Rhythm creates flow; it gives structure to expression. Speaking of the heart, S.D. Gordon writes, "The secret of its power is in the rhythm of action … we call rhythm of color, beauty; rhythm of sound, music; rhythm of action, work." The power of rhythm is everyone working together. Not necessarily faster, or maverick-like, but truly moving at a team pace – everyone and everything moving forward together. Consider a canoe ride with one rower in the rear of the canoe overpowering all other rowers. Not only does he wear himself out, he probably will send the canoe in circles or at least off course. This is inefficient work. How are you incorporating rhythm to blend your actions to your team and move your organization forward? How are you blending your vision and those of your loved ones into one powerful motion with small surges and small rests as you move forward together?

There's a divine principle of rest in work. ***The power of rest in work comes when we find rhythm that increases focus in driving forward!*** It's not busyness! Bid busyness a good-bye! Quickly! Busyness will disrupt rhythm and pace every time. Be prioritized and focused, and you'll find rest in work. One priority at a time. This is why teamwork and being a team player is so vitally important. You can be a maverick, but you'll probably reinvent the wheel a dozen times. It's like the speedster drag racing at traffic lights. You've seen them. In the grand scheme of things, did stepping on the gas, quick-braking, switching lanes, darting-in-and-out really get them that much further down the road? How much danger and angst did they cause in doing so? This isn't rhythm, yet it happens in many instances of our lives. Fitting is the John Sullivan Dwight's poem that goes,

> "Rest is not quitting
> A lively career:
> Rest is the fitting
> Of self to the sphere."

Gordon puts it this way, "True rest is in the unhurried rhythm of action." When you're focused on achieving a result in exchange for your actions; and, you work consistently toward your goal, you end up arriving at the finish line much sooner than if you'd been busy multi-tasking a dozen projects all at the same time. The satisfaction of achieving a result, seizing the victory, and realizing success releases chemicals in your mind and body. *This experience of motion followed by rest transfers energy into the next task and the next.* Gordon continues, "Rhythm is the secret of power." Find long-term power in your life by analyzing areas you can improve rhythm. Avoid busily darting here and there. Develop a vision, set goals and consistently take action!

Farmer Schmidt

Growing up, we'd cut, spin and bale hay from four fields. We owned the bush hog and spinner, but we'd hire Farmer Schmidt for the baling. I loved watching him work. Tall, dark-haired German farmer. Kindest face, strong hands and warmest heart. When the time would come for baling, it was long hours in the field to get it up and stored in the barns. Schmidt would work diligently and patiently. I remember time and time again the baler mesh would tangle, jam, or a tine would break. Schmidt never got in a rush or short. He worked calmly and steadily to get the hay up and baled so we could haul it to the barns.

Meetings

Consider two easily recognized causes for much wasted energy in business: meetings and email. Apply rhythm in these areas and you improve organizational rhythm tremendously. Meetings. The dreaded word. Why? Think about it. How many meetings drag on and on? How many meetings are poorly run and how much energy is swindled? How much time do we spend running around to figure out what everyone is supposed to be working on? According to statistics: non-engagement, dozing, daydreaming and simply skipping out of frustration are at all-time highs. Have you ever thought about excusing yourself from a meeting you didn't feel you could add value to, or asked to be emailed the bullet points and objective outcomes? If you are needed and can add value, then make meetings fun! Verne Harnish states, "30 to 60 minutes: one or two topics." Always assign "WWW – Who, What and When" he continues. Setting expectations on who is to do what by when helps people leave empowered. They can implement the Energy Equation of saying, "Yes," and giving their all to drive for a result!

Emails

It bugs some people to no end to have an email in their inbox. Internally, there's this alarm that goes off every five minutes to check theirs. To complicate matters, email servers have this "Whoohooo, you have no emails in your inbox!" congratulatory message. Let's own our energy and create an Energy Zone by setting healthy boundaries. Unless you're a dispatcher, receptionist, secretary or another type of gatekeeper, you can get by with a couple check-ins per day. Even in a role where frequent messaging is necessary, setting healthy times when you can unplug and focus elsewhere is crucially important! When you use the tool of email, set healthy expectations that save others' mental, physical or emotional bandwidth. Mental: You can add something like this to your email, "Just FYI – no need to respond." Emotional: if any part of an email can come across harsh, call instead and seek resolution voice to voice, or, better yet, face to face. Physical: writing something like, "Doesn't have to happen immediately. Let's discuss next time we meet." Save energy by creating an Energy Zone around your email. Just like social media or any other communication medium, learn to run it so it won't run you.

Get in the Zone

Create your zone. *Visualize it so you know what it looks like. Think through it. Also, think deeper than just tangible workspace. What's your space like? The space you create when you walk into any room?* Gracious? Calm? Sharp? Ready? Joyful? Compassionate? Think of your physical space and your vibe space. It's up to us to create our Energy

Zone and live energized. What's it going to take? Claim it now. I like how George Bernard Shaw said, "People are always blaming their circumstances for what they are. I don't believe in circumstances. The people who get on in this world are the people who get up and look for the circumstances they want, and if they can't find them, make them!" Create your Energy Zone at work. *Avoid separating who you are and what you do. They must coexist, the one leveraging the other to maximum effect!* Here are a few ideas you could graciously implement that will increase your energy – guaranteed. Add to this list. Create your "Energy Zone."

- Shorten meetings and stand. Do some calf raises while standing. Stand and stay engaged. Simply state you'd rather stand. It's super effective and keeps you sharp. There's a time and place to sit. I think we'd agree sitting happens more than standing already.

- Think crazy; be the one to speak up and think big at company meetings.

- Take notes. Never again attend a meeting to simply attend. Either engage or dismiss yourself.

- Set healthy expectations that save others' mental, physical and emotional bandwidth by defining "who, what and when" leaving meetings and in communications.

- Short walk or run before or during lunch.

- Workout. Perhaps your company has a workout room you could crank some irons, grab some pullups or something to get your heart rate up.

- Quiet time; focused time posted for others to respect.

- Have a place and time to think. Where do you go to think? At work, at home? Where? Dark room, thinking chair?

- High five a coworker.

- Start your day saying "Good Morning!" to coworkers.

- Bring cookies or a healthy snack to share.

- Have fun. If you're not having fun; you may not be working correctly – analyze.

Your "Energy Zone"

On a personal note, what are the things that reenergize you? If you could put all your favorite, energizing memories or dreams of life into one gigantic space, what would this Energy Zone look like? List these places, things, relationships and ideas and activities. Go ahead and start. You can always come back and add to it. Once we create our Energy Zone list, we can consider how many little things we could easily add to our environments and routines to ignite our energy. As you jot ideas down, ask yourself, *"Will this truly energize me – body, mind, soul and spirit?"* Create your list. Have fun and imagine. I'm going to encourage you to add more of this into your life. Share your list with someone you love. They'll probably find ignited energy in some of the same activities as you. What a great way to proactively find common ground!

We've created this simple exercise to help us visualize this zone. Think of energy as your flow of power. What puts your entire person into a super-energized and top-performing state of mind? How do you imagine this? There are certain things that we love: favorite flower, candle, inspirational quote, etc. This exercise is named "Energy Zone – When Life Feels Amazing List!" (also available with training module at www.timehooper.com) Simply, list an activity, an environment, an aroma, a person, an idea, or recall a time when you felt amazing! Do you love music? What smells make you happy? What pictures evoke the best emotions? What quote reminds you to think higher? What word reminds you of the essence your life is or desires to become? Are these visuals plastered over your office or maybe on your coffee mugs? Imagine spending the next decade of Christmases finding out these secrets of friends and loved ones and creating these environments for them in some way. Just an idea.

As you fill out your "Energy Zone – When Life Feels Amazing List" ask yourself, what makes you feel energized? What makes you feel alive? I love seeing corporate cultures encouraging energizing activities in and around the day's tasks. What could you change in your life to make you feel more energized? Stop right now and think. Think with me of a time, a moment, or a memory where you felt alive. When was this? Where were you? Who were you with? How did you feel? Why couldn't you recreate or do more of that? You might say, "Tim, that was on vacation, or that was when I was young." What could you do to recreate it? Maybe there's some promise, verse or song that in posting it would not only keep you centered, may just bless someone visiting your office space. Maybe it's been a long time since you rearranged or freshened things up. Try it; we were made to move and grow. Try changing something up. We've talked energy zone at work since we spend much of our lives there, but what about the home office, our reading nooks, our favorite seat we share with our spouse or kiddos. *Make your workspace and every environment one of an Energizer! It's your zone. Make it an Energy Zone!* Anything that enhances positive energy flow is Energy Zone approved! Get in the zone, stay in the zone! Your Energy Zone!

Think

We mentioned thinking when we discussed sources. When do you pause in your daily routine and life rhythm to think? "In the attitude of silence the soul finds the path in a clearer light, and what's elusive and deceptive resolves itself into crystal clearness," Gandhi profoundly said. Verne Harnish, in his masterful work, *Scaling Up*, states, "It's not sufficient to schedule thinking time just once every quarter or year." Peter Drucker has called our modern labor, "knowledge work." We have a lot of management jobs that bring with them mental fatigue. What are you doing to rest the muscle you don't see – your brain? Yes, rest it by giving it back its amazing concentration and focus. Un-inundate it, today. Let it work single-tasked, and then, allow it to rest. Give it some time to imagine, think and create. Let it solve the problems that have you baffled. When do you think? Where do you go to think? Have you cultivated getting all alone, by yourself to deeply think? McGinnis pointed out that, anyone looking carefully at the biographies of Jesus cannot help becoming impressed with the intentional times of being alone with which he conducted much of his ministry. McGinnis continues, "he steadfastly set his face forward and achieved more than anyone who has ever graced the face of this earth." Quiet time and alone time for some may be a scary place. Sometimes, we're afraid of the very voices in our head, or even getting alone quietly to think. We don't like what we hear and what our spirit is requiring of us. Decidedly, we live loud and stay social. We find the urge at work to get up and office hop, interrupting others' thoughts to think with us on something we may already know how to get done. We need everyone's "buy-in" on our brilliant idea, instead of just doing it and moving on. Quietly working to achieve results in life is true nobility. Focus on making results happen. Love the work and overcome challenge. Find security in your pricelessness. Know who you are and be okay to occupy quiet spaces of no applause, no noise, no partying, no crowds. Come away to think and plan; return to engage in power and precision. Like Jesus, Moses, the great and meek leader had much of his life marked by solitude on the backside of the desert herding sheep. King David watched sheep and like Carl Sandberg said of Lincoln, that "his greatness came in part from the years spent in the woods with his solitary companion, the ax." Washington journaled many a lone ride atop his horse surveying the countryside. Those who are content with intentional times of aloneness find a centering, a focus and a space so vast that they desire to visit it often.

When do you close your eyes to just simply imagine? When do you ask, "What if?" Do you have some daily imagination space? Are you a day dreamer on purpose? Did you get yelled at growing up for "day-dreaming"? The fact is, many of us feel like we're not accomplishing anything, but let me tell you something. Anytime you give your mind the room – just some quiet room – to channel its thoughts and imagination to generate ideas toward the realization of your worthwhile goal, you are at that moment doing your greatest work! Practice mental focus so you can perform greatness in stillness. ***Put your mind to work for you by affording it the opportunity.*** Many great thinkers, world leaders, and inventors of times past have utilized quiet spaces, dark rooms, shutting out all light and only taking a pad of paper and pen to manifest what came into their mind by way of creative imagination. What is it you desire out of life? Do you have space in your day and space in your mind to go think about it and create value to generate ideas? Creative space is one of the most energizing spaces!

Breathe

We are most energized when our emotions are flowing freely. We can gage this negative or positive flow, and better yet, we can improve it. You'll hear me state this over and over because it is that important! We can improve our emotions and ignite our energies if we'll just take some time to notice and think about what's really going on Until we unbox our hearts and break defenses down, I can guarantee our emotions aren't flowing freely. Moving past hurt, unforgiveness and fear allows us to experience deep joy and connection in all relationships. Once you move past deep wounds and are flowing, practice constant forgiveness. *Small emotional upsets happen throughout our days and without warning. Create emotional resets.* Perhaps every time you sit down in your chair, or take your stance at your workstation, you pause and take a deep breath releasing all negative thought and tension. Tony Robbins calls something similar "**RMT**" – release meditative technique. Check in with your emotions and encourage the positive emotional generators to maximize production! Navy Seal, Mark Divine says, "Breathing practice is an art mostly lost to the Western world. Warriors have known and practiced this art for centuries, making breathing practice central to their training – the ability to stay calm … creates the conditions necessary for courageous acts." You want to amplify everything you do? Breathe! I interviewed pilates instructor and flexibility and strengthening coach, Dr. Jen Esquivar. She stated doing two very simple things will increase your energy. **KEY:** Move and breathe. Two things many of us don't do. We sit or stand hunched over our technology and don't breathe properly or deeply. Singing helps open your lungs. Running fast gets me breathing deeply. I love it. I have felt my lungs expand running and I find such calm when settling back into my daily routines – especially when I worked a desk job. Research proves most people only use a small percentage of their total lung capacity. This is simply leaving a ton of energy on the table – not transferred! Untapped energy resources lying dormant. All it takes is some practice expanding a muscle ready and willing – your lungs. And, you might live longer, too. Stronger muscles tend to last longer. BOOM!

Move

Moving your physical frame sets off wonderful chain reactions throughout your person. *When you move your body, you stimulate your mind, invigorate your soul and awaken your spirit!* Thomas Bradberry states, "When you take time out of your day to get your blood flowing and keep your body healthy, it gives your mind an important break … while vigorous exercise does it best, even a stroll through the park, deep breathing and other exercises can "release serotonin and endorphins that recharge your mind and keep you happy and alert." Verne Harnish also shares a Steve Jobs technique called walk-and-talks. "Walking is found to have a similar calming effect that brings the brain down from an agitated beta state to a more focused and calm alpha state." Learn as you move! Work and move. Walk-and-talk! Create Energy Zones in life! Don't conform to dead and dry environments. Our modern bodies are crying out for relief – they want to move. Technology's too abundant to be tied to a chair all day. Move about and stay in flow state!

Ashley Benson, founder of B&B Sports is a highly trained consultant to professional tennis and golf associations. She is also a firm Pilates believer, trainer and sponsor of our global "Got Energy?" campaign. We shared a coffee and I heard her passion for helping people. She loves people and works to give them a painless life increasing mobility through stretching. She gives some basic advice for keeping your body moving and increasing mental focus, inspiring your spirit and invigorating your soul:

- Break the habit of leg crossing. In this position, the lumbar spine is in side bend position, internal oblique muscles are inhibited from firing, pelvis is in a postural tilt, there is stress on the lateral side of the hip and stress on the static nerve. This is a very difficult habit to break.

- About to launch is a product called Smart Seat that was designed to help. I have tested it and highly recommend it! (physcialmindinstitute.com)

- Upper body posture: bring shoulder blades (scapula) together and pull them down towards your hips.

- Lengthen the back of the neck and and keep face muscles soft and relaxed.

- Stand up and walk around every hour or so.

Fuel

When I worked in the office, I'd often skip lunch or miss out on a morning shake because I was running behind. Circumstances will come up, but you must fuel. Avoid running on fumes. Mentally throughout the day you must fuel. Place some empowering quotes throughout your office. Brendon Burchard coached me to set a midday alarm in my phone with three empowering words that take you to an energized mindset! Mine: love, decisive, courage! You must physically fuel and refuel as well. Make this a priority. *Too often, we let our moods get out of whack* because we don't eat, or we eat poorly. Hangry is a real deal. Snickers commercials that "You're not the same when you're hungry," are very true. Choose a high octane. Study and fuel correctly. Know good sources. Set reminders to eat a snack. Consult a nutritionist. My coach Rod Key states you should be snacking on quality fuel every three hours. He and I developed some planned snacks that are healthy and easy to make. Stuff like peanut butter oat balls, fruit, etc. Think about it. Avoid packaged vending machine chips and unhealthy fat-filled foods. These aren't nutritious and full of empty calories. The initial rush you feel is not lasting and isn't real energy! They'll cure the munchies, but they won't truly fuel you, or bolster your energy.

Laugh

Whistling, singing and laughing can be some of the most stress releasing and enthusiasm enhancing forms of expression. I know! I have them in my Energy Zone. Og Mandino said of laughter, "I have the gift of laughter and it's mine to use whenever I choose. Henceforth, I will cultivate the habit of laughter!"

"Humor is by far the most significant activity of the human brain," said Edward DeBono. I like how author M.J. Ryan points out, "We take ourselves and our problems so very seriously. We use our will-power and our won't-power. Don't forget to throw in a little wit-power as well!" Kids don't question whether they should laugh and have fun – it comes naturally to them. Do you ever wonder why this changes? Fear of others' opinions, maybe? Just food for thought. Why walk around all up-tight and serious, worried what people think of you? It's simply not worth the huge amounts of energy swindled from you! Laugh and let others laugh at you and with you! By the way, clients love to laugh, too!

Gracious Non-Conformist

None of us have to conform; we conform because it's easier. To experience life to the fullest usually means breaking out of the status quo and getting past our comfort zone. The nail that sticks up gets hammered down. And sometimes doing something to energize your life makes you stick out like a sore thumb. Sometimes, when we stick out, our defenses go up. We put on the hard hat expecting the badgering. Mark this down as a huge key. Let the looks, the badgering or the remarks roll off of you like water from a duck's back. Most times, people will badger because you've made them feel uncomfortable – without your even trying. People badger because they feel insecure. People badger because – get this – you give them hope, but they're going to make absolutely sure what you're up to is real. So, be ready to forgive. Just expect the badgering, the looks, the stares and the jokes. Be gracious. Chuckle. Laugh with them. Recently,

Energy Zone

I wore my new Brooks running shoes that my friend bought for me, a nice pair of Tom James Legacy jeans, and blue blazer to an event. Someone asked if I was trying to make a fashion statement. I chuckled and told them my ultra-flat feet are like space heaters on high of a hot summer day; dress shoes don't offer a ton of breathability. I also feel so much more aligned physically, and with my spine/pelvic misalignment, my back takes less stress this way. Better on the back, breathability and energy – why not? You've got to be ok with being you, but make sure people are ok with them being them. Sometimes they just get their defenses up because they think you doing something different means they need to as well. Put them at ease. Call yourself crazy about energy, blame it on me. Tell them you read "Got Energy" and are just more mindful of staying at peak performance – epic energy all day long! Laugh. It's ok. Don't stifle the synergy – energy happening between two people – by defending yourself or getting defensive. *You never need to apologize for living fully. Just purpose to love deeply as well.* Live in your Energy Zone so you can consistently live fully and love deeply!

CHAPTER 15
BALANCING ACT
the amplitude of wholeness

"My life is an indivisible whole, and all my activities run into one another ... my life is my message." – Ghandi

Riding Mower

My first riding lawn mower was given to me. It was a non-running riding lawn mower, but it was free. What young guy doesn't like a, "If you can get it to work, it's yours" challenge. Oh yeah! I started by changing the oil, draining and replacing the fuel, and making sure the fuel filter was clean. I WD-40'd the spark plug. I tried wire brushing the crank-case magnets. I replaced the air filter. I tinkered with the throttle levers; and, this tinkering went on for weeks. I'd come inside evening after evening smelling like gas.

The mower simply wouldn't crank. This was getting old. Finally, after spending weeks. I stopped in and chatted with our shop foreman, Doug. "Will you help me?" I asked. Doug listened and asked me to bring the fuel pump in the next day. Sure enough, when I brought it in to Doug, he took a paper-clip from the center, top drawer stuffed full of MacGyver-looking odds and ends. Doug stuck it into this tiny hole in the bottom, and "Ping!" …. We heard it. *A spring that was stuck came loose.* "Try that," Doug said handing the fuel pump back to me. Eagerly that night, I went out, reinstalled the fuel pump, and "Vroooooooom! The mower ran for years after that.

Life can be just that simple – and difficult. One thing, one dimension of our wholeness as a human being gets out of whack or left undone and everything else suffers. *Our wholeness as a human being is extremely important; yet, for different reasons, we'll experience deterioration in a dimension of our lives – an area that suffers and gets left undone. In contrast, when we grow as whole beings, and when we operate out of this fortified position, everything we touch and everything we do is amplified!*

Balancing Act

Have you ever experienced tremendous wobble and shake in your car's steering wheel while driving? Or maybe the bouncing feel of the entire vehicle? My friend's truck used to vibrate so badly his coffee would literally slosh in the cup holder as he drove. Obviously, in these cases, the tires needed some attention. One tiny balancing weight missing on one wheel and the whole vehicle suffered. What about that ride that was so smooth you almost didn't realize you were going as fast as you were? Thankful for the quick glance at the speedometer to (hopefully) correct this amazingly smooth high speed before peaking the hill in the road to discover the public servant's patrol car waiting in the median to help us make the correction. We as humans are not entirely different. For life to run effectively, for the maximization of our capacity and for us to truly thrive, we must look at life as a whole: mental, spiritual, health, family, occupation, recreation and social. We tend to look at these dimensions as separate entities instead of realizing these interact simultaneously; they are intertwined and complement each other never working alone. The all famous "Wheel of Life" gives insight into what famous psychologists, medical professionals, and scientists have discovered as the makeups of our lives and interactions. I'd highly encourage you to evaluate where you stand in each dimension of life so you can develop smart goals to fortify each one. You can become that smooth, efficient, shiny red Mustang flying down the road – each wheel balanced. The common seven dimensions of life wholeness are below.

Jot a percentage next to each one. From 0 percent representing "completely not doing anything", and 100 percent meaning "best in the world". Get an idea of where you're at:

Mental: _____

Spiritual: _____

Health: _____

Family: _____

Occupation: _____

Recreation: _____

Social: _____

An Act

Let's let go of a huge burden! Let's stop trying to be perfectly balanced. It's an act if we're trying. I heard speaker Don Day say it something like this. "You get up, go to work, spend 10 hours there, commute, get kids from school, get home for dinner and an hour or two in the evening to start all over the next day." Life balance seems so elusive to people and quite frankly, pretty hopeless. The **KEY** is not trying to tackle life balance, but to work on balance in each dimension. And in addition to balance, work to be fully present in the dimension you're currently in or working on: fully present at work when it's time to work, and fully present at home when it's time for family. Too many people are daydreaming about home when they're at work, and then stressing about unfinished work while they're at home. This is living out of balance. Balance one wheel at a time. *And just like that fuel pump, often there is one dimension of life that's off and negatively affecting all others.* This is out of balance, inefficient and exhausting. Identify and work most in the dimension that's wobbling out of balance and holding you back.

Balancing Dimensions

Balance should refer to being well-rounded in each dimension. Take recreation, for instance. You may like to golf all the time, but a balance may be taking up hiking because your wife and kids love this. Or, getting outside of your regular group or network to gain a different business perspective, etc. Learning a new trade to help develop your empathy – maybe like "Painting with a Twist" activity, or volunteering when all you know is leading a business. Balance in each of the dimensions, just like balance of individual tires, will contribute to greater life balance. Life's an ebb and flow and different phases call for greater focus in different dimensions. While we're working on one of our life dimensions, let's look for wholeness within that arena. So, if I'm to exercise for my body, do I pump garbage into my mind while I work out? Can I not find the balance of mind/body/soul/spirit in the arena of exercise? Quietly running into a sunrise can stir all of these and become a very balanced arena. At work, can I not find a flow and keep my body moving so my mind stays invigorated? Can I avoid gossip and think good, clean and positive thoughts? Do you see what balance in each dimension means? Do you understand wholly experiencing each arena? *Whenever you are whole and fully present, you amplify whatever you do!* Any dimension one of the seven dimensions of life you become more balanced in, you gain greater perspective and understanding and amplify that dimension. Therefore, when all the dimensions are being balanced, and we're engaging life wholly and fully present, we create this amplified Energizer state of being! We need to stop acting like we have a perfectly balanced life. Instead we can embrace our wholeness and find balance in each of life's dimension. Greater balance ignites energy as it naturally expands capacity and improves efficiency; imbalance swindles energy.

Being, then Doing

Being versus doing. Let's not confuse being for doing, but let's realize being will amplify doing. Here's what we mean. There are those that constantly work on themselves. Their being is important to them. They continually need a day of relaxation. They crave vacations and getting away from the stress of it all. Often, we're fooled by the leisurely pace. Lack of ambition seems to be a peaceful serenity. However, this kind of personality often suffers from deep wounds never healed, no vision, or fear of what others may think if they were to take action. Apathy usually plagues this life because of past wounds or emotional hurt. They've become inclusive and the state of "being" has become their drug. They show no proactivity at work and initiative is foreign to them unless it's something that excites their "being" state or appeals to an emotional need. Relaxation is often apathy's greatest smokescreen. I like how Brendon Burchard says, "We must beware of them, for they can make us fear the thing that advances our lives: effort."

On the other hand, there are those in life who are doers. They will never stop – or so they think. They are the energizer bunnies we talked about in the first chapter. They are hurt. You can almost see it, and you feel it by interacting with them – no real connection. To stop doing and even think about being means facing pain and hurt. It's easier to do. Religion is full of doers. People paying penance for past guilts or seeking some form of insurance for future doubts. These people do good work. They build great things and achieve amazing results in life. Work was designed to be gratifying and so they consume their life in it. Their state of "doing" becomes their drug and they misuse work. They are headed for burnout, or they become so calloused that work takes precedence over people and relationships. The martyrdom mentality takes over as they cope with a life of emotional disengagement. "I had to work to provide for you," is a common refrain. Doers pride themselves in making things happen. They inefficiently do life. They miss the leverage of full and overflowing love. They miss the amplitude of wholeness.

In this matter of doing and being, you cannot have one without the other; but you must have one before the other! This is key! Energy was made to be transferred. Just as the sun rises every morning casting its rays of warmth across our planet. Just as rain falls to the earth and rivers flow down the mountain and the waves roll up on the beaches. Just as heat from a furnace must be dissipated and just as the force from an engine must be transmitted to a driveshaft. Being without doing is implosive. Doing without being is explosive. Being, followed by creative, profitable doing – whole hearted work – gets things done. Being is the lever that amplifies everything you do! Yes, we must work on ourselves every day, for the person who adopts a mindset of effort – all in – understands you can't be all in if you're not your all. If you're not at your all, you will never be able to realize what maximum effort looks like. Being is more important than doing as being is the engine driving everything. Being is your energy. When your being is whole, your effort will not only be physical work, but emotional and spiritual work as well. When energy is flowing, you're pouring into your work and your work pours back into you. You know your work will have the maximum impact because you are at your best – you're whole.

Inside - Out

If we're not careful, we can catch ourselves thinking outside-in instead of inside-out. That's right. We want to change the world, so we get right to work. We quickly share the negative political post because, yes, a lot of politics are messed up; and through frustration, our emotions are triggered, and we respond.

We talk about the downfalls or negatives of others instead of looking inside at what we should change. It's so much easier to "point out" than to "work on." Stephen Covey wisely differentiated two categories of people. Proactive people focus on their "Circle of Influence" (things they can change and influence like themselves, their children, their environment, their responses, etc.). Reactive people focus on their "Circle of Concern" (things they have little-to-no control over like politics, others, the weather, etc.). When the next politically-biased post pops up or the gossip-filled text buzzes in, here's an exercise we all can mentally or verbally declare: ***"I'm committing to use this emotional trigger to take an inward look and use what might have been a hasty response to instead text encouragement or share a positive thought!"*** Remember the advice to draw a circle around yourself and change everyone in that circle! World-changers do this and all the circles their circle touches are better for it!

Simply reacting to life and living in the Circle of Concern swindles so much time and energy – sucks it right out of you! Run to the Circle of Influence! Start with you. Change the world from the inside-out! Live amplified by being, then doing!

Wholeness (Gestalt)

We've discussed being balanced in the different dimensions of our lives, but what should we consider for our overall wellness of life? Let's look at wholeness. Yes, that's right. Wholeness instead of balance, and we'll see why, soon. Accepting every dimension of your wholeness as that which makes you the strongest – gestahlt. Your wholeness is the complete person you are. When you're whole, you amplify energy. When you're whole, your capacity is full and can overflow to others. *As you invest in each dimension, you're becoming whole, you fill up and eventually overflow. As we reclaim our energy and set about owning our lives, we'll focus efforts in one dimension to repair and set it in order.* We'll spend several months focusing on one dimension if need be. The big hold up for you may be family. It may be health. Many of us are barely making it trying to survive life we don't have time or energy for what's most important – our life! William James said, "Most people live, whether physically, intellectually or morally, in a very restricted circle of their potential being. They make use of a very small portion of their possible consciousness, and of their soul's resources in general, much like a man who, out of his whole bodily organism, should get into a habit of using and moving only his little fingers." Jim Rohn said it like this, "Success is something you attract by the person you become." Wholeness! We've discussed the four parts of a person and have explored inner fullness. What is wholeness? Wholeness is gestahlt. Where the sum of the whole is greater than the sum of all its parts. Wholeness is abundance. When you are whole, you have inner peace, a powerful drive and are living vibrantly. You're not perfect. Perfection's not the point. You're growing intentionally in all dimensions of life. These dimensions work together to enhance your life. They support and strengthen each other.

Wholeness gives you the ability to stop running! I decided to start running in 2013. I loved it and picked up some medals. However, the end of 2014 found me lying flat on my back. Some of the childhood pains returned to my hip and back. I went to the chiropractor and found out I had no curve in my neck; and, my spine and pelvis were fused in front as opposed to on top. This caused one of my legs to be shorter than the other. Through a series of treatments, Magnolia Medical Center fixed me. It's been an incredible journey. I'm a stronger runner and person in so many ways and on so many levels because of signing up for my first 5K on January 1, 2014. I was literally scared out of my mind about it. Here's the deal. As we expand and grow in a certain dimension, say health, we find things out about ourselves, overcome and grow stronger. Brendon Burchard shares in his bestselling book, *The Charge*, that staying challenged personally is key to thriving and experiencing life more fully. It keeps passion flowing because of the investment in your wholeness as a person. ***Staying full and activating life within you amplifies everything you touch!*** You may try a new sport, play an instrument, eat a certain way, implement professional skill development, take a class, complete some big project. Take one area of your wholeness that's lacking – perhaps a big area of challenge for you right now – and scratch something you could do to challenge and grow yourself for the next thirty days:

_____

_____

_____

Since reading this, I've taken a single objective out of my annual goals and focused aggressively on it for a thirty day time period. There is magic to this monthly objective and it's long enough to accomplish great things, short enough to feel doable and repel boredom, and it adds a spice to life. A challenge will awaken dormant energies inside. Try this today and build your wholeness. You'll amplify everything!

Are you aware of the habits and activities in your life? Are they building you as a whole person to amplify value creation? Are you building valuable, energizing additions into your life? If you are, then you can create more value for others. Might your current habits be limiting your wholeness and stressing you out? I like how Lewis Howes states, "We think we can keep burning the candle at both ends because, well, nothing can stop us." We wonder where our friends and family went, we take the pills and push ourselves to burnout through poor exercise, lack of proper nutrition, little sleep. Our emotions go hay-wire and we become irritable and short tempered. It's no wonder. We are created as a whole being and must live as a whole being if we are to thrive. The hard work of being makes all the doing easier! Life and every action is amplified when we're whole. To be able to take care of others, you must first take care of yourself! We've heard it said, "hurt people hurt." Well, healed people desire to heal! When you're healing and living in love, life itself opens up to you, emotions are flowing, and everything is amplified.

7 Dimensions of Wholeness ... Mental

Are you mentally whole? Our mental dimension includes our perspective, mindset, thoughts, values & morals, self-esteem and emotional intelligence. Our development, intellect, lifelong education, readings, motivations, recovery and fulfillment are all a part of our minds and areas to consider as we ask ourselves, "Are we mentally whole?" Our mental aspect starts the list of the dimensions of wholeness. Our mental well-being, the thoughts and ideas that we allow our subconscious to muse on, our imagination and our beliefs will decide who we become. Then, persistence (mental toughness) continues propelling the body in the direction it must go to achieve the desire. What you think, you become. James Allen says it perfectly, "Good thoughts and actions can never produce bad results; bad thoughts and actions can never produce good results. We understand this law in the natural world, and work with it; but few understand it in the mental and moral world—although its operation there is just as simple and undeviating—and they, therefore, do not cooperate with it." *Too often, instead of exhibiting mental clarity by thinking good and empowering thoughts, setting goals around those thoughts and moving forward in the areas we can control, we complain about or explain away our situation.* Our mental wellness, in this case, is clouded. Zig Ziglar motivated folks to be meaningful specifics, yet many live as wandering generalities. It's easy to go mindlessly through life doing only what's required to live. Many get up each morning with lack of definite purpose, rush out the door to go build someone's dream, and then rush here, rush there, and never consider what life purpose is or take the time to paint their own future. You are blessed if you do exactly what you want to be doing in your career, however, a majority of people feel "stuck" in their job. The need for financial security causes us, so often, to trade all fulfillment and wholeness with the bank of "Maybe One Day." How do you not feel stuck? How do you find purpose and meaning? Change your mindset! Grow right where you are, right now. Great organizations encourage their people to grow and will train those who want to grow. Zappos, Health Corp of America and New York Life are just a few prime examples of companies that'll pay for workshops and continuing education for their teams. How about reading? Reading is to the mind what exercise is to the body, what prayer is to the spirit, and what love is to the heart! Earl Nightingale stated, "Books have meant to my life what the sun has meant to planet earth." How are you growing your mind with knowledge and exercising it through practical use of that knowledge? History shows some of the most educated and profound leaders of history were self-taught. They learned how to learn, and most importantly, they put their learning to immediate application in their life. Get in the practice of highlighting and marking practical applications in books when you read them. Learn to love learning and make application key! Let mental growth amplify your energy!

... Spiritual

Are you spiritually whole? Our spiritual dimension encompasses such things as morals, ethics, spiritual accountability, faith, our life purpose, stewardship, local church affiliation, and most importantly a personal relationship with God. Many choose to exempt themselves from spiritual fullness perhaps due to doubts about God or uncertainty of the unknown. Any amount of vision requires faith in some unknown. Those who won't seek spiritual truth and clarity will not live a fully experienced existence. *Those who exempt themselves from spiritual fullness dismiss what was intended for the mind to initiate and the body and soul to receive, that is, the energy of faith and the energy of hope!* You can live dead to your spirit. Many run from religion and rightly so. The problem is, we shut off our spirit to its desire and rob all other parts of our wholeness. A spiritual awareness will amplify your joy and fullness. Most of our hurts and wounds are those of the soul and spirit; unfortunately, when we close off our souls and spirits to life, we close off a majority of life. We live solely in the physical sense intoxicating our faculties with over-exercising, food, drugs, alcohol, driving desire to be rich, and so on. Anything that's a have-to-have, a habitual turn-to, or a crutch, may be our drug of choice to silence the spiritual and heartfelt hurts. It's when we allow the healing of our soul and spirit, that we allow for deep connection and fully experiencing life with our eyes wide open and minds raised to the highest frequencies! Spiritual awareness is the only way to receive true emotional healing. It's because faith transcends earthly trials and woes amplifying our strength to choose the correct emotional responses. When we only live as physical beings, responses must make sense. Responses give and get; they're tit for tat; and retribution and retaliation reign. When we only live as a physical being, we see others as simply physical beings, and if they can't benefit us in some way, then our response can easily be to hurt them. When we see people as spiritual, eternal beings with an emotional soul and beautiful mind, we transcend the tunnel vision of solely physical decision making. We're empowered to make choices with a deeper under-standing and awareness. The spiritually strong person amplifies the outcome of everything they do, every decision they make and every life they touch!

What are your virtues – the essences of your spirit? This is the ability to live at a higher consciousness. Living virtuously. So, what are you known for? When people enter your presence, what virtue vibrates around you? What would they sense looking deeply into your eyes with-out you ever saying a word? When we see ourselves as a whole being, it's not just a matter of what attribute works for one life situation at a time, or what attribute best serves a drive of ours. It's now a matter of whole-ness. Your mind's imagination harnessed by your spirit's virtue and one feeding the other. The Honorable J.T. Headley wrote of Washington's virtue, saying, "Virtues planted so deep in the heart are proof against the fiercest storms and severest temptations of life." Then, in his *Farewell Address*, George Washington urged our young nation to, "… cultivate peace and harmony with all … can it be that Providence has not connected the permanent felicity (intense happiness) of a nation with its virtue?" Virtue!

Could this be why the great Apostle urged us to think on virtuous things? Those who think virtuously will act in virtuous ways. The essence of your spirit shines forth about you constantly. Is your fragrance, your aura, one of virtue? Is your spirit healthy and virtuous? This is where oneness, wholeness, being real and genuine begins. It's an effort to be – not to seem – virtuous. In so doing, your spirit realizes deep, abiding joy. Happiness is only one of the rays on the wide array of glorious emotion flowing through a virtuous life. We must accept the wholeness of who we are.

I grew up in a military and religious home. We were taught mental and physical toughness mixed with spiritual dependence. However, we were conditioned to be emotionless. Unaware of our emotions can be a dangerous place. *Emotions connect us with others and hold the keys to all of our habits. Emotions generate the feelings which serve as triggers and gages for our energy. When we sear our emotions, we turn off a majority of life. We are whole beings and understandinhg our emotions will amplify everything we do.* Emotions can fluctuate and be triggered – especially as we practice and train them. Therefore, there should be a constant healing going on – a continual and daily time for renewal. Like my friend, Rob O. likes to say, "It's a jungle out there." For me, I practice meditation through reflection, gratitude and intentional silence, quiet focused visualization and thought. Prayer makes up a great portion of my meditation. The acceptance of a Higher Power, Divine Intelligence or Hand of Providence is an act of faith and proven to calm anxiety and worry. Why place such an emphasis on finding a still and quiet time in a place of meditation? A warrior is a warrior and should be about the affairs of battle, right? There's an ancient saying that the warrior is courageous first by building the true strength of the inner man. The inner person must be renewed daily no matter what state of affairs you find yourself in. Those in the battle are tempted to find a battle in everything, and those not knowing battle might run from healthy conflict. In matters of nourishing inner strength and fortifying mental clarity, one must meditate daily on their state of being and build inner strength and poise. Gordon writes, "…in the time of intentional quiet there comes, and comes ever more, the calmness for the brain, and the fresh fuel for the heart, and new steadiness for the will that holds all under its strong hand." Buddha said, "Your worst enemy cannot harm you as much as your own unguarded thoughts." Meditation allows you to step back and observe the traffic flow in your brain – your thoughts. What's working? What's debilitating? How do you apply truth to your current situation? Meditation is wisdom. Meditation affords you the chance to consider all paths, and upon consideration, choose the best one!

Personal peace happens when your inner conscience and your outward behaviors are congruent. Inner peace allows us to be at peace with others. In fact, when pointing out errors in others comes easiest, it's often a smokescreen or cover for lack of inner peace. Similarly, when we're afraid to give constructive feedback, but lavish flattery, it can also be a smokescreen to draw attention away from ourselves. Being at peace with yourself is foundational in all manner of relationships. You and I, when we are full of energy (at capacity and overflowing) produce feelings and emotions. We radiate this. When your energy – is depleted and you're hurting spiritually, it's easier to get sick, stressed, fatigued and much harder to show up and be there in force for others. To find deep, spiritual healing, to awaken our deepest soul, and to know only love, will require a daily progression in our spiritual journey. Let spiritual growth amplify your energy to live fully and to love deeply!

... Health

Are you healthy? Do you feel whole in your body and fitness? Our dimension of health includes physical fitness, nutrition, stress reduction, medicine and healing, mind-body wellness and healthy living. Physical health is in fact the easiest portion of personal wholeness to work on. It's the only tangible out of the four parts of self that we can both see and feel. I believe it's why Jesus questioned the religious ruler, asking him if he couldn't understand the physical and practical things of life, how would he understand the spiritual world? Understanding disciplines in the physical world – the one in which we live – allows us to better understand those of the spiritual world. Getting along with others leads us to greater connection with God. Physical understanding, first, brings what my coach calls transfer of discipline. *Transfer of discipline is powerful considering that we will never master anything, until we first master ourselves.* Many are failing physically being controlled by runaway drives. Many don't seek to understand their bodies, their desires or a proper balance in this dimension health. Let's focus on getting healthy. It's so important. Our physical health directly impacts how fully we live, how lively our experience, and how effective we will be while we're alive. Do you have a health plan? Did you know sound physical health beats financial security hands down when considering what constitutes true wealth? I have been guilty of saying "no" to fitness because of saying "yes" to something else: longer hours at work, sleeping in, etc. Business coach, Andy Bailey, says not taking care of ourselves hurts not only us, but others as well. *When we're physically unfit, we're not performing optimally for ourselves or others.* He states, "The first step to taking care of yourself is recognizing that it needs to be done … don't discount your own value … make a point of maintaining your own well-being." The days I'm active (workout, run, walk), I tap into more energy for work and for the kids when I get home! It's amazing how good you feel after just a short walk, meditation or prayer with the songbirds before sunrise, 15 mins in the gym, or just high intensity running the soccer ball through the yard with the boys! Let that good feeling and momentum unleash your energy to carry you to believe and keep taking the next small action toward your goals!

Notice I said small action. Through my running journey, I've learned the importance of slowing down, getting posture right, and enjoying exercise. Interviewing several fitness experts, their consensus is shockingly similar. People look to get results too fast. I was running with a UFIT trainer recently. Michael shared that with our modern bodies, we don't exercise like people did on the farm years ago. We come in to the gym to get bulked up, work out hard, and think the burn we feel is something amazing. While it's indicative that we wore the muscle out and will result in strengthened muscles, too many times, we are strengthening too fast and hurt ourselves in the long run, or create tightened muscles.

Rod Key, my running coach and owner of UFIT in Murfreesboro, Tennessee, advises runners to slow down and enjoy the journey. "Look up and around you, take in the beauty and progress slowly and correctly toward your goal." Rod also travels to corporations speaking on the *"4 Wheels of Wellness."* His approach is empowering and solid! Ashley Benson, founder of B&B Sports, articulates this fitness complex perfectly when she states, "If we are in training for a competitive sport or have challenging physical goal to prepare for, like a marathon, oftentimes the body is sacrificed for the sake of the end goal." When I interviewed her, she advised, "spend time defining your goal." Asking yourself what you want from your workouts and what you need are keys to starting down the right path. Knowing what fitness trends you are drawn to and are these trends helping you achieve your goal are also important to consider, she shared. Benson asks clients, "Is the time you're spending in the gym benefitting you long-term?" When we train, strengthen, or condition our bodies, we should first and foremost consider our posture. Benson continues, "Posture is KEY to aging gracefully!" She shares that pain and injuries decrease and you'll feel "awesome and energized after your workout." Remember, stretching and warming-up are important and often overlooked steps in exercise. *Working muscles in the proper form and a willingness to build slowly follows the Energizer's mentality for first being, then doing.* Enjoy the strengthening process and avoid hurting your body. I love her attention to this balance. Here's an example of Ashley's workout flow for anyone looking to start or improve their physical exercise:

- 5-min warm-up: jog / bike / light stretches.

- Warm-up in a way that corrects your posture.

- Stretch the small muscles along the spine and adjust the head to sit up on top of the body (recommend the HeadFloater™).

- Stretch, adjust and realign feet and wake up the important ankle stabilizer muscles (recommend the MIINS®).

- A few minutes to release muscle tension, knots, spasms in the back that can hinder proper form and alignment. Wake up the scapula area and deep stretch the chest and shoulders. Many use foam rollers (recommend the Parasetter®).

- Warmup spine and hip mobility (recommend the TYE4®).

- Lifting weights strengthens muscles — now we build muscle strength to hold the skeleton up right.

- Cardio / endurance — along with the heart and lungs, the

muscles are developing postural endurance and the joints will receive less wear and tear from repetitive movements because the small joint stabilizers have been activated and now serve as a brace around the joint.

Like one CEO told me regarding his health and lack of fitness, "Tim, if I don't do something, I won't even be around for the business in 10 years." Coach Rod Key states, "You can't delegate your fitness." You're either growing and stretching your capacity, or you're not. Stagnation feels bad. Physical exercise will put you into a flow state. It allows you to unlock energies and engage your mental, spiritual and emotional senses.

Some people run, some run really well, and some run so well it's intimidating to the rest of us. In fact, when I first considered taking up running, I was intimidated just by showing up to a 5K. The fear of the unknown held me back: how to start, how to finish, timing chips, training, etc. It took people like running coaches Rod Key, Jenny Hutchens and Wayne Burns, who didn't shove a lifestyle, or certain pace, or expectation on me; but, they came alongside and encouraged me to run my own pace and fulfill the distance that works for me! That's why to this day on an early morning, or late evening, or even mid-day at lunchtime, I'll plan to enjoy a run. Running can ignite your energy like crazy! Consider, though, someone who doesn't run. Maybe it's swimming. Maybe it's walking. Maybe it's 100 push-ups every morning like Jen's grandpa. For physical exercise, many think that I'll tell them they should run. In fact, many have asked if my book is about running because they know I run. *Simply put, I won't tell you to do anything. Here's what I'll ask. What makes you come alive? What gets your heart rate up and your lungs expanding for an extended period of time?* It may not feel great at first, but until your heart rate's up and your breathing harder than usual, you're not getting the cardio-vascular benefit of aerobic exercise Be it biking, swimming, dancing, taking a brisk walk, jogging or running – move! Experience what getting the cobwebs out feels like and what life flowing through you feels like.

What are you asking your body to do for you and are you giving it what it needs? Are you listening to it? When you work out, are you fueling properly, drinking enough water and are you sleeping properly? Educate yourself on proper amounts of water intake, good sources, of fuel and sleep. Yes, a good night's sleep! Vince Lombardi said, "Fatigue makes cowards of us all!" We all have shareholders in our lives to who we owe our best. Giving our best requires us to be at our best. The last client deserves the same amount of enthusiasm as the first, and our wife and kids definitely need our best – not the crumbs. What activities and investments in your wholeness allow you to operate at your best? Zig Ziglar made the illustration that if you had a multi-million-dollar race horse, you wouldn't let him say up half the night smoking cigarettes, drinking coffee or alcohol and eating junk food … no, you'd feed him the right food and drink and control his rest and exercise to give him a chance to perform like the Thoroughbred he is. Wouldn't we all? Friend, you're a winning Thoroughbred and have a billion-dollar body! Give yourself a chance to win! And, when you take care of yourself physically you amplify everything! Your mind is more alert and productive, your emotions find balance and your spirit is renewed.

I was reading spiritual leader and pastor, Dr. Paul Chappell's book, *Stewarding Life*, recently. He graciously shared some rather alarming statistics strait frrom the desk of the US Surgeon General:

- 34% of the American adult population is overweight.

- Poor diet and lack of exercise are associated with the top ten causes of death in the US, including the top four: heart disease, cancer, stroke and diabetes.

- Only 8% of Americans are getting the amount of exercise recommended for minimal health benefits.

- Only 12% of Americans had 80% or above scores in the USDA's Healthy Eating Index.

It's always a refreshing sign when leaders put emphasis on physical well-being as well as the importance of spiritual health. How can you fully understand one without the other? And if you say you have faith for eternity, but can't exhibit any faith for a month or year down the road for better health, better emotions, better life and mental awareness and clarity – all of which physical exercise is proven to give – then can one trust what you claim faith to be?

Physical wellness stimulates mental clarity, awakens the spiritual "muscles", and promotes emotional stability as your endorphins, serotonin, and dopamine kick into high gear.

This is not hearsay; its scientific. Some leave off physical well-being completely and try to develop all other aspects, while some leave off spiritual and emotional well-being to literally live at the gym pumping heavy iron. Don't get me wrong, these guys have a motivational effect on me to work out my comparitively puny arms, but the idea that we can divorce ourselves from certain aspects of our wholeness will not allow us to thrive! Here's the deal. We are human beings and thus, the mental and physical aspects are the easiest to comprehend. *I've found when I daily work on physical wellness, the other disciplines are easier to find.* You cannot get out of your skin. Your physical frame holds all else, and yet too often, we allow societal norms (tobacco use, over-eating, eating fast food versus whole foods, pulling all-nighters, etc.) to provide a false comfort that we're ok because "everyone else is doing it." Instead, we have to contemplate and think critically about what's happening.

Start mentally and decide to better your physical state! A good friend of mine, Becca, wrote me recently telling me of a 50-pound transformation she's achieved in just a year and half! Like a favorite quote states, she just "woke up one morning and decided she didn't want to feel like that anymore, or ever again," so she changed, just like that! She attests to the fact that running is beautiful, and it "wipes her emotional and mental slate clean every day." In turn, she's craving healthy food (fuel), and her family has come around her in support, and her focus and love of others and faith in God has never been stronger! I'm so proud of Becca and am encouraged to keep living wholly. We are all lights to those around us! I encourage you to find physical wholeness through some sort of activity.

Plan some form of exercise into your daily routine. A brisk 15-minute walk that gets your heart pumping and your lungs breathing deeply is proven to have so many health benefits. If that's all you did, the compound effect would be evident in your life. Mix that with adding some proven healthy fuel to your diet and budget your calories, and without any complication, you'll feel the benefits of vibrancy and physical health. It will affect every other arena of your life, too. Consume more protein, fruits, vegetables and grains. Lower your caffeine intake and drink a ton of water. There are so many tips in a quick Google search and you could quickly print a picture and stick it on your mirror for a reminder – install that switch! Let taking daily steps to improve your health amplify your energy!

Chapter 15

... Family

How's your family dynamic? How are your relationships with the ones you love? Do you get along with the ones you're closest with and tied to by relation? Our family dimension includes our spouse, children, parents, siblings and extended relatives. Parenting our kids is a tremendous responsibility and joy. With our spouse, deep relationship, passionate intimacy and the blessing of sex can literally create an oasis and haven in your home impenetrable by the outside world! Nothing will undergird and bolster your energies more than healthy family relationships; yet, the same relationships, when unhealthy, can swindle energy faster than anything. How does seventy years of marriage happen? I asked Mr. Busho, a distinguished WWII veteran. He stated with his soft, aged and beautiful voice, "Tim, you ready … listen close … two words: I'm … sorry." I often tell Jen that she and I will grow wrinkled and beautiful and walk into the next life together holding hands. Having lived fully, one night in our hundreds we'll take our last physical breath and enter eternity together. What belief can stimulate this positive thought? Is this crazy? Not at all. I have learned recently to look at my Jennifer with all her uniqueness and beauty as a complete human being: a physical body, spirit, soul and mind. *When we look deeply into the eyes of our family – our people – we see the sparkle and realize these are the windows to their souls!* There's so much beauty and treasure to which we'll never know the depth. This goes to a deeper and richer dimension of relationship. You can literally sit cross-legged in an empty apartment with a Domino's pizza, eyes twinkling at each other and knowing you have something special. It's the proverb that goes something like, "Better is a dinner of Ramen noodles where love is, than a freezer full of prime rib and trouble therewith." Build healthy and fulfilling relationships at home, and the wholeness of these relationships will amplify your energy!

... Occupation

How's your occupation? Are you giving it your all every day? Are you reaping the financial benefits because of the value you add and create? The occupation dimension demands a good chunk of our lives. I'd like to think at the end of my life, whatever I did for a living and how I did it was some of the best invested time ever! This dimension encompasses things like career planning, workplace relations, business skills, entrepreneurship, management, and leadership. *Most of us have no problem defining what a job is; but, to amplify everything in your life, determine whether you're on a career path that will put you in a job position where you will come alive!* Maybe your life purpose is being a mother, being a father, serving your country in uniform, being a community servant as a police officer or first responder, ministering or pastoring, building things, volunteering, being a nurse, musician, seamstress, and the list goes on. Maybe it's giving a smile, preparing a meal, or running a business. These are gifts, passions and life purposes. Work is a gift. We're able to fund life and hopefully thrive while we do it. Find the joy in work by taking your joy to work and not holding back! Be grateful for every chance of contribution you have. Like family, our places of work can either give us relational joy or stress. We are interdependent on our coworkers, right? Are you getting along? Is the work environment harmonious? If not, where's the pain? Are you choosing the highest responses possible if there's a stressful or toxic relationship? We can thrive in every relationship; we can. However, it will take the faith of choosing responses at the highest frequency – love.

Continually improve yourself no matter whether you're just starting out or have reached the top. I watched coworkers chase the raise instead of chasing the kaizen (continual improvement), or self-development that would have leveraged them ten times greater than what a raise could ever bring. While leaving for a better job opportunity may align you more to your life purpose (or you move geographically) we see job-hopping permeating a generation. It's easy to blame an employer or supervisor, while no personal responsibility is taken to grow one's self or better one's work environment. The vicious cycle of comparing, workplace gossip and looking for "greener grass" holds so many bound to the money chase.

Instead, start working on mental well-being. Grow your mind, your imagination, your outlook. Write down thoughts of what you'd like to do in life, make a dream board, read books, and then start planning. Plan on becoming better at work and shrink lifestyles now, if need be, to save to achieve those goals. Double blessing here as you'll probably end up getting a raise for bettering yourself professionally as well as having more from budgeting and saving. The plan itself doesn't need to be perfect as you'll refine this as you go along. It's the process of growth – the process – that betters us. Yes! And now, as you're working toward the goals you've set, you'll find focus and mental clarity! You'll be tapping into mental energy! Not only will you feel more bounce in your step at work, physically, your emotional well-being starts to improve because you're going places! You know it and you feel it! Mental, physical, emotional, and spiritual richness are priceless! Whether it's simply reading a leadership book, having a positive uplifting attitude, or spending quiet time in meditation and prayer, strengthening each area compounds so greatly over a lifetime. Becoming whole amplifies your energy! Couple that with a work ethic that finds purpose in anything you put your hand to, and before long, you'll be leading your field! The cream always rises to the top!

Remember, work is life; life is work. *Avoid looking to the mirage of balance between the two. Instead, be balanced by investing wholly while at work! Be whole and show up with fullness when it's time. Then, go home, and be home, when it's time.* The question then, is wholeness, and are we showing up fully and abundantly? Are we whole? Too many seek to find acceptance and fulfillment in work because doing is the quickest way to fill a void in our being. Often, someone from our past left a great big hole. Let's be honest with ourselves and ask why we're doing what we're doing. If we're burning ourselves out in our occupation, climbing the ladder and stepping on people on the way up, and find more fulfilment in our work than in the relationships of our lives, we can be sure there are past skeletons in our closets. Wounds we must face. We must stop putting a pretty bow on the lie – called an excuse – that sacrificing ourselves, our health, our happiness and our family are just part of the business owner's M.O. It's not, nor does it have to be! What's really driving you? The call to find healing – deep healing – is compelling us! For without healing, we won't show up whole – able to abound and

make greater impact in the time we choose to contribute and charge toward our vision. Carnegie shares the story of John D. Rockefeller Sr., who at the age of 43 had built up the largest monopoly the world had ever seen – the great Standard Oil Company. Yet at only 53, when most men are at their prime, his shoulders drooped, and he could barely walk. Carnegie states, "the ceaseless work, the endless worry, the streams of abuse, the sleepless nights and the lack of exercise and rest had exacted their toll … they'd brought him to his knees … he was now the richest man in the world yet had to live on a diet that a poor man would have scorned." Rockefeller's income at the time was a million dollars a week, and two dollars a week paid for all the food he could eat. "Nothing but medical care, the best money could buy, kept him from dying at the age of 53," Carnegie concludes. From this
wounded personality exudes an unrealistic ambition. Covey shares that those exemplifying wholeness "don't become workaholics, religious zealots, political fanatics, crash dieters, food bingers, pleasure addicts or fasting martyrs." When you work, be all in, so that when you're home, you're all in. Seek to find healing so you can become whole and operate abundantly! Let being all in at work – whole and abundant – amplify your energy!

... Recreation

Recreation's inclusive to arts and music, literature, rest and leisure, sports and hobbies, travel, vacationing, humor and fun. It's the time you get to enjoy the fruits of your labors. There's nothing better than sitting out on the veranda with a cup of crisp, cold water while looking out over the back yard in satisfaction. The roses pushing their blossoms out and over the lattices, the fragrance of spring in the air and the fresh blossoms of life all around can fill one's heart with wonder. Or vacationing in the mountains, travelling to Europe, playing tennis with a friend, running a marathon, or canoeing the river at sunrise. Some tap out of life always dreaming about recreation or recreating too much. They're not really living their dreams – they don't have dreams. *Their recreations are the norms of the societal class they belong to, and their recreation can turn into exhaustion.* One author wrote, "Those who are swept away by the popular current and learn to love amusement for its own sake open the door to a flood of temptations … they give themselves up to social gaiety and thoughtless mirth." When you become thoughtless and just go-with-the-flow, the temporal pleasure of recreation can become a drug like anything, and your life can drift. It's always great to check in from time to time and make sure you're the one driving what recreations you take part in, what's the purpose, and how do they engage you truly recreating you as a whole person. Avoid recreation that turns you off to connection and reality, becoming a numbing drug in your life. Flora Plummer said of this, "You lose … the capacity for a life of usefulness … the faculties of the spirit, and all that link people with the spiritual world, are debased."

Since life is a precious gift, choose your recreation as opposed to going with the flow. Be intentional – super intentional – with this gift called life. If I'm going to be lying on the couch, it's because it's in the plan for family fun night, or it's necessitated – sick, rest needed, etc. I will not seek comfort or coasting for the sake of easy. How do you balance recreation? Recreation is needed for wholeness. A workaholic is by-passing the pitstop. They're headed for a blowout, and if they're built rugged enough to stand it – some are – it will be at the expense of their team or family. Workaholics like busy, they thrive on stress. Why? They're finding fulfillment in work and much more – they're hiding in their work. They don't know how to experience life and let emotions of joy flow. How do you balance patience? Like the farmer, have you planted seeds? Plant seeds, toil long, and rest when the harvest is in the barn. Allow yourself the latitude to work hard and enjoy the fruit of your labor. Make friendships, spend time with your family. Travel. Live fully present to everything in life, today! When recreation doesn't build me in some way, should I be recreating? Recreating means just that – a chance to recreate. Analyze what you do for recreation and let it enhance everything about your life and your vision! Aristotle said, "The quality of life is determined by its activities." Let every activity of recreation build your wholeness and you'll amplify your energy!

... Social

Interacting with others in friendships, volunteering in our communities, and taking care of our environments constitute the dimension of our social lives. No matter how extroverted or introverted our personality types, we share this globe called Earth. We must interact at some level with humans or nature and the more harmonious this interaction, the better our experience and deeper our enhancement of energy! Some resist being social and some use social to solely benefit their agendas. The social dimension will energize those who truly seek to live together, connected through common interests and goals, people serving one another, giving back, and leaving our environments better than we found them. There's satisfaction that comes anytime we give back. Solomon said, "A good name is rather to be chosen than great riches and loving favor rather than silver and gold." How's your name in society? Are you known as a giver, a connector, a resource, a value-creator? Do you pride yourself in being anti-social? I'm not talking about introvert and extrovert and whether you're the life of the party or not. But, might there be deep wounds internally causing you to withdraw to some degree? Instead of letting connectedness flow from a whole being, some force being social, or they put on the social face. This only leads to exhaustion in living a facade. It happens. The term "fake it 'til you make it" can be catchy, but what you quickly learn about society is that there are a lot of fakes – those who aren't true to their word, those who will use you to gain their advantage. *We should all work to truly care for each other. This requires getting outside of our bubble to see the needs around us. It requires stepping up to the plate and not playing it small. It requires we amplify our efforts by disallowing the petty hurts and wounds we're holding onto. It requires healing. It demands wholeness.* There's a world hurting and there will be nothing more amplifying to your energy than to be whole, full and abounding in love towards all people! When this happens, amazing things happen – it all flows back in bigger and greater ways. Whether it's for one other human, or all 7 billion, let your social interdependence amplify your energy!

Chapter 15

Wholly There

Energizers are active physically, socially, mentally and spiritually. They live more abundant and synergized lives.! Being whole is a big deal! Wholeness amplifies every moment of our lives, every interaction with others and every action we take. Wholeness is the multiplication of effectiveness! More important than being rich, climbing to the top, being the strongest or smartest, wholeness will bring the satisfaction of a fulfilled life, and amplify your effectiveness in pursuing your life vision. In his book, *Think and Grow Rich*, Napoleon Hill shares the top twelve things that constitute true wealth:

- "Positive mental attitude,
- Sound physical health,
- Harmony in human relationships,
- Freedom from fear,
- Hope of future achievement,
- Capacity for applied faith,
- Willingness to share one's blessings with others,
- Being engaged in a labor of love,
- Open minded on all subjects toward all people,
- Complete self-discipline,
- Wisdom with which to understand people, and
- Financial security."

Consider these strong points that constitute true wealth. Each one of these can tie back to one and eventually to all of the dimensions of self. This is wholeness – the synergy of all dimensions of life working simultaneously together. For financial security to be listed very last is not surprising. To create lasting wealth means first being wealthy internally. Yet, many will run themselves, their families and closet relationships into the ground for another dollar. **When we accept the law of energy – first being, then doing – the whole person experiences the amplification of energy!** It's not so much the time at work versus the time at home, it's more of are we whole and are we fully present everywhere we are? This is effectiveness; this is balanced living. One moment of being fully present can change the world. Be whole and fully present wherever you are, and you will change the world! The only balance in life within your control is this: wherever you are, whatever you're doing, be fully there!

Fullness ... Order of Importance

Order is important: Mental, Spiritual, Health, Family, Occupation, Recreation and Social. Be whole for you, first. Be whole as a family unit, next. Your occupation, how you impact the world, and experience it through recreation follow. Then, you're whole, you're full and ready to share that fullness – living abundantly. Not saying wait 'til everything's perfect, but focus on healing in every area, thinking for yourself, what works, what doesn't work, imagining life wholly, mapping out a vision that's in alignment with wholeness. *Living fully so you can love deeply – experiencing an energized existence.* The beautiful thing about measuring and improving yourself as a whole person is beginning to see others as whole beings. The facade and fake quickly fade away and every human connection becomes an empowering moment. Everything you touch is amplified and turns to gold. Fight for your life takes on a whole new meaning. Swindlers become a little easier to say no to when we realize they are robbing us of our very fullness. The call to "Love your neighbor as yourself" no longer presents the problem of knowing how to truly love ourselves. Giving adds and multiplies. When you give to your wholeness, so that wherever you are, you can give wholly, then you are truly adding and multiplying! Living fully is giving; living fully is loving. What you do today to fill and fortify your energy compounds exponentially - why wait? Inner fullness is power - power to do anything. Take what you do seriously. You're an amplified Energizer. Let the way you carry yourself be of the utmost quality to say, "I value myself and I value you – you're important to me." Prepare yourself. Be at your best so that you can always be ready to give your best. The greatest enemy of thriving isn't dying, it's partially living. Seek wholeness; pursue fullness. You cannot give what you do not have; so, what will you have to give?

Measuring

Are you measuring where you're at in each dimension? To grow, we must first measure ourselves – an honest assessment of where we are and a vision of where we want to go. Brendon Burchard states, "If we are to measure, monitor and improve anything, let it be our story, our character, and our conduct – a mindfulness of who we are and how we are experiencing and relating to the world." Take a statesman as powerful as Ben Franklin. A man mighty in thought and deed. A man whose writings are still classics to this day. A man so curious he identified electricity in lightning (electricity well before its time). A man who could compel an entire French nation to aid a seemingly floundering, young United States. This man, after reading of life virtues, drew out ledger-like lines with virtues on rows and days of the month in the columns. He intentionally wanted to improve virtues in his life and in journaling his progress daily, he'd recall to his mind the virtue and take inventory of progress made, or not made. *This intentional measurement of growth depicts greatness. Show me a person intentional about virtuous beliefs and I'll show you a person of valuable behavior – behaviors that benefit the world!* Chart where you're at in each dimension of wholeness and commit to 1% better in each dimension. Repeat this phrase every day, "Today and every day, I'm getting better in every way!" Too often, we feel like there's so much growth and improvement we want that simply starting is challenging. Where do you start? I want to help. Think of roadblock number one in each dimension. What's holding you back mentally, spiritually, in your health, with your family, in your occupation, for recreation and socially? Jot one thing down and break this roadblock into bite sizes until you have one solid, actionable item for moving past this obstacle. Write this one thing down and go after it! Move the ball forward for your wholeness and fullness so you can amplify everything you touch and do! Increase your capacity. Become whole and operate from a place of fullness. Experience the abundance that follows and watch every thought, emotion, action and experience in your life carry the amplification of wholeness!
Becoming whole isn't something we try to make time for; wholeness becomes a non-negotiable and amplifying priority!

CHAPTER 16
TORTOISE TUFF

huge power in "little" consistency

*"No matter how many times I read 'The Tortoise &
The Hare,' the tortoise always wins!" – Dave Ramsey*

Our Friend, Tortoise

I was a young guy leaving the *EntreLeadership* conference! It was great!
One thing stuck out over all the other golden nuggets I wrote down.
One thing really resonated with me. One thing captured my mind and I
knew that by employing this one thing, I'd be successful in life. Yes, I was
certain of it! Probably the simplest and most child-like illustration of the
entire day, but the more I went back and implemented into my life, the
more I grew and the more energized my life became! It was a story Dave
Ramsey told with such passion and vigor that the hair on the back of my
neck stood up. It was such a simple story, yet it brought so much hope! It
was the David and Goliath victory. It was the Great Wall of China and the
Ironman! It was the flight to the moon and the marriage of seventy years.
It was the man against nature, the heroin against insurmountable odds! *It
was the story of that little, faithful tortoise – it was the huge POWER in
a little consistency!*

Dave tells the story like this, "One day, I was talking to a really, really
rich guy – I mean billionaire rich. We were having lunch, and I gave him

my standard billionaire question: 'What can I do today that will get me closer to where you are in your business and in your wealth building?' He leaned back and said … 'I want you to read a book. This is my favorite book. I read it several times a year. I read it to my children, and now I read it to my grandchildren over and over. It will change your life, your money, and your business forever.'"

Dave goes on, "Now, I'm a huge reader, so I was pretty excited at this point. This mega-billionaire is about to tell me the book that changed his life. Let's go!

'Dave, have you ever read *The Tortoise and the Hare*?'

Huh? A children's book? An old fairy tale? What does this have to do with wealth building? I sat there for a minute trying to decide if he was kidding or not. He wasn't. He leaned in and said,

'Dave, we live in a world full of hares. Everyone's racing around doing all kinds of crazy stuff. They're running ahead and falling back, running ahead and falling back. They're going back and forth, side to side, and all in circles. But the tortoise just keeps moving forward, slow and steady. And you know what? Every time I read the book, the tortoise wins.'"

It was the realization of this faithful, little, unstoppable, forward-moving tortoise that changed so much for me as a young guy. I decided instead of hopping from job to job like some of my peers, I'd stay faithful and maximize the position I was in at that time. By consistently putting in real work – not busy motion – but tangible results I could hang my hat on at the end of every day, I knew I could and would reap the reward. It's the amazing promise of self-fulfilling prophecy. What you think, you become. It's the consistency of great thoughts, an equally great attitude and faithful action! It's not pure thinking for a little while and then flopping back to old thought patterns. It's the resolute, tortoise toughness that sticks with the difficult decision even when the mood in which you made that decision wears off. It's creating your own mood through belief that doing hard stuff WILL pay off.

Non-Negotiable

A non-negotiable is something you've deemed absolutely a must! You won't even consider changing your mind! You won't deviate because the option to skip, miss, stop or give-up is simply off the table. Whether personal purity or physical fitness, non-negotiables are boundaries you set for yourself. *They keep your energy focused on creating the new and doing your plan instead of pushing on and fighting a moveable boundary.* Say your non-negotiable is going for a walk every day. No matter what, I will walk today! Say your goal is eliminating caffeine from your diet and you're meeting a friend for "coffee." Walk in and get a water (with lemons for added health) or decaf. Share your non-negotiable in a fun-loving way with your friend for support. They will gladly support you, I bet! We save immense energy by eliminating certain things that cause us mental turmoil every time we start the "should I / no I shouldn't" mind game. What do you want? Eliminate what's hindering you. Create a non-negotiable! Increase your personal energy and power!

Small (HUGE) Things

Did you ever lose one small, specially-threaded screw in the assembly of some device? This screw was the key to the entire project. Small thing or big thing? Well, it was a small thing that became a really big thing! J.T. Headley wrote, "On apparently trivial matters often hinge the greatest issues." Similarly, we miss big blessings in life by overlooking seemingly small things! This morning a minor setback occurred, and I almost missed taking in the sunrise while running. The sunrise! Think about this! Little thing, or huge splendid array of color that's easy to overlook because my mind was preoccupied? If we're not careful, we'll get so involved in a life venture or focused on a big goal that we overlook the small blessings taking place all around us! One runner friend, Miles, picks up pennies and even finds dimes along country roads. I've found a Craftsman wrench that lay on the roadside. Noticed or not, these small things are there. Many stress about everything being perfect at the wedding; yet, how many spectacular moments along the way were missed. It's a big day, yes! However, learn to laugh over the mess-ups and setbacks, and truly enjoy every hand-holding moment, dress fitting, flower selection, etc. Breathe in the experience of life. Even the small breath you just took was a HUGE deal. Imagine not having it! We weren't created robots. We have sensory nerves, feelings and emotions. Listen to your 6-year-old talk about how she learned addition in the tens' column. Celebrate the capital, cursive "T" that your son proudly displays. Pick the wild flower when you're out walking and tuck it in your wife's hair. Learning to notice and be thankful for the small, huge blessings in life will train our consistency. You believe that? We're simply rushing through life, too fast, and even the commitment to a better relationship, our fitness or a long-term dream stresses us out because we've been conditioned to look for a quick-fix. **KEY:** learn to love the process! Fall in love with the process. Love the journey. Enjoy the journey. The good and bad of the journey knowing that every small step is growth – it's progress! This is the POWER of small, huge things! ***Do the work to grow yourself, but be content that you're making progress every day, no matter how small a step forward!*** Stop to smell the roses from time to time! This is the HOPE of small, huge things! This is the POWER of consistency! Your energy is super-charged when your emotions get on board. Take in the beauty! Find joy and delight in the little things that are really huge!

Why discuss these small, huge things? Because, just like the tiny, small blessings we overlook in pursuit of our destination, we also discount the small, huge steps of progress in the consistency of pursuing our dreams. For instance, how do you get active? First, believe! Believe your continuous efforts will count! Believe they will make a difference! Patience is a must. The 5-minute microwave meal has undermined a patient mindset; so has the time lapse of TV paid programs. Getting fit, achieving a goal, or making headway on a project will not happen overnight. You must first believe that continuous effort will reap the reward, and then commit to never giving up no matter how small that action is! I love the quote Lao Tzu is known to have profoundly said, "The journey of 1,000 miles begins with a single step." In his famous book, *Poke the Box*, Seth Godin lays out the "Manifesto About Starting" defining the start as, "committing and going beyond the point of no return." Believe in your actions, no matter how small, and keep chugging onward like the little, blue engine! It will take this firm belief to keep you moving. The momentum we gain by this consistent action is phenomenal! Darren Hardy masterfully says it like this, "Learning success is hard, the process is laborious, tedious and sometimes even boring. Becoming wealthy, influential or world-class in your field is slow and arduous. Most people don't know how to sustain continual forward achievement. We think we don't like it or can't. **KEY**: We can learn to love any process, but it starts with embracing long-term commitment. Get excited about small, huge things! Be the tortoise! In his must read, *The Compound Effect*, Hardy formulates it this way, "Small, smart choices, plus consistency, plus time equals a radical difference."

Navy Seals are instructed, amidst the great challenges they face, to stop and make their beds. Small things matter. With 14 kids, my Mom learned the importance of consistency and routine. It's when healthy routine fell apart later in our lives, our family did as well. When you exercise, you are doing several things. You're affirming your value. You're telling your body that while you make demands of it for living life fully, you will also strengthen it and take care of it – it appreciates you greatly for this! When you pray, you may not see the effects today or tomorrow, but you are letting your spirit know that you will allow it to tap into the energy sources of hope and faith – your spirit will stay inspired and carry you through storms when physically, you can't walk any longer. Your spirit will blow on the embers of your soul when a wave of negative emotion takes you by surprise and threatens to stamp out your very fire and zeal for living fully and loving deeply. When you make time to exemplify your love in a small way every day through some kind deed or pouring your heart through the channel of a note, text or phone call or just beaming and radiating joy into someone's eyes, your soul will vibrate and pulsate feelings of love so strong that the attraction field will grow stronger and stronger around you! *The small – HUGE – things you do on a daily basis compound and combine into a synergistically whole person to carry you abounding through life as THE ENERGIZER!* Fall in love with small, HUGE things!

Leading Indicators

You ever notice the tortoise had a couple things he did – ONLY a couple? The tortoise prepared and plotted steadily forward. You need to spend some time getting super clear on what you want out of life.

Why? By considering what occupation, activities and contributions add the most value to your life and the lives around you, you can shed some clutter and some of the busy things that are simply swindling your very energy! It's ok not to be maxed out. You believe that? Let me type it again – it is ok NOT to be maxed out. It's ok. The hare was busy. The hare dashed off here, ate a snack, slept, ridiculed, etc. He was always busy it seemed. *When you gain clarity, you will be able to determine busy from important work!* THIS IS **KEY**! If you feel like you should be busier, don't go pick up something else, do more of YOUR plan – your high valued activity. Massive action on YOUR vision! Don't be busy with busywork; be focused with important work! The Great Wall of China and the Great Pyramids are incredible accomplishments especially in ancient times when stone was hewn by hand. These wonders are simply magnificent and breathtaking. Yet, these man-made wonders are simply one stone on top of another.

In sales, what makes us great relators – our friendly, creative, and flexible personalities – can also distract us from the important work of systematic follow-up and process. I believe the biggest issue is we don't realize the power of the drip; the insurmountable amplification of a little bit of faithfulness. Here's a **KEY**: do the boring process, fall in love with the small touches, and unleash your strengths in this by becoming super creative in how you reach out, how you follow-up, etc. Build a system or build a system that's fun! But have a system that REQUIRES daily action. No matter what it is in life: goals, your workout, your eating, relationships with your kids, your spiritual walk. Create a daily system that's creative and invokes your best emotions. You'll feel better and look forward to engaging your client. Create something for them, write them a text, call them, put a note in the mail. Be consistent. It tells them you truly want to build a relationship. It tells them you're not the flashy hare, but a consistent tortoise. Engage your heart into every interaction, and your heart will ensure you interact – it will remind you!

In sales, you have those who'll spend Friday afternoons calculating and recalculating their commission's checks. They'll spend more time arguing pennies instead of making a potentially million-dollar phone call. Which has the most chance for huge payoff? One's a lagging indicator (commission's check) and one's a leading indicator (phone call). One's past and over; one's future and contains potential. Things that are past and won't affect the outcome are lagging indicators. Revenue is a lagging indicator. The number of phone calls and visits you make - these are leading indicators. Focus your energies here! We know we'll win if we do these certain, strategic activities. Friday, then, could've been invested in the leading activities instead of wasted in the lagging squabbling. What leading indicators do you have in place that will result in great things for you and your family? Build great, meaningful, energizing habits. Then, consistently work hard in silence and let success make the noise! Someone said it this way, "Outcome is God's responsibility; obedience is ours." Like Dave's story, it boils down to doing a few basic things – the important things – over and over and over again. Day in, day out … faithfully plodding forward in the right direction. Focused, undistracted by all the hype, noise and fads. Like my coach, Rod Key states, "It's faithful obedience over a long period of time." Then, in time, and when it really counts, the tortoise steps across the finish line and wins!

Show Up ... Consistency

The victory is not to them who show up once in a while although they run their hardest and shout the loudest (remember the ones who look like energy); instead, it's to the faithful culmination of daily effort. I used to say I was a runner because I ran every now and then and ran a couple races. 2014 was my first year of running. I realized when I really wanted to dig deep and beat my previous time, I didn't have the depth and fortitude to last and would tank on the last mile of a 5K. I was a sprinter. I wasn't a runner. Not until running every day in 2017 did I become a runner. Every day going out to run. Wow! What a difference. My 1-mile, 5K, 10K, half marathon and full marathon personal best records were all broken within a nine-month span of time. I was doing interval and endurance training, but the daily consistency hands down built running fortitude like nothing else. What actions will enhance your energy? Make these deposits into your energy on a consistent basis. Like water stead-fastly carves rock, steadfastly carve your vision! When I was a kid, we had several trout ponds. The water that fed these ponds came from a small mountain stream. In this stream's path were some of the smoothest and beautifully carved rocks. Lightning may strike quickly and shatter timber, but I'd rather be steady, consistent and powerful like water hewing the rock. This power is far more beautiful and is the glory of patient perseverance – the power of consistency. I love the lyrics written that go:

> "Not to the strong is the battle,
> Not to the swift is the race,
> Yet to the true and the faithful,
> Victory is promised through grace!"

The power of consistency is the one small step. You want to change careers, learn a new skill, build a relationship, start exercising? Figure out the first small step and take it, then figure out the next small step and take it, and then another and another. Like Joe Girard said, "The elevator to success is out of order. You'll have to take the stairs … one step at a time." The beauty of small steps is that we don't have to take on the enormity of the goal or dream that seems daunting. Often, when intimidated by size of obstacle or task at hand, we're tempted to fight or flight. When we break it down into small bite-size pieces, this small consistency allows us to be creative and have fun enjoying the process! Small steps build momentum much faster. It's like the easiest gear on an 18-gear bike. Like the gym, or your accountability partner, or the new business - show up, do the work, be consistent and results happen. *Most drop off too quickly, not sticking around long enough to watch the tiny seedlings push through the soil.*

Mid-term and finals can come up and bring two responses: confidence and calm for those who showed up, engaged fully and did the work of learning each day throughout the semester; and, stress and anxiety for those who were hit and miss, disengaged or scrolling social media during class and discounting of the learning process. My buddy Joseph and I were balancing newborns, long hours at two jobs and trying to exercise. We joined the gym and held each other accountable. One thing I found that limited us and eventually saw us abandon our gym going was our hour-long regimen. Many times, I didn't have more than 30 minutes, so I didn't go. Years later, I successfully implemented gym consistency when I decided I'd go by every morning after my run and whether it was 15 minutes or 45, I'd pump some iron, or get some full reps in, and then shower and head to the office. Even 15 minutes gave my muscles fresh power and helped carve a channel of habit in my brain. The consistency allowed me to operate in peak performance condition for my team. This is the power of consistency – the nonnegotiable. You simply must! Stephen Corbert and Brian Fikkert wrote in their book, *When Helping Hurts*, that "change is difficult and in order for people to be willing to go through the pain of change, they must have adequate enthusiasm and drive to motivate them to make the initial changes and sustain them throughout the process … people's enthusiasm and drive are directly related to the degree they are participating in the planning." Why did this gym regimen work much better? It was my internal idea and planning and I knew it would work. ***Make sure, when you implement a change in your life, that it will work for you.*** Diets come and go because someone came up with a system that worked for them and will somewhat work for everyone else for different lengths of commitment. Is there a process you can design that fits your life much better? Run that regimen by your coach, counsellor or friend. Then DO it. You may be surprised how well it works and how energizing it is. Design the change you wish to see in your life!

I saw a short YouTube video about Michael Phelps and his consistency in practice and it's literally stunning! Working with his coach, Bob Bowman, Phelps developed his talents over the course of 12 long hard years. They built routines and rhythms for Phelps to develop his consistency of performance. This consistent preparation was met with opportunity and gave Phelps momentum just at the right time – the Olympic Games. Who's someone you know? Someone who exemplifies this consistency in your circles. Get around them. Learn what makes them tick. Chances are they have a "ball of WHY's" – several strong reasons to stay faithful! Darren Hardy cautions, "When you start thinking about slacking off … consider the massive cost of inconsistency; it's not the loss of a single action but the collapse and loss of momentum – your entire progress suffers." Eating crackers and taking a nap when you're supposed to be running is what hares do. Be the tortoise, be consistent, and refuse letting anything distract you! Consistency's key! Consistently resolve to be consistent!

... Daily

Synonymous to consistency is daily. Are your daily habits centered around your goals? Do you make forward progress daily? Are you employing the power of daily? This is the juice! This is taking it one day at a time! When I first stepped into a gym October, 2013, I watched a school administrator, Kenton, run the treadmill for 45 minutes. Every day after, same time (except one day of rest), he was there running. He has run the Middle Half in Murfreesboro every year for several years. His daily actions keep him consistent with his goals. Coach Wooden said, "When you improve a little each day, eventually big things occur!" Here's the deal. We wake up and go to sleep daily. We eat every day, we drink every day (hopefully a majority of water), and the list goes on. To be consistent with our goals, a broken down achievable plan needs to be written. Nothing complicated. If the plan is so bulky or too hard to come up with, chances are we're overcomplicating and over perfecting the plan. Further, it most likely won't fit into our daily routine. Create a simple plan with achievable, impactful pieces that fit into your daily routine. Daily activity equals consistency and ignites energy! ***Instead of the dreaded, vicious cycle of unaccomplished goals, focus on simple daily actions aligned with your goals!*** Rock your daily routine! Consistently crush your goals! Running daily taught me the depth of strength this consistency creates. When the race came up, I wasn't "flying by night." The daily work was there and strength was found. "Discipline is the spark that ignites the fire of habit," says Navy Seal, Mark Divine. Consistently flip the switches of energy sources on a daily basis! Just as sure as there's power in consistent daily action, there's also a joy and peace that accompanies this gentle way of living. It's finding joy in small blessings. The small actions that propel the best results and the small blessings that pop up along the way are equally noticed. The Tortoise Tuff mindset not only propels you forward, it allows you to enjoy the journey – to trust the process – and this enjoyment serves as a reserve fuel tank! You actually enjoyed the steak because you chewed small enough bites and chewed slowly enough! Laddie F. Hutar says, "Success consists of a series of little daily victories!"

... Training

Slow down to speed up. Slow down? Who wants to slow down? Why slow down? Slowing down means you understand there's a process. A coach of mine told me muscle soreness after workout means you worked out too hard. We're looking for immediate results, so we overwork our muscles instead of committing to a slow, steady and consistent process that pays off over the long run. Slowing down is what the long-term perspective understands. Avoid being in a rush. If it's important to spend the rest of your life doing, it's important enough to slow down and train properly and not skip the process. This produces muscle memory. Slow down and be deliberate about form, about the right notes, about the right processes, the right place, the right groups of people. Get the actions right and the results will start showing up in a profound way. Pace yourself! Be Tortoise Tuff!

Accuracy before speed. I'm a learning swimmer and I still growing faster than a "hunt and peck" on the typewriter. Both skills I'm honing, but it means intentionally slowing down and practicing the foot strokes instead of jumping in the pool and flailing my arms and legs just to stay afloat. You want to perfect your gift, you want to build a process, you want to make something repeatable. We're so busy speeding through life we don't take the time to test what works and what doesn't work. Whether this is testing different phone scripts at work, arranging a work-space so we can touch things once, finding out a loved one's favorite color, or learning to run properly, accuracy is a very important aspect of life. *Slow down and get it right, then make it repeatable. You'll save a ton of energy and become more effective and efficient.*

Do you practice? Sport teams practice. Athletes practice. Pros practice. Do you know why we don't know how to focus or how to perform our gift at a highly effective level? We're not practicing. Show up to practice every day. As I began speaking, I'd make my way to the Embassy Suites in town twice a week to practice. I'd find an empty room and present to the walls. It's actually harder, I've found, doing this, but I get to practice my keynote, transitions, memorize points and in time, have become confident on stage and able to hone and fine tune skills with my speaking coach's input. Learn to love practice – it's part of the process. Don't miss practice in your life. Play with your kids often. Practice being a Dad. Don't wait for an issue to arise to jump in and have to be Dad. Daily, consistent practice builds character. This is putting in the work when it really counts. Then, when opportunity intersects preparation, you're ready! David faithfully cared for the sheep and practiced on his sling shot. He'd be ready for that lion. Little did he know the practice he had reserved for lions and bears would conquer the unconquerable Goliath. Practice prepares you for greater things than you can imagine!

Mental Toughness ... Comfortless Zone

Comfort's okay, but not all the time! Comfort won't change us; it won't grow us! Getting out of our comfort zones causes us to explore & find new ideas, solutions and yes deeper reserves of energy! So much growth and good is possible if we'll simply move beyond our comfort zones! Our brains are hard-wired for survival – to find safety and comfort. Getting out of our comfort zone often yields a "kicking and screaming" reaction! Verbally affirming what we're doing is going to fortify our resolve to continue to push past fear. We must create new habits of excellence in our minds. It can be done. Tell yourself, "I look forward to this growth!" Reaffirm, "There is so much good that can happen if I'll just stretch a little! Starting a new semester at school, every class for a student is the same vast feeling of "getting out of the comfort zone." I say, "Way to go!" A new career, a new city, a new habit – they're all unexplored territory and we feel small in a vast new world. *Lean into it! Keep an open mind to always go and embrace living in the comfortless zone! It's where growth happens!* Every step for the Tortoise was comfortless, but only one step at a time was required. Focusing on reading a book with the intent to learn a new skill, getting up early to run, jumping up to the next set of dumb-bells, or adding to the number of prospect calls each day doesn't always come naturally! Yet, wonderful things await us beyond the comfort zone! Let's get our brains to be OK with the comfortless zone! Massive energy happens in this zone! Best-selling author of, *The 5-Second Rule*, Mel Robbins, calls it "Imposter Syndrome." You're carving new neurological pathways in your brain, and your brain's screaming that this isn't you!

By faith, you must lean into the "Imposter Syndrome" and passionately claim your new identity! Take courage and lean into it. I like to call this **Mental PE = pathway etching**. Be strong and very courageous. Charge into your comfortless zone! When you see a gorgeous oak tree in the fall time with its brilliant array of color, it makes you feel inspired inside doesn't it? That tree, so mighty and among the hardest of woods, took years to grow. What's more, imbedding its roots deep into the soil took conflict. Yes, conflict day in and day out to push into the soil and past the rocks.

Conflict is good if it's the right kind. Too often, we're getting distracted in the wrong kinds of conflicts in life. After all, someone else's stuff seems easier to fix; their conflict easier to decipher. *Embrace the right kind of conflict. The good pain that means your muscles are growing.* The pain of shutting everything off cold turkey to meditate – this indicates your spirit is growing. The pain of saying "thank you" as opposed to getting defensive next time someone offers criticism – this indicates your emotional muscle is growing. My coach Rod Key says, "Embrace the suck." Sure, the first mile may be waking the limbs up, but feel that circulation and flow by the second and third mile! Whoohoo baby! Embrace growth! Brendon Burchard states it perfectly, "Breaking from conformity and pursuing our own dreams will bring some discord upon us. There will be personal struggle and sacrifice. There will be fear and misfortune as we exert ourselves in the world … dedication to our genuine nature and our dreams will annoy people, injure egos, step on toes and force breaking from the company of those who would stop our march." We may be called upon to confront the bullies, leave a toxic work environment and challenge those around us with a higher standard. It will be hard work. Hard work because the nail that sticks up gets hammered down. He continues, "Let us take stock of what lies ahead. This work will require – demand – new levels of presence and power." We must be willing to take extreme and resolute ownership in the role we play in our own lives! To invest our energy into worthwhile growth and meaningful efforts in life. To constantly advance! Are you willing to develop the mental toughness to achieve a life full of vibrancy? Put today's date here if you are: _____

... Resolve

When we make a decision to do anything, there is a journey from our head to our hearts. That is, a journey that blends our soul and our minds into firm resolution to achieve the goal! Let's look at the definitions of commitment, determination and resolve according to *Cambridge Dictionary*:

- Commitment – "a promise to give yourself, your money, your time, etc., to support or buy something."
- Determination – "the ability to continue trying to do something, even if it is difficult."
- Resolve – "determined in character, action, or ideas; strong determination in bringing about a result – resolution."

With commitment, there must follow the determination of consistent effort. This daily action and follow-through builds emotional equity in our souls This emotional equity takes time to form. This emotional equity is called resolve! It's the cementing of the mental "know-I-should" with the soulful "and-I-must." It's when the going gets tough we can call on this equity for the resolve to see it through! This is the beauty of consistency! It literally builds our inner strength, our emotional equity – our resolve! To master endurance, realize your pain is temporary, but your reward is eternal. Embrace good pain. Navy Seal, Mark Divine, said, "Pain is your body's way of telling you that security is threatened because something is out of whack. However, when you consistently experience the personal growth that accrues from deliberately putting yourself out of balance ... you begin to embrace the temporary pain for the rewards it brings." *Stretching capacity is painful – but, you become more of an Energizer being able to transfer more energy and ignite more and be more!* Where's your focus? You can change your mindset even in the time of trial by shifting all of your focus to the reward, the benefit, the vison that you will at last unveil. Focus on the positive. Turn pain into joy! If I'm breathing, I have the potential for growth; therefore, failure does not exist. Success does not exist. One step or ten, I grow!

When we travelled America as a family, our caravan rolled into this

New Jersey camp. Since it was expensive to put twenty people up in hotels, we'd usually end of staying in gymnasiums, ranches out west, auditoriums, and summer camps. Every now and then, a very daring family would open up their home to us. On this particular day as we put the bus in park and stared out into the dingy Northeastern camp ground, we saw three large buildings – two of which were taller and actually leaning kind of like the Leaning Tower of Piza. Where we were instructed to stay was the smaller, brick building that, mind you, had broken windows and a door that hung ajar. We cautiously walked into the dank building to discover cobwebs, spiders, and very insanitary beds. We'd been on the road all day and this was not the oasis we'd envisioned a camp to be. We hit the doldrums very quickly. I remember my sister-in-law, Jessica, calling a sibling meeting together. She literally took charge assigning rolls. We were to find the cleaning supplies or find the nearest town and buy some. Sure enough, we made a list and before long, my oldest brother had found Wal-Mart and returned with Lysol spray for the mattresses, new sheets, new shower curtains, bleach, etc., Before long, we'd moved in. Finding some plywood and screws, we boarded up the broken windows, fixed the hinge on the door, and even found an old riding mower that we fixed up and turned into a go cart. We discovered a soccer field a mile down this trail through the woods and better yet, it was soccer season, so three of the afternoons during our stay, we popped hundreds of bags of popcorn and went to the stands on our "go-cart" selling the popcorn to hungry parents. It became one of the best stays we had on our fourteen-month trek cross the forty-eight contiguous states. Why? Embracing the comfortless zone. *Making meaningful moments out of every moment. Not waiting for the right circumstances to show up, but instead creating them. Leaning into the pain and growing. Changing perspective – turning trial into joy!* We could have wallowed in the dingy camp conditions for the two weeks we were there or experience fulfillment and joy by bettering the situation and finding or creating the good.

Many a good person becomes a by-stander in life because they stopped growing. We level off and become ok with good. Resolve to always take a step forward in any situation! My friend and exceptional business leader, Randy Boyd, says it's his life creed, "To make things better than they were when I found them!" Better takes resolve! Better means getting discontented with just doing ok. It's easier to want greatness when you're doing badly than when you're doing ok; true warriors fight for great-ness when they're doing well – they refuse settling for the mediocrity of "okedness." This is where a tried and true, Tortoise-Tuff mentality comes into play! What do you think the tortoise thought when he passed the hare and saw him sleeping? This is when the real mental battle came into play, and this my friend, is where the tortoise won the day! What are you desiring from life? Are you resolved?

George Herbert said, "He begins to die, that quits his desires." What do you desire out of life? Who do you want to be? What do you want to do? What impact do you want to leave? And what do you want to be known for? Les Brown says that all of us have been given a dream, but not all of us demand this dream become reality! Failing, then, is not the tragedy; ceasing to chase your dream is! You mustn't let anyone take your dream from you! You must hold onto that dream forever! In their book, *Do Hard Things*, brothers Alex and Brett Harris share that at each new challenge we face, it's a step outside of our comfort zones. After a while, the activity that once scared us, now "barely generates a yawn." Although we gain the experience of possibility, we shirk from the next challenge. However, the price of mediocre living is too high! ***The cost of choosing the comfort zone is missed opportunity and wasted potential!*** Run to the challenge! Learn to love the challenge. Challenge yourself! Challenges stretch and grow us. Constantly challenge yourself and by exercising this muscle often, you get used to simply stepping into comfortless zones every day. Every day and in every way, purpose to get better – to grow! Small steps in the right direction – upward – may prove to be hard steps. Hard things are hard for a reason – the reward is only guaranteed to the persistent and faithful!

Chuck Norris said, "Today we live in a culture that promotes comfort, not challenges. Everything's about finding ways to escape hardship, avoid pain, and dodge duty." Have we possibly given up on a dream at the first sign of trouble? Another writer said, "It's not the strength we lack, but the will." Napoleon Hill said, "What a different story men would have to tell if only they would adopt a DEFINITE PURPOSE, and stand by that purpose until it had time to become an all-consuming obsession." The beauty of Tortoise-Tuff mentality is that when you push through and overcome obstacles in achieving your dream, you are less distracted by daily annoyances. Things that once triggered you or swindled your energy don't even have a prayer. You literally chuckle thinking, "I just conquered 26.2 miles, I don't mess with piddley arguments like those anymore." When you raise one bar of expectation in your life, every other bar gets raised across your whole person!

... Perseverance

Failures will happen in life; therefore, flexibility must happen! *Expect failures. Embrace them. They are great teachers. Just get back up every time.* I love the story of Abraham Lincoln. What a calm leader he was, but might it have been from the patience learned through failure? Consider this man whose example of persistence can challenge and encourage us all. Born into poverty, Lincoln was faced with defeat throughout his life. He lost eight elections, failed twice in business and even suffered a nervous breakdown. He could have quit many times – but he didn't and because he didn't quit, he became one of the greatest presidents in the history of our country. Lincoln was a champion and he never gave up. Here is a bullet pointed summation of Lincoln's journey to lead our nation during a devastating and trying time:

- 1816 – His family was forced from their home and he had to work to support them.
- 1818 – His Mom died.
- 1831 – He failed in business.
- 1832 – He ran for state legislature and lost.
- 1832 – He lost his job; tried to get into law school but couldn't.
- 1833 – He borrowed some money from a friend to begin a business and by the end of the year he was bankrupt. He spent the next 17 years of his life paying off this debt.
- 1834 – He ran for state legislature again and won.
- 1835 – He was engaged to be married, but his fiancé died. Literally broke his heart.
- 1836 – He had a total nervous breakdown and was in bed for six months.
- 1838 – He tried to become speaker of the state legislature and

was defeated.
- 1840 – He pursued the position of elector and was defeated.
- 1843 – He ran for Congress and lost.
- 1846 – He ran for Congress again. This time he won and going to Washington, he did a good job.
- 1848 – He ran for re-election to Congress and lost.
- 1849 – He sought the job of land officer in his home state but was rejected.
- 1854 – He ran for Senate of the United States and lost.
- 1856 – He sought the Vice-Presidential nomination at his party's national convention and received less than 100 votes.
- 1858 – He ran for U.S. Senate again and yet again, he lost.
- 1860 – Abraham Lincoln is elected as the 16th President of the United States.

Something tells us that Lincoln embraced the journey understanding that every seeming setback was actually steps forward because he grew, he learned, and, he never gave up or quit the dream! Michael Jordan said it this way, "I have missed more than 9,000 shots in my career. I have lost almost 300 games. On 26 occasions I have been entrusted to take the game winning shot, and I missed. I have failed over and over and over again in my life. And that is why I succeed."

My very first marathon, the Nashville St. Jude's, I was forced to quit training from pulling a peroneal tendon. At mile marathon 18, I was forced to walk. By 19, I'd started to slowly jog and from that point into numbness and across the finish line, you have to literally look out in front of you, pick some landmark like a tree, a water station, or another runner and just run toward that repeating, "just one more mile … just one more mile." Then, when you pass the landmark, or the mile marker, you think, "OK, just one more mile, one more step, one more mile … " Rest at the finish line is coming, I must press on. *Perseverance is key! Resolve is unstoppable! It's at this point, the mines of energy are opened to you and you draw from power deep within.* Ralph Waldo Emerson is credited with saying, "Our greatest glory is not in never failing, but in rising back up every time we fail." Pat Summit, the most winningest coach in NCAA Division 1 women's basketball history who led Tennessee's lady Vols for 24 years straight said it as simple as this, "You can't have continued success without experiencing failure – so get used to it."

In reaching your goals, allow yourself flexibility. Let your methods evolve with your life and life phase. Ask yourself, "Do I have a life vision and am I daily progressing toward becoming that person?" David Niven PhD, says that goals are important, but they can do us a great disservice if they aren't flexible. I remember stating I was going to run 3 miles every day for a year and I did for eight months. Scheduling Pike's Peak Marathon into the journey left me slightly injured and taking three days off to recover a strained calf muscle. Then, jumping back in too fast, I knotted up again two months later in a half-marathon. My coach told me over and over, "I really wish you'd allow yourself a day of rest and recovery." There were also mornings of travel and to get my run in meant running when Jen and I needed an evening together. She was gracious for my goal's sake, but I learned through this process to analyze life's phases and your overall vision of where YOU want to be. Then, be flexible with your methods. Put goals of being into place – I want to be a certain speed of runner; then, establish the doing goals that fit life – I'll do training Tuesdays and Thursdays with this day for recovery. Know what you want to be and get some wisdom, guidance and perspective for the doing.

We must ask ourselves, "Am I jumping on everything and looking busy, or do I seek meaningful, real, productive endeavor with clear outcomes?" Brute force and speed can slow you down; many confuse this with perseverance. *Perseverance and stubbornness are not in the same family – one's a con. Perseverance is positive energy flowing in the correct direction and staying cool, calm and collected.* No one likes the rushing, overpowering and pushy salesperson any more than they like them in a partner, employer or acquaintance. Stubbornness, pressuring and rushing sounds on our lower instincts of fear – "run the sky is falling; act now!" Instead, empower yourself and others with calm decisiveness, confident faith and patient persistence! You'll persevere when you KNOW your decision was confidently based through faith on your life vision. You'll fight for the client who you know is the right fit. You'll stay in the relationship that wasn't manipulatively put together. Patient persistence is faith. Faith is alive and energizing, does good work and produces results! Weeds are stubborn; oaks are persevering. Weeds rush; oaks take time. Weeds benefit themselves; oaks benefit others. Persevere in faith my friend! Be an energizer – calm, cool, collected and persevering! This is why quick riches are worse than poverty because it breeds a false sense of value. It's artificial value and in fact, a large majority of our materialistic society, our relationships and even our learned and developed emotional states are derived from a jaded sense of value. Those who are quick and lazy, guess or follow the crowd. Those who are diligent will learn and acquire the facts so that they can think for themselves, think accurately, and be decisive. Here's what will keep you Tortoise Tuff – knowing your WHY! Your WHY gives you the best chance for consistency. Your WHY is who you are. Whatever you decide to do, do it with all your might! BOOM! Simon Senek, in his wonderful book, *Start With Why*, shares that without clarity of WHY, everything we do is just something to do. ***When there's no greater meaning past simply doing something, then your soul and spirit aren't invoked, meaningful remembrance isn't harnessed, and consistency is lost.*** This is why adversity and pain are so necessary. They force our hand and cause us to dig deep for our WHY! "Persistence with the right attitude is the key to success," one author wrote. Jeffrey Gittomer, author of, *The Sales Bible*, and phenomenal sales trainer, said it like this, "Obstacles can't stop you, problems can't stop you and most important of all, other people can't stop you. Only you can stop you." Let's understand that persistence is our commitment, determination and resolve to pursue growth, embrace pain and press toward our life vision. "Never give up on a dream just because of the time it will take to accomplish it. The time will pass anyway," said Earl Nightingale. This is a poem I heard as a kid and I've never forgotten. I include it here to encourage your heart, Energizer! Tortoise Tuff!

"When things go wrong, as they sometimes will,
When the road you're trudging seems all uphill,
When the funds are low and the debts are high,
And you want to smile, but you have to sigh,
When care is pressing you down a bit-
Rest if you must, but don't you quit.

Life is strange with its twists and turns,
As every one of us sometimes learns,
And many a fellow turns about
When he might have won had he stuck it out.
Don't give up though the pace seems slow -
You may succeed with another blow.

Often the goal is nearer than,
It seems to a faint and faltering man;
Often the struggler has given up
When he might have captured the victor's cup;
And he learned too late when the night came down,
How close he was to the golden crown.

Success is failure turned inside out,
The silver tint in the clouds of doubt,
And you never can tell how close you are,
It might be near when it seems afar;
So stick to the fight when you're hardest hit -
It's when things seem worst that you must not quit."

Trust the Process

The hard thing about consistency isn't always the habit you choose, it's all the other habits you gave up on, said no to, or the other perfectly legitimate things you could go do. *The process of what you said was going to be your activity can get boring. You don't see immediate results, you get discouraged, you want to give up and try something else. Keep planting – the harvest will come.* I love the story N.H Davis told about "The Rose Beyond the Wall." It goes like this:

"The fruits of our labor may be blossoming somewhere unknown to us. A lady once received a beautiful rose plant and planted it in her yard beside a stone wall. She watered it and dug around its roots and kept it free of insects. But she was much disappointed when it did not bloom. She thought her care for it had all been in vain and was very sad over what seemed to be a failure. But just before Autumn, while cleaning some undergrowth from around the wall, she discovered a crevice which admitted a ray of the setting sun. There, to her surprise, she beheld a branch leading from the rose bush to the other side. And when she climbed up and gazed over she saw that her labors had not been in vain, for her bush had sent out a tender and beautiful branch which had brought forth the fruits of her labor. It had blossomed on the other side of the wall!"

Dear friend, know this! Your consistency gives hope to people you may never learn of. You may not see the immediate results, but the harvest is coming! Your life is a fertile field amidst other lives of fertile fields. What you plant in this fertile soil will spring forth and blow into the fertile soil of other lives. It's an irrefutable law – the law of sowing and reaping. It's with this belief we heed the promise that states, "Be not weary in well doing for in due season you will reap if you don't give up!" What you plant, you reap! When you're internally whole, no one in the whole world can take that from you, and when the whole world comes down around you, you are still whole. Build you. Build your mind. Every day in some small way. Having no insurance, Thomas Edison lost a laboratory worth millions in a fire. Someone asked him, "What in the world will you do?" He answered calmly, "We will start rebuilding tomorrow morning." His attitude of goal-striving and goal-oriented disposition allowed him to keep an aggressive attitude. People noted that he never was very unhappy about the loss.

Your mind will be so resolute and resolved in the enjoying daily small steps that setbacks will never seem big. You just simply keep practicing your daily routine. The Energizer embraces the journey and while on journey forgets about the destination. The people so focused on the destination and trying to hurry up the process take shortcuts, complain and get super busy. They feel like they're moving – sometimes, they're going backwards. Every setback is blown out of proportion because they simply can't wait another minute. The Energizer, on the other hand, adopts Tortoise-Tuff thinking and trusts the GPS. The destination is plugged in, and the Energizer trusts the process and embraces the pain and pleasure. Happiness and sadness are part of the journey in becoming the person they're meant to become.

Bigger Than You

I remember growing up, my siblings and I loved to ride bicycles. We'd bike some 30-mile trips at times across the farmlands of Bavaria. One route was a 5 mile loop up this mountain to our horse coral. We had some land on this mountain that was just gorgeous. It was our horses' summer romping ground and being Halflinger breed, they thrived on the slopes. We'd bike up there a couple times a week to check on them, fill the water troughs, dump some more hay and feed them grain. The hill to the top was taxing. We usually pumped our legs until we could pump no longer, then, we'd jump off and walk. I remember the day as a young teenager where I pumped all the way to the top. Slow, steady, and barely moving a foot each pump, it became a mindset of just one more pedal pump. Sometimes I'd move more sideways to keep momentum going and get my pedal position up top for a powerful pump. It was an out-of-breath, exhausted, triumphant feeling when the last bend in the road and the steepest portion of asphalt finally levelled out and I could see the top. In life, it's the same mentality. You absolutely want something and commit to go after it. You're pointed in the right direction and challenges and obstacles come. It's life and they will happen. *The fact of the matter is this, it's not the time when everyone's there cheering and seeing the great strides you're making that count. It's those times in secret when you barely feel like one simple decision has any significance on your journey.* It barely feels significant at all and you decide one breach in your integrity – what you promised yourself – won't affect your journey. Friend, the simplest decision for right, in the quiet and obscurity of your own company, is the greatest decision of all. One foot of private mastery equals miles of public clarity, power and fullness! Don't ever forget this!

Why are the decisions in private the toughest? The Tortoise-Tuff longing inside is speaking to us. Our higher conscience, our self-awareness is pleading with us to stay resolute. It's not flashy, it's not noticed – yet – and may never be noticed, but the Energizer knows that next pedal pump of struggle gets them closer to personal wholeness.

You know what was so amazing? When I finally broke this mile ascent, the second and third time grew easier until the pump up the mountain became easy. I KNEW I could. Then, the next phase happened. My younger sisters grew up and rode with me. I had the vision of the top and when they were about to give up, I'd ride up alongside them and tell them, "Breathe in, breathe out, breathe in … rhythm with your pedaling." "You can do it." "You got this." I'd get them as close to the top as they could, then we'd walk together. One day, the final and most glorious phase happened for me. After my regular encouragement wasn't enough and I could see they were just about spent, I turned back, down the hill, swooped around, pumped really hard, got up alongside of them reaching over to the back of their bike seat, I pumped for thirty seconds. Their load got lighter, and their muscles recouped just briefly enough in their legs and they caught some breath. Then, back to encouraging and another swoop, then another, until, we both arrived at the top of the hill. This is when Tortoise-Tuff embedded itself deep in my soul! Know this, your decision in private to stay faithful and true to what you promised yourself will carry you and propel you to the top! This character will build so much strength that you'll be there for others when they need it most! You will not only win your race, you will help others win their races as well. You're not the flash; you're the faithful! You're Tortoise-Tuff! *Go bigger than you and watch perseverance yield a greater depth of meaning!* Realizing there are others needing your light and your love causes us to answer the call to bear one another's burdens. It gets us looking up and out; not just in.

One Word

Rekindle your WHY daily and you'll stay consistent. I like how Les Brown said, "when you feel like quitting remember why you started."

Tortoise Tuff

One word can literally be to you what "Charge" would mean to a battalion of skilled warriors. What's your battle cry? What's your one word? In 2017, I resigned from my 10-year position and we launched *Time4Energy*, finished compiling this book, and finished a degree over three, fulltime semesters. My word for the year was consistency. *Time4Energy*'s mission? To "ignite energy"! This mission is so needed and invigorating that I'm in it for the long term. Morning after morning, when I just wanted to NOT have another assignment due, was tired of writing papers and ready to complete my degree and finally be fulfilling my calling fulltime, I'd state to myself, "Be consistent, Tim ... be the tortoise ... ignite energy everywhere you go, be it the classroom or corporate global ... be consistent." Many mornings, my vision and my word kept me focused, fueled and Tortoise Tuff! Tortoise Tuff realizes that it's the long term. There is huge power in a little consistency. You become dependable and trustworthy when you're consistent. *What's your word for this year? One word that will carry you through? It will scream louder than any alarm clock, compel you to give your last drop of energy each day, and keep you calm, cool and focused!* This poem came to me one day when running and it stuck:

> What's your one word that inspires your morning
> And gives your heart a song?
> What's your one word that brightens your day
> When things are going wrong?
> What's your one word that encourages you
> Through days, however long?
> What's your one word for your entire year
> That'll keep your energy strong?

You may have a couple meaningful words; one needs to lead the pack! My words for 2017 were: Consistent, engaged & faith. Consistent every day, engaged fully present and focused with the person/people I'm with (ie: wife, kids, colleagues), and a faith that dreams big, believes big and acts big! Consistent leads the pack! BOOM! Consistent, consistent, consistent! Tortoise-Tuff! Keep going – just one step, and then one more!

CHAPTER 17
W.W.I 1.D.

becoming CEO

"*Nurture your mind with great thoughts, for you will never go any higher than you think.*"
– *Benjamin Disraeli*

It's Your Company

It was a frigid cold day, and the president's office was a bit too hot, causing condensation on the long, narrow windows. I remember watching the secretary's eyes close and pop back open a couple of times. I was tired myself and really tried to focus on the project updates that were being delivered in somewhat of a monotone. It was a Monday morning, and the meeting format had become so predictable that some of us were tuning it out wishing to get back to productive work. Some Mondays would see heated conversations regarding timeline demands and limited human resources; then, some meetings would seem to go places and were fun. I wasn't sure if the previous night's Colts' Superbowl win under Tony Dungy and Peyton Manning's leadership had anything to do with the tired faces – and voices – but, it was hot, and grogginess hung in the air that morning. Just then, the secretary's hand left her notepad and her gel pen was streaking sparkles across the conference table as she dozed off. Our CEO stood from behind his desk and called a time-out. His challenge was short and to the point. *"When are you all going walk into this company in my shoes?* What if you were to pretend – just for a day – like you're the CEO, like you have to make payroll, like you have to carry the weight of the lives of these people and the families they represent on your shoulders? Look! Half of you all are sitting here not even taking notes! Why are we meeting anyway? Could you just act like you cared?" Wow! At first, I became defensive in my heart. Didn't he see my note pad? Certainly, he knows I care! After we resumed the meeting, it hopped along and most everyone was engaged. I walked from his office that day going quickly from upset to empathetic. I couldn't imagine the weight of his position. At nineteen years old, I couldn't say I could even fathom it, but I decided to get to know his pain points and how best I could offer solutions. Shortly after, I was promoted to lead the purchasing department and we became close friends.

Do you want the tremendous opportunity of leadership? Then, first, own whatever arena you're in, today. This ownership is extreme. You simply don't make or accept excuses. Empowerment is your byword. You engage all your mental capacity and unleash your energies into each task at hand. Let's look at how to think like a leader - literally becoming CEO. *It's the one who asks the question, "What would I do if I were the CEO?" that realizes there's more personal power available to us then we like to admit.* It's a simple change of perspective and taking extreme ownership! To the one who takes ownership – becomes the owner – impossibilities become minor challenges. Excuses fade. This mindset doesn't only work in business, it can work anywhere in life. This mindset forces you to take responsibility!

A Message to Garcia

Over coffee one morning, my very first, executive-coaching client, Ray, shared this story with me as we engaged in a lively conversation about taking extreme ownership of life and occupation. I place parts of Elbert Hubbard's story here as I hope every high schooler, college student, trade school graduate and aspiring business professional will read it. Hubbard penned this 1899 narrative in passionate terms that I felt fitting. A bit condensed from the original version, the story goes like this:

"When war broke out between Spain and the United States, it was very necessary to communicate quickly with the leader of the Insurgents. Garcia was somewhere in the mountain vastness of Cuba - no one knew where. No mail or telegraph could reach him. The President must secure his cooperation, and quickly. What to do! Someone said to the President, 'There's a fellow by the name of Rowan who will find Garcia for you; if anybody can, he can.' Rowan was sent for and given a letter to be delivered to Garcia. How the fellow by name of Rowan took the letter, sealed it up in an oil-skin pouch, strapped it over his heart, in four days landed by night off the coast of Cuba from an open boat, disappeared into the jungle, and in three weeks came out on the other side of the island, having traversed a hostile country on foot, and having delivered his letter to Garcia, are things I have no special desire now to tell in detail. The point I wish to make is this: McKinley gave Rowan a letter to be delivered to Garcia; Rowan took the letter and carried it to Garcia.

Here is a man whose form should be cast in deathless bronze and the statue placed in every college in the land! It is not book-learning young people need, nor instruction about this or that, but *a stiffening of the vertebrae which will cause them to be loyal to a trust, to act promptly, concentrate their energies; do the thing – 'carry a message to Garcia!* ... Civilization is one long anxious search for just such individuals. Anything such a man asks will be granted; his kind is so rare that no employer can afford to let him go. He is wanted in every city, town, and village - in every office, shop, store and factory. The world cries out for such; he is needed and needed badly—the people who can carry a message to Garcia."

This story describes the person so deliberate in action and courageously decisive who, knowing what to, or asking for something to do, boldly follows through and completes it! This is the clarion call to anyone willing to enter and truly engage their organizations and perform their best work! These are the proactive, initiating Energizers who don't wait for life to happen to them; they go and happen to life!

Up for a Challenge

Are you entering your place of work with the attitude of "Trust me with a challenge"? Challenge changes your capacity; you can fight and shrink or embrace and grow. To love challenge is to love growth. "Expectations are self-fulfilling. People who aspire to less get less," says Chester L. Karrass. Why don't we naturally aim high? Well, aiming high involves risk. Risk of failure and embarrassment. Setting high targets demands we work harder, carefully plan and unleash a dogged persistence to achieve our targets. "Aim high and you'll do better." Karrass declares! Challenges keep team members empowered and engaged. "Keeping talent engaged is a key role of management," says Verne Harnish, "and great managers can keep a team happy and engaged, more so than free lunches and yoga classes, or trivial give-aways." **People want to grow. People love challenges**. Chief Engineer of the first Lexus, Ichiro Suzuki said, "Even if the target seems so high as to be unachievable at first glance, if you explain the necessity to all the people involved … everyone will become enthusiastic in the spirit of challenge, will work together and achieve it!" If you're a team member, be bold! Ask for a challenge and solve it! Are you showing up in fullness and asking for challenging stuff? Are you engaged and unstoppable?

Two Dollars Neck Down

Lift your perspective to that of ownership mentality and your mind-set will literally move into a room of exponential size. A mindset shift to becoming CEO, even if it's just imaginary, will cause you to think.

You may feel inadequate, uneasy and even fearful to assume more leadership. Speaking up with your opinion, your solution or your idea can be intimidating – at first. Embrace it. Lean into it. You're now calling on mental faculties that may have been slumbering up to this point. The most valuable thing you'll find in leadership is the ability to think critically. To analyze situations and make good judgment calls. It's an exercise of the mind. In his day, Henry Ford said a person's manual labor was worth two-dollars neck down. By this, Ford indicated that creative ideas and problem solving were "above the neck" activities and couldn't always be equated into dollars. Consider the assembly-line idea. The potential to uncover, discover, or invent exponential value lies within all of our mental grasps. New value is created in the mind. What process, what idea, what practice, what product, what new way of thinking could add value to your organization? What could you think of? If someone handed you the reigns of the company tomorrow, what would you do? What would you start, what would you stop, what would you continue? Chances are you have some amazing ideas. By becoming CEO, you unleash your mental capacity to think bigger, on a grander perspective and you understand things better.

Question with Intent to Listen

What does this mean? First, most don't ask empowering and powerful questions. Too often, we make statements, then we make defensive statements and then we ask indicting questions. All to prove our stance and fortify our position. Instead, do the hard work of thinking with intent of asking the most empowering and powerful question. The energizing leader doesn't have to talk much. Energizers realizes that if they can get people to think for themselves and discover beliefs on their own, they have achieved the highest level of leadership. It's unwavering leaders like George Patton in the field of battle, consistent coaches like Nick Sabin on the white-striped football turfs, calm protestors like Rosa Parks on a bus in Alabama's capitol city, and kind teachers like Jesus who instilled vision so deep and empowered their followers to think and feel for themselves. *When we ask empowering questions, we'd do ourselves the greatest disservice by not listening and listening well; for our question was given with the intent to listen – was it not?* In becoming CEO, how do you create the most value in your team? If below the head is only worth two dollars (figuratively speaking), then realize that all the heads around you have infinite value-
creation ability. Realize that the mind isn't a vessel to fill by talking and

barking commands; instead, the mind is a fire to ignite by asking empowering and powerful questions with the intent to listen, learn and map out growth. Remember, that more powerful than a hundred answers is one powerful question. Learn the **PERK** of asking powerful, educated, revealing and kind questions:

> **P** – Powerful in that they result in powerful answers,
> **E** – Educated in that you're desiring to learn more by what you're asking,
> **R** – Revealing in that they're open-ended and will reveal the most information for reason or causality, and
> **K** – Kind in that they don't demean anyone but always give benefit of the doubt.

Fuel the Vision

Immerse yourself in the vision and be a promoter of it! Encourage others around it. Every leader needs a champion in the ranks. Be this champion for no other reason than to give back and embody extreme ownership! You control more of the company dynamic and culture than you'll ever know. Own your influence and use it. Become an encouraging follower. No longer does hanging out on the sidelines fit your leadership mentality! Your chiefest aim will be to hold the vision clearly before your team at all times. Let it be the spark that lights the fire, the bellows that fan the coals, the wood that feeds the flame the hope that inspires belief. Let it be a vision greater than any one person or any one organization. Let it be eternal vision tied to the well-being of humanity. *Let it induce the deepest energies stored up in the mental warehouses and locked away in the souls of your people. Let vision be the beacon that casts its bright light over the waves when the waters turn rough.* Corporate executive, what's your vision? Mom, dad, what's your vision? Friend, what's your vision for your life? Will it inspire all who enter your waters? Will it light the way through the rocky cliffs and lead them safely to the shore? My vision for my life is, "Living fully and loving deeply!" An empowering vision aligns all effort behind clearly defined goals. One business leader told me, "Tim, move from CEO to **CVO – Chief Visionary Officer**!" Let your vision encompass your WHY! The best leaders light a powerful flame of vision within their bosoms, it shines brightly from their presence, and all come to light their candle by its radiant glow!

Not a "Yes Man"

Becoming CEO means thinking on your own two feet. In your mind at least, you should trial and error every decision you make. Think things through. Engage in mental exercise. Especially if you're a trusted advisor to the leader. Think through the problem and opportunity, analyze your solutions possible outcomes, speak up, and keep an open mind. Voice your opinion in a respectable manner. Even taking a stand for something you believe in shows that you're willing to take a stand. Be gracious. David Mamet said it like this "Do not internalize the industrial model. You are not one of the myriad of interchangeable pieces, but a unique human being, and if you've got something to say, say it, and think well of yourself while you're learning to say it better." *By empowering your team, your people or yourself to think, you ignite team energy and develop self-sufficient problem solvers/solution finders.* Complaints transform to idea-generation. Jack Daly, in his book, *Hyper Sales Growth*, states, "To truly empower your employees, you need to create an environment where the people who work in it feel comfortable making decisions as if they were the owner." This is CEO mentality, right here! I remember a retired Colonel I worked for, Dar. He told me as a young manager, "Tim, think of two, great, possible solutions for every problem you bring me. Chances are we'll use one of them or part of them but get in this habit." This is life-changing thinking in every arena of life! I call it the **TASK** Method of turning prolems into opportunities:

    T – Think through the problem and opportunity,
    A – Analyze your solutions and possible outcomes,
    S – Speak up, and
    K – Keep an open mind.

Never Have to Ask for a Raise

With an extreme-ownership mentality, you'll never have to ask for a raise. You lead, encourage and influence and you'll attract the roles, opportunities and raises to you. I'm living proof. In ten years, I never had to ask for a raise. Passion puts your name at the top of the pay-raise list every time. *Passion pays! Make a difference; the dollars will follow!* Deliver the message to Garcia every day and you'll be the president's Chief-of-Staff before you know it. If the raise hasn't happened or doesn't seem to be coming, consider your investment of labor. Is it the right kind? Are you all in? Think of tangible and valuable ways you're going to amplify every role you're in, starting now!

Deference (Think "We")

Deference is the necessary component of harmony. Napoleon Hill said, "Every manager knows what a difficult matter it is to get employees to work together in a spirit even remotely resembling HARMONY." In order to be a great leader, one must first learn to be a great follower. Are you a deferent leader? A leader never has to have it his way. A selfish stubborn-ness is a sign of insecure leadership. Being deferent to another good idea is a bad idea to the immature leader. As managers, they criticize; as leaders, they dictate. We've all seen them, but instead of highlighting immature leadership, let's analyze our own followership. Are we deferent? Are we able to contribute to a good idea even if it wasn't our own? Are we hyper-critical? Are we undermining leadership? Becoming CEO requires the ability to subject our own ideas and agenda to the collaboration of a team to emerge with a win/win solution. A deferent mindset is a collaborating and team building mindset. This makes an inspirational leader. As a follower, jump in, collaborate, and share your ideas remaining deferent. *Put as much heart into the team decision and go-forward objectives as if you'd derived them yourself. This mindset is contagious and synergistic.* This mindset is not opposed to challenge when it's the right time to challenge, but is also the quickest to throw vim and vigor into moving the team forward. This mindset becomes CEO. It's taking responsibility and looking out for the good of the whole.

Delegation

As dental coach and speaker, Penny Reed told me, "You must know it, believe it and live it before you can delegate it." Until you immerse yourself in any business with a mentality of extreme ownership, you won't grow to the capacity of delegation. The mental energy required to map out solutions and bring clarity from the complex is enormous. Would you be one willing to learn? Then start right now demanding more engagement from all of your energies – physical, emotional and mental and spiritual! Show up to the next meeting with fresh ideas and really put your mind and heart into it. Do this on a consistent and courteous basis and you'll be surprised at the leader that's longing to come out. Lean into the fear your likely to experience and take courage – expand your capacity! Become CEO by thinking and acting like the CEO. Extreme ownership! "Nothing's stopping me but me."

Patience

CEOs have a lot of people to lead. Understand if change doesn't happen right away, it's not that you weren't heard. Sometimes, it's just not the right time. Be careful not to get discouraged taking ownership. Sometimes, you might feel like cold water is being poured on your zeal. The bigger the organization, the more patient one must be. Make compelling cases for change and be patient. Keep positive energy flowing as an abundant source. Be a patient and encouargaing follower!

Praise

How do we help people thrive in their talents, abilities and gifts? Praise accomplishment and growth. We see a tendency in leadership to hold back lest praise spawns complacency or "goes to their heads." W. Somerset Maugham said, "the common idea that success spoils people by making them vain, egotistic, and self-complacent is erroneous; on the contrary, it makes them for the most part humble, tolerant and firm. Failure can make people bitter and cruel." My speaking coach, Gale, tells a story of this joyous receptionist who ushered him into a manufacturing plant. Upon meeting his client, Sam, Gale asked him, "What is that lady's name? I was impressed with her joy, attention to detail and cheerful greeting upon my arrival." Sam shuffled through some papers with a snicker. Pulling a resume from a to-be-filed stack of papers, he replies, "That's Sara ... she's new. Give it a couple weeks and she'll give it up ... they all do." What? While Gale saw some real opportunities for manage- ment growth in this scenario, the sad news is, this actually happens. Why praise people when we really want them to level off and not show us up? *Those becoming CEO will praise the good and inspire more of it! Want your team to succeed? Empower them by praising them and giving them the credit.*

Caring

You know how to get people to care for your organization? Show them you truly care about them. When people feel – yes feel – like you care about what they care about, they start to care about what you care about. This may be through appreciation, noticing them, taking interest, supplying needs, securing their buy-in, etc. When people feel – there's that word feel again – they are appreciated, they are bound to give their best! Do they feel your care? Great leaders are willing to perform any task when the occasion demands it. Nothing is below them. This is ego-less leadership. Jesus led the way in this when he said, "The greatest among you shall be your servant!" I remember a former employer going in on a Saturday with t-shirt and baseball cap to work with the guys on the floor. Do you realize the camaraderie and loyalty this act garnered him? He could've been on the golf course or vacationing. He loved working and often told me it was a relief from the administrative side of business to go out and see something tangibly get done. I remember one of the machinists bragging about how the boss proved to be a better machinist than him, "I had no idea, Jeff was so good." I remember him saying. At the Thanksgiving, company-wide dinner, you'd find him pouring the drinks and keeping the food line going. I watched a perfect role-model of servant-leadership! Again, coming from the restaurant business, he knew food service and was good at it!

Question is this, what do you love doing that your people can count on you jumping in, getting in the trenches with them to show them you care? My team can count on my communication advice. I love communication and I love crafting powerful messages. They call me and we brainstorm together. They can always count on me to speak with them for one of our clients or visit to develop a relationship. I love relationships! Jen can count on my washing the big stuff after dinner, sweeping the floor, cleaning toilets and giving kiddos baths. These are tasks I love to do! I shared many a sweet dish-washing moment with my Mom and I still find powerful thought-space over the steam of hot water and smell of Dawn fruity soap suds. It may not be a physical activity, either. I remember one manager of mine, Randy, would stop by my office every morning with his coffee and great big grin asking if I needed anything. He'd wish me the heartiest "Good Morning," and move down the hall to some others on his team. I always took Randy's coaching and advice to heart because I felt he cared! *It's time to get real and let the people that work with us and do life with us feel we care; let them sense that we feel blessed to create value in this world with them.*

Becoming CEO means you begin caring for people and not simply reprimanding behavior. This is a tough one. As managers, often, we can hide behind quotas and make demands. We can reprimand behavior easily. Seeing potential in others and building on their strengths takes time which means a couple of things: we must learn how to better manage our own work (be less controlling and delegate) and yes, learn people skills. Ken Blanchard says in his runaway bestseller, *The One*

Minute Manager, that "it's very important when managing people to remember that behavior and worth are not the same things ... what is really worthwhile is the person managing their own behavior." See, this goes deeper and is the hardest work – it demands we become emotionally intelligent. Whoa! This is Energizer stuff right here! There is what's called positional authority and relational authority – the latter garners trust and full engagement!

There's this story I read of a brilliantly arrayed lieutenant barking orders at some Continental regulars retrieving a cannon from a muddy ravine during the American Revolution. They were apparently struggling; thus, the lieutenant increased the volume and intensity of his demands. Several minutes passed bringing with them the hoof beats of a passer-by on the wooded trail. The hoof beats thundered up, abruptly stopped and the rider dismounted and hurriedly brushed past the lieutenant and into the mud with the regulars. With coordinated effort, the cannon's retrieval was quickly completed. The black-caped rider turned and to the dismay of the onlooking lieutenant, his general, George Washington himself, stood there with the look of displeasure on his face. Saying nothing, he mounted his white stead and was quickly lost to sight. This story struck me hard as a young guy! Do we shirk from the less glamorous tasks and let position and power go to our heads? Sure, there's high payoff activities, but sometimes the call to jump in the trenches with your team is sounded – do we jump in? *When we do, I guarantee our teams begin looking at their careers a bit differently. Career no longer; calling forever!*

Conflict

Too many energies are pent up in a worker's heart when they really have something to say, have a disagreement, or they feel they've been wronged, yet they have no safe channel for feedback or chance of redress. When there's no healthy environment for feedback or meaningful, safe conversation, workers will converse amongst themselves over how bad management is and so on. However, when leaders take the time to sit down and ask for the good, bad and ugly without any recoil, employees feel heard, and trust is built. High growth and healthy organizations have corridors of conflict built in. They are systematic, so people know a conversation is on the horizon. A team member knows a small grievance can wait for that conversation. They trust you as the leader will have this promised discussion with them. *Encourage healthy conflict and you encourage energies be transferred into valuable action and away from feelings of hurt which lead to gossip, discord, disgruntlement and turnover.*

Take Blame

Taking blame doesn't necessarily mean saying, "It's my fault," unless, of course, it is. Taking blame means, take the blame right off the table. It doesn't matter. If there's a serious violation of trust that simply requires reprimand or removal, then this must be handled in a professional manner. Too often, however, fear of blame over the smallest mess-ups runs rampant in business and we spend so much time and energy covering our tails. If we'd instead take the blame off the table, take responsibility for the actions or corrective actions, and move forward, we'd save so much energy!

I remember one of the most freeing moments for me as a young guy. A big issue happened on the shop floor. It was my fault, the supplier's fault and the engineering department's fault. A part number on a bill of materials was wrong which originated with engineering. I was the last set of eyes, and as I was buying these expensive cylinders, I should've noticed that something about the price looked off. The supplier on the other hand gave us a ten-week delivery that already pushed us to the limit. When they finally arrived, we realized what happened. These pneumatic cylinders were five feet too long! To get the correct ones would take at least six more weeks expedited, and this piece of equipment was already running behind schedule. A meeting was called. I could sense the anxiety and all that was about to break lose. I saw the file folders being pulled and through the windows, the case was being formed against me. Now, before I go any further, I used to get very defensive! I could argue my point very aggressively. Engineering and project management knew they needed to formulate a compelling argument – I was swindling energy. In fact, fear hung heavy and thick from the ceilings that day. My direct manager was called into the meeting and ... the CEO. What was my saving grace? A business coach by the name of Andy Bailey. A couple months earlier he had looked over some goals I had written down and noticed my reading list. I thought it should've impressed him. As he looked over it, he said, "Hey, swap that last book with *Emotional Intelligence 2.0*, instead." I snapped back. "Thanks, but no thanks. These are the books I've committed to read!" He calmly and deliberately replied, "My point exactly." I was so intrigued by that calm, knowing response, I picked the book up immediately and read it. Now on this day of the imminent meltdown, I walked in and let them know I took full responsibility and we needed to work with the supplier to get the corrected parts expedited. The supplier ended up taking the cylinders back – amazingly. The ease of handling that conflict came from accepting blame that was rightfully mine. When I did, all the fight was sucked out of the room, stacks of file folders, printed-off email chains, and all the "proof" went untouched as we all focused on tackling the solution together.

People skills are called "soft skills" in business. I believe this is backwards thinking. Hard skills are those that apply directly to the job function. However, soft skills, should be renamed something like critical skills. *If we are to become CEO's, then to truly lead and inspire people, we must make a priority of emotional intelligence and relationship building expertise. It's needed now more than ever. Bolstering our own energy so our emotions flow properly and we choose optimal responses is so key.* Build your "soft skills," or as I like to call them critical skills, like attitude, communication, creative thinking, teamwork, networking, decision making, positivity, problem-solving, critical thinking, and conflict resolution.

Training

Begin training. If you want your team to grow, grow yourself. I remember telling our company's CEO as a very young guy that I wanted to own the company one day. Now, it's not what I really wanted; I wasn't sure what I wanted at 19. But, do you think he despised me, or that he saw ambition and potential? Becoming CEO means a paradigm shift and all of a sudden, you create urgency in your life to learn and grow. I remember stepping into the lead sales position recruiting candidates. There were some Top Grading, leadership and sales books I thought would align with my role and I began training myself. By becoming CEO, you don't settle or level off. You learn, train and continually hone your leadership skills. The mindset of "What would the CEO do?" empowers you. You use this questioning not only in becoming more of a leader and moving toward full ownership of decisions, but it also gives great guidance for those decisions as well as decision recommendations. Becoming CEO means you get to know leaders and your team at a deeper level. Ask what's keeping the CEO up at night. Ask what their current top pain points are right now. Ask them what activities energize them and do they have the bandwidth to do more of these. Ask them what big or exciting thing is coming up for them or the business. You'd be surprised how many external pressures are placed upon leaders where they don't always get to open up or feel safe to open up. Ask what they're passionate about. Ask where they see themselves and the company in 5 years. Ask what they're studying and the reading they'd recommend. These questions are great to ask of yourself and of your team as well. Not only will you get to know them better, you help them appreciate their wholeness as a person. Strive to get to know the heart and mind of the people you serve whether that's your leader or those you lead.

I found, many times, I could join in reading a great book to be better aligned with leadership, I could know pain points and be on the lookout to eliminate or divert them and I also got a higher perspective of the most valuable activities. It was moving into this space after reading Larry Linne's, *Make The Noise Go Away*, book, that I took a huge step from purchasing manager into sales. "Sales," our CEO had told me, "is my biggest pain point." Looking back, nothing grew me more than sales. Stretch your expectations and look for ways to become CEO and again, we're meaning THINK like a CEO would think. Become the master of your destiny! "As you think, so you shall become. ***Our organizations are looking for the team members who will arrive to the scene so full of life and wholly unleash all their energies, not into a career, but into a calling.*** The Energizers of our organizations are as Rowan on the mission to find Garcia. They possess the depth to fuel the vision, inspire enthusiasm and achieve great results as they become CEO!

CHAPTER 18
200 PERCENT HEART

living like it's your big moment

"Enthusiasm is the greatest asset in the world. It beats money and power and influence." – Og Mandino

Overachiever

Jill worked for a prestigious manufacturing firm that supplied parts to BMW and Mercedes. I was privileged to meet her for the first time as she greeted me and my team. Offering us water and making us feel right at home, Jill exemplified a keen awareness of her company's business and more impressively, displayed a passionate belief as she shared their core values and why she loved working as executive assistant. She had a professionalism and tenacity about her that was attractive. When I dug deeper and learned her story, I found out that *this single mom had simply showed up to her previous job, the local car dealership, with a ton of enthusiasm!* She was thankful for a place to work and gave it her all when she was there! One day, a distinguished, German gentleman walked in to buy a Jeep. She put all the documentation together for him just like she would on any other day. As he signed the final paper, "he made me a job offer," she recounted gleefully. Jill had no idea he was the president of a large manufacturing plant. She attracted the opportunity of executive assistant by giving two hundred percent right where she was at! We'd call her an overachiever – the term used to describe the rarity of this level of contribution.

Perhaps your job – your life's work – is very gratifying and very fulfilling. If you love your job, you form a minority of the twenty percent who do. Forbes indicates eighty percent of people hate their jobs. Of this percentage, I wonder how many don't find fulfillment in their work simply because of holding back and not putting in their full effort and ability. I've found that once people decide to start giving their current situation everything they've got, something amazing happens. The situation actually improves, and they begin to find fulfillment through passionate contribution. Does an "overachiever" really over achieve? Or, are they simply finding the joy in living every moment like it's their big moment? Might they actually enjoy unleashing 100 percent and expanding their capacity towards 200? The rarity in this world, called Jill – or each one of us who so chooses – will show up whole and in fullness so that we can unleash a genuine enthusiasm into whatever we decide to do!

Purpose

Do you believe accomplishing work – having a purpose – is a gift? Perhaps you've viewed work as a necessary evil. In this book we learn that work – meaningful contribution and achieving a result – is actually part of the energy definition. *We learn how to shift our mindset on work as we ignite our energy. With a changed perspective on life and work, we purposely bring more passion into our life and work every day.* Fulfillment comes to those who give their all. Many of us have a dream job in our minds; our current job may feel like an anchor holding us back. We've heard of the "greener grass syndrome," and I believe it's inherent in humanity to want more. This desire is completely legitimate. Whether that's more responsibility, more money, or simply more purpose, we feel unfulfilled for a reason. A good portion of our unfulfillment stems from unfulfilled expectations we had of our jobs. So, we check out mentally, daydreaming about our dream job.

Finding Your Dream Job

Here's a secret. When you start working at your current job as if it were your dream job, you will attract your dream job. Several things happen. You either begin loving the job you thought you hated, you get promoted, or you get hired away. You attract exactly what you are. If you're complaining about your current job, you're only speeding up the merry-go-around of a vicious, unfulfilled cycle and again, several things will happen. You either stay in your current position feeling stuck, leave for something that seems better, or quit altogether. Someone once said, "If the grass looks greener on the other side, it's time to water your grass." *Do you know what happens when you decide to show up in force at whatever you're doing, today? You'll be impactful and realize the fulfillment of giving your all, you'll have the energy to learn the skills you need for your dream job, and finally, you'll watch the dream job or role attract itself to you.* Finding purpose in our work, today, is so very crucial.

Many greats we've studied in history books like George Washington, Abraham Lincoln, Harriet Tubman, Henry Ford, Sochiro Honda, J.C. Penny, Amelia Earhart, Steve Jobs, Francis Nightingale and Jonas Sulk are proof. Proof of women and men who took all their gusto, their two-hundred percent, and, because of this, enabled expansion for themselves and so many others. Expansion happens when your effort has been maximized and can no longer be contained. You must expand your effort in your current role. This expanded effort alone can be purpose, and purpose sown grows greater purpose. Call it growth, expansion or promotion, you and I are in control of finding purpose.

Finding Purpose in Work

Work must give purpose if it's to be viewed as a gift and joy. If work's purpose isn't evident, people pull back and become disengaged. Our jobs as managers and team leaders must be, first and foremost, facilitating purpose in the objectives, targets and activities we lead our teams to accomplish. I've heard people call millennials lazy – I disagree. I've personally witnessed some of the hardest working, passionate people among millennials. We'll do something for absolutely hours on end, stay up all night, take part in an activist movement, and so on. Sure, laziness exists, but I believe, too often, there's a lack – an enormous void – in leadership's ability to communicate vision, describe work as meaningful, or define its purpose and assign tasks to match personal gifts and desires. In his powerful book, *Bringing Out the Best in People*, Alan Loy McGinnis wrote, "The leader's challenge is not to take lazy people and make them into industrious types. Rather it is to channel already existing energies into the most worthwhile endeavors." Seth Godin states, "Excellence isn't about working extra hard to do what you're told, but taking the initiative to do work you decide is worth doing!" *People don't like being bored and lethargic and will welcome the leader who can sincerely teach them to enjoy their work, or the teacher who makes learning fun.* In his book, Tribes, Seth Godin states, "The secret of leadership is simple: Do what you believe in. Paint a picture of the future. Go there. People will follow." In his book, *Good to Great*, Jim Collins defines great organizations as those with the ability to get the right people on the metaphorical bus and then in the right seats of the bus – doing their gift, their passion! In fact, he further expounds, "If you think you have the wrong person, first give the person the benefit of the doubt that perhaps he or she is in the wrong seat. Whenever possible, give a person the chance to prove himself or herself in a different seat, before drawing the conclusion that he or she is a wrong person on the bus." The wisdom of Mr. Collins is evident. Help individuals find purpose in their work.

Finding Work with Purpose

If you're reading this book and you're currently giving your absolute best, yet you still feel stuck or see nothing moving at all, chances are you're not "turned on" because that's not what you're designed to do. Start thinking about where you really want to be. Where do you belong? Take time to analyze what you love to do, and what you could be happy doing the rest of your life. In his transformational recording, *The Strangest Secret*, Earl Nightingale says it this way, "Success is anyone who is realizing a worthy predetermined ideal, because that's what he or she decided to do … deliberately; but, only one out of twenty does that!" Finding purpose and meaning in your work will naturally increase your capacity – your energy – to do that work. Why not sow some seeds to finding a ton of purpose, meaning and profitable endeavor by following some ancient advice from none other than Napolean Hill:

- "Decide EXACTLY what kind of a job you want. If the job doesn't already exist, perhaps you can create it.
- Choose the company, or individual for whom you wish to work.
- Study your prospective employer, as to policies, personnel, and chances of advancement,
- By analysis of yourself, your talents and capabilities, figure WHAT YOU CAN OFFER, and plan ways and means of giving advantages, services, developments, ideas that you believe you can successfully deliver.
- Forget about "a job." Forget whether or not there is an opening. Forget the usual routine of "have you got a job for me?" Concentrate on what you can give.
- Once you have your plan in mind, arrange with an experienced writer to put it on paper in neat form, and in full detail.
- Present it to the proper person with authority and they will do the rest."

Times change, but what remains the same is the longing for value. *Every company is looking for virtuous people who can add or create value.* Their value may be resources, ideas, services, connections, communication, inventions, expertise, etc. Every company has the room, or will make the room, for people who enter the scene with a definite plan of action which will be advantageous to the orgainzation. Be bold and open your mind to develop what you'd love doing. Until you find your purpose, you'll struggle getting your enthusiasm meter over 100 and on the way to 200 percent!

200 Percent

Working on ourselves and on something productive is energizing. It's being and doing. But, there's a constant pressure in our environments to hold back, conform or settle for the status quo. Giving your all feels good; but, it's not required. Mediocrity's pull is so strong. We enjoy comforts of life – especially in our modern day – and our endeavors and contributions in what we do, too often resemble just that – comfort. Not too little, but not too much! But what's too much? If you're showing up fully present, then why not give your all! ***Know what direction to go, know what the outcome looks like, then charge into the tasks you decide on with vim and vigor!*** They say the day before vacation is always the most productive day. Why? It's because we want to line everything up perfectly. We know things have to be done, we delegate, we look ahead, and we plan. Ah! Plan. In this situation, we should all be taking more vacations, right? Well, maybe that's not the real issue here, but I can attest sometimes one day of determination can be as fruitful as a week or two (or three) of good intentions. Why? Your back is against the wall. You know you must focus and finish a lot of things – and you do! Imagine this same level of intensity every day. Imagine that today was your last day and what you did today would be the last set of memories people had of you. Today would form the legacy you leave.

A sign I used to have hanging on my office door as a constant reminder to never wait to own something, but to be proactive, an initiator of all that is good and truly responsible person read something like this, "The Rare Responsible Person":

Self aware
Self improving
Self disciplined
Self motivating
Acts like a leader
Doesn't wait to be told what to do
Picks up the trash lying on the floor.

Note: If you're a young guy, print this and stick it on the door. Winston Churchill said, "I'm just an average man willing to work harder than the average man." The person committing to extreme ownership of life – the 200 percent heart – leaves it all on the field. Imagine living every moment like it was your big moment. You know why you get nervous when you're about to sign a mortgage, go on stage, meet a friend, get married and anything that we call "big" in life? Because, your mind is sizing up what's in front of you and calling on the reinforcements. So in life, when you commit to 200 percent, your mind will summon your deepest reserves of untapped energy. You will move like Wonder Woman and Superman! All hands on deck! All in! You're living every moment like it's your big moment!

Charging into Mile Two

At the start of mile two is where duty stops and desire begins. Its where careers turn to callings and journeys turn to joy. Its where process turns to pleasure. Its where little turns to a lot! It's the very point that the mind connects to the heart and magic happens. A mentor and motivational friend once challenged me with this thought, "You don't have to, but what if you did?" What if you went the second mile? The first mile represents the requirements and expectations. Most will travel mile one. To get paid, to earn the degree, to have the family, you name it, the first mile must be travelled. The second mile is often less travelled. This is the zone of the "little extras!" And in this zone is where magic happens! You planned the date before your wife asked, and you had the baby-sitter lined up. You went over and above on the work assignment adding value. You reached out to encourage your fellow students. You thanked the McDonald's cashier for her smile. You volunteered to help in the community or through your church in some area.

These are simple examples of stuff no one requires, but this "stuff" is the little extra that creates the juice! We recently went to Michigan, and in the hotel room at night my fellow sales associates and I sent handwritten notes to our clients. No one required it, but think of their faces and the joy they'll receive opening a heartfelt thank you note! A friend and I shared coffee recently and he shared how he adds a little encouraging quote to his field reps' weekly priority sheets. He doesn't have to, but he's going the second mile! Are you willing to be proactive and go the extra mile? Zig says, "There's no traffic on the extra mile." What is one thing you could do today that is not required but could mean the world to somebody? Do one little extra thing today and watch the energy happen! BOOM!

Calling Instead of Career

When you put all your heart in, your career becomes a calling. *The powerful perspective of "Get-To" drives this rare type of ownership – extreme ownership! No one will force you to step up to the plate, and in olden time, neither would the law demand your going the second mile.* This was a choice – your choice. Will you operate in the temporal realm of making money in a career, or will you operate in the eternal realm of creating connection, relationships and healing in every realm of life – your calling? One is first mile requirement; the other is second mile choice! Here's the key – passion pays! I like how the authors of the *Go-Giver* stated, "Your true worth is determined by how much more you give in value than you take in payment." Charles Francis Adams said, "No one ever attains very eminent success by simply doing what is required; it's the amount and excellence of what is over and above the required that determines the greatness of ultimate distinction." Jack Daly, speaking about Southwest Airlines, says, "They have created a culture where their people act in the best interest of both the customer and the company." At organizations such as Southwest, Zappos, Google and others, it's far greater than just a job!

Creating Opportunity

When you're all heart, you're brave, you're courageous and you're all in. Enthusiasm is the abundance of an energized life. A life on fire; a heart that's pulsating love into every action. S.D. Gordon called enthusiasm, "the heart burning." These people are springing forth, not just from 100 percent heart – the point of fullness – but expanding towards 200 percent – the abounding life! You take life on with all the ardor your heart possesses. Therefore, if the phone's not ringing, you're making it ring. You are bold. You create opportunity! My friend who's a real estate agent and broker, Monte Mohr, invited me onto Nashville's WSMV - Channel 4, recently. Why? I told him I'd love to share my experience of him selling our first home. When his six-foot, six-inch stature walked through our door, he barely spoke a word, and moved through our home, room to room, in deep contemplation – fully present. Then, sitting down with Jen and I, he addressed Jen. He included me but made her the target of his feedback. He picked up on our having three kids (at that time), the toys and her sewing studio. He told her with as much as she had going on, he knew it would be tough to ask; but, we had to – absolutely had to – put some of the big toys and furniture in the garage for showing our house. "Trust Uncle Monty, when I tell you, this is how to sell your home." The past few realtors hadn't demanded this of us and naturally, we kept doing regular life. With the radical change that Monte kindly demanded, our house sold on the eighth showing and he saved us two grand. All of that, and he called us more throughout the process and loved on us. To this day, we call him Uncle Monty. Why? *There are those people who take business beyond a transaction by fully engaging their clients with inner fullness and personal power – energy. Energy attracts! These people take business beyond the transaction.*

Emotional Manufacturer – Our Hearts

Has your heart been squeezed recently? Do you feel touched? There is a proverb that states, "Keep your heart with all diligence, for out of it are the issues of life." The wholeness of your heart – this manufacturer of all your emotions – is the greatest key to living an energized life. Many walk through life with a closed-off heart. They've been hurt and wounded, and instead of forgiving and restoring emotional flow, they've plugged a portion of their heart. Scared to relive the hurt, they venture far away from anything that might open that emotional artery. They've literally boxed their heart up, built great walls around it and go through life feeling neither pain nor joy. Often, pain must first be experienced to know full joy; softness and calm to know strength and courage. The greatest generals of all time have been the emotionally stout kinds. J.T. Headley wrote of the invincible general George Washington, " … that great grand heart, which made him so terrible on the battlefield, was yet full of the tenderest affections, and clinging still to his dear mother, whose love for him was deep and unfailing as the ocean-tide, he wept like a child when told he should see her no more." How's your emotional state? Are you flowing? Are you ok leaving it all on the field for something worthwhile? Have you experienced that joy?

Enthusiasm – Eternal Force

Deep energy drives an eternal enthusiasm! Heartfelt emotion propels this enthusiasm outward – it's contagious! *The beautiful part is when you throw your whole heart into something, energy is released in the greatest ways possible.* Companies hire passionate people – no doubt. Imagine, though, through the amplitude of wholeness, if the passion you showed at work was truly your passion. Not the borrowed passion of the leader you love and would do anything for. Not the passion from motivation you listened to on the way to work. While both are important, where is the deep, heartfelt, truly energized labor that refuses to even remotely accept anything in life as a J.O.B. or career. Instead, everything you decide to put your hand to is a calling. It's a matter of transferring your livelihood, your lifeforce – your energy – into, and no matter what it is, you're all in! Like Dr. Martin Luther King Jr. said, "Whatever you are, be a great one!" Enthusiasm comes from the Greek work entheos, which means "inspired, filled with divine power." The biblical account of the passion of Christ is incredible. What love! What Divine Power carried this deeply wounded and physically battered man up a rugged hill? Enthusiasm calls upon an internal force – an eternal force – that rarely gets tapped. When it does, though, things happen! The marines have this theory that when you feel like you're tapped out, you're only at 40 percent of your potential.

When adrenalin kicks in, a superhero-like ability comes over you.

One of my favorite movies is, "Facing the Giants". It's a small country high school and it comes down to the quarterback's attitude of failure. Everything he does breathes inability to win. No belief, no faith and no hope inspired. His team sticks around him because he's the biggest, strongest and the most contagious – in a negative way. The coach picks up on this and challenges him to get down into the bear crawl position. "I'm going to blindfold you and your only job is to start here in the end zone and crawl to the 50-yard line." The coach continued, "You'll carry your team mate on your back, and you must promise me one thing." "What's that?" Brock asked.

"You have to promise me you'll give your absolute best."

Long story short, Brock made it to the 50, 60 and 70-yard line. At that point he's shouting through the blindfold at the coach that he can't go on. The coach screams, "You're best, Brock. Just your best, you can do this! Just give me one more." 80, 90 … 93 … 97 … wobble … wobble …. 98 … arms shaking … 99 …. Collapse into the end zone. Crying and face in the ground, Brock mumbles, "We've got to be at 50. That had to have been 50!" The coach says as tenderly as possible, "Look up, Brock! You're in the end zone." Things changed for the team that day. Why? Brock realized that he hadn't even tapped into his potential yet, and what's more, his contagious spirit when changed to enthusiastic belief inspired hope and belief in his team and carried them to victory!

To engage the feelings of the people in our lives like our families and clients, to gain entrance past their naturally raised defenses, and to see their energies engage with ours, we must lead with spirit and passion engaging our feelings and emotions into our work. Dr. Harvey Cushing said, "Nothing great or new can be done without enthusiasm. Enthusiasm is the fly wheel which carries your saw through the knots in the log. A certain excessiveness seems a necessary element in all greatness." Hill states, "Without enthusiasm, one cannot be convincing. Moreover, enthusiasm is contagious and the person who has it, under control, is generally welcome in any group of people."

Possible with Courage

Igniting our energy and unleashing our enthusiasm into our work will require courage. *A great deal of passion is lost to our world for want of a smidge of courage.* Most people are fearful of what others will think if they stand out or overperform. Yes, it feels uncomfortable. Fear will hold us back in life if we don't possess courage, and courage starts when we have a big enough WHY. Courage starts internally. The fears and voices in our minds tell us it's not worth it. Overcoming these fears and voices is the real battleground. The voices will mockingly ask if living fully awakened and energized is all it's cracked up to be. Replace these negative, fear-based emotions – immediately. Replace them with the emotion of courage! Courage to no longer stand on the sidelines and observe the game, but to jump in with both feet everything else following behind! Courage to rise above the other voices I know will seek to pull me down and cool me off! Courage to love my work and embrace it as my calling! I love how Florence Nightingale said, "Courage is the universal virtue of all those who choose to do the right thing over the expedient thing!" Courage is identifying the fear and doing the right thing anyway! Why not give life our all? Remember the 4,000-year-old secrert also known as the Energy Equation? We've all seen sports players literally spend themselves on the basketball courts, football fields, ice rinks, and so on! Not to belittle sports as this is part of their lives and exciting entertainment, but consider the people in your circles of life, your kids, and your coworkers. Do they deserve any less contribution? It'll take courage to unleash everything and pour your 200 percent into your family, your workplace, a cause, or your community! The opposition will put up a fight, calculating fears will tell you to hold back, yet courage will see you through. Speaking of the biblical account of Gideon's band, S.D.Gordon writes, "three hundred young men fresh from the farm, who were willing, courageous and hot-hearted – all heart qualities. They stood every test and they faced a foe that humanly they had no chance to overcome – they were known." Like a trainer of mine, Chris Hocker, once told me, "Courage stares fear in the face. Courage is recognizing the fear and doing it anyway."

Passion Pays

Why is turnover an issue for a lot of organizations? A big reason is unmet expectations. People expecting out of a job more than it can give, or more than they're willing to give. So, we hop from one job to the next, settling in and putting in what's required. *But, when you're created, designed, and capable of so much more, settling in will be the most unfulfilled work you ever perform. Giving your all will take you further, faster; and, it feels good and the feeling lasts.* In fact, meaningful contribution was wired into us to feel good; but, passion does so much more for you than a mere feeling. Passion pays! Passion pays in perpetuity! Make a difference and the dollars will follow is a principle we teach sales people. When you focus your energy on making a difference for your client – meeting their needs – they will naturally turn their spigot to your channel and they'll hire the most heartfelt service every time! Passion pays. You ask any business leader what they'd take first, talent or tenacity, they'll pick tenacity. Aptitude or attitude, and attitude will win every time. Unless you're in such a specialized field that training takes years, most business owners and execs climbed to that level through passion. They know passion pays and they pay for passion. Be the nail that dares to stick up. Make the leap to expand into the 200 percent! Make a difference and the dollars will follow! Godin points out that successful organizations are paying for people who make a difference. The business owner who doesn't value passion won't pay for passion. They need bodies. If you're committed to show up with passion and make a difference, find the employer who values passion.

Passion brings thoroughness. When you invoke passion – that's putting your 200 percent heart into your work – you won't settle for mediocre results. You demand your best and your presence demands the best of those around you. Give your best! We feel our best when we give our best. Wouldn't you love everyone around you to feel their best? Encourage them to give their best by giving yours and they're much more likely to catch the feeling. Passion is contagious – positive or negative. You effortlessly bring out the best in those around you. Football coach, Lou Holtz, once said, "Ability is what you're capable of, motivation determines what you do, and attitude determines how well you do it."

When I was in fifth grade, I struggled with English. Math, History, Science – fun. English – ugh! One night, I was going through the Red X's all over my English book and noticed a handwritten note. It was my Mom's handwriting. I still have the curves of those red-penned letters etched in my brain:

> "The hand of the diligent shall bear rule, but the slothful shall be under tribute. Prov. 12:23 … Timothy, I've been praying that you become more diligent in your school work. I love you, Mom."

Wow! That note tugged tears right out of my heart and I gave my all in school from that day on. The story of the power of one heartfelt, hand-written note is my Mom's; and, the story of a passionate life can be every-one 's who decide to unleash their whole being into that which they do!

A passionate life is a powerful force! ***Everything you do with your whole heart carries your heart forever.*** You become thorough. In customer service, you're tuned to the feelings of the client and listen to them. You care and show empathy. You travel the second mile every day because your heart's in it, you're whole and your energy – that capacity to do work – is abundant and drives your passion! As the executive assistant, you're loving, gracious and understanding. Short tempers don't phase you. You forgive, you love and your abundance demands a respect and offers healing even at the highest levels of leadership and among some of the most exhausted people. You serve with a heart of gladness because your passion transcends merely holding down a job. Your passion is your very essence. It's your pleasure to serve. That's who you are. You're not doing it for acknowledgement; therefore, your passion doesn't quit when no acknowledgement comes. In sales, your passion leaves no stone unturned. You know you can help and you look for alignment of prospect's needs and the value you're creating. You aren't at odds with your organization or your client, for you realize you're simply the conduit between both. Your passion is the amperage behind the flow through the conduit. You are whole, abundant and attractive because your heart is apparent, and you truly care. As a teacher, mother, father or friend, your passion shows up with overflowing love. People never forget you because you made them feel amazing about themselves. People like to be around you because your emotions are whole, and your passion splashes those wonderful emotions over to them.

Finally, passion brings useful creativity. This is the highest frequency of passion, and it's only attained after invoking your whole heart, your 200 percent and exhausting passion's thoroughness. When you're emotionally sound and abounding – ignited energy – your passion is fueled keeping you in a consistent state of proactivity! Flora Plummer says it like this, "Enthusiasm born of true love for the cause enables the worker to do better." *Doing our best means we are continually looking for ways to do our best, better! You're thinking of opportunities, you're creatively imagining what not yet is and you're developing solutions. Your heart and mind are in sync creating joy for others, you're open and looking for the opportunities. You spot them and when you don't see any on the immediate horizon, you create them.* Your passion builds a powerful mentality.

When 200 percent of your heart is engaged, you're not holding anything back! Because you believe that full engagement is the only kind that counts, then you will constantly be pushing against and breaking through the proverbial glass ceiling. You will constantly expand opportunities for you and others. You will see potential where others don't. New heights will always reveal themselves to those climbing the mountains they're already on, but never to the ones who stand waiting.

We must ask ourselves. Have I given more and better service than what was required? Did I show up passionately because I was blessed to get to perform the work? Did I make a difference for someone today? Energizers are fully awakened people who go happen to the world; they don't wait for the world to happen to them. Imagine the difference we could make in our lives, families, schools, businesses, churches, communities and our world if we'd show up with 200 percent! Energizers are all heart and expanding! They are reaching for the 200 percent heart! The second hundred percent comes when your first hundred percent is given! You want to experience life and feel love like you've never experienced life and felt love before? Give your whole heart. Squeeze it all out! Leave it all on the field! Don't save anything for the swim back, for you have an ocean of opportunity and unlimited power available to you when you reach the difficult place and achieve the height of giving your whole heart. When you give your all, your heart will expand, your horizons will extend, and your potential will multiply as you begin to live climbing toward 200 percent! Live today as if it were your last! Live today as if it were your life's greatest masterpiece. Celebrate and thrive today! *Yesterday's in the books, tomorrow's an empty guaranteed. Today, right now, open your heart to new levels. This is your big moment! Step into it living fully and loving deeply!*

ACCOUNTABILITY

Embracing vulnerability by building a Scrum cheering you on, & enthusiastically engaging your life shareholders creating raving fans.

Imagine
the fulfillment
of deep relationships
valuing others,
learning constantly,
and being a caring,
confident leader.

CHAPTER 19
SYNERGIZE

energetic learner – all are my teachers

"The learners shall inherit the earth while the learned will be beautifully equipped to live in a world that no longer exists." – T. Harv Eker

Get Your Boots; Go See

"Get your boots; go see?" Huh? That's exactly what it sounded like my Japanese client was saying. In fact, it stuck in my brain this way. The meaning of what he said and how I heard it actually made sense. Engineers in manufacturing and other industries have this practice, adopted from Toyota, called, "Genchi Genbutsi," or like I heard and remember it, "Get your boots; go see." Simply put, this mindset means, "get up and go see." Engineers can sit at their desks, hypothesizing and theorizing, when a quick trip to the manufacturing plant's production floor, where they can put their hands on the actual product or problem, saves so much time and energy. With this practice, one accepts that they can learn more from a real-world experience than from a mechanical drawing, computer software or their own expertise. *The underlying foundation to this principle is keeping an open mind, going to learn, seeking to understand, and embracing the synergy that all people can teach me something!* So, an engineer gets up from the desk, gets his safety gear on: steel-toed shoes or boots, safety hat and goggles, and walks to the floor to discuss the design or issue with the people assembling it or dealing with it. They ask questions, listen and get the assembly teams' buy-in. They were committed to energized learning. A story Jeffrey Liker shares in his book, *The Toyota Way,* is that of the 2004 Toyota Sienna's design. Engineers were sent from Japan to travel the United States from coast to coast. They observed. They listened. They saw people eating in their vehicles much unlike Japanese culture. Fold down seats, trays, and a lot of cupholders – check! They saw people at Home Depot loading a 4x8 sheet of plywood on top of their van and tying it down. Fold down seats and a wider body at the floor of the van that could receive this – check! The 2004 version of the Toyota Sienna revamped the entire industry's van sizes. They did something different because they allowed all people to teach them. They embraced energized learning! Further, the Toyota Motor Corporation heralds relentless reflection known as Hansei and continuous improvement known as Kaizen. These are the keys to becoming a learning organization. They say, "We view errors as opportunities for learning. Rather than blaming individuals, the organization takes corrective actions and distributes knowledge about each experience broadly …"

Those who stop learning, in T. Harv Eker's words says, "will be beautifully equipped to live in a world that no longer exists." If you want to get left behind, stop learning. *Accountable people possess a sincere desire to learn! Accountability is after the truth.* Those who embrace accountability will live in their truth no matter the cost – even though it may temporarily embarrass them. Self-examination and continual improvement are essential to all who demand of life more than mediocrity! Embracing accountability means you're a synergistic learner. This type of learning opens your mind and grows your heart in understanding.

Learning Leverages

Think for yourself, learn from all people in your life, and know how to apply what's already been learned to current life situations. Leverage the resource of learned knowledge and wisdom. Synergy happens when people share and are open to each other's input, knowledge and wisdom. A mastermind comes into play when your mind and another's mind bond on the same common goal and solve for the unknown. It literally creates a third mind that didn't previously exist – called a mastermind. Both minds are focused on the outcome and pouring all energy of thought into it! Energized learning leverages so much cognitive energy.

Synergy

Synergy's definition is simply, "The interaction of two or more agents or forces so that their combined effect is greater than the sum of their individual effects." This is powerful! *When I finally stopped entering relationships of life trying to prove myself; but instead, entered with an understanding heart, all relationships changed. Relationships grew richer, became stronger, and all relationships became a synergistic experience.* Two can create more together than what they could have possibly created by themselves. Who are you creating value for the world with? Many great endeavors have blessed this world because two people knew how to value each other and get along in a spirit of unity! Oneness! Synergy! Gestalt! Where the whole is greater than the sum of the parts. There are eight notes in an octave of music and each note is a key instrument in creating harmonious music: **A,B,C,D,E,F and G.**
Let's call the following the **Octave of Synergy**. Following these steps creates a harmony of synergistic relationships:

> **A –** Aligned. Aligned with each other does not mean thinking the same way but thinking together. Putting both minds together to create more. Alignment thinks in terms of "we and us" not "me and you." Alignment makes decisions based upon vision and with the goals of the relationship in mind.

> **B -** Being. Being is the freedom to be yourself and exercise your gifts; and letting others be free to be themselves and exercise their gifts. Being looks at who the person is and amplifies that, not at the what the person's currently doing.

C – Creative. Creativity finds ways to create and add value to the relationship. This is proactive and chooses to act based on principles not on circumstances. Competitive, comparative and condemning attitudes only result in calculating and controlling relationships – unhealthy relationships. Creative relationships are proactive, healthy and growing!

D – Defenseless. Defenselessness embraces healthy conflict, encourages feedback and listens. No defense. Too often, we say we encourage conflict and as soon as someone trusts us enough to share something bothering them, or a possible irritant we're bringing into the relationship, or something they're simply concerned about, we quickly retort to save our image. We hear the first line and begin formulating our counter-argument like we're before the grand jury! We can and we will prove them wrong! We make them the enemy for telling us the truth, or maybe what they sense is the truth. Think about it. If there wasn't any truth to what was said, it wouldn't bother us so deeply. Usually, our reaction validates the truth. Author, Josh McDowell, in his book, *The Father Connection*, shares an insightful story of moving his family from California to Texas and his fifteen-year-old daughter struggling with the effects afterward. One night, his daughter, Katie, made a comment expressing her struggles and he came on strong, got upset and said some cruel things to her. "She went to her room and I went bed," he shares. His wife told him truthfully what she saw and recommended he apologize to Katie. Josh told his wife he'd make amends in the morning, but she insisted he really needed to right then. So, Josh went to Katie's room, told her he was wrong, he responded in the wrong way and that he was sorry. "Here's what I want us to see," Josh states, "I believe that those moments of painful honesty with my daughter accomplished more for our relationship and for her understanding of honesty than anything else I may ever do." Wow! No defense. Synergy!

E – Energizing. Energizing means you're *whole, full and abundant.* This means you're capable of achieving results in the relationship. You're emotionally strong and empowering to the other person. You pour encouragement into them. You're fully present. An energizer is intentional in relationships. You pour your heart into the other person. It's not checking your cell phone, email, or halfway listening. You've assigned this time to this person and you are fully present during that time to make the most of it. Real and deep connection rarely happens; however, real and deep connection is really the only time progress and forward-motion happens. When training works best with my kids, are the times I stop, get down on the floor on their level, look in their eyes totally quiet, wait, then softly speak and ask them questions to get them thinking. The quick, snappy, short-fused, often loudly-barked commandments in passing only produce fear and more of the same activity.

F – Forgiving. A continual, consistent and constant forgiveness is necessary to keep relationships synergized. Most of the big issues we refuse to forgive are a result of small instances we didn't pro-actively forgive – let go of completely. One of my good friends, Vinnie, said it this way, "Most people wear their feelings on their sleeve waiting to be hurt; instead, wear your whole heart on your sleeve looking to love and be loved!" Instead of the grudge, let it go. Give your heart without recourse. Let your getting be in the giving! Someone said it like this, "A broken heart is better than a boxed heart." Forgive constantly and completely! Give love no matter what!

G – Grateful. Gratitude for every person, their gifts, uniqueness and beauty. When we stop trying to "fix" everybody and start projecting belief over them through our gratitude for the beauty we see in them, everything changes. The good is amplified and major things happen – together! *With genuine gratitude, ego simply can't exist, and thus, everyone shares equally in the finality of what's created.* A unified sense of gratitude persists.

Learn from All ... Curiosity

Energetic learners love putting puzzles together. Laughingly, I'm kidding a little bit. Here's the key, though. Be curious; always looking to learn. Avoid grabbing one piece of the puzzle and contentedly leveling off believing you have the whole picture. Poke, prod, explore and seek to understand more. Albert Einstein claimed, "The important thing is not to stop questioning. Curiosity has its own reason for existing." One of my friends is super successful in real estate and investing and has also authored some books. Whenever he meets someone for the first time. He'll ask them for one piece of life wisdom. People say all sorts of amazing things and then Joe closes by saying, "You can learn something from everyone, if you'll only ask." In his book, *How to Become a Rainmaker*, Jeffrey Fox describes a great sales person as one who is willing to ask enough "dumb" questions. Be curious and commit to learn Move past the fear of a "dumb" question. Guess what? They don't exist! Ask questions. Then, listen to learn and to experience. Do we listen to learn, or do we listen to respond? I've been guilty of the latter many times. *Work in life to be curious. Explore, ask questions and then listen. Let life be a grand, experiential adventure – one that would give Curious George some healthy competition!*

... Humility

Humility can't coexist with stagnation. Stagnation means one is unwilling to learn and grow. Stagnation is opposite of growth. Pride says "I'm greater than" or "I'm the greatest" and therefore, pride sees no need to learn from anyone. Pride can't see blind spots and won't accept someone else pointing them out. Pride reads books and frames the lessons into everyone else's life situations. Pride stems from basic insecurity. Humility never thinks ill of oneself – not even for failing. Humility learns from everything and everyone. Even King David humbled himself to hear the counsel of the prophet Nathan. Humility isn't bashing yourself or thinking any less of yourself. It's simply appreciating others' perspectives. It's appreciating wise counsel, thinking for yourself to apply counsel and growing! One of our clients is an amazing executive and a couple decades my senior. When she hired our firm to coach her and her team, I told her we hoped to get just as much out of the arrangement as she did. Some would argue you should be coached by someone who's your senior. Is this argument correct? Not necessarily. All people can teach me something, and there have been people younger than me who've exemplified discipline or a behavior that I was working towards; and, I allowed them to speak into my life. Being a synergistic learner results in a powerful life! "All people are my teachers" mentality doesn't look to power play. It doesn't abuse and corrupt power as it opens the power of knowledge and understanding to all! It makes for powerful living when you realize all people are priceless and therefore, I can look for virtues in someone that looks completely different than me and learn from them! *Seek out authorities in your life – people well versed and exemplifying virtuous living – and be accountable in learning from them.* Allow wise authority to speak into your life. I like how McGinnis put it, "Everyone, no matter how highly placed, needs to be accountable to a few wise people."

... Criticism

Criticism usually happens because of one's own insecurities. Sometimes, though, it happens constructively by an industry expert or someone with our best interest at heart. Know this. In life, criticism will come – both good and bad. If we'd commit to learn and grow continually, we'd save a lot of energy swindled from us by responding incorrectly to criticism. Our own tendency towards a critical attitude would dwindle as well, for we'd see even the negatives of life as learning opportunities. The organism that's growing, whether it's a sapling or other plant, displays a confidence and non-apologetic attitude. It's when it stops growing that it droops and becomes a stagnant eye-soar in the garden. When you're growing and proactively moving through life with initiative and ambition, you're less likely to criticize. The stagnant ones criticize, and "criticism is the one form of service, of which everyone has too much," wrote one writer. I've heard many people say, "Expect the critics in life – they'll come." I agree. Being critical is nothing more than hyper negativity bias. We're all capable of nit-picking and pointing out seeming flaws. We must exercise wisdom listening to criticism. As we filter out the nay-sayers, we musn't stop receiving valuable criticism. If we stop receiving critcicism, we inflate our own sense of what's right and look at others' opinions as wrong. Dale Carnegie said, "Show respect for the other person's opinions. Never say, 'You're wrong." You don't have to succumb to criticism, but you can accept and filter it. Always be open to some nugget that you hadn't thought of. If nothing else, let critics' opinions be your litmus test for keeping a gracious attitude. Be so ok with yourself that anything can simply be like water off a duck's back. They're entitled to, and perfectly human for offering their opinion. Be ok with people voicing their opinions and beliefs. *What if instead of thinking, "You're wrong," we tried thinking, "I appreciate the fact that you feel the freedom to voice that opinion." Big difference, and very telling of whether we're energized learners or possibly insecure.* One of my high school teachers shared a story of an executive who walked off the elevator of his high-rise to be greeted by a man who'd been waiting in the lobby. He wasn't very happy and seemed to have a bone to pick about a recent situation. My teacher, John, who worked for this executive at the time thought he was about to witness a fight. The words used by this man were severely harsh! Without saying a word, the executive pulled a notepad and pen from his pocket, opened it, and wrote down what this man had said. "Would you jot your number right here?" asked the executive as he handed the note-pad and pen to his critical friend. Stricken with unbelief and an awkward silence, the man wrote it down. "Thank you for letting me know. I'll look into this." With that, the man felt heard and the strife ceased. Learn, grow, and be ok with the critics. Help them be ok with them, too. They might be shocked as many critics are used to getting a fight when picking one.

Without pain your muscles don't grow, so without conflict, relationships don't grow. Know the difference (pain vs. injury). Abusive relationship versus arguments. One is physically dangerous and harms you – never grows you. Seek professional help if this is your situation. Do you run from conflict? Do you defend against conflict? Or, do you open up to conflict with an understanding heart? Seek to understand. Listen to what's really being said. *Pain ceases to be pain when we name it something else – learning. When you have an understanding heart and you're not defensive, you become super approachable.* You will also learn to craft criticism in the most beneficial way. I've found that those harshest with their criticism or reproof are often the most defensive when approached with criticism and reproof. Chances are, when you drop your defense and listen to the whole sentence or reasoning behind that person making a complaint, you'll be able to identify the points that stung and learn from them so that when you're called upon to give constructive criticism, you can offer it in the most gracious way. If someone has a new suit on with a tag on the back, have enough confidence in how you'd approach them and know that they'll respond in so much thankfulness because you've said something like, "Hey man, love the suit. Perfect fit! Wanted to let you know about a tag I bet no one has even noticed. Figured you'd appreciate me saying something." When one can overcome the fear of criticism and moves courageously through life, they no longer resent critics, they simply appreciate them. They give proper appreciation to criticism – sometimes it's worthless and other times it's priceless. Overcome fear of criticism by beating critics to the punch. That's right. You can when you commit right now to be a lifetime learner!

... Wise Counsel

The energized learner is constantly on the lookout for a lesson and its application. They learn from everyone – what to do and what not to do. They go a step beyond this to intentionally initiate learning. They learn specific skills from specific people. There's a great proverb that goes, "He that walks with the wise will also be wise." Who are your five closest friends? Those you text, message, follow, or spend the most time with? You'll become like them – question is, do you want to become like them? Accountability understands that learning and growing is stewardship of a greater impact on this world. Therefore, in this matter of energized learning, we should work to be all ears. Learning constantly from people. Think about it. What are you currently listening to today? Will this increase your energy (capacity to do work)? Will it grow you? A quick analysis may identify some poor listening choices: talk radio, negative commentary, immoral lyrics. What is it? We walk through this world and there are negative messages – even in advertisements – that speak to our fears and our egos. Sensationalism, celebrity gossip and political bashing becomes addictive to so many. Negativity bias sets in, opinions form and now you must share and probably tear friendships down, etc. Energized learners don't succumb! Pick wisely. The media allowed into our minds should ignite our energies. If we simply could care less about learning and tune into just any source, then it may be indication we've levelled off and aren't demanding more out of life. I love how Sharon Lee says, "The moment you say 'I know everything' is the end of your growth."

Learn from Things

Nature and events can teach us things. All of us have someone in our life that we learned a lot of what not to do from. Have you ever considered some of what they did that was beautiful, that was unique and good? When we look for the good, even in the people or events of life that threatened us, we fortify positive energy through forgiveness and gratitude. Similarly, when have you unplugged from everything and sat for hours pondering the beauty of a mountaintop or meditating in nature. *There's so much to learn right at our feet, if we'd simply look for natures' lessons. There's much to learn after every activity in life if we'd simply reflect.*

... Books

Energized learners are intentional readers. What books are you reading? You'll become like the people you hang around and the books you read. Read for learning and apply the knowledge you learn. Be careful your reading isn't driven by the fear of missing out. This fear will start a dozen books within a short amount of time and struggle finishing any. Energetic learning will start and complete a book and specify how that book's principles will be applied. We've heard all our lives, "Readers are leaders." Someone else said, "Readers aren't always leaders, but all leaders are readers." Titles attract our attention; and yes, we feel the huge necessity to add that information to our brains. It's bound to help us and offer great perspective. Yes, yes, yes! All books are written by a different voice than ours and we should be life-learners.

I love how someone said, "The person who does not read has no advantage over the person who cannot read." Just learn to decipher between the fear of missing out and energized learning. Energized learning knows they are consistently growing and remains fully present in the current book, it's teaching and how to make application. Even before this, the energetic learner is considering parts of their wholeness that could be strategically built and bolstered. They research and choose what to learn. Slow down and read to heed. Heeding what you're reading sometimes means you stop eating so that you can digest, implement and grow. So, I propose that *readers who are heeders make the greatest leaders*. I'd rather intentionally hand-select 12 great books to read this year and be an energized reader, than brag about the dozens I'm reading – grazing and not truly implementing. Do you read to learn or read to complete? Slow down. Avoid simply absorbing; instead, energetically engage!

... Failures

Accountable people – energized learners – make mistakes and admit them. "He is a little man who is afraid to admit he has been wrong," said Maltz. Gladstone shared, "No man ever became great or good except through many and great mistakes." And Sir Humphry Davy attested, "I have learned more from my mistakes than from my successes." I've found that thanking people when they correct me does phenomenal things. It's not easy to do, but once you get to this point, you no longer fear the "fail." You know that it's neither failure or success – it's all growth! Pat Summit, in her book, *Reach for the Summit*, said it like this, "You learn as much from getting it wrong as you do from getting right. But you must be willing to take responsibility for failure and be willing to examine it closely no matter how excruciating or embarrassing." Overcome the embarrassment by being an energetic learner. Learn from everything, every event, every success, every failure and every person. Learn and grow!

... Successes

I remember leading sales, it was easy to learn when a big failure took place; but, it was easy to get a bit lax when everything ran smoothly. Forgetting to look for a learnable lesson was easiest when the presentation or client visit was a huge success. However, successes can be great teachers! What to amplify, do more of, opportunities to capitalize on, etc. After hosting our initial *Energy4Life Signature Workshop*, I met with John Turner who let us pilot the program with his team. John's a phenomenal leader in life and real estate. I asked him, "John, give me the good, bad, and ugly." He was very kind and gracious in his feedback that we were able to clearly identify strengths and weaknesses to learn and grow from. Why? To make the next one, and the next, better for those attending. *Learning from successes allows us to build upon what's working to make it even better.* This is innovation. John Maxwell stated, "We didn't come out of the Stone Age because we ran out of stones." Someone innovated! Innovation looks into the future and doesn't level off. It's learning from success, what worked, anticipating future needs and adapting and creating forward value. This is energized learning!

Learner for Life

Live life as a continuous learning adventure – a journey – as opposed to some physical destination to arrive at and settle into. When you become a lifetime learner, you won't be so hard on yourself because you know you're progressing – it may be ever so slowly, but you won't give up no matter how hard the going gets. You'll laugh; you'll have fun learning – you know you're growing! Hill claimed, "The person who stops studying merely because he has finished school is forever hopelessly doomed to mediocrity, no matter what may be his calling. The way of success is the way of continuous pursuit of knowledge." Benjamin Franklin said, "If you think education is expensive, try ignorance." John Maxwell says of Da Vinci, "His talent was extraordinary – but so was his teachability. And the evidence for it can be found in his notebooks. They are physical record of a mind that never stopped discovering and never ceased learning!" Energizers are teachable. They read a wide range of topics, love wisdom, and listen intently. They commit to learn from every experience.

Growth happens for the energized learner. *They are wholly involved in learning; therefore, their spirit, soul, mind and body all benefit from every learning experience. They are quick to alter course or apply new knowledge. They possess an understanding heart, and wisdom graces their steps. They realize they are not only a lifelong learner but are also gaining life from learning.* That's right! When we seek to understand, listen and respond by taking action toward growth, we find that life greatly improves, our relationships improve, and results are achieved at a faster rate because of applied knowledge. It's what happens when we determine how to apply the knowledge of a great book. I love how Jesse Lee Bennet said, "The man who adds the life of books to the actual life of everyday, lives the life of his whole race. The man without books lives the life of one individual." The energized learner receives more life as capacity expands! Accountability's tremendous resource opens to the one who is open and willing to learn – the Energized Learner.

CHAPTER 20
SCRUM TIME
unleashing vulnerability – 10X accountability

"Vulnerability is the ultimate form of accountability practiced by the ultimate form of power – inner strength!"

4-Degree Origin of "Scrum Time"

BRRRRR! It was 4 degrees on a January morning. We were outside doing what we should've been doing on a treadmill – running. Yes, running at 4 degrees. You don't lick your lips running in this temperature. In fact, our exhaling breath froze on our hats and face masks, and the ladies' eyelashes formed little ice-cycles. After the run, we did what all 21st century runners do – took a selfie. Our faces were so numb it was difficult to tell whether we were smiling or not, so our coach, Rod Key, declared, "Scrum Time!" and we linked arms, huddled up and snapped the most resolved picture I think I've ever posed for. I'll never forget that morning and that feeling! *The feeling of insurmountable strength when your freezing cold but surrounded with the warmest hearts!* The six of us that morning formed an inseparable team. A team wanting one thing – momentum towards the goals we said would improve our life experiences. We didn't want to miss a beat and that morning, we all texted each other and rolled – slipped and slid a little – down to the Murfreesboro square where we'd run four miles – slipping and sliding some more. Not saying you have to go run at 4-degrees, but having someone with whom you can share your deepest struggles is the insurance policy of an energized life. You don't have much to hide when you share brutally revealing moments of life together. There are runs you miss, runs you feel terrible through, runs you don't get the PR, and runs that you simply just don't feel like running. The power of "Scrum Time" is that someone is on the mountain when you're in the valley.

Scrum

What's a scrum? Scrum is a shorter word for scrummage, and where we get our football term scrimmage from. A scrum is a common formation in the sport of rugby defined like this, "A scrum is a method of restarting play in rugby that involves players packing closely together with their heads down and attempting to gain possession of the ball." *Here's how a scrum applies to life. Each of us need people who will lock arms with us to achieve the goal. Be it in your career, mothering, fathering, teaching, pastoring, running, dieting, going back to school, starting a new business, volunteering or growing spiritually, success becomes predictable, results become expected, and life becomes fuller by forming a scrum of strength and power in our lives!* There is great strength in numbers! Like the proverb says, "Two are better than one." Our winning at the line of scrimmage often comes down to who's in our scrum! A coal by itself can grow dark & cold, but placed with fellow coals will spark, energize & generate a roaring fire! Lock arms with great people who will inspire, encourage & motivate you daily – form a scrum! Strengthen! Energize! Win! In the Scriptural account of Saul being anointed king, the story tells of a small band of strong-hearted men who formed around this humble king. Later, during his demise, you don't see this band. He became proud, lost his scrum and was alone and by himself. Darren Hardy says there are "few things as powerful as two people locked arm in arm and marching toward the same goal." Who are you accountable to? Bob Proctor says, "Accountability is the glue that ties commitment to results." Someone else said, "You'll hold yourself accountable for the goals others know about; tell someone what you're up to."

Form your scrum today. Not just a casual scrum – a scrum scrum! People you meet with, check in with and hold yourself radically accountable to! Establish how often you will meet and how to make this meeting mutually beneficial and fun! You may find an accountabuddy for walking, running, going to the gym, playing tennis, sharing a coffee and great development book like this one. It may go deeper than an accountabuddy. You may hire a coach, see a counselor, ask someone to mentor you in a certain area, or look for a specialized trainer like Mr. Miagi of "The Karate Kid." Build this scrum as intentionally as a President would fill cabinet positions. Like Dave Ramsey advises, find people with "the heart of a teacher." Verne Harnish states, "What a shame to have a high-powered executive or middle-management team that doesn't take even 15 minutes each day or an hour a week to focus its collective intelligence on the opportunities at hand." In business, this synergy of cognitive power can account for massive growth. Why not take the same huge advantage, embrace accountability and develop a scrum in your life? "Two are better than one" seems like a basic idea; often though, there are obstacles and difficulties we decide to handle ourselves. We decide to set a goal and muddle towards it alone. We don't take advantage of the huge resource of accountability! *Find someone who loves you deeply and wants to see you succeed in life. Someone willing to push you. Give them permission to offer advice and always welcome it! Check in with them about your successes; be brutally honest when you fail. They'll help you to reflect not on successes and failures, but on growth!* They'll help you build and bolster great desires to avoid the pitfalls and stay on track with your goals. Find a tribe and tap into its power! Overcome mediocrity; live to your full potential! Abraham Maslow said, "The story of the human race is the story of men and women selling themselves short." It's harder to sell someone else short on the potential they see in us! Get someone who's looking out for your potential! It's the power of the scrum! It's the song, "You Raise Me Up." It's true connection and trust. It's being willing to accept places you're weak and beautifully allowing someone else's strengths to compliment you. Key is this! Build your scrum now, when you can and while the sun is shining. That way, when trials come, they can help raise you up. Solomon states, "In the multitude of counselors, there's safety!"

A good coach knows how to challenge you and focus you on the right activities! Sometimes we want to tackle too much and perhaps not the right things. Sometimes we're so close to the trees of our own lives and know everything we want and everything that needs to happen, yet we can't see the entire forest. Mix all that with other obligations and the relationships that take time in life, we either demand too much of ourselves or give up and coast. Prioritizing and focusing are easier with outside eyes. In today's rush, it's even more crucial we gain this added perspective. Having our scrum's perspective can keep us centered and open-minded. We're in this together and we learn to drop the defenses! Sometimes in life we feel like we're being crushed by this giant boulder; to your scrum, it's a grain of sand. One simple perspective shift is all it takes to change anything. David Niven PhD. states, "When we're alone, problems fester. By sharing (either through prayer or to a trusted friend) we can gain perspective and find solutions." Jim Collins advises CEOs to "recruit several pairs of eyes (and to have frequent contact with the market) to help you navigate." Jeff Bezos says, "Think complex; speak simply." A good coach can take something that seems complicated because you're in the midst of it and can make it simple. One or two empowering questions can reframe a complex situation so nicely and bring everything into perspective.

Mind Power

In the universe there is matter and there is energy. Man's mind absorbs energy from the universe by way of thought impulses. It is the coordination of our physical, emotional, mental and spiritual states. Two minds joining may form a mastermind and generate more thought, therefore absorbing more energy than could have been absorbed by one mind. There is a synergistic power that happens in the harmony of combined thought. Hill describes this as, "The coordination of knowledge and effort … a spirit of harmony between two or more people, for the attainment of a definite purpose." *Much like a group of batteries that will provide more energy than a single battery, the power of the scrum is that when a group of individual minds coordinate together and function in understanding and harmony, the energy absorbed is multiplied through this powerful alliance of cognitive power.* This multiplied energy becomes available to every individual brain in the scrum. Scrum-time, therefore, generates and inspires an enthusiasm which is much greater than the sum of the parts! Family therapist and best-selling author, Alan Loy McGinnis writes, "An enthusiastic person can ignite others and create a fine fire!" He states that many kids go out into the world to function at levels far above average. Some people mistake these children's success to an inherited I.Q when it is due to far more than intelligence. It is a super-intelligence! One that comes from the energy and enthusiasm generated within the family group. There is power in minds dreaming, thinking and working together – harmony! Synergy! Scrum-time! Great things can happen through open-mindedness within a powerful scrum! I know that when my brothers or sisters and I get around each other, nothing's impossible; in fact, everything's possible! My business coaches and life mentors make obstacles look like speed bumps. They offer tremendous perspective and we infuse each other with power. Who are those people in your life? Get around them. Think with them and get on the higher frequency of shared intelligence. Who's in your scrum? Is it coordinated and harmonious thought? Is energy ignited and action more common and frequent because of your scrum?

Tribe Power

A great form of a scrum that will add power to your life is joining an existing tribe. Seth Godin wrote the book, Tribes, with the basic principle that "one another + a leader + an idea = a tribe." Question is, what group, leader and idea do you identify with? What tribe aligns with your vision? THIS IS KEY! What tribe is headed in the direction you want to go? *Tribes keep you energized & growing! Your tribe can either make or break you; for we become like those we spend time with. Identify with an idea your passionate about and join or start a tribe.* Igniting energy is my passion and calling! Inspiring people to see how valuable they are and how amazing life is! This is why we call this shared passion the **Energizer Tribe** – igniting the energy daily to live fully and love deeply! This tribe is a global family of people wanting to live wholly energized and high on life! Who are you following? Are they challenging you to grow? Are they helping you reach your goals, or pulling you down? Find the right tribe; change your life. The right tribe can help keep the momentum going in your life. In her book, *This Year I Will*, M.J. Ryan states, "Find someone who's doing what you want, and imitate them." I'm more likely to run every day when my tribe is holding me to it. My tribe gives me additional power! You become like those you follow. What's your goal? Does your plan incorporate a tribe reaching for the same?

Growth Power

Be committed to your own growth. Your scrum should be a tremendous resource to you to look out for anything hindering your growth. They are not responsible for our growth, though – that's where each of us must take individual ownership. Failing feels taboo in our lives. We go to great lengths to tell people how great things are going for us in life. We wear masks and put on facades. We often see patterns of failure in life, but we're unwilling to name them. Someone said, "When you name it, it no longer holds the power over you! This is so true. Remove the taboo of failure by naming your mistakes and empowering yourself to choose another course of action. When I first began my journeys as a salesman, my coach would travel with me and my team. We'd head out super early most mornings and shared a lot of life behind the wheel. There were the long trips to southern Georgia or Detroit, Michigan. The last thing you wanted to do was mess up. Travel all that way and blow it! Never felt good. So, David, our sales manager would tell us to fail. He encouraged the mindset that nothing was failure when you learned something from failing. The visits with a prospect or client became empowering. You had nothing to prove. You had no pressure. If you researched, put in the work and practiced beforehand, then you could show up and trust the process. Trust formed so much faster when you could say, "No, I don't know about that. Tell me more," and so on. *As far as failures went, we didn't have any! What we had instead was an empowering growth mechanism. Failures – zero; learning moments – every moment!* Every Monday morning, we'd have round table and share "Fist bumps and gut checks." The gut checks were the learning moments. We got vulnerable with each other and we even named our learning moments. Good, bad and ugly. What we found out was this – failures don't exist, unless you stop learning! Another thing we learned is that learning moments aren't good or bad, they're all good. So good, in fact, that David and I launched *Energy4Sales*, a sales coaching platform, and are co-authoring the sales playbook, *DAFT ... Stamping out daftness in the sales process.* Trust me. I was the beta test! It's all about being alright with failures and mistakes by realizing they don't exist. They are learning moments. Name them – summarize the life lesson. Empower yourself. Be vulnerable and build a powerful scrum!

While the best friendships form when two people become deeply vulnerable, the goal is driving together for results. *It's not chum time; it's scrum time – grow! Accountability's not laziness. You're responsible for you! Accountability allows for a different perspective and someone who can help you see your blind spots. Accountability ensures you stay driving for results in the event you just get off. It doesn't mean you check out of critical thinking or become dependent on your scrum. It's an interdependence – a gestalt mindset.* Your scrum helps you process and get concrete in complex decisions. Sometimes, a complex decision in life won't make sense to you. In these instances, I like how Jack Daly says, "model the masters." If you can see the outcome someone else is getting, and the fruits of their lives are good, then trust the process and model the behaviors they've tried and tested. Kind of like seal training – they've been there and have your best interest at heart. If it grows you and you trust your scrum, then model their behaviors and grow! Always apply your own critical thinking skills; however, avoid stalling. Learn to embrace growth – even the uncomfortable kind. Know that if you do ____ then it's likely you'll get _____ result. Like CEO of Amazon, Jeff Bezos says, "Most decisions should be made with about 70% of the information you need; if you wait for 90% or more, you're moving too slowly."

If your scrum is constantly trying to get you to grow, you don't need a coach as badly as you need honesty. Be honest with yourself. Your amazing and nothing you do changes that. Avoid falling into the trap of trying to impress your scrum with how hard you're trying or telling the little white lies – known as excuses – to your coach. You're not going to let them down being completely honest about where you're at. Be honest so you can grow! No success. No failure. Just growth! Challenge yourself and grow. Get ok with failure. Fail fast and learn faster! Seneca said, "If thou art a man, admire those who attempt great things, even though they fail." Theodore Roosevelt said, "The only man who never makes a mistake is the man who never does anything." Jack Lemmon once said, "Failure never hurt anyone; it's the fear of failure that kills you."

Vulnerability

Vulnerability is a deep word! It's a scary sounding word, but why? Our fear of what others think, perfectionism, being in control, past hurts we don't want to face, fearing, and unwillingness to face the truth about what's holding us back, and the list goes on. Here's the deal, vulnerability is viewed as a liability. We must change this paradigm in order to succeed. *Vulnerability allows us to dig deep, identify patterns of limiting beliefs, and be super accountable as we break free and charge forward. Accountability gets you in the 90th percentile; blunt, open vulnerability with a trusted coach can get you almost all the way guaranteed* (depending on when you get that coach involved along the process). Vulnerability is never easy. Tommy Spaulding who wrote about deep relationships in his book, *It's Not Just Who You Know*, states, "We're most vulnerable with those who extend to us their grace. When we offer it – or find it from others – we're able to let go of our pride and take some risks when it comes to letting other people see us for who we really are – not just the parts we'd like for them to see." Vulnerability is accountability on steroids – 10X accountability! Vulnerability is super intentional. You must purposely ask someone to be in what my friend, Jack Daly, calls the "boardroom of directors" for your life. You must start with vulnerability and form deep trust by revealing what's holding you back. Set up guidelines. Ask them to check in with you on a specific area. You must work at vulnerability. We all have a tendency to want to impress others. Whether a rigid upbringing made you feel inadequate and you live your adult life overcompensating, or you're simply a perfectionist and can't handle someone finding out everything's not perfect, we're all faced with the same fears. Break free by making sure your scrum is empowered with your tendencies and vision, so they can help you – yes, HELP, you – overcome the tendencies and press toward your vision! Ethics writer and scholar, Arthur Holmes, stated, "A community is possible among friends where their lives become like open books, they admit to each other their failings and bring to light each other's faults." This is a community of high trust. They discuss what they're working diligently to become and how each can help the other grow. This kind of accountability – your scrum – encourages self-examination, strengthens moral resolve, clarifies vision and builds good habits. Crave accountability and embrace vulnerability in your quest! Next, set specific goals and share these with utmost commitment. Nothing halfway. The beauty of an empowered scrum is them asking if what you're going after is really what you want. They may ask you if it's reasonable. *Yes, empower your scrum to call you out when they spot anything less than reaching for your full potential.*

When I was at a very dark spot of addiction in my teenage years, I remember a time my brother John, who was just about to get married, picked up on my external attitudes and sensed where I was at. He found me in the barn and said three very firm words, "Tim, saddle up!" Within ten minutes, we were trotting down the road, turning left onto the trail just outside of town and past the "Second Bridge." It was actually the second bridge from our house. We lived in a small, German village full of bridges, water-wheels and dams, as the WaldNaab river sent smaller creeks all over the countryside. As we turned onto the trail, the horses were very familiar with what came next. A minute of trotting past some ditches and then full gallop, out past the waterfall, through miles of fields and then up this beautiful road to the Hof (bed and breakfast farm). We didn't say a word the entire ride. I remember his look, though, when he told me to saddle up. It was firm yet empathetic. I knew he knew the struggles I was facing. Sure enough, we came to a halt just at the edge of some trees where the grass was green and lush. We let the horses chomp some grass as they rattled the bits in their mouths and blew the breath from their nostrils while shifting from hoof to hoof in anticipation of the ride home. "Tim, I know what you're up against; I was there, too." …. Thirty minutes of talking and sharing, and John opened, cleaned and dressed some emotional wounds that day that over the next few months and years would slowly heal. I began to understand vulnerability that day. Build a scrum of high trust. People you can get vulnerable with.

Relationship - Deep

Our scrum can help us experience emotion and stay connected. Our scrum is made up of people who care. I highly encourage you to pursue relationships with your scrum – deep, trusting relationships. *Relationships with which you KNOW you can share epic, universe-sized ideas with – big dreams, monster-sized goals.* Why? When you speak it, your RAS filter will test you by laughing at you. That's right. You may even laugh at yourself, get clammy hands or a shaky voice. Sound familiar? When you have someone that says, "Tell me more," and they sincerely want to believe in you and listen, they help you put clarifying details on our dreams. This is the power of the mastermind. Their mental energy and yours join forces and what may have been a lone, twinkle of a shooting star, now hangs in the sky for us to reach for. It's locked in, its claimed, its spoken and if pursued with full faith and unwavering belief, it will come to fruition. Do you have someone you create mental synergy with? Simon Senek, calls vulnerability something that must be willingly expressed. People only express vulnerability – the greatest stage of potential growth – when they feel a surrounding of immense trust. Most corporations can't even boast coming close to this. Typically, you sense and feel a ruthless competition, walls, and barriers of communication among teams. On the other hand, a common purpose, healthy channels of conflict and harmonious communication led by trustworthy leadership can create a togetherness mantra – no runaway, unhealthy competition. Some of the greatest leaders surrounded themselves with circles of people and inner circles of confidants. Nick Vujicic suggests, "when you're stuck and can't find a way out, look for help. Seek guidance from those with a wider perspective: a friend, family member, professional counsellor, or a public servant." Know this! There is always a way out. There are people in your life that love you and want to see the best in you! No matter what your mind is telling you, no matter what fears you're shrinking from, there is someone created for this unique moment in your life. Finding that person and trusting them to help you will be your deliverance and breakthrough! We become super grateful for the scrum and it makes us super thankful for all the people we get to do life together with. Your scrum helps you be ok with you; you in turn, tend to stay ok with others understanding everyone is fighting some kind of battle. The deep feeling of gratitude, nurtures relationships inside and outside of the scrum.

Resource - Huge

Vulnerability will completely change your life – if you'll let it. It can be your greatest asset! Huge power available to us when we open up! Do you nurture mentoring relationships? Do you have a accountabuddy, scrum or tribe you do life with? You're worth it! Guaranteed! Welcome the power of accountability and take your life to new levels! Realizing the huge resource that vulnerability is, let's build our scrum! Richard Koch states, "you alone cannot make yourself successful. Only others can do that for you. What you can do is to select the best relationships and alliances for your purposes." Here's the Energizer Accountability Declaration:

> "I embrace vulnerable accountability, and I purpose to seek out wise counselors and teachers. I will take advantage of their enhanced perspective, skills and advice that'll maximize my life and impact other lives."

If you are in the position or practice of hiring coaches in business or for your life, be careful of coaching programs that are merely cookie-cutter systems. While systems are so key, they were designed to create habitual repetition while tracking results. A good coach will have solid systems in their toolbox, but face-to-face must happen. The proverb says "Iron sharpens iron so the countenance of man his friend." Get a scrum around you with whom you can check in on the good, bad and ugly. Get a small band of people around you that make it impossible not to grow. Many people get stuck in ruts of actions they thought at one point were important, but due to the vibrant and volatile nature of ever changing business and life, some systems and even actions in business becomes antiquated. YOU should be empowered to come up with the solutions. Make sure you're checking in with skin and bones and **KEY** – they're getting you to think. Keep this in mind. Your scrum should offer ideas, solutions and fresh perspectives, but should never discount your amazing mind to the point of thinking for you. Does your coach or mentor get you to think? Do they ask questions? Do they listen? Building a scrum is not building a team. You're not delegating your work to your scrum. You're getting powerful minds and caring hearts that will get you to think! Pick your coaches wisely and find someone you can have fun with! Our *Energy4Execs* coaches have this mantra,

> "If you stop feeling heard, and if I stop inspiring you to think, find someone who does."

A great coach sees you for all your potential and possibly dormant energies. They breathe on your coals and you burst into life! More of you should come alive each time you encounter your scrum. A coach brings a different perspective to your life, serves as a great listener and sounding board for you and is a trusted confidant for accountability. Someone you can fully trust so that with complete disclosure you can truly move your life and business forward – not just have a "feel-good" session. A good coach will create synergy with you. Your two minds equal a greater force together. They always get your **VOTE** because these things happen naturally with them – you're not forcing a fit. You become a team:

V – Vulnerability is easy.
O – Openness is a two-way street.
T – Trust is easily established; they offer trust.
E – Easy to get along with; they know themselves and aren't insecure about their own strengths and weaknesses.

A good coach's METHOD looks something like this. It's so simple. Not easy – simple:

P – lifts your perspective; inspires you to think bigger.
O – clarity on ownership; defines next steps for results.
A – accepts 360-degree look; encourages relational connection.

When you leave, you feel refreshed, recharged, energized and inspired. It's like you took a drink of refreshing water - **H2O**. This is the feeling:

> **H** – Hears you; they listen deeply, ask questions and truly care.
> **2** – Two are better than one. A strong relationship forms. They want you in their life; you're more than a transaction.
> **O** – Only has your interest at heart; not manipulative.

And for the final ingredients defining what to look for when building your scrum, a good coach will look out for you. This is the **MAP** for what to look for in the person of the coach:

> **M** – Models the trait, connects you to the skill, or can get you to the place you wish to be.
> **A** – Abundant mentality. Invests and pours part of themselves into you. Loves you.
> **P** – Purpose drive. They help you dream, believe and achieve. Their eyes are fixed on your goal. They're your lifeline!

Think of the different roles in your life. Think of someone you know, love and trust that role-models what you're looking for. Are you a young person, married man or woman, manager, leader, business owner, or corporate executive? Obviously, every level of life brings different levels of challenges and opportunities. Write down your roles of life and then write someone's name next to that role. Some roles will require an accountabuddy, some roles a mentor, some roles a "Mr. Miagi" and one or two perhaps a paid coach. Jot these names down as they come to mind. *Schedule time to share a coffee or phone conversation and present them with your plan for adding value to their life while they work with you in and on life. Ask them to join your scrum, set healthy check-in frequencies, and start embracing accountability on steroids – vulnerability!*

CHAPTER 21
160,000 EYES
lighting the way for others

*"What you are thunders so loudly that I cannot
hear what you say to the contrary!"*
— Ralph Waldo Emerson

Breathing Confidence

"This ain't no practice life!" I remember this highly enthusiastic guy speaking at the front of the conference room. His black turtleneck under the olive-brown blazer gave a sharp appearance to the gathering of our company's leaders. He called attention to the front of the room by asking, "What do you want out of life?" He was sharing a Jim Collin's concept from Jim's book, *Good to Great*! The premise is that you can never be great at something unless you are passionate about it, can be the best in the world at it, or it satisfies your economic needs. I began thinking hard that day of what I wanted at 19 years of age. I decided I loved people and would bring harmony to the workplace. I decided I loved promoting and would align myself behind everything I could at work that would build my coworkers and encourage them to get involved and grow, too. I loved to inspire and so, I'd inspire everyone on the team to their best by being my best. *At 19, I was struggling with confidence and other emotional limiting wounds, but one thing I know, Michael Burt breathed enough confidence into me that day* to let me know my life and my light could light the way for my colleagues. I would strive for excellence and be the best in the world at what I did. Michael, to this day, is lighting the way for sales people all over the nation doing incredible things, never settling or cooling off – staying hot. He gave me a little book that day, and I highlighted page 23 were he wrote, "When you can enjoy your work then you will have the enthusiasm and energy to lead others." That quest for energy never left me. That day, was a pump priming for me the pump into discovering what true energy – wholeness, fullness and the abundant overflowing of real enthusiasm for life – was and is.

Ten years later, I met Michael again and we embraced like brothers. He was still up in front of the room inspiring people – this time it was hundreds of real estate agents. Michael and a host of mentors have lit the way for me. Every life I touch as I coach or speak, or through my books is fruit to their lives. *It's a victorious inspirational cycle that keeps on giving. When you choose to light the way for one person – just one person – you never know how far that one life may reach. The lasting effects and dividends are eternal.* Here's the amazing thing about accountability, though. When you accept all those counting on your light, you will run to form the scrum in your life! You want to be the best light you can be!

360 Degree Accountability

You can Google "best leadership books" and get a plethora of experts' titles: Maxwell, Covey, Collins, Burchard, Gladwell, Senek. There are many levels of leadership and great authors have and will write wonderful resources we should dig into. Why? We're all leaders! That's right. Did you know on average, a person meets 80,000 people in their lifetime? Wow! Leader you! Every single one of us who'll take a 360 degree look around us and scan the roles and relationships just a little closer than normal will realize we're leading someone. Even those with poor character still influence and lead others. Working with inner-city kids for seven years proves that even the drug dealer is a leader. You name any life role, unless you're the man on the moon, well, you're still a leader! Mom, dad, teacher, pastor, police officer, nurse, employer, employee, you name the role, and we can find at least a dozen people at this given moment in your influence of leadership. In my favorite Book on leadership, Paul the Apostle wrote, "Be an example," and Solomon admonished, "Walk with wise people and you'll be wise." I like how a *TIME Magazine* author said, "Leadership is not an image, it's a quality!" Can people call you an example or a wise person?

Look at yourself in the mirror. Look past the image, and look at your heart! You are a leader! Who will you impact today and how will you impact them? At this moment, a small portion of your life-time allotment of 80,000 people are watching you! Will you let them down, or will you go the way and show the way? Taking a 360-degree look around us, we'll find multitudes following in our footsteps, people counting on our example and someone not giving up right now because of our light. *Doing the right thing and making the right choice isn't always easy. At the point we're tempted to give up, let take a 360-degree look around us and recall this energizing and inspiring thought, "Someone is counting on our light, today."* McGinnis writes, "In every arena there is a vacuum waiting to be filled by some person who can impart vision and steer people's energies into the best endeavors." Sometimes you step up to the plate, and you feel like people around you don't believe in you. In fact, many will criticize you and pour cold water on your zeal. Why? Do they want you to fail. I believe they don't want you to fail as much as they don't want you to show them up. Yet, I believe something deeper is going on. I believe they really want you to succeed, because if you can do it, maybe – just maybe – they can, too. Those who hope you succeed may be your toughest critics initially. They've been burned and hurt before. They want to poke you full of holes and deflate you – that is, if you're deflatable. When you withstand it and rise above, even your critics draw hope from your life. Sometimes, lighting the way for others means your light shows up shortcomings and makes others uncomfortable.

Don't turn your light down to cover your own shortcomings or those of others. As a leader, demand excellence – yours first. As a leader, be first to admit failure – and grow. This demand for excellence and culture of growth won't always mean you're the most liked leader, but like Vince Lombardi put it, always "… hold it more important to hold the player's confidence than their affection." When the going gets tough and the party's over, people know who's held firm to excellence and who's integrity has always rung true to strive for peak performance! Their confidence will be in the tried and true every time. So, never apologize for being firm in your commitment to excellence. Never apologize for your dedication to growth. Never apologize for your resolution to live an energized existence! If the temptation comes to turn down the light, turn it up even brighter. Expose your own faults so you can grow and with your light, excellence and growth, others will follow. *Lift people to higher standards by raising your own.* Charles Schwab convinced the most acclaimed business men of his time to rethink industry standards. Those who are articulate must first listen, really hear, seek to understand and then desire the outcome and move in confidence to articulate the plan in the language of the beneficiary. Yes, if you're a sales professional or a mother, an executive or a teacher, your ability to hear and understand pain points of others and articulate a plan of action to overcome them in their language is crucial. Be willing to learn about them so you can light the way for them. Let not our goal be to change people for then our air becomes that of superiority; neither let us acquiesce to the insincerity of "accepting" everybody. Instead, let us call on ourselves to daily strive for excellence. Let us help others to clarify growth in their own lives and on their own journeys.

Our chief aim in lighting the way for others should be to enlighten their thinking. Tom Mullins said of leaders, "they must be good managers, but most managers aren't necessarily good leaders." John Maxwell profoundly said, "A leader must know the way, go the way and show the way!" In lighting the way for others, help them see possibilities in themselves. In lighting the way, we should get people to think and help them to see. That's it. And the best way to do it is by living it in your life consistently! Seize the day; light the way!

1 of 7 Billion

You and I can change the world! Like any dream, though, it's easy to succumb to the "elephant complex." It's just such a big idea – changing the world! Have you considered some very small bite-sized pieces like: smiling, complimenting, loving, praying, having manners, being polite, giving, small acts of kindness, etc. Some have said, "I've tried smiling, it didn't work." Wait! Don't discount you! Don't discount that you're one of seven billion people. Last time I checked, brilliant men like Fibonacci documented "1" as a counting number! Therefore, you count! If YOU smile, you're changing the world. You are one of the world! Your smile lights someone's world and in turn, it'll light your world. Your smile may just be the spark someone's fire needed before it went out. Your smile may be hope in a hopeless situation. You never know how something as simple and free as a kind-eyed smile might do. Albert Schweitzer said, "In everyone's life, at some point, our inner fire goes out. It's then burst into flame by an encounter with another human being! We should all be thankful for those people who rekindle the inner spirit." Are you a rekindler of people's spirits? Are your life and words lighting the way for others, today? What example do our kids see? If we discount ourselves, they'll likely discount themselves. Know this! *Changing the world starts with believing you can; then, realizing that you only control you is vitally important! Sure your actions are going to have ripple effects, but if you were the only change to ever occur, that would be enough.* Smile today because you're worth it!

Aesop said, "No act of kindness, no matter how small, is ever wasted." If you have a good thought about someone, or remember something they did, or they simply cross your mind, text them. You never know why they crossed your mind at that moment. Chances are, you were fully present with them when you met, and they mentioned something was going on that day, and your subconscious mind is signaling you to remember. It could also be your Creator signaling your heart to encourage another of His children and since you've been growing in spiritual wellness you're open to receive this prompting. Many simply shrink from the vastness of humanity and underestimate the POWER of one life. I love the story of the boy throwing starfish back in the ocean. Loren Eiseley writes it so beautifully:

> "Once upon a time, there was a wise man who used to go to the ocean to do his writing. He had a habit of walking on the beach before he began his work. One day, as he was walking along the shore, he looked down the beach and saw a human figure moving like a dancer. He smiled to himself at the thought of someone who would dance to the day, and so, he walked faster to catch up. As

he got closer, he noticed that the figure was that of a young man, and that what he was doing was not dancing at all. The young man was reaching down to the shore, picking up small objects, and throwing them into the ocean. He came closer still and called out "Good morning! May I ask what it is that you are doing?" The young man paused, looked up, and replied "Throwing starfish into the ocean."

"I must ask, then, why are you throwing starfish into the ocean?" asked the somewhat startled wise man.

To this, the young man replied, "The sun is up and the tide is going out. If I don't throw them in, they'll die." Upon hearing this, the wise man commented, "But, young man, do you not realize that there are miles and miles of beach and there are starfish all along every mile? You can't possibly make a difference!"

At this, the young man bent down, picked up yet another starfish, and threw it into the ocean. As it met the water, he said, "It made a difference for that one."

A story was told where someone asked Mother Teresa if the years and countless heartaches and ceaseless toils were worth the sacrifice. She stated, "I never think about the sacrifice." Instead, she looked into the eyes of the person she was serving and saw their beauty. Every life mattered to her, and one sparkle of joy, one glass of water received was worth ten times the struggles. *Oh, that we'd get past our own self-centered ambitions and agendas to realize the power of touching just one life. Just one life carries so much potential and possibility! Look for the miracles of one touch and let every action you take and every response you choose be one that lights the way for others because, it makes a difference!*

160,000 Eyes

Every life counts; every action counts. 80,000 people are affected by our lives on average. That means 160,000 eyes are watching us! Do the right thing no matter where you are – in public or in secret. Tears fill my eyes and my heart is squeezed every time I hear the Rodney Atkins hit- country song, "I'm Watchin' You, Dad." It's powerful! It ends with the young son telling his dad, "I wanna do, everything you do, 'cause I'm watchin' you." *Are you a person of resolute integrity? Are you true to what you believe in?* Do you alter your beliefs to what you think people want to hear? People will sense flaky all day long. People are used to chameleon sales people and have no higher defense. People will buy from the person who moves with integrity – they are the same all the time. Like my friend Jeff Carlton likes to say, they are "Solid!" These people can be counted on to be there like a mighty oak! They are true to themselves. Sales professional, have you been taught to be a chameleon, blending in with prospects and clients? I call you to a higher perspective. Value your client by listening to their needs and then create or add value to them. People don't buy from people that are just like them. They buy from people they sense are real and can be trusted. Schwab condemned the steel mill's unjust and unfair practices of the time in front of Andrew Carnegie himself. He called them what they were and won the affection of Carnegie – someone who believed Schwab's idea was a better way and bought into it. He trusted Schwab's integrity. This is an Energizer – to be; not to seem. "No man, for any considerable period of time, can wear one face to himself and another to a multitude without finally getting bewildered as to which may be the truth," said Nathaniel Hawthorne.

I used to struggle getting up to run. Part of the reason was saying yes to a late night the evening before. Getting up isn't magic; we actually want to get up when we get enough sleep. The bed felt so good, though. Comfort in bed; discomfort awaiting at the gym. Hmmm. The comforter was very deceptive! A decision to stay in bed is short-sighted. Falling back to sleep meant waking up in a rush, running out the door and eventually placing more discomfort in my life. Then, there's heavier traffic, getting to work late, stressing out, etc. Choosing the discomfort of the gym or the morning run would have been long term thinking. The main point here is this. The calm mindset I could have showed up to work with because of a run, exercise and quiet time that morning would have centered me, and I'd have been a calming force for all the people around me. Instead, my rushed sense had the same effect on others and made the day much harder. *One small decision, though never seen by anyone, was experienced by everyone!* And eventually, they all are. I've always loved the quote that says, "More is caught than taught." Authority on family relationships, Dennis Rainey, puts it this way in his book, *Pulling Weeds, Planting Seeds*, "As an impressionable young boy, my radar caught more of my Dad's life than he ever knew. During my perilous teenage years, he was the model and hero I needed … He taught me the importance of hard work and commitment … I felt secure and protected. Most importantly, he taught me about character. He did what was right even when no one was looking. He never cheated, or grumbled … his integrity was impeccable. The mental image of his character still fuels and energizes my life today." *When we allow anything to fill us that won't serve us and others, we lose out and rob ourselves and others of what could've been a powerful transformative experience. Whether we want to accept the accountability to the eyes watching our lives or not, the fact is, they're watching. Are we lighting the way?*

Underestimated Ripple Effect

Every action we take, every decision we make has a ripple effect. Someone will either be advantaged or disadvantaged by the choices we make. There are two principles that we should never forget. One is called 6 degrees of separation and one is called the butterfly effect. Both are the science behind the ripple effect. The butterfly effect is a concept that states that "small causes can have much larger effects". The term was coined by Edward Lorenz, regarding the formation of a tornado being influenced by small amounts of air being perturbed weeks earlier by something as small as the flapping of butterfly wings. Six degrees of separation is the idea that "all living things are six or fewer steps away from each other". Within six steps, a friend of a friend can connect any two people on this planet. Think about that for a moment! Wow! Lest we think our actions are insignificant, it would only take two people to pass on your one smile compounding quickly to equal 4, 8, 16, 32 … !

How do the names of Betsy Ross, Mary Pickersgill and Francis Scott Key relate? Well, here's a story of small, consistent, even seemingly insignificant actions that had tremendous, ripple effects. I sat contemplating the other night as Jen tediously stitched the final beads on a bridal gown's bodice. "Small, consistent actions compound quickly and result in beauty," I thought, admiring the sparkling beads. BOOM! That's when Betsy Ross came to mind. Not a president, yet she was working in her center of influence sewing flags for ships when George Washington approached her about a much-needed standard for the patriots. The *History Channel* reports that Congress had loosely designed the flag, but Ross finalized its brilliance (one of the reasons the stars have five points – not six). Do you know how Mary Pickersgill comes into the picture? Being inspired by Betsy Ross' flags, Mary sewed one of the largest star-spangled banners. Her flag was hoisted atop Fort McHenry where, just outside in the harbor, Francis Scott Key was negotiating an exchange of prisoners aboard a British ship. Trapped on the ship, he watched the eruption of a deadly bombardment on the fort and his countrymen that night in 1814. He watched Mary's flag "gallantly streaming" as the cannons lit the sky. After hours of emptying their arsenals of warfare on the newly formed America, the guns of the large fleet of British ships finally ceased. In the blackness of night, Key and others aboard the British ship waited with bated breath for the dawn to determine the fate of their countrymen and this symbol of liberty. As the early light began to chase away the darkness, he saw it. This banner of liberty stood, waving proudly over the fort – furling with hope in the morning breeze. Inspired, he penned, "The Star-Spangled Banner." Think of the ball games, ceremonies and grand events you've heard opened with our glorious anthem. Did your heart swell up in reverence? *What are you doing today mother, teacher, pastor, doctor, nurse, police officer, business owner? Do the "threads and needles" seem insignificant at times? Don't be weary in doing well; you're bound to reap the rewards! Consistent actions of integrity in your center of influence will compound greatly!* Like Betsy Ross, imagine the enormous ripple effect your actions can have! Let this vision energize you today!

I spoke to Jack Henry associates as we launched *Time4Energy*. It was my first large-scale, corporate presentation, and I was terrified. Mel Robbins was giving the main keynote next door and I was the breakout session. She was eloquent; gorgeous voice! Powerful and getting better every minute intensifying the internal fear I was sensing. When the two teams of agents flooded into the breakout room and I met them, they were going on and on about Mel Robbins keynote. "Oh no!" I thought. "I'm sunk." I asked, "What was the powerful take away for you?" Shannon stated, "Mel has this real simple formula for when you feel stuck or fearful, just count '5-4-3-2-1' and just start! Lean into fear and if you can count '5-4-3-2-1,' you can do anything!" Wow! What great advice and internally, right then and there, I applied it. I calmed myself, walked to the front of the room and began my presentation. *When one of the agents hugged me after and said she needed the message of ignited energy – living fully to love deeply – right then at a difficult moment in her life, I inwardly wept. My heart was squeezed and never stops being squeezed.* The ripple effect of Mel Robbins' keynote was immediate and compounded. I met Mel exactly a year later and this beautiful soul was still inspiring hope through 5-4-3-2-1! The powerful truth is this: you never know who you're touching!

Og Mandino, in his book, *A Better Way To Live*, shares a touching story. We've all probably seen the beautiful, "Praying Hands," in a card, a memorial-service handout, an ornament, a picture, or portrayed in some other hope-giving way. Have you heard the story? Here it is:

> "Back in the fifteenth century, in a tiny village near Nuremberg, lived a family with eighteen children. Despite their poor condition, two of the children had a dream. They both wanted to pursue their talent for art, but they knew full well that their father would never be financially able to send either of them to Nuremberg to study at the Academy. After many long discussions at night in their crowded bed, the two boys finally worked out a pact. They would toss a coin. The loser would go down into the nearby mines and, with his earnings, support his brother while he attended the academy. Then, when that brother who won the toss completed his studies, in four years, he would support the other brother at the academy, either with sales of his artwork or, if necessary, also by laboring in the mines. They tossed a coin and Albrecht Dürer won the toss and went off to Nuremberg. Albert, his brother, went down into the dangerous mines and, for the next four years, financed his brother, whose work at the academy was almost an immediate sensation. Albrecht's etchings, his woodcuts, and his oils were far better than those of most of his professors, and by the time he graduated, he was beginning to earn

considerable fees for his commissioned works. When the young artist returned to his village, the Dürer family held a festive dinner on their lawn to celebrate Albrecht's triumphant homecoming. After a long and memorable meal, punctuated with music and laughter, Albrecht rose from his honored position at the head of the table to drink a toast to his beloved brother for the years of sacrifice that had enabled Albrecht to fulfill his ambition. His closing words were, 'And now, Albert, blessed brother of mine, now it is your turn. Now you can go to Nuremberg to pursue your dream, and I will take care of you.' All heads turned in eager expectation to the far end of the table where Albert sat, tears streaming down his pale face, shaking his lowered head from side to side while he sobbed and repeated, over and over, 'No ...no ...no ...no.' Finally, Albert rose and wiped the tears from his cheeks. He glanced down the long table at the faces he loved, and then, holding his hands close to his right cheek, he said softly, 'No, brother. I cannot go to Nuremberg. It is too late for me. Look ... look what four years in the mines have done to my hands! The bones in every finger have been smashed at least once, and lately I have been suffering from arthritis so badly in my right hand that I cannot even hold a glass to return your toast, much less make delicate lines on parchment or canvas with a pen or a brush. No, brother ... for me it is too late.' More than 450 years have passed. By now, Albrecht Dürer's hundreds of masterful portraits, pen and silver-point sketches, watercolors, charcoals, woodcuts, and copper engravings hang in every great museum in the world, but the odds are great that you, like most people, are familiar with only one of Albrecht Dürer's works. More than merely being familiar with it, you very well may have a reproduction hanging in your home or office. *One day, to pay homage to Albert for all that he had sacrificed, Albrecht Dürer painstakingly drew his brother's abused hands with palms together and thin fingers stretched skyward.* He called his powerful drawing simply "Hands," but the entire world almost immediately opened their hearts to his great masterpiece and renamed his tribute of love "The Praying Hands." The next time you see a copy of The Praying Hands, take a second look. Let it be your reminder, if you still need one, that no one - no one - ever makes it alone!"

Subsequently, Albrecht Dürer became a leader in the movement known as The Graphical Renaissance. I often wonder if the depth of his works – unparalled at that time, and still today – stemmed from the depth of love for his brother? *Every action in life has a ripple effect; often times, it's a much larger effect than could have ever been imagined at first. Will this thought of the enormous potential we all possess energize us? Will we let it?* That by dropping a small, insignificant pebble in the pond we know the ripples will hit the bank on the other side. Everything we do, how we speak, carry ourselves, and touch others can have an enormous ripple effect!

Underlying Reality

Deeply in the heart of every human is a longing. Longing to be valued. Longing for identity. Looking for hope. When you've found healing, and you accept your priceless value; when you possess identity through vision and purpose, and when you take ownership and your actions are consistent and constantly valuable, you broadcast all of this and more to every life you touch! Your life gives healing and hope! When you choose virtuous acts, you tend to see the same virtue in others and in so doing, you either verbally or non-verbally communicate encourage-ment and inspire them to be more of the same. You find and inspire more of what you are. Our actions then carry a multiplication effect so enormous in fact, that if we truly realized the benefit of one small noble deed, we would set forth to do ten thousand more of the same.

Smile, light the world with your eyes, love and think purely. Work diligently and effectively. Encourage and inspire always. Similarly, a choice to hate, to fight, to accuse or to argue multiplies into more fighting, bickering and arguing. Your choice in the tiniest event and in the darkest night will either breathe life into fellow coals or be another stomp to stamp them out. It's the fable of the cold cinder and the burning lamp. They took a long journey together to see what they could find in the world. That night, the cold cinder wrote in its journal that the whole world was cold and dark. It didn't see a ray of light anywhere; only dark-ness everywhere. The journal the lamp kept told a completely different story. Wherever the lamp had gone it was bright and cheery, it had found no darkness. Buddha said, "If you light a lamp for somebody, it will also brighten your path!" *Light a lamp for somebody by helping them see their beauty. Help them see their value. Help them feel worthy. Give them identity by appreciating them! Sure, hate exists in the world. Many good-meaning people fight hate with all of its kin: judgment, anger, and even more hate. Instead, we can realize the underlying reality that there are hurting and undervalued people in this world. When your life speaks healing, identity, hope and inspiration, people will hold on to your example for all they're worth.* How do we best give people identity? Appreciate them. Find the good! There is nothing more worth giving to another than genuine appreciation! Here's another acronym for aiding our memory. **SAINT**:

S – Sincere
A – Appreciation
I – Is
N – Needed
T – Today

William James said, "The deepest principle in human nature is the craving to be appreciated." Mother, appreciate your child. When it seems like nothing more than whining, appreciate them for the times they've expressed gratitude. You will get more of what you focus on. Period. Leader, inspire your followers. Your life lights the way and your words breathe hope that they too, can progress upward to heights of living in abundant joy! May our lives breathe, "I believe in you!" May our eyes broadcast, "I'm looking for the best in you because I get to!" And, as we walk through this world lighting the way for others, may passionately proclaim this **Energizer Proclamation**:

"I want someone to look at me and say, 'because of you, I kept going!'"

There will be people your life touches that you will never learn about. I've heard countless stories of people who looked to someone for hope and inspiration and never told the person. Your kids will tell stories of you to their kids and grandkids. Your life story never ends! You are leaving a legacy every moment you live! What legacy are you purposing to leave? How bright is your light and are you lighting the way for others? Perform small acts of kindness everywhere you go! Drop pebbles; anonymously change the world! "Be kind, for everyone you meet is fighting a hard battle," said John Watson. Regarding this matter of kindness, we must work hardest to perpetuate kind deeds to those in our lives we've grown accustomed to or are familiar with! We must work to become emotionally whole and empowered so that we overflow emotional kindness to every human being! Travis Bradberry states, "Your emotions are powerful weapons, and continuing to think that their effects are instant and minimal will only do you disservice!"

When I was a teenager, I was casually walking back through the horse corral after picking up hay-bail twine. Out of the corner of my eye, I caught the flare of nostrils, the nipping of one horse towards the other, and a vicious kick which turned into several hundred pounds of a golden-brown horse hurling toward me! Wham! Down I went feeling the punching impact of a fleeing hoof jar my left shoulder. Fortunately, it had rained, and the corral was muddy breaking some of the hoof's impact. Emotions get going and tempers flare – and not just in the horse corral. It happens in our homes, workplaces, communities and the world! People get hurt. *We lash out and whether intentionally or not, we ding people's identity and worth. By-standers suffer, too – more than we'll ever know! Critical words cut deepest to those near us because those near us trust us the deepest – they've lowered their walls of defense. Friend, work to create kind habits of gesture, communication and life! Speak kindly!*

The common denominator in human longing and universal language screams identity. We all long for more life and greater meaning! Maltz says, "More living means among other things more accomplishment, the achievement of worthwhile goals, more love experienced and given, more health and enjoyment, more happiness for both yourself and others." One of the most important and eternal channels of energy is other people and our connection to them! Let's not refuse their help, nor the happiness and joy others may bring us. Let us not pause or hold back when we can give to them. Let's name pride for what it is, not self-worth or esteem, but insecurity that builds the facade of a greater importance or accepts lesser worth whimpering behind fear and victimization. When pride is rejected, and a self-worth is accepted, we will gratefully accept help from others, and we won't be too cowardly to give ours. We shall then annihilate prejudices, judgments and perverted ideas of self-importance. We will be yielding the highest relational dividends of identity, belief, acceptance, and the deep love of genuine appreciation!

Ultimately Relationships

Life ultimately comes down to the health of our relationships. *Relationships can be the greatest source or the greatest swindler of energy.* We are created for connection. In case we want to fool ourselves in drawing back, becoming reclusive or adopting a hermit-mentality, know that these, too, are also masks. They're more permanent masks. People who feel judged, criticized or scorned typically draw back. People who are stuck in a vicious cycle and lack the courage to reach out for help, begin living in a tight bubble. Connection is painful because it means facing broken promises. But, humans are created for connection. All of nature proclaims and encourages connection. Without connection, we limit our experience of living fully and loving deeply. John Andrew Holmes Jr. said it this way, "It is well to remember that the entire population of the universe, with one trifling exception, is composed of others." None of us are islands to ourselves. Think about your neighbors. Do you know them? I know times have changed from the "good 'ole days", but how much fear are we actually projecting into our communities making it easier for fear to thrive? Prudently reach out to introduce yourself and explore possible connection. It's one of the best and most human things you can do. You'll also feel happier at home, which is where many of us spend a good deal of time. Overflow blessing on your neighbors! Get excited about sharing spaces of our globe with people! Get as happy as a puppy gets when it sees a human-being! Why not? What stops us from enthusiastically connecting? Dig deep here and you'll very likely find some fears and prejudices. If you'll make becoming a connector a priority in life, you will change your life and your energy condition! When we connect, emotions happen in the greatest way. This means we're calling upon more or all of our energies (mental, spiritual, emotional and physical) when relating to others. Human connection is powerful! Relationships are so vitally important; in fact, they're the key to greater fulfillment and joy in life! Often, Jen and I walk the neighborhood at night and pray for our neighbors. It's a great feeling and you literally invest yourself into their well-being. Throwing leaves over the fence or senseless bickering with your neighbor won't even cross your mind when you're invested in them. It's shocking how much of our energy is swindled in those relationships – family and neighbors – designed to be the best, but where something's gone radically wrong.

There have been multiple moments of clarity, along my journey of emotional healing, where this 360-degree accountability principle has been etched deeply into my soul! It's realizing that life is ultimately about the health of our relationships. Our relationships with God, with ourselves and with other people. *Relational health and our trustworthiness are inextricable. 360-degree-accountability is realizing that we must be who we say we are – genuine, authentic and sincere. True to ourselves and a light for all those coming after us. Someone true and dependable; someone others can count on!*

As a young guy, my heart had been broken. I'd boxed it up and had divorced deep, emotional connection from all relationships. My emotional arteries were plugged; stopped up. I was afraid to be hurt again. A decision for pornography as a teenager turned to addiction, haunted my adult life and stalked my marriage. The desire grew, and because I couldn't find myself being vulnerable with anyone about my imperfect emotional state, I fell deeper and deeper into the hopeless chains of bondage. On the outside, I'd created this "perfect" life. Inwardly, however, fear, emotional disconnect and a longing to be valued ruled my soul. Sexual desire to me was an objectified, marketed, physical form – no deep emotional, spiritual and mental connection. Just physical fantasy. This allowed me to remove all emotional connection from it. Here was the most beautiful and strongest drive known to man, created to powerfully unite two humans in a spiritual, emotional, mental and physical bond; yet, in my life it was being ruined by this painful and lonely experience. Way before my addiction and even after finding freedom, countless relationships and homes have fallen to the viscous grip of pornography. But, is it really pornography? I've coached both men and women who struggle with its addiction. I've heard people rationalize it and remove its taboo, saying it's ok. So, let's remove the taboo. Yes, remove the taboo by realizing that pornography isn't the root issue. Both men and women's bodies are beautiful creations! Amazing and perfect in every way. A molecular formation, so divine, it can literally connect emotionally to other human beings and spiritually to a Higher Power. *Deep emotional wounds and spiritual hurts leave loss of identity and devaluation in our lives and here lies the real issue.* We are taught to wear masks in our society and measure up to someone's standard of perfection.

I remember finding the first magazine and literally becoming upset towards the person in whose possession I'd found it. Then, I'd seek it out on my own, and resentment toward that person grew to bitterness. I was stuck, emotionally wounded and addicted to mental and physical fantasy. Why write about this very "touchy" subject? Because it's treated as taboo and kept a touchy subject – so we don't touch on it or talk about it. Being completely honest, we'd have to agree it's not pornography that people struggle with the most. It's the lack of worth, loss of identity and emotional disconnection in relationships that form the real issues. We won't even give our own thoughts credibility because we feel little to no worth. We simply succumb to the oldest and strongest emotional stimuli instead of, by faith, installing new, mental programming that's pure and powerful! Someone or something is holding our worth over our heads and it's time we take our worth back. Many struggle with this addiction and want freedom. They've bought into the "ease" of pornography and a quick high. It's no different than overindulgence in food, wine or sex. It's no different than tobacco or drug addiction. There's a thrill, and a temporary happiness that, for a short while, numbs the emptiness and disconnect we feel.

There's a ton of energy in our sex drive. When we embark down the path of cheapening human connection – the deep connection – this wonderful gift of sex was designed to give, we waste our energy and drain our emotional bank accounts. We objectify another human being and literally become physical, empty shells moving about. Anything that takes the wholeness of a beautiful mental spiritual, emotional and physical being and objectifies it is wrong. Dictators have done it with people groups they wanted to annihilate. We do it when we look at someone's physical frame and glorify it with no regard to that person's spiritual and emotional state. We do it when we name-call, stereotype and disrespect any other human being. Isn't this what mediums such as magazines, television and the internet allow us to do? We aren't in the presence of another human being, we only see what's shown. It's not their whole being. It's not entirely true. It's not real. It's a mirage; a fantasy. The hole in our hearts that social media, TV, and the internet can never fill is the longing for being valued and deep connection! We attack one another in business, politics and religious circles. Do we think we can cheapen our fellow man in such disregard and be found blameless?

When we finally realize wholeness, we finally realize connection! If we are to leave a legacy and light the way for others, we must embrace our wholeness and the wholeness of every human being! We must realize what we think affects those around us; your eyes and body language speak your thoughts way before your words catch up. We must realize how we feel affects those around us; our emotional wellness will dictate the health of every relationship. We must realize our physical actions and spiritual connection all combine to create connection or disconnection with every life around us. This is paramount to creating healthy relationships – engage every relationship wholly!

While many have dampened or tuned out their sex drive because of poor lifestyle choices, or emotional wounds they're unwilling to face, the drive remains one of the most powerful. It's the only way any species continues to exist. Our drives within the corridors of natural design are healthy; any runaway drive can present danger to our thriving. Healthy boundaries allow any drive to remain strong, beautiful and bountiful! Healthy drives maximize and create value. Runaway drives break natural laws established from the beginning of time. Runaway drives break common sense if we're honest enough with ourselves to analyze and address where we've gone out of bounds. Runaway drives don't create value, not even for us – if we're honest with ourselves. If you're struggling with addiction, I understand. I've been there. It's simultaneously the easiest and hardest path! It's a mirage; a never ending black hole! All addiction is toxic.

Addictions result in a huge amount of lost potential, living in a fog instead of clarity, broken relationships and too often, loss of life. My first wakeup-call in this matter of addiction was my wife, Jennifer. Here was a princess of a lady. Someone I didn't want to hurt. She was beautiful inside and outside. Other than my mom, who I watched pray over me, write notes to me and believe in me, even when she was forced to disown me at nineteen, Jen is the lady whose spiritual walk revived hope in my spirit that life can hold deep, spiritual connection. Compared to the priceless gem she was, my addiction glared at me! I knew it had to go. Yet, the deep lack of self-worth made the struggle a dozen times harder than had I accepted my priceless value as a whole human being. *When I finally realized that life was awakened to fullness when the spirit, soul, mind and body were in congruence, then I found walking in integrity in all parts of self, made much more sense.* Understanding wholeness of integrity and the congruence of the parts of self that make up our entire being is key – absolutely **KEY**. Even in the beginning of our relationship, Jen and I didn't know how to deeply and emotionally relate to each other. The journey was slow and tedious – but totally worth it! Seeking to understand each other was important; getting to know ourselves was the secret.

Three years after being married, we decided to have kids. Here came my second wakeup-call which catapulted me headlong into the wonderful discovery of embracing accountability and deep vulnerability. The doctor visits, the ultrasounds, the beauty of a little soul being formed inside of Jen began unboxing my emotions. Little by little I began to feel again. As Jen's tummy grew, and I'd sing through her stomach feeling our feisty daughter kick and do cartwheels, I remember feeling the hot tears stream down my face. Then, came week thirty-five. It was a standard, weekly, checkup, but one they told Jen she was in active labor. Since we had already been to the hospital at week thirty-three to stop labor, we asked the doctor if we could return home to labor it out. We lived twenty minutes from the hospital and they agreed but cautioned us to get back as soon as the contractions became close enough, signifying delivery time. Talk about excitement. We laid everything out, again, and got the house cleaned top to bottom. My pressed, white shirt with stripes and a nice pair of jeans were ready. Around midnight, I collapsed onto the bed falling asleep to the rhythmic contractions Jen was having. Around 3 a.m., Jen shakes me awake and says two of the most excited words, "It's time!" We jumped in the car and literally flew toward the hospital. The highway's 65 MPH turned to 55 and then 45 MPH. When it's your first kid, though, everything's an emergency. And, at 3 a.m. there weren't any other cars on 231 North heading up to the town square and down to the old hospital on Highland. Coming into town, we passed a gas station and sure enough, blue lights flash! I didn't know what to do, so I put the flashers on, kept going, but rolled the window down and motioned my hand out the window. The officer pulled alongside of our Toyota, Yaris, glanced over, and at that moment in perfect timing, Jen had the contraction of contractions. She's raised up in the seat and I have a young, pale, scared, first-time-dad look as I look back his way. He motioned me to go – we did! We arrived to the hospital and by 6 a.m., Jen had done an amazing job of giving birth to our sweetheart, Nikki! Nikki was a preemie and after NICU gave her an examination and announced a healthy baby, they swaddled our four-pound, twelve-ounce, soft-skinned baby girl and brought her to Jen and me. That moment, a lot changed in me! My spirit, soul and mind were altered that night. From guarded and perfect, I changed to open and vulnerably imperfect.

My mind raced. I saw faces of the daughters of this man I know. He struggled with the same addiction and emotional disconnection that ultimately caused him to leave his family. These daughters became rugged fighters, strong, and rigid – they had to be. They made something for themselves in this world – carved their niche. But, deep down inside they had the same gaping hole for connection that I had inside of me. I heard some of them say, "I never want to see the man again!" The violated trust was sensed; it was real. I now get to support and encourage them in their individual journeys of forgiveness and emotional healing. *These thoughts were a huge wakeup-call for me. Here, my little four-pound, twelve-ounce, beautiful, first child and daughter, Nicole, lay tucked against my chest, her tiny soft head in my hand and her even tinier purplish feet barely reaching the bend of my elbow.* My mind raced. I saw her first birthday; and, watched her take her first step. I felt her hug me, snuggle with me, kiss me, and climb up on my lap dragging her favorite Precious Moments book behind her for me to read to her. I watched her tie her tennis shoes and start kindergarten. I watched her ride her bike without training wheels. I kissed her first boo-boo; and, I watched her walk confidently into the world with a sparkle in her eye. Then, I saw a different story – it was a horrid thought. All the beauty of what a little girl's life should be vanished – poof. My living in insecurity and fear cast an evil spell over her upbringing. There she was in my mind's eye living in fear of how she looked, insecure, and low self-worth – same as she saw in her dad. I realized that my emotional hurt and wounds cut off a deep, loving and pure relationship with her. This disconnection left her unconfident and seeking affection anywhere she could find it, instead of KNOWING her worth and walking into life with her head held high like the princess she is! I saw her suffering the same way I suffered – not knowing how to genuinely and emotionally connect with people. Images of her graduating high school flashed in my mind; then, cold chills as and I heard her scream in my face that she never wanted to see me again! I'd already watched this happen in real life; now, my ghosts of the future painted these drastic stories. One was young, innocent and peaceful. A beautiful and loving depiction of blossoming life. Life was meaningful and connection safe and deep where the castle walls were strong and secure. The other picture was cold, bleak and broken. This moment, as Jen and I lifted Nikki up and gave her back to our Creator, we promised to love her and raise her to the best of our ability. Inwardly, I promised to reach out and become vulnerable with some good people to help me replace old thoughts and emotional generators in my mind. In fact, a few months later, I reached out to my brother, then to a spiritual advisor, a parental mentor, a marriage counsellor, a purity accounta-buddy, a professional fitness coach and eventually a leading business coach – a powerful scrum with people that literally love me and I love them! *The overwhelming awareness of the shareholders in my life caused me to open myself to vulnerability. I couldn't risk failing my shareholders. All of a sudden, protecting my own ego by hiding behind a "perfect life" mask seemed ridiculous. I had to get vulnerable and quick. Name my pitfalls so they'd no longer have power over me and live in a new paradigm – one that these trusted people insired me to dream of and paint! I'm indebted to my counselors – my scrum!*

This is **KEY:** When you look all the way around – 360-degree accountability – and realize all the eyes looking your way – the shareholders of your life – you'll embrace vulnerable accountability! You'll run to find and build your scrum! I wanted so badly to be an emotionally sound and pure father who could connect deeply and wholly with my kids. Author Josh McDowell conducted two studies. Both strongly indicated that sexual woes were "less likely among teenagers who reported close relationships with their fathers." He continues that a married couple has the best chance to guide their children toward personal wholeness. "If open and positive communication channels are maintained, the richness of your own sexual security will strengthen the relationship. Your son will learn from you what it means to be a man and how he should treat a woman. He will feel comfortable about himself because he has one of the best guides available. Your daughter will gain self-respect and cherish her femininity." When she hears you praise her genuinely and express appreciation for her wholeness of character both inside and out, she receives a huge advantage as she searches for real, genuine love in world full of paper-thin men. McDowell states, "She'll be less vulnerable to the exploits of men because the authority of your life and love will provide a defense." Dad and Mom reading, *your life has authority. A genuine life, a real life, a person who is whole speaks volumes without ever saying a word. You live in your truth and get along with people. You don't have to change, because you're whole. Are you whole? Are your four parts of self in congruence. Is your internal dialogue matching what people see on the outside.* People are counting on you being genuine, authentic and sincere! How's your relationship with yourself? How's your relationship with your kids? How's your relationship with others? For the couple who can't have kids or don't have any yet, know this. Those of us from broken homes and broken relationships are looking at you and even more so since we need double assurance that relationships can work. As a hurt teenager, I watched couple after couple. I prodded extra deep as I was sure it was all fake. What is it really like behind closed doors? Fortunately, some couples stood the test. Yet, many families confirmed the same hidden turmoils happened behind their closed doors, too. Others sounded shocked and told of wonderful lines of communication and understanding with their parents. This gave me hope – hope I never let go of. I watched and re-watched my father-in-law's relationship with his daughters, and with my wife. I watched re-watched my parental mentor, Joe, and his relationship with his four daughters.

It's when we realize the impact our lives have that we'll go get vulnerable with someone. It's when we realize people are watching our life for hope and inspiration that we'll build the Scrum of our lives. There is no neutral ground. We don't act alone. Every action effects someone else.

Chapter 21

Every thought vibrates into someone else's thoughts. Every emotion either hurts or helps those we do life with. The level of our wholeness correlates to the wholeness of our family and our friends. Realizing that we're inspiring for better or for worse will require us to take life more seriously and open ourselves to accountability – the vulnerable kind. *Looking deeply into the 160,000 eyes watching us, seeing the sparkle and realizing those eyes are windows to an eternal soul will force us to realize we must be people of integrity – deep, whole and true energy!* Our life may only be the flicker of a candle today, but it can be a mighty lighthouse tomorrow! There is a powerful song I played on the piano as a kid. While pecking the notes, I struggled finding the right rhythm; but, the words imbedded themselves into my mind forever! They've had a lasting impression on me, and they sum up this principle of lighting the way for others so beautifully:

> "I would be true, for there are those who trust me;
> I would be pure, for there are those who care;
> I would be strong, for there is much to suffer;
> I would be brave, for there is much to dare.
>
> I would be friend of all—the foe, the friendless;
> I would be giving, and forget the gift;
> I would be humble, for I know my weakness;
> I would look up, and laugh, and love, and lift.
>
> Who is so low that I am not his brother?
> Who is so high that I've no path to him?
> Who is so poor I may not feel his hunger?
> Who is so rich I may not pity him?"

Every action, every touch and every connection lights the way for another! Don't ever lose this **KEY**! Dale Carnegie tells a story about how one nurse profoundly changed a life. He tells it so well and so heartfelt that I share it in its entirety below. The story is of a man, Martin Ginsberg:

> "It was Thanksgiving Day and I was ten years old. I was in a welfare ward at the hospital and was scheduled to undergo major orthopedic surgery the next day. I knew that I could only look forward to months of confinement, convalescence and pain. My

father was dead: my mother and I lived alone in a small apartment on welfare. My mother was unable to visit me that day. As the day went on, I became overwhelmed with the feelings of loneliness, despair and fear. I knew my mother was home alone worrying about me, not having anyone to eat with and not even having enough money to afford a Thanksgiving Day dinner. The tears welled up in my eyes, and I stuck my head under the pillow and pulled the covers over it. I cried silently, but oh so bitterly, so much that my body racked with pain. A young student nurse heard my sobbing and came over to me. She took the covers off my face and started wiping my tears. She told me how lonely she was, having to work that day and not be with her family. She asked me whether I would have dinner with her. She brought two trays of food: sliced turkey, mashed potatoes, cranberry sauce, and ice cream for dessert. She talked to me and tried to calm my fears. Even though she was scheduled to go off duty at 4 p.m., she stayed on her own time until almost 11 p.m. She played games with me, talked to me and stayed with me until I finally fell asleep. Many Thanksgivings have come and gone since I was ten, but one never passes without me remembering that particular one and my feelings of frustration, fear, loneliness and the warmth and tenderness of the stranger that somehow made it all bearable."

I'm dedicating this story to my sister Rachel and aunt Judy who are nurses as well as the millions of nurses, doctors, physicians and all in healthcare service who meet people at the most basic level of sustaining, prolonging or enhancing life. Perhaps the noblest of professions this must be. Consider though, where your profession intersects humanity. *Any time you are touching a life in some way, what kind of way are you impacting that life? Are you life-giving? Are you hope-inspiring? Are you a channel through which flows abundant blessing? Do you believe in people?* Or, do you have walls of defense up and constantly find yourself condemning, comparing or competing with others? What if everyone you met wasn't on some imaginary pedestal; instead, they were on a hospital bed needing a touch of hope. It doesn't matter what industry you're in, like someone said, "If they're breathing, they need encouragement." Are we lighting the way for others, today? Living fully and loving deeply?

CHAPTER 22
PAYING DIVIDENDS

creating raving shareholders

"The deepest principle in human nature is the craving to be appreciated." – William James

You Always Come Find Me

"What's the one thing you're thankful for, Jeremy?" The question came as we drove home one dark night and the kids were getting a bit restless in the back of the van. I had posed the question to myself and Jen to lead the way expressing gratitude for one thing each member of the family did or meant to us. Nikki's turn came and she expressed she was thankful for dates with Daddy, Mommy teaching her to cook (at seven, she loves to cook), Playing with Jeremy and Ethan each day, and having the little sister, Kaylee, she prayed for. Now it was Jeremy's turn. I was expecting the regular things parents do to be recounted. But, Jeremy's a deep thinker and took me by surprise. *The next thing Jeremy said I hadn't even thought of as a big deal, but his words squeezed my heart that I inwardly wept the rest of the drive home.* Here's what he said in his paced and deliberate, six-year-old way. "I'm thankful that you always come find me when you get home." What?! Wow! Jeremy is the guy who'll be in the middle of building a Lego robot, or some other invention where he'll stay, super-focused, even as his siblings run for the door when they hear me arrive home. Kissing and hugging Nikki, Ethan and Kaylee, I look around and go find Jeremy to kiss and hug him, too. Only a couple of strides to find this big teddy bear usually in his room or upstairs. A minute, maybe two. No big deal to me – HUGE deal to him! Apparently! That night told me more about emotional deposits of love than any of my readings or trainings. My heart did somersaults as this innocent picture of affectionate love, my kid, told me exactly what meant so much to him. I felt the tears start coming, and they didn't stop until we pulled in the driveway. This six-year-old kid who just spoke a simple piece of gratitude taught me so much that night! *How many small acts do I discount that mean the world to my people? How much love don't I express that could mean so much to another! I was challenged to amplify the connection and pouring deposits of love into people!*

Create Raving Shareholders

When's the last time we sat and listed the shareholders in our lives? Yes, wrote their names out. Those who are counting on you to succeed, those who want you to succeed, those who believe you will and those who have invested into your success. What about the names of everyone who's formed any sort of relationship with you, has invested in the corporation called "You". They really want you to do well, and your doing well will spill over on them in some form or fashion. When the corporation call "You" is whole and flourishing, you're leveraging all the investments up to this point in your life and you're living fully present today! Your living fully and loving deeply creates value and the shareholders in your life receive consistent dividends! This is the ultimate form of accountability – shareholders. Accountable to take responsibility for all those in your care. Accountable to maximize life for you so you can maximize life and love to them! Most think of accountability as their relationship with a mentor or coach and they stop here. This, my friend, is only the start. This is only the step up to the platform – yours. That's right! The people in your life are counting on you; they're counting on me! Are we sending them dividends very regularly?

Reality of Bankruptcy

When the corporation called "You" is languishing, you're overextended, constantly asking forgiveness, begging for investors and empty. This can last in business and relationships – for a short time. If a business fails to finally realize a profit, it will fold. Many relationships profess the same fate. It's interesting how we form relationships. We build relationships for a reason: friendship, love, networking, business endeavors, partnerships, etc., if for the most part, both parties feel they can offer something to the relationship. We call these relationships mutually beneficial. Further, a healthy relationship is a growing relationship. Mutually beneficial and growing relationships are what we should start out with! Sure, there are those people that look to use everyone they meet. After offering chance after chance, some of us have had to leave an emotionally toxic and hurtful, possibly even a physically abusive relationship. But, by and large, most relationships do not form with hurtful intent. So, what happens? How do tensions fester? How does distrust grow? What happens to make it easier to skirt around some very important issues that prevent growth from happening? What causes employees to criticize an employer, a child to disdain a parent, a husband to disregard his wife, a wife to dread her husband, or a friend to desert a friend? ***Relationships, our understanding of them and our interaction in them, are in direct relationship to our relationship with ourselves.*** Relationships can either bring the best or worst out of us. Relationships form at the sensation of trust and end at its desertion. Relationships too often are entered into with both parties wearing masks. As time goes on, we lower our masks. It's really hard work to wear a mask, so in our private spaces and out of exhaustion, we let them down. When we do drop these masks, and let our guard down, we become the truest form of ourselves. Too often, the other party begins to judge the things they either didn't know were there, or the things they don't like and believe should change. Instead of encouragement and gratitude for the good that's there, negativity bias sets in and we begin attempting to fix the other person instead of loving them unconditionally and encouraging them to become the best version of their unique selves.

Lack of self-awareness means lack of social awareness. Many are searching for themselves and for fulfillment. They're drained and looking for energy externally instead of becoming whole and energized internally. We're insecure deep down inside, because our value is based on others judgements and what they think of us. We may be holding ourselves to an unrealistic standard or have past emotional hurts that we've never healed. So, when someone opens up and trusts us with their emotions, we go to fix in them what we see in ourselves. *When trust is given and an openness occurs, violating this trust is the quickest way deep emotional wounds are formed. And it happens so quickly in the deepest relationships because walls and barriers are down. We know the weaknesses of the other and they're the easiest to hurt.* When we feel attacked and our trust has been violated, we feel betrayed and hurt. Deep wounds left unforgiven and unhealed suck our emotions into a negative flow. We operate life holding back, mistrusting, judging others, cynical, skeptical, hurt, resentful, taking advantage of, hating and even lashing out. This is how abuse in relationships begins. Sociologist Murray Strauss states, "The true rate of physical abuse within marriages involves approximately fifty or sixty percent of all marriages rather than just the twenty eight percent who report it." Whether it's physical abuse, verbal abuse, financial abuse, or emotional abuse through intimidation, humiliation or going silent, we somehow form resentment where once we found rejoicing. In compelling men to be the loving fathers and husbands their families are inwardly languishing for, Tony Evans proclaimed, "Never before have we needed such urgent intervention … just last year alone, nearly one million students failed to graduate high school. Over one million prisoners were high school dropouts. Over 750,000 teenage girls became pregnant. Close to one million marriages ended in divorce. All of this cost our nation over $300 billion in lost revenue, public assistance and expenses. Not to mention lost fortunes and lost hopes." Fikkert and Corbett write, "Poverty is the result of relationships that do not work, that aren't just, that aren't for life, that aren't harmonious or enjoyable. Poverty is the absence of peace in all its meanings." When there's discord in relationships, no one has fun. Basically put, we entered a relationship with high hopes and expectations that weren't met. Blaine Lee, author of *The Power Principle* claims, "Almost all conflict is a result of violated expectations." We went into a relationship looking for emotional healing that didn't happen. Silently, we demand too much from the relationship.

No one hears us, but they sense and begin to feel a growing resentment. The relationship we planned on satisfying us whether friendship, marriage, career, church, social group, and so on, turns out becoming an emotional drain, a nightmare in which we feel trapped. We focused so much on the golden egg of what this relationship should be producing (our expectations), we stopped creating value of investing in the goose. We kill the goose and the golden-egg production stops.

This relational over-expectancy and emotionally-wounded tradition affects kids – greatly. Again, Tony Evans says, "In suburbia, many fathers have gone 'missing' either through divorce, neglect, or overindulgence." The people who were supposed to teach connection have become disconnected. Oftentimes, leaders will carry airs about them and remain disconnected. This affects followers – greatly! Rivalries and factions form – the leader's emptiness and pursuit to fill emotional voids through ego or fame is to blame. Many religious leaders bite and devour one another. The ones who should hold the greatest responsibility of spiritual connectedness model fighting instead. Self-righteousness and judgement exude from many religious organizations. Instead of loving people, a disconnected, discounting and divisive atmosphere prevails. This affects spiritual followers – greatly! The world languishes for worth; instead, we compare and compete to be the greatest. *This facade of self-righteousness is a vicious traitor. It has sent many into shameful and fearful obscurity – completely disconnected.* I empathize for leaders who either hold themselves, or are held by others, to some unrealistic standard of perfection and the glass-house of disconnectedness. Instead of humanity marching forward together in pursuit of deep connection and loving relationships, we've allowed ourselves to believe that conflict and strife are normal and should exist. When they don't, we create exactly what we believe should be. Instead of adding or creating value together; we hold back, calculate, languish and wither up heading for relational bankruptcy and lonliness!

Relational Dividends

When a corporation is profitable, it can invest the net profit into owner's equity or send dividends to shareholders. Too often we're running on "E" and aren't able to add a lot of value to what we touch and do. Further, we've not even thought about how to add value. We've not laid out any plans of adding value to our circles. Adding value is not difficult at all; but, it does take the right mindset and intentionality. Further, having a game plan will prioritize those things that make us whole and flourishing so we can show up wholly and fully! So, if you're on "E" start by asking yourself how you can create value. Ask your Scrum and listen. They may have insights you haven't thought of before; or, they may see things in you that you don't even see in yourself – yet! I hope these two words sink into our hearts for the rest of our lives and literally permeate every relationship. If you need to remember it by **CV**, then think about letting the core value of your life be "Creating Value." *Ask, "How am I valuing this person, adding value to them, and creating value in our relationship?"* If we let this question guide us, then, every relationship will benefit and we'll create raving fans in our homes, our families, our friendships, our circles, our networks personally and professionally. Life is then seen as the gift that it is - one you can give over and over! Nothing other than value. It's utilizing the **Triple A** of relationships: **Always an Appreciating Appraisal**! Never depreciating the other. Always building-up, bolstering, encouraging, inspiring and uplifting one another!

Most of us have at least one relationship where things are not working properly. Could it be that what we've learned is off a bit? Could it be our own beliefs are limiting us? Could it be that we're calculative instead of flowing love freely? As a young man, I've heard some fathers say you should never apologize to your kids, "you're the king of your home", etc. I've watched the adverse effects of dads unwilling to admit mistakes and sincerely apologize. While I believe strong leadership is key, this mindset doesn't really depict strong leadership. It's emotionally wounded leadership. I believe the strongest leaders are those who are the most human, connectors, authentic and okay with being imperfectly perfect. There are times when apologizing to our kids or those under our leadership is absolutely necessary! Dale Carnegie shares the story of a father constantly finding fault with his son. Instead of keeping up this guilt-driving behavior, the father apologizes to his son. This story is so impactful, it's hanging inside my bathroom cabinet door for a daily reminder. I will also share it here:

"Listen, son, I'm saying this as you lie asleep, one little hand crumpled under your cheek and the blond curls stickily wet on your damp forehead. I have stolen into your room alone. Just a few minutes ago, as I sat reading my paper in the library, a stifling wave of remorse swept over me. Guiltily I came to your bedside. There are the things I was thinking, son: I had been cross to you. I scolded you as you were dressing for school because you gave your face merely a dab with a towel. I took you to task for not cleaning your shoes. I called out angrily when you threw some of your things on the floor. At breakfast I found fault, too. You spilled things. You gulped down your food. You put your elbows on the table. You spread butter too thick on your bread. And as you started off to play and I made for my train, you turned and waved a hand and called, "Goodbye, Daddy!" and I frowned, and said in reply,
"Hold your shoulders back!"

Then it began all over again in the late afternoon. As I came up the road I spied you, down on your knees, playing marbles. There were holes in your stockings. I humiliated you before your boyfriends by marching you ahead of me to the house. Stockings were expensive - and if you had to buy them you would be more careful! Imagine that, son, from a father! Do you remember, later, when I was reading in the library, how you came in timidly, with a sort of hurt look in your eyes? When I glanced up over my paper, impatient at the interruption, you hesitated at the door. "What is it you want?" I snapped. You said nothing, but ran across in one tempestuous plunge, and threw your arms around my neck and kissed me, and *your small arms tightened with an affection that God had set blooming in your heart and which even neglect could not wither.* And then you were gone, pattering up the stairs. Well, son, it was shortly afterwards that my paper slipped from my hands and a terrible sickening fear came over me. What has habit been doing to me?

The habit of finding fault, of reprimanding - this was my reward to you for being a boy. It was not that I did not love you; it was that I expected too much of youth. I was measuring you by the yardstick of my own years. And there was so much that was good and fine and true in your character. The little heart of you was as big as the dawn itself over the wide hills. This was shown by your spontaneous impulse to rush in and kiss me good night. Nothing else matters tonight, son. I have come to your bedside in the darkness, and I have knelt there, ashamed!

It is feeble atonement; I know you would not understand these things if I told them to you during your waking hours. But tomorrow I will be a real daddy! I will chum with you, and suffer when you suffer, and laugh when you laugh. I will bite my tongue when impatient words come. I will keep saying as if it were a ritual: "He is nothing but a boy - a little boy!" I am afraid I have visualized you as a man. Yet as I see you now, son, crumpled and weary in your cot, I see that you are still a baby. Yesterday you were in your mother's arms, your head on her shoulder. I have asked too much, too much." - W. Livingston Larned

The person who understands that relational bankruptcy can occur and seeing the devastation on the horizon will take brutally honest steps to apologize and re-establish trust, will be on their way to creating raving fans! Lest you fear a relationship is too far gone, realize that many of us do not know how to give a sincere apology. Most apologies are given with calculation or expectancy of response. And while this story is from the perspective of a father, please hear me well. If you're a wife, mother, executive, manager, leader, business owner, sales professional, politician or other official, educator, child, sibling, or another husband or father like me, face the elephant of relational tension in the room. Everyone knows it's there. My friend, Andy Bailey, tells the story of the bison. When there's a thunderstorm on the horizon, the bison embrace it and run headstrong into the storm. They get it over with and in the past so they can move on in life. Cows on the other hand run from the storm until inevitably being overtaken by it. By running from it, they only prolong the pain. *Be the Energizer who embraces conflict, makes peace and humbly allows the emotions of others to flow – good and bad emotions at first, until love is the prevailing result.* Open the pent-up tension and take the initiative to allow healing to happen. Take full responsibility –

calculating nothing; or, this advice won't work. Too many of us are after building our fortunes that we won't even stop to consider the devastation we're leaving in the emotional bank accounts of our relationships. Og Mandino said, "It's good to have money, and the things money can buy, but it's good, too, to check up once in a while to make sure you haven't lost the things that money can't buy." At the end of life, what's going to be most important to you? Consider.

You may have fairly loving and healthy relationships right now. What are you doing to deepen and strengthen these? The time you spend with your family and with people should not be second thought, it should be first thought – always! Fully present! Efficient with your time, but not with people, as Covey once said. In business as in life; it's ALL about deep connections and loving relationships! Bob Burg and John Mann powerfully share in their book, *The Go-Giver*, that "a genuinely sound business principle will apply anywhere in life – in your friendships, in your marriage, anywhere … the true bottom line is not whether it simply improves your financial balance sheet, BUT whether it improves your life's balance sheet." These are the lessons we learn of how to be a friend, how to care, how to make people feel good about themselves, and like Burg and Mann point out, these are things "the marketplace wants very much – always has, always will." Will we take responsibility and embrace the truest form of accountability today? *Will we practice and practice and practice until we're realizing consistent emotional profits and able to yield dividend upon dividend into our relationships?*

Cultivating Sincere Relationships

Cultivating relationships takes time. Cultivating relationships takes a desire to responsibly step up to the plate and light the way for others. There are professional skills learned to enhance a client relationship, sure. But, what about a deeper formed relationship because you genuinely value and love the other human being. Expressing that love sincerely is key in paying dividends to our shareholders no matter if that's in business or life – it's all one! Here are the **7 T's** to cultivating sincere relationships.

Time Invested

At the end of our lives, we won't wish we made more money or put more hours in at work. What we'll wish is that we'd have spent more time with the people that mattered most in our lives. Dr. James Schaller wrote the book, *The Search for Lost Fathering,* and recounts the story of a man who spent an entire night on a fishing trip with his son. That night, the father – who was a nationally known figure and commanded a lot of influence – wrote in his diary, "I went fishing with my son today; it was a day wasted." The son also kept a diary and also wrote about the trip; except, what he wrote was completely different, "Went fishing with Dad today – best day in my life!" *For many of us who are fathers, mothers, business owners, leaders and friends, we don't realize the amount of power we hold in our own hands. We limit our perspective and don't realize what our life means to someone and what investing some of that life into them and with them might do for them and mean to them. Time invested into an eternal being is an eternal investment; are we investing wisely?* Dads, when we get home from work, our real work is just beginning. If it means taking a shower or hitting some pushups to get the heart pumping or sitting in your car in the garage for ten minutes to defrag your brain so that you can fully engage your family, it will be well worth the effort to show up fully. Dr. Meg Meeker, in her book, *Strong Fathers, Strong Daughters,* states, "You will influence your daughter's entire life because she gives you an authority she gives no other man." In fact, she goes on to say it would terrify most men if they really realized just how significant their influence on their daughter's life is. It would catapult you off the couch. You'd switch off the television and you'd snatch her up and take a walk, color a picture, plan her college hunt, whatever it is. Whatever your role in life, you hold authority – someone's watching you. Someone needs your investment.

Focus on investing time on common interests in relationships. Accept that there are always going to be differences between any two people. Just look in a mirror with any other person and it'll confirm this. Focus on what the other person likes, wants and needs and the relationship will blossom. It's a proven statistic that each common interest between people in a relationship increases the likelihood of a lasting relationship. Most of the people who attest they share very little common interests probably haven't explored all of their own interests, written them down, and compared notes. Try it. It might surprise you. Jen doesn't care for Chinese-food or fish. She's graciously offered to cook them, but I asked her not to. These categories for me can be covered at lunch with friends or on trips. At home we thrive in common interests. I love riding bicycles and did this growing up. Most cycling groups take more time out of Saturday than running does. So, I chose running back in 2014 and it's been a wonderful form of exercise for me. Most times, unless it's a marathon, I can get out early (as early as I like) and run, getting back before the kids are waking. Jen and I love building business together, taking walks, travelling, watching Hallmark movies, and raising our kids. We have dream boards full of stuff as life phases move from toddlers to teens and so on. Before kids and after, intentionally cultivate common interests.

Total Listening

When's the last time you intently listened to another person. You showed up into their life, their space just to listen. No agenda. Ask open ended questions to learn more. If you could … If you had … How would you … What is something … When did you … When have you … When was the last time… and so on. "Why" is more indicting of a question and should be used in deeper and more crucial times of decision. It's power-ful. Why does this mean so much to you … as opposed to … Why did you do this. A question like, what caused you to make that decision … is easier. See the difference? Ask open ended questions and be genuinely curious. *Most of the time, especially today, our kids, our coworkers, our friends, our employees, and our networks are competing with technology for a piece of us.* We have one eye and ear on them and the other eye and ear on our cell phone, Bluetooth watch, computer screen, email inbox, or cluttered desk analyzing what we must do next when they leave. This competition is ongoing. Kids often will act – good or bad – to simply see if their parents are watching according to Dr. Meg Meeker. They want to be noticed; they long to be listened to. When you halfway listen to anyone, it's an emotional hurt – very small. We've gotten used to it in society. The time halfway listening hurts the most is when kids are real little. They grow up learning to do and accept the same – this is shallow connectivity; poor listening.

If you run, walk or drive through any city, you're bound to see vivid colors and paintings on bridges, buildings, train-cars, etc. I remember getting upset when I saw graffiti. It was such a disturbance to what was once a pretty structure – well, maybe not the train cars. "Vandals" and "gangsters" are the labels we've given these destructive expressionists! But, have we stopped to ponder the lesson in graffiti? Since working with inner-city kids and having kids of my own, I realize that too often I'm the one to blame. I arrived home a couple months back and Nikki greeted me at the door with a huge hug and said, "Daddy, I drew this story, wanna hear it?" My quick response was "Sweetheart, give me a second to put my things up, and I'll listen to the story you wrote," I was about to close my eyes to sleep that night when I sat up to full attention – I'd forgotten. Redemption happened the very next moment we had together; but, the thought of the times I haven't taken the time to listen remains a wrench in my gut. *Maybe we've allowed life to get too busy with everything else besides scooping up a loved one to do NOTHING but listen. Ask questions about how they're doing, feeling, what they're thinking about, etc.* Imagine the difference in these "vandals" and "gangsters" should some leader in their pasts have taken the time to listen. Listening is caring. Listening is powerful! We've heard the saying that we have two ears and one mouth for a reason. Take it from someone who enjoys speaking, the most powerful words are the ones you hear – not speak!

Interpersonal communication (IPC) is a huge deal for any relationship in life and any business or industry. It's especially important for physicians, physician's assistants and doctors to master! *The Reader's Digest* once said, "many people call a doctor when all they want is an audience. "Studying patients and doctors, interpersonal communication experts state that just the feeling of being rushed versus the feeling of being heard holds a huge contrast in the outcome. A patient's level of satisfaction is greatly reduced if they simply feel they weren't listened to. How many lawsuits are filed simply because people felt they had no other recourse – they weren't being heard so they resort to this option of being heard. How do you make people feel? Maxwell says, "Immature leaders lead first, then listen afterward." Many a professional will learn the professional graces of listening to those he leads or listening to the clients he serves; yet, when entering the door of his abode, the farthest thing from his mind is listening to his wife and kids. Some of this is simply a physical plea for retreat to a quiet place. Then, let us retreat to a quiet place of thought, rest and recharge before entering in to greet the greatest shareholders of our lives. Too often, though, there is no financial gain to us in sincerely listening to those we love – so, we skip it, or halfway listen.

Real, deep communication. Listening deeply and responding lovingly with value. When does it happen? Tommy Spaulding calls communication a "super routine" in his life. No wonder he understands, practices and speaks on **ROR – Return on Relationship**! In his book, *The 5 Love Languages*, Gary Chapman paints the picture of quality conversation shared with your spouse like this, "focusing on them, drawing them out, listening sympathetically to what they have to say. Asking questions, not in a badgering manner but with genuine desire to understand their thoughts, feelings and desires." Think in terms of their outcomes - needed service. *Create value for your spouse, kids, colleagues by giving them a safe environment of deep and total listening! Seek to understand! Listen to understand.* The psychologist, Carl Rogers, wrote in his book, *On Becoming a Person*, "When someone expresses some feeling, attitude or belief, our tendency is almost immediately to feel 'that's right,' or 'that's stupid,' 'that's abnormal,' 'that's unreasonable,' 'that's incorrect,' 'that's not nice,' and so on … rarely do we permit ourselves to understand precisely what the meaning of the statement is to the other person. My business partner and I are publishing the book, *Sales Daftness*, basically recounting stories from our days in sales and making it ok to fail – aka learn! Too much pressure is put on sales people to be perfect. Be human, I say, and constantly learn. Make mistakes and grow. One chapter in the book is "Catering to Cato." Simply put, a client complained to me about my voicemail greeting, which I change every day to include the date and a quick inspiring word – usually 15 seconds long. I jumped right in to defend my greeting and how so many people appreciate it, yak, yak, yak … David interrupted me and asked our client if she knew the asterisk trick? "What's that?" she asked. "You can push the asterisk and go straight to the beep," David explained. "You mean when I call my brother, and my mom, and my other suppliers I can get straight to leaving a voicemail?" she asked surprised. "Sure can," David said. He sold technology in a past life and he would know. He also coached sales for years and knew that she really wasn't complaining at Tim's voicemail. He heard her – her pain. It wasn't about me at all; I was the one who made it about me. Seek to understand. Listen, not to the words being said, but the pain being expressed. Listen from your shareholder's point of view! Empathize with them. Put yourself in their shoes. A wise business coach of mine, Mark LeBlanc, told me once that he's part of the "Listener's Association." I chuckled and thought he was jesting until I looked them up and joined myself. I figured becoming a better listener would be a top skill to learn and fine-tune the rest of my life. *Raving shareholders won't be made as long as the gift of truly listening is at the top of their wish lists and continously undelivered.* In fact, they may stop believing it's ever going to happen unless we inspire the belief again by practicing it, today!

Talk About Them

People love to talk about their dreams, goals, feelings, likes and dislikes. We all do and we often listen to someone's story until a similar story is sparked in our mind and we begin to process how we're going to share when they finally finish. We've all been there. Know who you are and where you're going so well, that you aren't using every conversation to talk about yourself. Then, be courteous to those people who do use every conversation to find themselves. Help them by asking them about their dreams, their passions and their feelings. Our conversations today can be so very superficial. We talk in terms of possessions and favorite sports teams. We talk in terms of what we know and commonalities we share instead of being curious and just finding out something new and obscure about another human being. We rarely talk emotions and deep feelings. This is where an Energizer's ears perk up. When you're emotionally whole and abundant, you have emotional service you can render. You can offer a safe conversation because you know what hurt and healing look like and you can talk about feelings without judgment.

Here's where those of us as dads and moms can succeed. Cut past facade and allow your kids a safe zone to share anything with you without getting in trouble. Root for them!

Superbowl rolls around. Millions of people will watch two teams battle for this notable, American championship! Living in Germany, football wasn't even a thing; well, it was – soccer! Football is so interwoven with American culture and does a ton of good for young people, colleges, team spirit, charities, business, etc. Most Americans will make time to watch football! We make time for the things that matter to us. ***Here's the million-dollar question, though. Do the things that matter to us hold eternal value?***

Last week I visited one of my inner-city kids. He was tossing his football vertically into the air and catching the return. "Junior," I hollered, "right here!" Within 10 minutes, 20 kids were out playing with us. Simple example, but here were a group of kids just waiting for someone to take time for them! Eternal value! That's it! I want to make time in my life for people, for inspiring and encouraging others wherever I'm at. People are eternal beings, so making a difference for somebody is eternal work! While rooting for whichever team is yours, think about who you're making the time in your life to root for? Eternal purpose ignites our deepest spiritual energy – guaranteed! BOOM!

Quality conversation requires not only listening, but also talking and sharing what's going on with you. Allow your spouse the blessing of feeling your joy and pain so they can unite with you, bond in strength and sense such sweet unity that is designed especially for marriage. "Most people are more concerned about the Middle East and a hundred other friends than they are concerned with their spouse," Gary Chapman points out. While this may seem absurd, it's evidenced by our disproportionate news watching and scrolling of our social media. Are we instead talking about them?

I read a story Dale Carnegie shared about a salesperson that tried to sell a product to the head manager of a hotel for two straight years. Finally, in desperation and having invested in human relation training, the salesperson decided to find out what the manager loved. He loved talking about professional greetings having joined the Hotel Greeters of America. The sales person approached him on the subject of greeting, said nothing about his product, and before two weeks were up, an order was placed by the hotel manager. Disraeli, who Carnegie called, "one of the shrewdest men who ever ruled the British Empire," said it like this, "Talk to people about themselves, and they will listen for hours." Get to know your shareholders. When's the last time you asked your partner about their dreams? What ignites their energy? When's the last time you asked your kids what they wanted to do? What they wanted to be when they grow up? When's the last time you asked your client what they love doing in life? What aspirations they have? What hobbies they enjoy? Get to know your shareholders – radically. Just because you can and since people love when you take genuine interest! Seriously, think about it. *You may ask a question they literally never thought of or asked themselves and you may open an avenue of life up to them they never lived or thought about; thus, you will have helped them live a little more fully by simply caring a little more deeply. You cared enough to ask. BOOM!*

Perhaps the simplest key to remembering to talk about someone is remembering their name. Phillip Bossert said, "Interest level is measured by how much we remember." Have you ever met a stranger or prospect or community member at a social gathering and a minute after introducing, you forgot their name? I have. This is because I was thinking about what to say, instead of engaging in fully listening and deep connection. The importance of remembering and using names is not just "the prerogative of kings and corporate executives," says Dale Carnegie, "It works for all of us." Value people and talk about them by first remembering their names.

Touch Empoweringly

I've had to cleanse my mind of a society's disregard for not just women, but all kinds of people. We see an advertised Hollywood agenda or Playboy model that does nothing more than take a creation of amazing emotions, soul, spirit and physical beauty and objectifies and exploits it. We see sports stars elevated to stats and literally worship what they can do with inflated leather. Awe inspiring – absolutely. Back flip over the defender to catch the pass in the end zone? I'll jump off the couch cheering at the top of my lungs every time. Problem is, this talent runs skin deep many times and we hear the sad reports, the abuse, the drug use, the failing relationships. My heart hurts for these dear souls. The pressures of society to look a certain way, be a superstar or model all come with a hefty price tag. Dr. Meg Meeker shares a sad statistic that the majority of girls crave their father's touch, especially as a teenager, and they never receive it. Whether it's because a dad feels awkward because of society's objectification of women, or afraid of connection, or whether pop culture tells us, "girls need their space," Dr. Meeker says, "Just be her dad: be confident, defend her and be supportive, and don't back away from hugging her." Dads and moms, we have the incredible responsibility to wage war on the media messages that fly fast and furious to destroy our children's purity and innocence! Talk with them openly about their physical bodies and beauty and always tie it to a more glorious and wonderful emotional, mental and spiritual wholeness. The physical is what we can see; teach them, by the eye of faith, to see, feel and sense the whole picture. Help them understand you can't act in one dimension without affecting the whole! *Keep physical touch the wholesome and connective gift that it is. Discuss the glorious spiritual, emotional and mental connection that accompanies all physical connection. Purify your mind. See people as the beautiful creations they are.* Think at this higher frequency and you'll realize the wonderful ability and tremendous power to tune out a lot of media messages that pervert touch. Your touch, your connection, your hug, your eyes will all be pure. And, the best part. Your kids can tell! Whether they can define it now, or it dawns on them later as they mature, they WILL know. Your thoughts and your mind send vibrations that are either pure or impure; whole or objectifying. When our minds and spirits are impure, our shareholders suffer the consequences. Keeping a pure mind pays – trust me! Hugging, looking into someone's sparkling eyes, and feeling deep connection is amazing. It's reserved for the pure and wholesome in heart. Your wholeness will dictate how whole your spouse, kids, friends and relationships feel. Raise your thought standard and you increase the availability for healing, hope and wholeness for all those around you. Think wholesome, empowering thoughts; and your touch will empower!

Try Spontaneity

Sometimes in a relationship, there are hurts you sense in the other person. When you've found healing and forgiveness and your emotions are flowing in a positive direction, you simply want to help and give healing as well. This is the heart of an Energizer. One of the best things you can do for someone is get them to feel again. People box their hearts in to keep them safe from being hurt again. Opening this box takes trust, patience and nothing but love. Love people. Perform acts of kindness. Be spontaneous Do something to break the rhythm from time to time. Get a little crazy. Sometimes all it takes, husband, is to break some relational boredom by dating again. Remember the movie-nights, picnics in the living room when it rained or down by the country lake in the summer? Remember working your hardest to rush home, clean up and whisk her away to go ride bicycles, or hike? What changed? *Rhythmic, habitualized, relational boredom set in. Shake yourself from this and deliver your relationships today.* Go do something spontaneous and be ready for a guarded reaction. Guarded reaction just means that she doesn't trust you – yet. Keep it up and she may realize you are doing something for her without any hope of anything in return. Be spontaneous, today!

Trust Built

When we break a promise, it's because we didn't value ourselves properly, since our words are part of who we are – how we think, process and speak – we discounted our own words and broke what we said. In speaking of children, Josh McDowell writes, "Many of us break promises … because we don't recognize how important our promises – both implicit and explicit – are to our sons and daughters." We don't recognize the profound effects that breaking our word as well as keeping our word have on our kids, our wives, our friends and our relationships. One of my coaches says, "Be your word!" Too often, we aren't true to ourselves because we fear what saying "no" sounds like, so we say "yes" when we really shouldn't. Or, because we don't value our own emotional state, we discount the emotions of others as well and trample on their emotions by making and breaking promises over and over.

I struggled with this for a long time. I'd say "yes" to everything due to fear of conflict, fear of what others thought, fear of just chilling and taking time to replenish (feeling undeserving of this), and fear of displeasing someone (disease to please). These fears are trust's nemesis! They destroy trust as we overcommit and constantly move through life without clarity. People don't judge our character by our intentions; rather, we are judged by our actions. *As you journey to becoming an Energizer, it's a matter of wholeness. Getting so clear about who you are, what you're up to, and how best you can create value and get things done. Saying "yes" and following through works when these pieces are whole. You have the capacity to do the work, and you do it. Energizers are whole and true.* They value the consonants and vowels as they exit their mouths to form words which form promises, and they keep those promises. This is the completion of creating value. Your word has value until you break it. Creating value means every word you speak is valued. Dennis Rainey says of character, when you speak truthfully, "your eyes will demand the same truth in return."

While trust goes hand in hand with synergy, I believe trust should be more of a proactive activity than it is. Many people don't offer trust. Perhaps we aren't sure how to clarify healthy expectations, seek to understand the other person's point of view, or maximize value by letting each other work in individual strengths. Most often, though, we've simply not exercised ourselves in being trustworthy. Exercise yourself in it. Allow yourself to make promises (small ones at first) and commit to keeping your promises. Relationships are strengthened and fortified when we make a promise and come through on it. Kids learn to hope and dream when they can count on a promise being kept. There are two kinds of promises: implicit and explicit promises. Both are both important – come through on them. If you explicitly state you'll take on a project and complete it by a certain time, don't procrastinate or over-complicate it. Start it and complete it. Place value in your word and back that value with the gold bullion of action. On the flip side, if it's implied you are to be a friendly receptionist, commit and verbally promise to be the warmest and most cheerful gatekeeper your company will ever have. With any relationship, there are both implicit and explicit promises. Implicit promises may be expected, like nurturing the relationship, doing your part, and communicating with each other. It may be spending time together. Too often, this implied promise goes unclarified, so one person makes spending time less a priority than the other. Two perspectives of one implied promise. Most relationships have trust deteriorating as we speak because people haven't taken the time to put definition around the implied promises. What a lady thinks "Prince Charming" will remain is never discussed or defined. He doesn't know he's missing a beat, and has become a workaholic because he assumes (again, no definition) that she wants this, that, and the other. The workaholic may not feel like they're breaking any promises; however, you'd get a different feeling from the wife or kids who claim, "Dad's never around." Many sense a huge letdown of missed expectations – implied promises that were never clarified. Venture into the proactivity of turning implicit into explicit promises like, "Son, we're going to hang out and spend some time (implicit); so, let's build a go-cart this Saturday (defined – explicit)." To build trustworthiness, state implicit promises as explicit. Ask of your relationships what their expectations are, or voice what your expectations of yourself are. This is **KEY**. Let them know what you can commit to. That way, you're sure to fulfil both kinds of promises creating amazing trust!

Avoid letting a hyper and busy technologically-saturated world pressure you to over-commitment. You owe no one anything but the fulfillment of the promises you make. Keep your promises to your kids. This is the first line of trust your kids will learn. If you prove trustworthy they will learn what it looks like and be able to detect phony! Think of this strategic advantage you will give them! Be your word and let your word be you. Work to get these in congruence.

As a leader, you will spend energy absorbing complaints of people. In every arena of life, build healthy corridors of conflict. Allow anger or grievances to be voiced. Not having trusted space of touch communication is equivalent to clogging emotional arteries or sealing off a boiling pot of water – it's the exact same outcome. Hurt. Anger. Venting. Explosion. Many a harsh response is to blame for scarred emotional arteries. Allow emotions to flow, even if they're negative at first. It's easier to cleanse flowing water than it is to purify stagnation.

Therefore, it's easier to listen and help find a positive remedy than closing someone off by not allowing conflict. Exercise the muscle of conflict. Sometimes, a simple, "Thank you" when someone expresses a concern will do more good for that person." Basically, we must ask ourselves, "Do we care?" Rene McPherson, a past CEO of Dana Corporation said this, "The way you treat an employee is closely observed by all other employees. They decide whether you and your company can be trusted on the basis of that data." Truly caring builds trust! Napoleon Hill predicted the relationship of employers and employees would evolve into more of a partnership than it has been in the past stating that all leadership-by-force passes away, but leadership-by-consent of the followers is the only kind that endures forever. Do your people feel you care? They may know it, they may have heard of instances of it; BUT, do they feel it on a consistent basis? Do your kids feel you care? They will care to follow when they feel you care about them. Trust is built by being true to your word, by being your word, and by caring enough to be both!

Transformational Belief

Believing the best for people even when they can't believe it for themselves may be the most abundant gift we can give another human being. Think bigger. Think about what you can both become together. It's your belief someone may need at a time when they can't even see how to believe in hope. This is faith. This is big thinking. It's abundant living. It's what Energizers do! *We find, in history's crises, women and men who stepped up to the plate and courageously stood in the gap for someone or something they believed in. Will you? Who's suffering in your life? Will you choose to thrive now, so you can offer them deliverance?* Our founders did it years ago for us. Men and women so immune to fear they took decisive action. One man calling on another and initiating the first Congress of thirteen colonies. Who were these two brave souls? Samuel Adams and John Hancock. Yes, it was their idea to form a Congress, and we know the rest story leading up to 1776 and after. We read how Heaven and earth moved on behalf of these champions of freedom. Will you stand in the gap for someone? Do you choose to see the best and believe the best for someone? Goethe states it like this, "Treat a man as he appears to be and you make him worse. But treat a man as if he already were what he potentially could be, and you make him what he should be." So many people want to carry all the baggage of past paradigms into relationships and rehash. What if you breathed healing and hope by forgiving and offering someone a fresh start. Covey called it "changing someone's paradigm." You can literally change a life. When I was in sales, I'd ask a potential client if, "once we're doing business and I see to it you're a raving fan, will you refer me to your business colleagues?" I'd not talk in terms of a prospect, but I'd look down the road as if we were already friends. Why not? Speak and cast a vison. You can do this for anyone and at all stages of life. Speak to kids as the genius that they can be. Inspire people to greatness. Look for the trace of good and magnify it! In business, we call it Win-win! Win-win can happen when both sides go beyond a transaction and understand giving. That's why a handshake used to mean so much and trust was so valuable. Chester L. Karrass, founder of Karrass School of Negotiation says that you can take the stress out of conflict and negotiation when you think win/win. Mutually beneficial ideas show you care and will keep people interested and talking. *Finding a better way for both parties is the basis of creating raving shareholders. Both can benefit. At the core of our fear-based and lesser drives, we tend to pull back, fold our arms and think inwardly. Let's purpose instead to cast a vision of what we can be together!*

When I managed purchasing in the past, I decided to stop picking up the phone and squabbling over shipping costs, meager discounts, etc. There's a good bit of expenditure, here, for sure, and you can spend so much time and resource fighting something instead of thinking of a better, more mutually beneficial way. I noticed how many suppliers I had, and how widely scattered they were – hundreds of suppliers in all different states and countries. In the past, a vendor account was created to save a few dollars – for a transaction. By pulling reports and looking at spend, I decided to have my top 30 suppliers in to tell me what more they'd like to have of our business. Wow! They claimed more vision over supplying to us and in so doing, leveraging deeper discounts and phenomenal terms. Most all of them found something more we could consolidate with them, or some service they could provide that perhaps we weren't taking advantage of. Before I left the department, we had negotiated most all shipping costs away simply by increasing the size of the pie – more product orders. We'd freed up valuable team member time by allowing suppliers to manage inventories, and we consolidated at supplier warehousing for JIT delivery; thus, we extended our accounts-payable days and better leveraged cash flow. Instead of calling to squabble over little stuff that was really happening, we'd have these top 30 suppliers visit quarterly for appreciation first, and then collaboration on ways to improve. Just a few of the names still stand out: Michael, Mary Lee, Pat, Renso, Tim, Marcus, Kay, Jay, Mike and others. We built such great relationships with our suppliers, and they attested that they loved coming in to see us. Create win/win in every arena of life and you will create raving shareholders!

Guy Kawasaki says there are two groups of people: eaters and bakers. One wants a bigger slice of an existing pie, and the other wants to make a bigger pie. "Bakers think that everyone can win with a bigger pie." Be a resource. Think win/win and always bring your energy full and overflowing so you can add and create value! *Help people expand their potential. Help create value that previously didn't exist in their life. Get them to see something that you see in them. Something that maybe they haven't noticed in themselves or they have, but it's going to take some outside credibility to inspire a deeper belief.* Did you know that most people will place more stock in what someone else says about them than what they think or say about themselves? We are our own worst critics. Believing in someone's potential and helping them expand their potential is a great gift.

Leaders, managers, help your teams expand their potential by giving them a challenge. Keep work interesting and exciting. Let them solve things for themselves. Let them know you know they can do it and you trust them. Empower people by believing in their potential. Frederic Herzberg, a credible and deeply-researched behavioral scientist studied people from manufacturing laborers to corporate executives. The most important factor of any job – the most energizing part – wasn't money, benefits, vacation package, bonuses, recognition, prestige, title, or even type of job. The most invigorating, exciting and energizing part of all work is this – the work itself. Many, who start into one form of work they love doing, end up doing something far different and more robotic. We fall into boredom and dullness. We don't live in creative spaces and with challenges that excite our deepest energies. Every successful person loves the challenge of work. Figuring it out. Solving for "X", or the equivalent in your field (if you dislike math). People want challenges. Try this with your kids, "I've got something for you to do … wait a minute … hmmmm … this may be too difficult …" The response will inevitably be, "No, no, daddy … I can do it." Even the first breath of life was a challenge and pulling up on the side of the couch and taking the first step – a challenge. Stop challenging a person and some of that person dies. Some of their energy lies dormant. In fact, the worker who lives long without a challenge will either find another place of employment – a challenge in and of itself or the promise of a challenge – or, they'll create business – the entrepreneurial challenge. Transformational belief sees what both parties can become together, it sees the best in somebody and it casts vision and creates value! Who's receiving inspiration from you? Who's receiving the great gift of transformational belief, today!

Raving Fans; Resounding "Yes!"

Too often in life, we create calculation tablets. These tablets are held very sacred in our relationships. We usually round up on our deposits and round down on others'. Just the opposite happens to withdrawals. We deflate our own withdrawals and inflate those made by others. Our accounts receivables are huge and aging. We have so many expectations we've created, and we're headed for bankruptcy. We stop giving because we're waiting to receive. We calculate, calculate, calculate. We developed the mentality of "If I do _____ , then I expect you to do _____ ; or, when you do _____ , then, I'll do _____. This isn't living truthfully. When you live truthfully, you know love forms the most nurturing environments and is the highest frequency of operation. You make your choices consistently based on your principles, not on circumstances or others' responses. *Living with a calculating mentality makes someone else responsible for why you can or don't take the action you know you should.* Trust will never grow with this mentality. It's not living in the truth you know. You allow others' responses to make you alter your truth. Daniel Smith wrote in his book, *Romancing Your Wife*, "There is probably nothing more appealing to a woman than selflessness lived out on her behalf." This may mean pitching in on the house work when you don't feel like it, grabbing a dishrag and scrubbing the big pans after dinner, changing the diapers or hanging out with her to listen, instead of hanging with the guys. Investing in a relationship means mutually creating value for each other. There's nothing more rewarding in the long run. It means letting go of comparing this relationship to any other relationship. Everyone is different. When we focus on what we see as shortcomings, we only invoke more shortcomings. Instead of placing a guilt-trip on someone, imagine jumping into the relationship fully present with a full heart of understanding. One author wrote, "The trouble in a relationship often starts when people get so busy earning their salt they forget their sugar."

Relationships are too valuable and too short to not make every action and every word count. Use your amazing vibrations of sound called voice to stimulate positive emotions in your loved ones! This means speak good things, be kind, show love! One of my morning affirmations is this, "I'm a proactive husband and dad covering my Jennifer and my kids, Nicole, Jeremy, Ethan and Kaylee with unconditional love! I see, inspire and believe the best in and for them! They know I love them, they hear I love them, and they sense and feel I love them." Covey says, "The more we can see people in terms of their unseen potential, the more we can use our imagination rather than our memory with our spouse, our children, our coworker, our employees." Dag Hammarskjold, past Secretary-General of the United Nations, made this statement so powerful, it makes me stop and examine every relationship I'm pursuing every time I read it. He said, "It is more noble to give yourself completely to one individual than to labor diligently for the salvation of the masses." Especially nowadays with technology and our constantly being plugged-in, this statement's difficult to comprehend. *Consider though, if you even have one individual you do give yourself completely to when you're with them – and we're talking wholly: physically, emotionally, spiritually and mentally.* This is why sex is never truly and deeply fulfilling to so many couples, and it's why religion can become as dry as a dirge.

Imagine spending a day completely unplugged and totally focused on romancing and meeting the needs of your spouse? What would that look like? Imagine becoming so immersed in prayer that we forgot about time and gave our Creator such undistracted and wholehearted worship? We are so fast-paced that this journey of deep relationship is rarely explored.

Instead, most relationships remain superficial – propped up by societal expectations. This is why two partners in a firm will quarrel and violently part ways leaving thousands of workers in a tail-spin. This is why two people can storm out of the house leaving little kids to form emotional callouses in order to cope. All of the world's problems can be traced back to broken relationships. This is why many executives feel more trust around their workaholic associates than they do with their own wives and kids. This is why religious leaders can inspire each other with visions of saving the world and return home to a family in distress. *It's wonderful to aspire to reach the masses, build clientele, or thrive in social spaces, but be fully present and know your closest people!*

One day I made a statement to Jen that completely changed my mindset and life. I told her that my hope is years down the road, I could get back down on one knee asking her to marry me. After years of getting to know me at my worst and at my best, I'd hope that I'd paid enough dividends of love to her that she'd not even have to think long at all, but instead, grab my hand and looking me deep in the eyes with a heart bursting with love and emotion say at the top of her lungs, "Yes! YES! Of course! I will! I couldn't imagine it any other way!" Would your employer say the same if given the chance to rehire you? Your manager? Coworkers? Would your kids say the same if given the chance to pick their parents? Would your business partners say the same? Your friends? The people in your group, your association, your circle? What dividends are your shareholders experiencing from your life? Here's the **Energizer's Shareholder Declaration**:

> "I will create raving shareholders among the closest relationships of my life by paying dividends of living fully present with them and loving them deeply – unconditionally!"

Are you an Energizer? Applying the principles of perspective, ownership and accountability daily will raise our frequency to higher living, will expand our capacity, and will ignite our deepest energies to live fully and love deeply! The time for energy is NOW!

CHAPTER 23
SECOND BONUS

the beginning of a journey

"Come unto me, all ye that labor and are heavily burdened, and I will give you rest." – Jesus

I Believe in You

Driving down the gorgeous, lush and shaded Natchez Trace Parkway heading for Mississippi, I was deep in thought. Maybe the mandatory 50 MPH speed limit of this 444-mile stretch of roadway brought me into this unrushed, pondering state. Maybe it was the brilliantly blue sky. Or, perhaps it was my meditation that morning about the lady who Jesus met at the well in Samaria about 2,000 years ago. Additionally, I'd listened to Darren Hardy that morning after my run. He challenged all listeners to *reach out to three people in their lives who really needed to hear the four most powerful words, "I believe in you."* As I drove along this beautiful day, the lush forests, green grass and yellow and purple budding flowers along the route called on the best of my emotions. Since leaving the gym, I had messaged two people: Jen and Kevin. Jen had invested herself recently into deeper devotion and prayer as she crafted the well-being of our three precious kiddos (before Kaylee was born) every day and was strategically reaching out to encourage other moms! I was super proud of her and wanted to send her this boost of four powerful words. Kevin, my accountabuddy, had invested so much of his love into me, believed in me, and was Head-Mastering a school of eight hundred precious kids! He made an easy second. Now, I was pondering who the third person should be. My dad kept coming up in my mind, but this couldn't work – I'd tried to re-establish a relationship after leaving home, but that didn't work. At least, he wasn't responding the way I thought he should. The bitterness I tried to eradicate through a calculated forgiveness was still there – deep down.

Not long before this day of pondering, my Aunt Judy had visited my family in Tennessee. We didn't grow up around our relatives since we lived in Germany. Learning my family history and origins opened my eyes to some things. I learned of the ways my granddad (who I met only once right before he passed away) had treated my dad. Unfortunately, the harshness I was raised with couldn't even come close to the brutality my dad endured as the only living son of his dad – a retired, Marine Corp. colonel. An unworthiness had been engrained so deeply into my dad. That day, driving down the Parkway something dawned on me! I realized that although my dad projected a very low self-worth over his kids, it was a higher form of worth than he'd been given. To the best of his ability, dad had filtered a good bit of what he knew. My heart immediately gushed a wave of emotions through me as I realized Dad spent his life trying to feel worthy. He overcompensated, drove hard and turned off all emotional pain. He was invincible and while thousands were impressed with him and with our large singing "perfect" family, there was very little real, authentic connection – very little love. It was a dutiful existence.

Weeping, I pulled up Evernote, and through tears, I recorded a letter of forgiveness. I told Dad exactly what had caused the feeling of hurt and engrained such a bitterness for him. I told him I forgave him unconditionally. I told him that I realized how stuck he must feel, and that I promised my love unconditionally. I told him that I believed in him! "I believe in you, Dad!" That's it. *By projecting unconditional love and belief over him my heart opened a little deeper and bitterness turned to forgiveness – the unconditional kind.* I wanted to hug his neck and let him know how amazing of a human being he was and is. I wanted him to know that he's a beautiful person!

In writing this book, I've hesitated sharing any personal stories, but as lives crumble about us, as human worth is stomped on in our society, and as a I meet young kids, domestic violence survivors, single ladies and young men looking to fall in love, husbands and wives struggling in marriages and even leaders trying to connect with their people, I realize the search for worth is universal! I must share my story because it's so much greater than me. It's greater than Dad. It is literally a matter of abundant life or slow death. Every personal story I share in this book has brought emotions of love so strong, in fact, that I literally move to a greater place of love for my dad and others. It's in this heart that I share the stories asking readers to claim the same forgiveness, unconditional love and belief for someone in your life who so desperately needs you! I rejoice that at the time of this writing, my journey will take me to see Dad for the first time in twelve years. I can't wait to hug his neck!

Journey of Worth

Friend, thank you for reading my book and investing in your energy - living and experiencing life wholly, fully and abundantly! My journey has been freeing and healing to say the least. Loving all people deeply has amplified every connection. My prayer is you've been blessed, challenged and helped by reading. Perhaps the corporation where you're employed purchased this book for you. Perhaps you've found this resource yourself through the internet, a traditional bookstore, or a friend's given to you as a gift! Out of respect to all parties involved, I don't claim faith in Jesus Christ as a prerequisite to living wholly, fully and abundantly in any previous chapters. *I believe, with a heart of understanding, we can choose best options and practices to live virtuously.* I quote many scientific thinkers, spiritual leaders, and brilliant, business leaders throughout these pages whose research, teachings and advice can lead to massive amounts of success and abundant life. I've made many statements where you've sensed the presence of faith; that's who I am. And, I believe we all have faith to some degree. I've used many physical, every-day illustrations and examples to make sense of living an energized life. I firmly believe when we understand physical principles, we're better equipped to understand spiritual truths. All truths are parallel. Jesus asked a spiritual leader, Nicodemus, this question, "If you don't believe the earthly things we know to be true, how do you expect to believe the heavenly things I'm telling you?" I'd be dishonest if I didn't admit to you my own human limitations and share the power for a higher perspective, the amplification of life, and the abundant joy for living that I've found and experience daily in my Lord Jesus. I've intentionally left my personal testimony of faith for this chapter for those longing for a rich connection with God and a deep, spiritual awakening. Faith in Jesus is the oxygen of my spirit. His example and life speak volumes! He's my connection to God Almighty who, because of Him, I get to call, Father!

Friend, I share in these next few pages what overflows from my heart. Not some religious code, but a relationship with God through His Son, Jesus. Many strive for some pre-determined level or standard of perfection. We do. We try to do the right things and make sense of this world. We're asked to be tolerant of people's positions and beliefs. Where does this stem from? People come into our lives all the time and we make an internal judgment call whether they're ahead or behind us. We feel threatened for a reason. Positioning is a real thing – it happens in families, in corporations, in politics, in religious circles and the list goes on. Here's the deal. We all form beliefs and ideas – many similar beliefs and ideas, and some that differ. *Therefore, measuring our value by man's ruler or our own, we will always come up short – devalued. This is why we see comparing, competing and condemning in our world today.* Religion begins with good intent and at some point, crafts an unbearable book of codes by which we measure one another. Religion says you must do all of this. Religion shows inadequacies as awful flaws. Religion promulgates fear into hearts and lives of boys, girls and adults of what's going to happen if you don't measure up. Religions in our world bicker, battle and war. Many reject religions and set out to seek peace; yet, we have inward contempt toward somebody, some group, or the religious people we abandoned. Jesus came and made some strong statements. The religious factions that had taken divine laws of the worth of life, respect of our fellowman and worship of God and added to them rituals and man-made ideologies attacked Jesus and any disrupter of the lucrative, political system. When Jesus simply wrapped everything up into "Love the Lord God wholly; and, love your neighbor as yourself," he was hated by the ritualistic and religious crowd.

As a young man, I wanted to turn my back on faith. To live in the here and now and abandon my belief in anything eternal. *However, an isolated humanistic idea can never lift us to the highest form of worth – pricelessness. Because, who gets to set this standard? This belief can never fulfil or satisfy the deepest longings in our spirit for awakened and abundant life.* It's as if the eternal spirit within us cries out for redress and never stops pleading deep down in our emotions. I couldn't silence the need, the desire, the longing, the craving for deeper meaning, infinite purpose, fullness of life and deepness of love. I looked at the teachings of Confucius, Buddha, many world leaders. I studied hundreds of business leaders' books, and read after and followed other, great influencers. I noticed similarities between all teachings, and too often, the radical differences when a religion was used to cloak a manmade agenda. The common denominator led me back to this – deep, unconditional love is the most powerful force in the universe. Simply studying the life of Jesus for an entire year blew me away and recaptured my heart! He became so much more than the mascot of Christianity. Why? He's the one who claimed to be God's Son. He made some powerful claims disrupting an entire system of calculative, comparative, competitive and condemning structure of religion and politics. If Jesus is the Son of God and He claimed we could have a relationship with God (through Him), then I would pursue a relationship with Him. If He were true, then He'd have no problem coming through on His promise.

But wait! How in the world would He want a relationship with me? A God so big and so great that man will never comprehend. A God who spread out the vast universes – just the outskirts of the grandeur of His kingdom. A God who decided to create man and place him on a planet supportive of life – unlike any other planet. He who called the earth His footstool, and says He has amazing plans for us. What? But alas! If I can't measure up to the most rigid standards imposed my man, how will I ever gain acceptance and measure up to God's standard of worth? I could never measure up growing up. Even straight A's didn't feel to be good enough. Similarly, when will I ever know my own attempts finally measured up? I constantly fell short of my own expectations. The vice I sought to overcome held a firm grip on me. I gave up again – a failure. I realized that many successful people get to the end of their lives having lived in splendor, but in death they find a perplexing loneliness. How could this be, I wondered.

It's then I realized that God said He's a rewarder of them that diligently seek Him. Not please Him, seek Him. Jesus said, "Seek first the kingdom of God and His righteousness, and all these things – physical things – will be added to you." He's the one that came to earth and touched the unworthy. He didn't condemn those who religion called guilty. He said he came to take away the sin of the world. Imperfect, I want to fear and shy away from connection with God; Jesus said by Him I have the power for constant connection – regardless! "Whoever believes in me is not condemned … when you come after me, you're my brother, my sister," Jesus said.

It's then I realized that salvation isn't simply an eternal place in Heaven that we can easily define and some religions distort. Salvation isn't being rescued from some awful, evil punishment in the future. *Salvation is the acceptance of identity, worth and hope. Salvation is deliverance from emptiness – right here and right now! Salvation from the awful punishment and fear that crushes our spirits every day. Salvation from the hopelessness of evil that exists. Salvation is faith in all that's good, loving and possible. Salvation is a changed perspective: a changed mind, soul and spirit.* All of our emotions rushing and running in fear of coming up short, doing and doing – our batteries quickly rushing towards "E." The excuses, the judgements, the criticisms, the better-than-them, the pride, the ego, the undeserving, the fearful, the afraid, the distrust, the hate, the bitterness, and the sinning against eternal souls all around us. Salvation from all of this! Salvation from living a false identity – identity in my own self-righteousness and how much better I am than everyone else. This is bondage and pride; a false sense of worth that's shaky! This is living competitive, comparative and with condemning tendencies. Salvation, according to Jesus, is immediate completeness – in Him. Salvation is Jesus perfect, holy righteousness covering us. Salvation is immediate redemption to our priceless worth as His creation. Study the life of Jesus and everyone He touched, every miracle He performed and every statement He made backs this up!

Could it be we struggle believing a God could be so kind and loving? Naturally, we want there to be some sort of standard because then we can feel like we achieved something and take pride in our achievement. Or, we don't accept His righteousness because we hate ourselves and won't forgive ourselves. We hate others and don't want to forgive freely – we live a calculated existence. We can glory in accomplishment and our own righteousness. God's righteousness, however, is a gift – true gift of salvation! *Immediately, it changes our perspective and we begin giving up our own self-righteousness. We tap into pricelessness and Heavenly drive. We tap into the most powerful force that ever was and ever will be – love. Love heals, and we can't measure it. It's the harder choice.*

Wow! Jesus offered worth freely and it makes sense. He went to every "unlovable" in society when He walked the earth, and He touched them taking away their shame and giving them worth! He met physical and spiritual needs. He constantly challenged people to think. Many felt threatened in their false security of self-righteousness. Why do we continually deal with unworthiness? Someone else's standard at some point was, is, or will be better than ours. Humanly speaking, wouldn't they be worth more? Friend, our Creator set the standard of worth – priceless. It's when we decide to prove our value through our own righteousness, we fall short. Who values us then? By faith, we accept that Jesus took that old standard of man's worth, the crushing weight of self-righteousness, and a law so heavy not even the one who professes to measure up could stand to carry it. Jesus – the priceless gift of God Almighty – took that horrid standard of self-righteousness, all sin, and the knowledge of good and evil and nailed them, with Himself, to a rugged cross. Author Doug Reed states, "When we take our eyes off our own misdeeds and look at who Jesus is and what He has done, our shame flees. Sin consciousness disappears, and God consciousness takes its place. We become a new creation that once again bears God's image." He continues, "We've all felt shame and to avoid it, we wear masks and tell lies to maintain our worth among our neighbors." What is our measure of worth tied to? Self-consciousness or God consciousness? Jesus restored relationship with our Creator – direct access to God! Let us embrace His power to walk into the throne room of Heaven boldly as worthy sons and daughters. Let us put on His robes of righteousness and find our priceless value two-fold. Once by creation, and twice by the fact that he bought us back! He gave His everything, so we could have everything!

There are some things I've noticed on my journey through life. This journey has taken me into contact with some of religions' toughest task masters, and some of the most hurt people. I've also met those with great intentions, huge commitments, and even greater hearts. Every now and then, there is a spiritual leader who emerges not through title, not through prestige or position, but with a clear message of healing. It's not a message of condemnation, but a message of life and of hope. Jesus said, "I am the light of the world … the very bread of life." He said, "I've not come to condemn the world, but that the world, through me, might be saved." Saved from what? Fear, religion, judgment and condemnation because of self-righteousness and a fluctuating standard of worth!

Living in this fear is no way to live. What we can apply to any and all of these situations is love. Perfect love that casts out fear. But how can we know how to show perfect love without a perfect example? Jesus was this example when he laid down His life. *Instead of turning my back on faith, I turned my back on religion and pursued a relationship. Let me tell you something.* My pursuing a relationship wasn't and hasn't always been a faithful pursuit. What I found was God pursued me in return. He says, "You will seek me and find me, when you seek for me with all of your heart!" Jesus said, "I've come to seek and save those that are lost." We all crave something more – a deeper relationship. When we understand the phenomenal, unfathomable work Jesus did to give us God-awareness (priceless worth), we realize the gift of salvation, the Bread of Life and this Living Water Jesus is to us. Maxwell Maltz put it like this, "Let us not limit our acceptance of life by our own feelings of unworthiness. God has offered us forgiveness and the peace of mind and happiness that comes from self-acceptance. It is an insult to our Creator to turn our backs upon these gifts to say that his creation is not worthy, or important, or capable. The most adequate and realistic self-image of all is to conceive of yourself as made in the image of God."

A relationship with God is possible; every moment of every day. And He enables and empowers us to live through consistent love! He gives us all power to forgive any one who has wronged or hurt us – His is the highest power and eternal power! He empowered me to see things from a different perspective and forgive my Dad. He calls us worthy! We have faith, whether in our ability, our good deeds, humanity, government, etc. I choose to believe the best about people, and I put my faith in a lot of things that appear to be true from all tests of genuineness. *I choose to put my highest faith in One who has fulfilled all promises, who's given me a deep peace, personal forgiveness and enablement to forgive others. The One whose mercy has allowed me to make peace with the past, the One whose truth gives me unwavering faith to dream dreams and make plans for the future, and the One whose love and peace fills me each day to live fully present today making a difference in this world through love for all mankind!* Rick Warren says, "When you remember you're loved and accepted by grace, you don't have to prove your worth." You're worthy and worthy people do worthwhile things! Dr. Frank G. Slaughter says, "You cannot believe yourself created in the image of God, deeply and sincerely, with full conviction, and not receive a new source of strength and power!"

Journey of Identity

God said, "I will be a Father to the fatherless, and a Husband to the widows." Wow! Both a husband and father offer deep emotional connection, yet so many who we should have been able to trust let us down. Why trust anyone else? When we give trust, we show faith. Faith in something greater. Sure, people let us down; but does that mean we should draw back and never experience the joy of someone receiving and safe keeping our trust? I encourage you to look up to Heaven and ask God to show Himself to you! He said he is a rewarder of them that diligently seek Him! I love the song that says, "He's a good, good Father!" He's proved true and faithful to me even as I cut through thick religious code to realize my identity is in Him – I'm His son! We are the sons and daughters of God because of Jesus taking away the barriers. We are adopted into a royal family. *Clothed in His righteousness, we're a child of the King – clothed in royal robes! Jump, skip, dance and sing, for you are perfect! The only person to disallow this daughter-ship or son-ship is you! Jesus said the only thing limiting His fullness and presence of peace in our lives is us. Our unbelief.*

As we claim our identity as sons and daughters, let's look at the veracity of Jesus' identity. There are things Jesus claimed and events that happened that many an atheist and scholar, upon close examination, have come into drastic realization, that Jesus and all He taught aligned perfectly and fulfilled all that was foretold. Here was the greatest teacher walking the earth and many only saw Him as this. Yet, veiled in flesh, here walked Jesus – God with man. Let's consider some of the profound effects of Jesus:

- Miracle birth in Bethlehem.
- Most celebrated historical figure.
- Fulfilled approximately 353 previous written promises that God's Son would come to earth.
- Our calendar revolves around His birth and life.
- Taught peace and love – beatitudes and virtues.
- Healed disease, fed and clothed people and gave them spiritual healing as well – no condemnation.
- Greatest servant leader of all time.
- Master teacher.
- Every religion has some trace to, or resemblance of His teachings, and leaders today replicate them in some ways.
- Corporations are full of "golden-rules" and the sensitivity – seeking unity and harmony – he taught in "Love your neighbor as yourself."
- He claimed to be God's Son.
- Political and religious factions fearfully and treacherously put Him on a cross and crucified Him as foretold and written hundreds of years prior.
- Miraculously rose from death, ascending from a sealed and guarded tomb after three days as He promised; and, he was seen by hundreds of people.
- His unconditional love and gift of perfection – His righteousness – takes all competitive, comparative perspectives away replacing all fear with faith, hope and love for all people for all time.
- Kids loved, trusted and ran to Him. His essence was divine. His virtue flowing freely to all those who reached out to touch Him.
- Evil is present in this world while everything about Him radiated goodness.
- Why is it that only His name is cursed in language? Is there not another powerful force of evil in this world opposing Him?
- Even as God's Son, he embraced accountability by speaking to and through many women and men throughout time, pursuing a relationship with them, and thus fulfilling our deepest need – a higher sense of relationship. Taught twelve men and even called

the one betraying him "Friend."

- Gave us a model of unconditional love. The only model that can truly heal emotions deeply and offer forgiveness completely voluntarily.
- The strongest and most proud of us turn to Him when troubles come, or we face death.

Why did He die willingly? How do we resolve the "Passion of the Christ" if it wasn't truly to restore relationship to God by drinking the bitter cup of punishment to take away all the sin, shame and fear in the world – past, present and future?

His promises haven't failed. He said that He gives us the power to be the daughters and sons of God – the very power! He took away the sin of the world. By faith, we accept the paradigm he has given us – perfect, royalty and worthy! Because of his full and complete surrender on the cross to bear the awful weight of all that's evil, he lifts us to perfect standing with God. We're good by Him. Complete in Him. Feelings of inadequacy are tricks of all that's evil to cause us to distance ourselves from Him out of shame. He asks that we simply do justly, love mercy and walk humbly with Him. Walking with God doesn't sound like any mean task to me. That sounds like royalty, angelic and glorious. *It's when we accept a discounted, human paradigm and live in that, we feel unworthy and forget our King's robes and our sonship and daughterhood*. It's time we claim our power to be His sons and daughters, today! Nick Vujicic pronounced, "Even if at times you feel alone, you should know that you are unconditionally loved. God created you out of love. Therefore, you're never alone. He doesn't love you if …. He loves you always!"

Journey of Healing

It's when I realized that hurt people hurt, I began to scrape off the emotional calluses from my heart for my Dad and others I felt animosity towards. I realized that at some point in their life, they were pained, shamed, devalued, or made to feel unloved. Hurt people may not have had the blessing of feeling love or experiencing acceptance. Our call, through Jesus, is to live at peace with one another and turn the other cheek. He didn't just ask us to, he backed it up by going all the way to the cross. When we argue and fight, we do our royal identity the greatest hurt. Simple faith and true belief in what Jesus said stops our fighting right away. He can make our hearts whole, he can quicken our spirits to come alive and fill us with His goodness. He can empower us daily to be abundant sources of love and light to our world! Forgiveness is a Heavenly guarantee. "TETELESTAI – It is finished!" He cried from the cross! There's now no condemnation, Scripture shares. Jesus work on the cross ended the divide that sin and shame had placed between God and man. Now, forgiveness, worth, identity and unity with God was immediately possible! Let us never cheapen "so great a salvation" that we've been given – yes, given! Let us daily reflect in the divine worth Heaven gives us! What if we lived offering this same gift to everyone? Wow! What a concept, and this is the journey of forgiveness and healing that leads us to complete emotional healing and an outpouring of radical, unconditional love!

The strongest and toughest of us have some deep emotional needs that only Jesus can fulfill. The best and most accomplished of us have something shameful in our past. *It's when we accept His unconditional love for us that the energies of a quickened and eternal spirit begin to move in us. It's then that the overwhelming nature of His forgiveness and love overtake us and we surge with life like we never thought possible. It's a deep and abiding healing – we become whole!* There's this disparity we face in life. The balance of doing and being. Some people are doers. They feel they can never do enough and find their value in doing. Often, sacrifice is easy and feelings of inadequacy and insecurity rule. They're afraid of what being themselves looks and feels like. Taking time for yourself or sitting still seems absurd. Mary and Martha were two sisters who loved to host Jesus. One day, Martha was bustling around the house and would huff every time she came through the room. It perturbed her to see Mary sitting there spending time with Jesus. Martha finally blurted out her frustration that Mary needed to help her. Jesus kindly reminded Martha the importance of quiet devotion with him, saying Mary had chosen the important function. Just take inventory of where you're at in life. Hurried? Busy? Carrying a load and doing all the time? Jesus said,

"Come unto me all ye that labor and are heavy laden and I will give you rest, take my yoke upon you and learn of me for I am meek and lowly in heart. For my yoke is easy and my burden is light." We see a yoke and a burden that would have been symbols of a mule's work in history. *Learn of me, however, is a mental well-being. Meek and lowly shows an emotional intelligence indicative that the great Teacher was showing how much more effective and efficient our life's work can be when we first be, then do!* Like S.D. Gordon writes, "only what the warm current of His love draws out does Jesus desire from us. It is to be a free and voluntary service." I love how Flora Plummer writes, "There's only one way to look for all the rest, joy, love and light – up. There's life in a look – a look into the face of Jesus. The joy, peace, comfort and courage – everything for which we long is there. In His dear face we see love in its fullness, divine pardon, tender guidance, and complete salvation. The past, the future, that which is going on around us, our own weaknesses – all are forgotten as we look up into His blessed face." She continues, "And when we look up, He is looking down, and directly at each one of us, and every promise His lips have uttered becomes ours personally. And – more wonderful than all else – by beholding the face of our Savior we are changed. With invincible courage we press forward." His promise that the hairs on our heads are numbered means he notices. He notices when a sparrow falls to the ground! What an infinite, a miraculous God; and yet, a caring Father! We will never fathom the depths of the richness of His mercy. I think king David penned it beautifully, and I believe that divine love and supreme intelligence and wisdom for life is ours when we simply decide to thrive by the Shepherd's side:

> "The Lord is my shepherd, I shall not want.
> He maketh me to lie down in green pastures,
> He leadeth me beside the still waters,
> He restoreth my soul!
> He leadeth me in the paths of righteousness for His name's sake.
> Yeah, though I walk through the valley of the shadow of death,
> I will fear no evil; for, Thou art with me.
> Thy rod and thy staff, they comfort me.
> Thou preparedst a table before me in the presence of mine enemies.
> Thou anointeth my head with oil,

My cup runneth over!
Surely, goodness and mercy shall follow me all the days of my life,
and I will dwell in the house of the Lord, forever."

Journey of Abundance

I love the quote that says, "Do all the good you can, in all the ways you can, by all the means you can, in all the places you can, to all the people you can, for as long as ever you can – because you can!" Yes! We can, and we get to! It's our joy to abound! It's when we begin living at a higher frequency and realizing that we don't need anything more – we're complete in Jesus – then, we can be whole, full and overflowing. *The fruits of God's Spirit overflow as He fills us. This is the glorious and divine energy of His Spirit! Love, joy, peace, patience, kindness, goodness, faithfulness, gentleness, and self-control are produced by our lives. These are the emotional generators installed. We get to choose our responses through the power of God's Spirit and overflow His love to the world.* Our overflowing is all to His glory! If we're holding back or empty it simply means we've not taken the time for spiritual connection and renewal. He's faithful! He calls us to meet Him every morning for the fresh supply of manna only He can give. He rewards our consistency. The problem isn't God's insufficiency; the problem is our inconsistency. What result are you looking for in life? Let our actions show faithfulness – full of faith. Pray expecting an answer. Walk trusting the process. Live peacefully, confident in your Father's love. Meet Him daily. David said, "Morning, evening and at noon will I pray and cry aloud, and He will hear my voice." Jesus promised abundant life saying, "I am come that they may have life, and have it more abundantly." Abundantly means "plentifully, in large quantities and overflowing." We simply fail to come to Him. Jesus said to the woman drawing water at the well, "If you knew the gift of God, and who it is that says to you, 'Give me to drink'; you would ask of Him, and He would give you living water … an internal well, springing up eternal life."

Most possess a disproportionate fear of punishment. Friend, have you thought that God wants to punish you? He doesn't. Instead, He sent His

Son, Jesus, because He cannot lie, and He says He is merciful and full of compassion. He stated that which is not of faith is sin. The very fear that grips your heart about your worth, your identity, the ability and availability of full healing and the life of abundance is all earthly fear. Full faith realizes that God is everything good, lovely and just; and, only by faith will eternity and unconditional love be opened to us. *It's when we remain trapped in a comparative, competitive and condemning warp that we punish ourselves and others. When we lift our eyes to see the glory of His redemption, we see a Creator who's made a way for us to live shameless and perfect in His righteousness by faith! Abundant life!*

The time we live in pride against Him is the time we spend living in dependance of the standard of our own goodness. Human standards will always end up coming up short, get modified, etc. There is always some-one who's wronged us in some great way – too great for our own ability to forgive. We are imperfect; we're in this body and feelings of hurt happen. We can strive for perfection or to be better than someone else. Who sets this standard? Who says, "OK, you've arrived." On the other hand, we can, by faith, accept His perfection and cease to strive altogether. Faith in Christ puts us at the top; there's no more striving. You're good and begin to live life abundantly! We can let everything we do bring us joy unspeakable! Every task, be it glorious or grim, can have eternal meaning! Didn't even Jesus declare, "When you give a glass of cold water to the least of these my brethren, you've done it unto me?" When we realize we're perfect in Him, then we will come before Him in faith, full of confidence, peace and joy. The same joy with which my 3-year-old daughter runs to me screaming, "Daddeeeeee!" when I walk in the door.

Is your time with God transactional or relational? An event? A transaction? Fire insurance? And, in insecurity, do we continue in fear to live in our own self-righteousness? Condemning this person, judging that person, hating this group, speaking evil of another? If there is an eternal hell, are we simply becoming "Christians" breathing its very fire? Salvation is a way of life – saved from the paralyzing deadness of fear to living abundant in faith. Every action has eternal value. I no longer have to choose my actions based in fear of what I know at the moment; instead, I get to choose divine actions based in faith of a process so much greater than me, a promise so much stronger than I can make, a Force so infinite and unfathomable. I get to choose love-based actions. Salvation is an eternal and Heavenly perspective. *Salvation is an awakening from a merely physical existence to a spiritual awareness. Salvation is a God-consciousness that moves past the scowl of judgment, insecurity and temporal problems to the smile of love, security and endless opportunity.* In one word, the weight of the law, all self-righteousness, competitiveness, comparison and condemnation have been consumed – this one word is love! His love is measureless; let's channel it abundantly! Love the Lord God with all your spirit, soul, mind and body; and love your neighbor wholly as yourself!

God breathed into man the breath of life, and man became a living soul. There was fellowship with God that sin and shame broke. Jesus redeemed mankind; put us back into direct relationship with God. Our spirits will live forever. Jesus' power quickens our spirits. He can bring us to life and promises His continual presence. He spoke of:

- Powerful perspective – having a grain of mustard seed faith, only belief and condemning no one.
- Overflowing ownership – his only response was love and leading a peaceful, abundant life.
- Authentic accountability – invested in his followers and deeply in every human interaction.

Carnegie shared his abandonment of established religion to that of pure faith for pursuing a greater relationship with God. He said, "the fact that we don't understand the mysteries of our bodies, or electricity, or of the gas engine doesn't keep us from using and enjoying them." He continued, "the fact that I don't understand the mysteries of prayer no longer keeps me from enjoying the richer and happier life that it brings." Like Carnegie, I've moved past the trivial, fear-based differences that divide humanity. I've forsaken religion in pursuit of relationship – deeper, closer, and constant spiritual connection! I'm tremendously interested in what faith will do for our world! Just like electricity and good food and water help us to lead richer, fuller and happier lives; so also, faith goes far beyond simply giving me spiritual values – it literally empowers me to live fully and love deeply! William James said faith gives "a new zest for life, more life, and a larger, richer and more satisfying life! It gives me hope and courage. It vanishes tensions, anxieties, fears and worries! It gives purpose to my life and direction; it vastly improves my happiness. It gives me an abounding heart, and it helps me to create for myself on oasis of peace amidst the whirling sands of life." Jesus said, "Abide in me, and let me abide in you; your life will bear fruit!" Let the sap of the eternal and divine power of God flow through you! Only His love; nothing else. Accept completion in Jesus eternal work. Abound because you are blessed to! Live fully because he gave us everything; love deeply because he loves us relentlessly!

Powerful Perspective

We're priceless; valued highly! More than just a positive thought we cling to until losing faith in ourselves or being condemned by others, Jesus' finished work is the gold bullion to back up our worth! Change your perspective. You're priceless by declaration of Heaven. He's clothed you in King's garments; you're perfect. "Abide in me," He says! "Take my yoke, learn of me, I'm meek and lowly, and you'll find rest for your souls, because my yoke is easy, and my burden is light." We've been given the POWER to be the daughters and sons of God through Jesus! Open your heart to the perspective of being a beautiful creation and your life matters right now! *What's possible in and through you is unimaginable so begin imagining and dreaming right now.* Every day is an amazing journey, good and bad things will happen in life and both make us glisten brighter, Life lived abundantly every moment can be yours because you're not out looking for the perfect moment or longing for the perfect house, kids, lifestyle, etc., you're making every moment perfect - your presence in that moment projects the glory and splendor of that moment! You're perfect because of awakening to God-consciousness. You're complete in Christ. His perfect child!

Overflowing Ownership

How will you live in your new identity as God's son or daughter? Some say that living in radical love tends to bring laziness - you don't have to earn anything, so why do anything? This is simply a myth. If this reasoning were correct, then why can kids go and go and go for hours? It's the names, harsh words, criticisms and negativity kids grow into that crushes their ambition. Growing up finds us misunderstanding our own value and therefore, creating it happens as a reflection of ourselves. It's calculated, comparative or competitive. Taking ownership of life based in duty will stop when we feel we've reached a certain level of success – not too little; and not too much. Or, we're harshly driven by the motivators of ego, greed and power. If we thrive and succeed, it's often from the ambition of proving ourselves, or having to work. Having to do anything eventually breeds hatred and brings burnout. *On the other hand, getting to do something from an overflowing heart brings fulfillment and joy and stimulates gratitude.* It's simply errant to claim love lessens responsibility when in fact, it leverages more responsible ownership! The only response to love is feeling valued and valuable thinking begins. Love leads to the best form of responsibility – service and being socially aware. Value creation gets us thinking addition and multiplication – not subtraction and division. With this multiplying and abundant mindset, we realize that maximizing our potential is the greatest way to love more people! Jesus said, "If I be lifted up, I will draw all people to myself!" This is abundant thinking! We understand that an extreme ownership of our one life can compound tremendously into others' lives. Radical love never stops compounding, growing, multiplying and maximizing! It can't. Radical love heals emotional hurt and turns negative energy – draining out – to positive energy – full, abundant and overflowing. Therefore, our only choice as this loved child of the King is whether or not we'll put on our kingly clothes every morning and walk into our world as a constant, passionate source of energy - creating value, doing good and serving others!

Authentic Accountability

When you realize you're priceless and learn to see yourself as the valuable, amazing creation you are, you start loving yourself properly. Your relationships with everyone are reflections of your relationship with God and yourself. "Love your neighbor as yourself" begins to make sense. In past times, every connection with another human being was an internal judgment call. To elevate ourselves to some position meant raising or lowering others as well. Sure, we admire those we've elevated until finding a chink in their armor. Then, inwardly we rejoice because we're better in some way. This positional jockeying is a constant struggle. *When our minds are renewed, however, we see every human as a brother, a sister, and a friend we haven't met yet and we love unconditionally – no judgment. We'll learn from all people and we'll accept our responsibility to all people to make this world a better place.* We uplift everyone. Everything we do is bigger than us. We're all equal. We're all beautiful creations. Pride, ego, judgment, positioning, bickering, arguing, mistrust, lying, facade can all go. We can value every person we come in contact with and offer an open heart of love to them Sure there'll be people who want to hurt you. Hurt people hurt. But you realize this, and it gives you an even greater reason to love! Every interaction with your wife, husband, kids or another human is perfect. You realize the ability for two spirits, souls, minds and bodies to connect is simply miraculous. You delight in everyone you meet and value them.

Divine energy is an eternal well of life springing up from within. Living in this abundance, we reach for greatness in life because we're unwilling to settle. We're priceless and perform priceless acts. We're dressed in king's robes and anointed by the King himself to go forth into the highways and hedges to carry His light, life and healing to all we meet! We're plugged into solid, pure energy sources and have built switches of habitual consistency to tap into these sources daily. When we get side-tracked or turned around, like we all do at times, we simply start anew in that very moment realizing the time is always now. We don't burden ourselves with the baggage of feeling behind. We're always "caught up." We've become vulnerable with good people to remind us of this. We've intentionally and proactively put a Scrum of accountability together with trusted advisors in our lives! We start new and fresh every moment and enjoy the journey of growth, authenticity and vulnerability! We're becoming a source of life to all those around us because we're living fully. We long to experience life to the fullest! We invest all our energy into everything His Spirit leads us to do. We say, "no" to anything we couldn't do wholeheartedly! We show up full of life! We're fun to be around! We're in constant flow state because we're emotionally whole and stable. We get results because we realize passion pays, and we don't buy into the lie of excuse making. We're whole in every arena of life and this wholeness allows for fullness and abundance and it amplifies every action! We love deeply and value every human being – realizing they're shareholders in our lives! We live at a higher consciousness of social responsibility and interdependence. We realize behind us comes another generation who will follow the legacy we leave, and we realize the life we've decided to live abundantly, not only matters for us, but it also matters for generations to come. Every choice we make lights someone else's candle! We realize relationships are the crux of accountability, and our emotional wholeness allows for deep connection and deep love deposits into everyone we touch. Our families, our friends, our clients, our communities are raving fans! Even our enemies feel our love. We live everyday signing the **Power Of Attorney** of our sacred possession – our energy – to the divine and eternal force of true love! Although positive energy will happen for anyone who lives at a higher perspective, takes ownership and embraces accountability in their lives, when we're plugged into the highest form of energy – God's divine filling and power – the ability to live in unconditional love is limitless! *This powerful perspective, overflowing ownership and authentic accountability empowers us, engages us and encourages us to live fully and love deeply!* Perspective, ownership and accountability – **POA** – are the keys to the awakened, abundant and deeply energized life!

INDEX

to these amazing authors, thank you for speaking into my life ... your words light the way for others

"Give me an understanding heart..." – *King Solomon*

Allen, David (2001). *Getting Things Done*
Batterson, Mark (2006). *In The Pit With A Lion on A Snowy Day*
Blanchard, Kenneth (1981). *The One Minute Manager*
Bradberry, Travis; Greaves, Jean (2009). *Emotional Intelligence 2.0*
Burchard, Brendon (2012). *The Charge*
Burchard, Brendon (2014). *The Motivation Manifesto*
Burg, Bob (2007). *The Go-Giver*
Burt, Michael (2005). *The Inspirational Leader*
Carnegie, Dale (1936). *How To Win Friends and Influence People*
Carnegie, Dale (1944). *How To Stop Worrying and Start Living*
Chapman, Gary (1992). *The Five Love Languages*
Chappell, Paul (2012). *Stewarding Life*
Covey, Stephen M.R. (2006). *The Speed of Trust*
Covey, Stephen R. (1989). *The 7 Habits of Highly Effective People*
Covey, Stephen R. (1994). *First Things First*
Daly, Jack (2014). *Hyper Sales Growth*
Darion, Joe (1972). *"The Impossible Dream"*
Davis, N.H (1920). *"Rose Beyond The Wall"*
Divine, Mark (2013). *Way of the Seal*
Drawas, Orna (2010). *How To Perform Like A Rockstar and Still Have Time For Lunch*
Eker, T Harv (2005). *Secrets of the Millionaire Mind*
Eldredge, John (2001). *Wild At Heart*
Ellis, Linda (1996). *"The Dash"*
Elrod, Hal (2014). *The Miracle Morning*
Evans, Tony (2012). *Kingdom Man*
Fox, Jeffrey (2000). *How To Become A Rainmaker*
Gittomer, Jeffrey (2015). *The Sales Bible*
Godin, Seth (2010). *Lynchpin, Are You Indispensible?*
Godin, Seth (2015). *Poke The Box*
Gordon, Jon (2007). *The Energy Bus*
Gordon, S.D. (1906). *Quiet Taks On Service*
Hardy, Darren (2010). *The Compound Effect*
Harnish, Verne (2014). *Scaling Up*
Harris, Alex & Brett (2008). *Do Hard Things*

Headley, J.T., Hon. (1860). *Life of Washington*
Helmstetter, Shad (1982). *What to Say When You Talk To Yourself*
Hill, Naploean (1925). *Think and Grow Rich*
Holmes, Arthur F. (1984). *Ethics: Approaching Moral Decisions*
Howes, Lewis (2017). *The Mask of Masculinity*
Jones, Charlie (2004). *Books Are Tremendous*
Karrass, Chester L (1996). *In Business As In Life - You Don't Get What You Deserve, You Get What You Negotiate*
Kawasaki, Guy (2011). *Enchantment*
Kiyosaki, Robert (1998). *Rich Dad, Poor Dad*
Koch, Richard (1998). *The 80/20 Principle*
LeBlanc, Mark (1999). *Growing Your Business*
Liker, Jeffrey (2004). *The Toyota Way*
Linne, Larry (2009). *Make The Noise Go Away*
Maltz, Maxwell (1960). *Psycho-Cybernetics*
Mandino, Og (1968). *The Greatest Salesman in the World*
Mandino, Og (1997). *The Greatest Mystery in The World*
Maxwell, John (2005). *The 360 Degree Leader*
Maxwell, John (2007). *Talent Is Never Enough*
McDowell, Josh (1996). *The Father Connection*
McGinnis, Alan Loy (1985). *Bringing Out the Best in People*
McKey, Zoe (2016). *Daily Routine Makeover*
Meeker, Meg (2007). *Strong Fathers, Strong Daughters*
Murphy, John (2012). *The How of Wow*
Newberry, Tommy (1999). *Succes Is Not An Accident*
Niven, David (2000). *The 100 Simple Secrets of Happy People*
Plummer, L Flora (1935). *The Spirit of the Teacher*
Rainey, Dennis (1989). *Pulling Weeds, Planting Seeds*
Ramsey, Dave (2011). *Complete Guide to Money*
Robert, Gerry (2017). *Multiply Your Business*
Ryan, M.J (2006). *This Year I Will*
Sanborn, Mark (2004). *The Fred Factor*
Schaller, James (1995). *The Search for Lost Fathering*
Scriptural Quotations referenced between the *King James Version, Amplified Version,* and *New American Standard Version*; and personalized or paraphrased in some cases.
Sinek, Simon (2009). *Start With Why*
Smith, Debra & Daniel (2005). *Romancing Your Wife*
Spaulding, Tommy (2010). *It's Not Just Who You Know*
Summit, Pat (1998). *Reach For The Summit*
Vujicic, Nick (2010). *Life without Limits*
Wagner, David (2002). *Life as a Daymaker*
Walter, Howard (1906). *"I Would Be True"*
Warren, Rick (2002). *The Purpose Driven Life*
Ziglar, Zig (1984). *The Art of Closing The Sale*

Growability™

ACCELERATE YOUR BUSINESS GROWTH.

A PLAN FOR YOUR BUSINESS

The ©Growability method and workbook provides a step-by-step guide to creating health, growth and stability in your business. Our 140 page ©Growabilty workbook uses the analogy of planting a tree to teach the 12 fundamentals for growing any business.

BUSINESS CONSULTATION

©Growability's founder and CEO Joshua MacLeod provides deep dive consultation for business leaders and owners of small to medium size businesses.

MARKETING EXPERTISE

From creating a comprehensive marketing strategy to designing your brand and website from scratch, ©Growability offers complete marketing solutions.

Growability™
ACCELERATE YOUR BUSINESS GROWTH

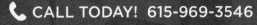

📞 CALL TODAY! 615-969-3546

joshua@growability.net | www.growability.net

GALE STONER

Portraits

SENIOR PORTRAITS

FAMILY PORTRAITS

SPORTS

galestonerimages.com

615 . 473 . 7674

gale@galestoner.com

© Gale Stoner

ASHLEY BENSON FITNESS

owner of BB SPORTS CONSULTING

TRAINING FOR THE MODERN BODY

Offering a unique Pilates-based conditioning and training program focusing on the fundamentals for sports performance.

CONNECT!

bbsports.team
@ashleybensonfitness
ashley@ashleybensonfitness.com

About Tim Hooper

Tim leads a speaking & coaching business, *Time4Energy LLC*, based in Nashville. His *Energy4Life Seminar*™ is ideal for people who want to perform at their best and put more life in their time. As a coach, he works one-on-one with executives who want to understand what makes their key people tick and inspire them to work together in reaching their goals.

In fact, he wrote the book, *GotEnergy? ... 3 Musts to Ignite Your Passion!* It provides ideas and best practices for overcoming the obstacles that get in the way of peak performance and relational harmony. People who attend Tim's presentations often share they have more passion for their work, create unstoppable momentum and experience more peace along the way both professionally and personally.

On a personal note, Tim's a St. Jude hero on a quest to run a marathon in all 50 states. When he's not speaking, Tim's spending time with his four kids and lovely wife, Jennifer.

Energy4Execs
Executive Coaching

Energy4Life
Signature Team Workshop

Energy4Sales
Sales Coaching

For dates and details regarding the *Energy4Life Seminar*™, or to reach Tim, Subscribe online @ Time4Energy.net, or email: **NeedEnergy@Time4Energy.net**
Mailing address: Time4Energy, LLC, P.O. Box 332798, Murfreesboro, TN 37133

CPSIA information can be obtained
at www.ICGtesting.com
Printed in the USA
LVHW02s1905200418
574328LV00002B/3/P